SHERLOCK HOLMES HANDBOOK

SHERLOCK HOLMES HANDBOOK

~ 2nd edition ~

Christopher Redmond

DUNDURN PRESS
TORONTO

Editor: Jason Karp
Designer: Jennifer Scott
Printer: Transcontinental

Library and Archives Canada Cataloguing in Publication

Redmond, Chris
    Sherlock Holmes handbook / by Christopher Redmond. -- 2nd ed.

ISBN 978-1-55488-446-9

1. Holmes, Sherlock (Fictitious character). 2. Doyle, Arthur Conan, Sir, 1859-1930--Characters--Sherlock Holmes. 3. England--Social life and customs--19th century. I. Title.

PR4624.R44 2009   823'.8   C2009-902993-6

1 2 3 4 5   13 12 11 10 09

We acknowledge the support of the **Canada Council for the Arts** and the **Ontario Arts Council** for our publishing program. We also acknowledge the financial support of the **Government of Canada** through the **Book Publishing Industry Development Program** and **The Association for the Export of Canadian Books**, and the **Government of Ontario** through the **Ontario Book Publishers Tax Credit program**, and the **Ontario Media Development Corporation**.

Care has been taken to trace the ownership of copyright material used in this book. The author and the publisher welcome any information enabling them to rectify any references or credits in subsequent editions.

J. Kirk Howard, President

Printed and bound in Canada.
www.dundurn.com

Dundurn Press
3 Church Street, Suite 500
Toronto, Ontario, Canada
M5E 1M2

Gazelle Book Services Limited
White Cross Mills
High Town, Lancaster, England
LA1 4XS

Dundurn Press
2250 Military Road
Tonawanda, NY
U.S.A. 14150

CONTENTS

Introduction   9

I. THE CANON   12

A Study in Scarlet   12
The Sign of the Four   14
The Adventures of Sherlock Holmes   16
The Memoirs of Sherlock Holmes   19
The Hound of the Baskervilles   24
The Return of Sherlock Holmes   26
The Valley of Fear   29
His Last Bow   31
The Case-Book of Sherlock Holmes   34

II. CHARACTERS AND ADVENTURES   38

Sherlock Holmes   39
John H. Watson   46
The Supporting Actors   49
The Unpublished Cases   56
The Rooms at 221B Baker Street   58
Holmes's Methods   59
Overtones in the Stories   62

III. SHERLOCK HOLMES IN PRINT   66

Sources   67
Manuscripts   70
Publishing and Textual Transmission   70
Copyright   76
Editions of the Stories   78
Annotated Editions   81
Illustration   84
Translations and Transcriptions   91

IV. ARTHUR CONAN DOYLE   95

Life and Medical Career   97
Literary Work   102
General Interests   115
Spiritualist Interests   126
Posterity   130
Biographical Writings   133

V. THE VICTORIAN BACKGROUND   139

London   142
Public Affairs   150
Money and Social Class   154
Daily Life   162
Higher Pursuits   167
The Empire and the World   172
Who's Who   180

VI. CRIME AND PUNISHMENT   188

British Law   189
Policing and Detection   190
Detective Stories   198

VII. HOLMES IN MODERN MEDIA 210

Pastiches and Parodies   211
Theatre   221
Radio   228
Film   232
Television   242
Other Media   250

VIII. FANS AND FOLLOWERS 257

The Baker Street Irregulars   257
Sherlockian Life   268
Overseas   277
The Printed Word   285
The Internet   295

IX. A LASTING INFLUENCE 298

Memorials   299
The Common Image   304
Academic Scholarship   310
The Appeal of Sherlock Holmes   315

Appendix: The Sixty Tales   322

Index   324

INTRODUCTION

HARDLY A VILLAGE LIBRARY anywhere is without some volume of Sherlock Holmes. Hardly a cartoon or show business figure has never dressed up in "deerstalker" hat and magnifying glass to communicate instantly to a universal audience that here is the great detective, known to North American toddlers as "Sherlock Hemlock" and to late-night movie watchers as the hyperactive, overcoated Basil Rathbone. If the creator of Holmes, Arthur Conan Doyle, was once identified as "the best-known living Englishman," Sherlock Holmes has a claim to be the best-known Englishman who never — quite — lived.

Everyone who is literate knows Sherlock Holmes, if only vaguely, and those who do may someday wish to know more. A few enthusiasts already know far, far more, to the point that they exchange trivia at the regular meetings of Sherlock Holmes societies from Tokyo to Toronto. When it first appeared in 1993, this book was intended for both kinds of people, and — despite the development of the Internet in the meantime — I respectfully doubt that any more comprehensive tool for either group has appeared. For the enthusiasts, the Sherlockians, this new edition may serve as a key to larger libraries, including their own shelves as well as to the burgeoning online library of Sherlockiana. It has been designed, too, as a ready reference for information currently scattered in often inaccessible places in the great Sherlockian literature. I hope it will stand beside the chief printed reference works for Sherlockians and the leading online sites. For general readers, it may be of use as a companion to *The Complete Sherlock Holmes*, or to whichever smaller volume of Holmes stories may be at hand. For a few of them it may even become an enticement into the Sherlockian world that has been my home for as long as I can remember.

By no means could I hope to include all knowledge about Sherlock Holmes in a single volume. But the essential facts are here, along with generalizations that provide a context for them, and a good many indications about what else has been said or written for those who want to know more. I welcome corrections, comments, and suggestions, and I am grateful to the many readers who provided such responses to the first edition (especially Roger Johnson, who kindly wrote that the book contained "an astonishingly tiny number of errors in such a densely-packed text").

I hope the style of these pages makes it clear that I take the stories of Sherlock Holmes seriously, but enjoy them at the same time. It would be a pity not to take them seriously, for they demonstrate such insight, and can teach us so much. It would be a disaster not to enjoy them as five generations have already done. As entertainment they generally speak for themselves, but perhaps this book will be a little help for those who hope to understand better the language in which Sherlock Holmes, and Arthur Conan Doyle, make themselves known, a language that is increasingly different from the one we encounter every day.

In 1993 I noted that the writing of this book had depended on many sources. At my elbow, I wrote, I had kept the Canon itself, and two essential reference books: *Good Old Index*, by William D. Goodrich, and the *Bibliography of A. Conan Doyle* edited by John Michael Gibson and Richard Lancelyn Green. Beside them stood, as sixteen years later they still stand, Jack Tracy's *Encyclopaedia Sherlockiana* and the Ronald DeWaal *World Bibliography of Sherlock Holmes and Dr. Watson*, as well as annotated editions of the sixty stories — the difference being that at the time there was one such edition of importance, edited by William S. Baring-Gould, and now there are four.

"Rarely," I continued then, "have I managed to write a paragraph without jumping up to consult some other volume: perhaps Steinbrunner and Michaels's *The Films of Sherlock Holmes*, Hugh Harrington's privately printed *Canonical Index*, *Bigelow on Holmes*, the indexes to the *Baker Street Journal*, and Bill Rabe's 1962 *Sherlockian Who's Who and What's What*." In this year's revision, too, I have consulted those and many other books, of which the most important new arrival is *Starring Sherlock Holmes* by David Stuart Davies. "Practically every other volume on my shelves," I wrote, "was needed at least once during the several months in which I drafted the pages that follow." Between 1993 and the present my study has moved two storeys upward, but most of my books have not, and I cannot count the number of trips I have made down the stairs to the shelves and up again to the keyboard.

INTRODUCTION

Many individuals, too, have been of great help. In 1993 I acknowledged Cameron Hollyer and Victoria Gill; I must now add Peggy Perdue, their successor at the Arthur Conan Doyle Collection of the Toronto Public Library. My good friend Barbara Rusch encouraged me throughout the original writing and has been a loyal supporter again. I take pleasure in acknowledging the help of Kate Karlson, who has, during my long friendship with her, contributed enormously to forming my view of the Sherlockian literature and the Sherlockian world, on which this book is based, and developing my knowledge of both. In the same way I am greatly indebted to my father, Donald A. Redmond, whose guidance and companionship have made my Sherlockian work possible. In addition, in the rewriting I have consulted many other Sherlockians — mostly by email — on points with which I thought they could assist, and I have rarely been disappointed.

The principal difference between the 1993 writing of this book and the 2009 updating has been the role played by the World Wide Web. The original edition briefly mentioned the existence of Sherlocktron, which in 1993 was a dial-up service; this edition has an entire section about Sherlockian resources and activities on the Internet. In addition to consulting Sherlockian sites many times (I am particularly indebted to Randall Stock, the online master of reliable information in several vital domains), I have been able to save myself much time, and repeated trips to a library, by drawing specific facts and background information from Web sources. I do not blush to admit that, for example, the essence of the paragraph about William Morris that I have added to Chapter V of this edition was drawn from the article about him on Wikipedia, and I gratefully acknowledge the editors on that site and many others who serve the cause of knowledge by their work.

My dear wife, Susan, still resists becoming a Sherlockian (a policy that helps keep me in modest touch with the world outside my study) but has provided affectionate moral support throughout the writing of these chapters. As I finished the first edition, our son Christopher was just reaching the stage of real literacy, with a special enthusiasm for *Nate the Great*. As I finish this one, he and his partner, Suzie, have made us grandparents. I look forward to the day, not so many years off, when young Swithin will be reading the best stories ever written (I'll recommend that he start with "The Priory School") and another generation will be added to the long chain of readers of Sherlock Holmes.

CAR
May 2009

I

THE CANON

THE STORIES OF SHERLOCK HOLMES, known as "the Canon" in allusion to a term used by Bible scholars, were written by Arthur Conan Doyle over a period of some forty years, from 1887 to 1927. They include four novels and five volumes of short stories, for a total of sixty tales. According to a report by Charles E. Lauterbach in 1960, the Canon contains a total of 660,382 words. Later, in the computer age, researcher Les Moskowitz was able to determine (2005) that they use 20,426 different words.

The sixty stories, and the collections in which they appear, are considered here in "Canonical" order, the order in which they are usually published in collected editions. It corresponds closely, but not exactly, to the order in which they were first published.

Sherlockians sometimes resort to a set of four-letter abbreviations for the story titles that were devised by Jay Finley Christ and first published in connection with his *Irregular Guide to Sherlock Holmes*, 1947. They are widely used in footnotes and sometimes even in text about the stories, either in all capitals (ABBE for "The Abbey Grange") or, less often, in the upper-and-lower-case format which Christ used: Abbe, Blac, Engr, RedC, 3Stu, and so on.

A STUDY IN SCARLET

The novel which began Doyle's writings about Sherlock Holmes was published at the end of 1887 as the principal contents of *Beeton's Christmas Annual* for that year, a paperback published by Ward Lock and Co., London. The magazine also included a couple of short plays, as well as advertisements. Few copies remain, and *Beeton's* has become the best-known treasure for which Sherlockian collectors long. Prices are high though not stratospheric; a newly discovered copy (without covers) sold for £18,600 at an auction in Oxford, England, in 2008. Three facsimile editions have been produced: one in 1960 jointly by the Baker Street Irregulars and the Sherlock Holmes Society of London, one in 1987 by British publisher John Michael Gibson, and a 1987 reprint of the BSI facsimile issued by Magico Magazine of New York. Descriptions of the original and the facsimiles, which can be distinguished from the real thing in subtle ways, appear on Randall Stock's website at *www.bestofsherlock.com*. *A Study in Scarlet* was subsequently published in a trade edition by Ward Lock (1888), and it, too, has been reproduced in facsimile (1993). The first American edition came from J.B. Lippincott Co. in 1890. Several magazine appearances are also recorded.

Detective stories not having been fully invented in 1887, it is hardly surprising that this first Sherlock Holmes novel does not follow what have come to be the conventions. Indeed, in an early chapter Holmes must virtually explain to Dr. Watson what it is that he does. Watson, as the narrator, devotes the first two chapters to introducing himself and the hero, whom he meets in a memorable scene in the pathology laboratory at "Bart's" (St. Bartholomew's Hospital, London). Only in Chapter III (of fourteen chapters, divided between two Parts) does a murder engage their attention.

The murder is virtually solved by Chapter VII of Part I, which is intriguingly subtitled "Being a Reprint from the Reminiscences of John H. Watson, M.D., Late of the Army Medical Department." The scene changes in Part II, "The Country of the Saints," which is narrated in third person rather than first. The action now takes place on the "great alkali plain" of western America, a region unknown to geography, and in the Mormon settlement at Salt Lake City, Utah. A sweet young romance is interrupted by the lecherous demands of the Mormon establishment, leading to events more characteristic of a Western than of a detective tale. There is much about horses, ravines, rifles, and the purity of womanhood. The vicious and colourful behaviour attributed to the Mormons in these chapters is less than historically accurate, as Jack Tracy has concisely shown in *Conan Doyle and the Latter-Day Saints* (1979), but provides splendid motivation for the murder that is finally explained in the last chapter of the book.

The crude dramatics of both Parts echo Doyle's other early novels rather than the more sophisticated Holmes stories he would write later. Similarly, the prominence of the love interest and frontier adventure detract, in a modern reader's mind, from what fails to be a pure detective story, although they will have striking echoes in *The Valley of Fear*, written almost thirty years later. But the introduction of the principal characters (and their delineation in such passages as the famous "Sherlock Holmes — His Limits") are entirely convincing. Watson is shown as a respectable doctor; Holmes as a brilliant, unsystematic, easily bored young man; and Lestrade of Scotland Yard as a self-important plodder. And such details as the comic constable John Rance and the moment when Holmes is taken in by an "old woman" show Doyle already in full command of his medium.

THE SIGN OF THE FOUR

J.B. Stoddart of *Lippincott's Magazine*, preparing to launch a British edition of his Philadelphia-based publication, took the young Doyle out for dinner August 30, 1889, along with another young author, Oscar Wilde. Both were commissioned to write novels for *Lippincott's*. Wilde's eventual product was *The Picture of Dorian Gray*, and Doyle's was *The Sign of the Four*, which appeared in British and American editions of the magazine in February 1890. Shortly afterwards it was issued in book form (no. 266 in the "Lippincott's Magazine Series") and that October in an edition from the firm of Spencer Blackett, classified by at least some bibliographers as the true first edition. There were also several newspaper serializations once the three-month exclusive rights purchased by J.B. Lippincott & Co. in England had expired.

In the United States, where Lippincott had rights in perpetuity, offprints from the magazine were also published, but the first identifiable American book edition was also the first in a long string of piracies (that is, unauthorized publications): a volume issued in March 1891 by P.F. Collier. Copyright protection in the United States did not extend (until July 1, 1891) to the works of foreign authors, and it quickly became open season on *The Sign of the Four*. Donald Redmond's 1990 book *Sherlock Holmes Among the Pirates: Copyright and Conan Doyle in America 1890–1930* is largely a study of how this one book was published and republished. He writes: "From 1890 at least until 1924 *The Sign of the Four* was never out of print. From 1894 until the eve of the First World War five to ten different versions were on sale simultaneously."

Because the piratical publishers worked fast and cheap, errors and verbal variations crept into their texts, some of which have survived into modern editions. The most famous, a reference to "crows" (rather than "crowds") at the

Lyceum Theatre, inspired Newton Williams, an early student of textual variations, to dub his work "the great crow hunt." Such variation even extends to
the title of this novel, which was *The Sign of the Four* in *Lippincott's*, but lost
a definite article to become *The Sign of Four* in the Spencer Blackett edition
and the Collier piracy (apparently typeset from the Spencer Blackett text). The
four-word title is more widely used today. Green and Gibson assert in their
Bibliography of A. Conan Doyle (1983) that "the author originally used the
longer title though preferred the shorter one."

Under either title it is a splendid novel, vastly more mature than its predecessor. Presenting Sherlock Holmes for a return appearance, though still clearly
not foreseeing that he had created an industry, Doyle crafted a tightly knit
plot that can be recognized as a detective story in modern terms. But the love
interest, linking Dr. Watson with the client in the case, Mary Morstan, is still
conspicuous, alternating with detective work: Holmes and adventure yield the
stage to Watson and love five times through the book's eleven chapters. Miss
Morstan makes an early impression on Watson, he moons over her, he sees
her become more and more responsive to his attentions, and at the end of the
narrative he reveals to Holmes that he has proposed marriage and she has
accepted. So neat is the tying-up of loose ends, after so brief a courtship, that
one recognizes the author's intent to write Watson out of Holmes's life, ending
their companionship and ruling out any future adventures.

The action again takes place in London, with rich scenes set in its foggy
streets and in a huge, mysterious suburban house, Pondicherry Lodge. The
case begins not with a murder but with a puzzle brought to Holmes by Miss
Morstan: she has been receiving valuable pearls from an anonymous source,
and now a mysterious message has arrived. Holmes finds the explanation only
after a murder does occur and requires solution, to say nothing of a fine scene
in which he and a borrowed dog, Toby, follow a literal scent through London. An even finer chase scene takes place along the Thames, through glinting
sunlight and evening fog. Explanations follow, but the inevitable flashback
(to India in the time of the 1857 Mutiny, an era that would appear again
in "The Crooked Man") is confined to a single chapter. Characters are excitingly drawn (Bartholomew Sholto is usually acknowledged to be a portrait of
Wilde), and despite many improbabilities and fumbled details — the action
shifts inexplicably from June to September within hours — the book can be
said to deserve its immediate success and its continuing popularity.

THE ADVENTURES OF SHERLOCK HOLMES

The title "The Adventures of Sherlock Holmes" is popularly and loosely used for any part of the Holmes saga; it was the title of the second film starring Basil Rathbone as Holmes, and it has provided such distortions as *The Misadventures of Sherlock Holmes* (an early collection of parodies), The Adventuresses of Sherlock Holmes (a society of female enthusiasts), and *The Sexual Adventures of Sherlock Holmes*. But strictly it is the title only of one book, the first of five cumulations of the original short stories.

These twelve stories appeared in twelve consecutive issues of the *Strand* magazine, July 1891 through June 1892, helping to establish the new magazine's reputation for first-class fiction. (They were also published in the American edition of the *Strand*, a month later in each case, and syndicated in American and British newspapers.) They also created a new genre: a series of stories involving the same character, each of which could, unlike the episodes of a serial, stand alone. When the sequence began, Sherlock Holmes was almost unknown; a year later he was the popular rage, and his creator was recognized as a successful author.

In October 1892, a collected volume of the *Adventures* was published by George Newnes, Ltd., the proprietors of the *Strand*, priced at six shillings (about $24 in today's money). The first edition, ten thousand copies, was sold out by early in 1893, and succeeding editions have been in print ever since in both Britain and the United States (where the first edition is that of Harper & Brothers, 1892).

The Adventures of Sherlock Holmes includes some of the best-known and, by general acclaim, the best of the Holmes tales, in particular "The Speckled Band" and "The Red-Headed League." By the time of "The Boscombe Valley Mystery," which is the fourth in the series, Doyle had established most of his bag of conventional tricks. That tale offers everything from the police baiting (in which Holmes mocks professional incompetence) to the obligatory moment at which the sleuth crawls about the scene of the crime with his magnifying glass. The formula "The Adventure of," which begins the titles of more than half the stories, was used for the first time in the seventh of the series, "The Blue Carbuncle" — it had taken Doyle that long to recognize that he was writing to a genre. ("The Adventure of" is often omitted by commentators.) The slowness of that recognition explains both the frequent cross-references among these early stories (each one mentions some that had gone before, as the author reinforced the connections in the readers' minds) and the peculiarities of the first story of all, "A Scandal in Bohemia," which is so little like a "typical" Holmes adventure.

A SCANDAL IN BOHEMIA. First published in the *Strand* in July 1891, this tale involves romance as much as detection. Its structure indeed suggests opera, and appropriately so, as the heroine, Irene Adler, is an operatic contralto, entangled with a flamboyantly improbable king. Scholarship about the story has concentrated on determining the intended identity of "the king of Bohemia," and on the logistics of Ms. Adler's blackmail attempt. The chief influence of the story, however, has been the fancy that Holmes meant something erotic or even spiritual by the label "The Woman" he applied to her.

THE RED-HEADED LEAGUE. This tale, first published in the *Strand* for August 1891, is a classic of detection (in it Holmes makes his celebrated remark about the importance of trouser-knees) and bank robbery. For grotesquerie, on which Holmes prides himself and on which Doyle so often relied for his literary effects, it would be difficult to beat the story's picture of Fleet Street choked with red-headed men of all tinctures. A striking reinterpretation of the tale is that of Samuel Rosenberg in *Naked is the Best Disguise* (1974), who identifies its motif of tunnelling, and its effeminate hero, as signs of a homosexual subtext.

A CASE OF IDENTITY. First published in the *Strand* for September 1891, this tale, with its curiously old-fashioned title, is nearly as insipid as its near-sighted heroine, Mary Sutherland — who, however, becomes the first of the "damsels in distress" whom Holmes rescues in so many of his cases. One might describe "A Case of Identity" as being Poe's deceptively simple "Purloined Letter" in a setting of middle-class tedium, in which, as some punster has observed, the Angel is a devil.

THE BOSCOMBE VALLEY MYSTERY. The fourth of the original tales, first published in the *Strand* for October 1891, may plausibly claim to be the perfect Sherlock Holmes story, offering everything readers have come to love, from a railway journey to a scene in which Holmes throws himself into the mud to look at clues through his lens. Once the mystery is solved and the innocent man cleared, to the discomfiture of Lestrade, Holmes arranges for the guilty man to go free, in view of extenuating circumstances. This tale is one of several in which an Australian background plays a part.

THE FIVE ORANGE PIPS. They are the sign of the Ku Klux Klan, whose American villainies (a favourite theme throughout the Canon) lie behind the violence in this tale, first published in the *Strand* for November 1891. The story also offers a particularly rich list of unpublished cases, and a revealing scene in which Holmes berates himself for failing to save a threatened client's life. Finally, it includes that splendid atmospheric line, "The wind cried and sobbed like a child in the chimney."

THE MAN WITH THE TWISTED LIP. Given to the world in the *Strand* for December 1891, this tale begins with a Watsonian domestic scene (the famous passage in which the doctor's wife calls him James rather than John) and moves on to an opium den before its main plot begins to appear. The story, one of double life and deception (and one in which Doyle gives full play to his fascination with deformed faces), is about a middle-class journalist who enters the dirty and unrespectable world of begging. Ugly economic truths come unusually clear to the reader as Holmes works out what is going on. Also featured in this tale are feminine beauty, in the form of Mrs. Neville St. Clair, and couture.

THE ADVENTURE OF THE BLUE CARBUNCLE. Christopher Morley called this tale "a Christmas story without slush"; it was first published, presumably just before Christmas, in the *Strand* for January 1892. The tale has to do with a holiday goose, which in pre-refrigeration days must be eaten promptly and which proves to contain a stolen jewel. The comic Henry Baker is only an incident, and the actual thief is of no account. What matters in the story is its seasonal framework, from the "compliments" brought by Watson to Holmes on "the second morning after Christmas" to Holmes's pardoning of the thief at the end because it is "the season of forgiveness."

THE ADVENTURE OF THE SPECKLED BAND. Best known and probably most often dramatized of the short stories, this tale brings Holmes to the assistance of another damsel in distress. Her sister has already died in mysterious circumstances in a lonely country house, and now she too is threatened. Freudians delight in this story, with the obvious sexual threat posed by a selfish stepfather, and the story's climax comes after one of those late-night vigils in the dark, when Holmes conquers an improbable snake, a "swamp adder." (Much has been written by Sherlockians about its species and the likelihood that it could drink milk and respond to a whistle.) The flavour of exotic India adds grotesquerie to the English countryside as it subtracts realism from the tale, which was first published in the *Strand* for February 1892.

THE ADVENTURE OF THE ENGINEER'S THUMB. Doyle becomes luxuriously gruesome in this story, beginning it in Watson's consulting-room as he (incompetently) treats an amputation. Then the patient — Victor Hatherley, whose profession of engineer was just the new thing for a smart, practical young man in the 1890s — tells the story of how he lost his thumb to a meat cleaver, and Holmes identifies the crime and the criminal for whom the attack on Hatherley was a mere incident. The story was first published in the *Strand* for March 1892.

THE ADVENTURE OF THE NOBLE BACHELOR. One can hear an echo of Doyle's early social and romance tales in this story, which first appeared in the *Strand* for April 1892. The title is a novelty, for there is no acknowledged bachelor in the story. At its centre is a society wedding; in the background, events no less romantic that took place in the American west. Holmes, seeming not to share the Victorian impression of America as uncouth, speaks of the future "quartering of the Union Jack with the Stars and Stripes" as the hope for civilization. The story includes such other beloved details as Holmes's snub of a nobleman who suggests that the detective has not worked at such a social level before ("No, I am descending") and the arrival of "ancient and cobwebby bottles" to accompany a catered supper at 221B Baker Street.

THE ADVENTURE OF THE BERYL CORONET. Unusual for being set amid snow, this tale — which first appeared in the *Strand* for May 1892 — is one of several jewel-theft adventures in the early Canon. It also has a spicy sexual subplot, and brings Holmes into indirect contact with one of those mysterious quasi-royal personages who figure in several of the stories. How plausible it is for any such personage to pawn state property (with a most respectable banker) for private advantage, and how plausible it is for a corner to break off such a coronet with an audible crack, it may be best for the reader not to inquire.

THE ADVENTURE OF THE COPPER BEECHES. This next of the "damsel in distress" tales, published in the *Strand* for June 1892, presents the first of the "four Violets," women — more or less distressed — who share that given name and appear in Holmes's cases. Violet Hunter, the governess puzzled about a household where she is compelled to cut off her beautiful red hair, is in fact a strikingly strong and interesting woman, whom writers have sometimes imagined as a possible mate for Holmes. The story is an admirable venture into the Gothic genre, with its isolated house, intimations of madness in the attic, feminine fear, and final bloodshed.

THE MEMOIRS OF SHERLOCK HOLMES

A second series of twelve "adventures of Sherlock Holmes," as they were first called, appeared in the *Strand* beginning in December 1892 and continuing through December 1893. Again, the American edition of the *Strand* carried them a month later, and they also appeared shortly afterwards in *Harper's Weekly* (except for "The Final Problem," which was published in *McClure's* as well as in the *Strand*).

As soon as the series was complete, it was published in book form as *The Memoirs of Sherlock Holmes*. The first American edition, from Harper & Brothers, contained all twelve of the 1892–93 stories, but the first British edition, from George Newnes, Ltd., omitted "The Cardboard Box," which was then dropped from all subsequent book editions of *The Memoirs*, including a "second issue" from Harper in September 1894.

THE ADVENTURE OF SILVER BLAZE. Set against the irresistibly colourful background of horse racing, and provided with some of the most dramatic dialogue anywhere in the Canon, this story is a favourite and has been dramatized often. It provides the "dog in the night-time" incident, which in non-Sherlockian contexts is the most frequently quoted of Holmes's sayings, and for Sherlockians it provides the vexing mathematical puzzle of the train whose speed Holmes could calculate to the nearest one-half mile per hour, as well as many interesting anomalies in the details of racing colours and regulations. Further, in the original publication, it provides the most popular of all Sidney Paget illustrations, showing Holmes and Watson in their railway carriage, in classic poses. The story, first published in the *Strand* for December 1892, and reprinted in *Harper's Weekly* for February 25, 1893, has a surprise ending of a kind that could hardly be improved upon.

THE ADVENTURE OF THE CARDBOARD BOX. First published in the *Strand* for January 1893, and *Harper's Weekly* for January 14 of that year, this story involves fine detective work and a very satisfactory outcome. It also involves a double murder (the severing of the victims' ears, a mutilation of the kind Doyle used again and again in his writings, is particularly grotesque) and one motivated by sexual jealousy. Presumably for such reasons, Doyle chose to suppress the story soon after its publication, not to restore it for twenty-three years. He told an acquaintance in 1903 that "a tale involving sex was out of place in a collection designed for boys." Later he called it "sensational" and (which it is not) "weak." It may well be that his real reason for suppressing the story was its grimness; unlike most detective stories, it has nothing like a happy ending.

THE ADVENTURE OF THE YELLOW FACE. This tale, first published in the *Strand* for February 1893 and *Harper's Weekly* for February 11, 1893, is one of the less popular of the early stories, perhaps because Holmes's attempts at detection in it are utterly unsuccessful. The background references to the American South are less convincing than those in "The Five Orange Pips," and what it says about relations between the races makes many readers uncomfortable. The story's greatest strength is probably its picture of life in London's rapidly growing outer suburbs.

THE ADVENTURE OF THE STOCK-BROKER'S CLERK. The *Strand* in March 1893 and *Harper's Weekly* for March 11, 1893, presented this tale of a clever robbery and a man who impersonates his own brother. It uses a theme that had already appeared in "The Red-Headed League" — distracting an innocent man with highly paid busy-work to allow thieves to have a clear shot at their booty. Perhaps because much of the action takes place in inelegant Birmingham, or because Hall Pycroft the clerk is so colourless, the story is not highly regarded.

THE ADVENTURE OF THE 'GLORIA SCOTT.' After ten brief paragraphs of introduction, this tale (first published in the *Strand* for April 1893 and *Harper's Weekly* for April 15, 1893) is told entirely in the voice of Holmes, reminiscing before the fire. It is as though the author, two years into his writings about Holmes, felt the need for some novelty. What he introduces is a flashback to the detective's youth, specifically to the incident that led him to make detective work his career. Like so many of the stories, the matter turns out to have its origin in distant regions and long-gone years — in a mutiny aboard a ship en route to Australia's penal colonies. The detection is of little interest, though there are some fine minor deductions about the person of old Trevor, and the most memorable aspect of the case in fact is the amusing if improbable cipher in which an important message is conveyed.

THE ADVENTURE OF THE MUSGRAVE RITUAL. A month after "The 'Gloria Scott,'" in May 1893, the *Strand* presented a second story about Holmes's college years, one with many strong features. It also appeared in *Harper's Weekly* for May 13. This tale offers royalty, sexual intrigue, a first-rate antagonist for Holmes in the person of butler Brunton, and the "ritual" itself, a series of solemn questions and answers, so easily memorized, so hard to forget. Although the solution to the puzzle is somewhat artificial, involving trigonometry and arbitrary pacing of distances, the climactic scene in which a corpse is found under the flagstones of Hurlstone Manor is a fine one.

THE ADVENTURE OF THE REIGATE SQUIRES. This tale, set among the gentry of Surrey, appeared first in the *Strand* for June 1893, titled "The Adventure of the Reigate Squire," singular. *Harper's Weekly* published it June 17, 1893, as "The Reigate Puzzle," perhaps because Americans could not be expected to know exactly what a squire was (although there is evidence that "Puzzle" was the author's original intention). In British book editions, the title became "The Reigate Squires," plural, but the "Puzzle" version has remained standard in the United States. By any title, the story is undistinguished, though it presents some memorable glimpses: of Holmes prostrate with depression even while Europe rang with his praises, of Holmes feigning illness to create a diversion, of Holmes knocking over a table and blaming Watson, of Holmes showing off his abilities at the analysis of handwriting. It takes no graphologist, however, to see that the fragments of a note that are reproduced with the tale, being the essential clue, are in the handwriting of Arthur Conan Doyle.

THE ADVENTURE OF THE CROOKED MAN. Published in the *Strand* for July 1893, and *Harper's Weekly* for July 8 of that year, this story returns to the Indian Mutiny as background, and gives full scope for Doyle's fascination with physical distortion: the "crooked man" is an ex-soldier who is hideously crippled as the result of torture by the rebels outside Bhurtee. The tale is notable for the presence of Teddy the mongoose, for the Canon's only reference to regular church going (in the Roman Catholic tradition, not that of the established church), and for the motive that lies behind the evil deeds it presents: a love triangle, the rivalry of two men for the love of the beautiful Nancy Devoy.

THE ADVENTURE OF THE RESIDENT PATIENT. When this story first appeared in the *Strand* in August 1893, and *Harper's Weekly* for August 12, it began with a brief episode now unfamiliar to most Sherlockians. Holmes is at work on an "abstruse" chemical investigation, but "towards evening" he breaks a test tube, gives "an exclamation of impatience," and suggests to Watson that they go for "a ramble through London." In modern British editions of the story, that incident has disappeared, and the "ramble" is suggested in the same brief paragraph in which Watson speaks of "a close, rainy day in October." In American editions, it is also missing, but in favour of a three-page digression known as "the thought-reading episode," a passage that had previously been published in "The Cardboard Box." That episode was transplanted into "The Resident Patient," at the expense of the broken test tube, when "The Cardboard Box" was suppressed, as it effectively was from 1894 to 1917. Such editions as the Doubleday *Complete Sherlock Holmes* continue to print it in full in both stories. In other respects "The Resident Patient" is less remarkable, though the opportunity it gave Doyle to use his knowledge of medical practice gives verisimilitude. The story deals with the mysterious behaviour of Dr. Trevelyan's resident patient, who proves to be in hiding from his former companions in crime; at last his sins find him out.

THE ADVENTURE OF THE GREEK INTERPRETER. This tale dates from the *Strand* of September 1893, and *Harper's Weekly* for September 16. It is of interest chiefly because it introduces Mycroft Holmes, the detective's brother, offering a long scene at the Diogenes Club in which he displays his eccentric brilliance. The case itself is set among foreigners rather than among Englishmen, and involves kidnapping and extortion of a most melodramatic kind. Little detection is involved, but there is a satisfactory rescue scene in which Watson has the opportunity to administer first aid in the form of brandy.

THE ADVENTURE OF THE NAVAL TREATY. So long is this story — some 12,700 words, compared with an average of 8,100 for the fifty-six short stories — that it was originally published in two installments, in the *Strand* issues for October and November 1893. *Harper's Weekly* also published it in two installments, October 14 and 21 of that year. (The first installment ended with Holmes's announcement that "We are now going to interview Lord Holdhurst, the Cabinet Minister and future Premier of England.") For the first time in the Canon, Holmes is involved with government secrets and affairs of state: a treaty has been stolen, and war threatens if it is not recovered. The story has elements of the locked-room mystery, with a rather improbable floor plan of the Foreign Office, and of the purloined-letter tradition, as the treaty is found very close at hand. Its most memorable moment is, however, a digression, in which Holmes admires a moss rose and reflects that "Our highest assurance of the goodness of Providence seems to me to rest in the flowers."

THE ADVENTURE OF THE FINAL PROBLEM. The title of this tale seems a redundancy — the more so as Holmes faces no "problem" in it, in the sense of a mystery to be solved. Rather, he has traced to his lair the mastermind of London criminality, Professor Moriarty, and must now conquer him or be conquered by him. To Watson's horror, detective and arch-criminal die together, falling over the falls of the Reichenbach, in Switzerland, to which the two men have journeyed in anticipation of a showdown. Doyle wrote this story and offered it for publication in the *Strand* (and also *McClure's*) for December 1893, simply as a way of killing off Holmes so that he might turn his authorial attention to other works. When it appeared, he told audiences later, "if I had killed a real man I could not have received more vindictive letters than those which poured in upon me." There is, however, no first-hand evidence that young men about town wore black mourning-bands on their arms that winter. Their grief, real or assumed, is a tribute to the effect of the earlier Holmes stories and the pathos with which Doyle, in Watson's voice, writes a final tribute to "the best and wisest man whom I have ever known."

THE HOUND OF THE BASKERVILLES

Determined for some years to write nothing more of Sherlock Holmes, Doyle weakened in 1901 when he realized that Holmes was the perfect protagonist for a novel he wanted to write about a demon hound on Dartmoor in Devon, in southwestern England. He did not, however, bring Holmes back to life, instead presenting his story as an adventure that had taken place some time before the encounter at the Reichenbach Falls.

It has become the most beloved and best known of all the Sherlock Holmes tales, the name *Baskerville* being easily recognizable even to those who have never read a word of the story. It is also arguably the finest of the novels, perhaps of all the stories, for it displays a unity in time and texture, and a splendid series of perplexities and rising climaxes, unknown in any of the others. It has no long flashback (a device which disfigures all three other novels, as well as some of the short stories) but it does indulge in the luxury of varying points of view, several chapters being told as extracts from Watson's diaries or letters to Holmes, while others are his usual more leisured narrative.

The case takes Watson, and then also Holmes, to desolate Dartmoor, in the vicinity of the fearful prison at Princetown, to investigate the mysterious death of Sir Charles Baskerville, along with some peculiar collateral events. The plot is simple enough, although two sexual subplots complicate matters somewhat, but in this novel the atmosphere is immensely rich. There is the moor itself, with its relics of prehistoric man (emphasized by references throughout the story to anthropological studies and themes). There is the lurking presence of the prison, with Selden, the escaped murderer, a constant threat. There is the suffocating pettiness of village life; there is the gloom of Baskerville Hall, where the new squire, Sir Henry, announces at the end of the story that he is eager to install electric lights. There is constant tension between science and superstition, and Doyle was not wrong when he famously wrote to his mother that the book was "a real Creeper." A textual analysis of *The Hound* by Wendy Machen (in *Canadian Holmes*, 1989) finds that the dominant colours in this story are the black and white of night, the grey of uncertainty, and the green of the moor's vegetation. Somehow this grim environment has appealed to Sherlockians, among them Philip Weller, whose 2001 commentary on *The Hound* is titled *Hunting the Dartmoor Legend*, and Brian W. Pugh and Paul R. Spiring, who produced *On the Trail of Arthur Conan Doyle: An Illustrated Devon Tour* in 2008.

Doyle attributed the idea for *The Hound of the Baskervilles* to his friend Bertram Fletcher Robinson, declaring in a dedicatory epistle (of which three different versions appear) that Robinson had told him of "a west country legend." But scholarship has not turned up any Devonshire legend involving a dog, a wronged woman, and supernatural vengeance, though there are "black dog" legends aplenty. Tradition has pointed to a legend associated with the Cabell family of Buckfastleigh, Devon; but that legend cannot be traced before 1907 and may itself be based on the Baskerville story. The Baskerville and Vaughan families of Herefordshire apparently are associated with a longstanding Black Hound story, as Maurice Campbell argued in the *Sherlock Holmes Journal* in 1975. The safest conclusion is that *The Hound* has overlapping and multiple sources — as Janice McNabb argues in *The Curious Incident of the Hound on Dartmoor* (1984).

The difficult question is just how much Fletcher Robinson contributed to the creation of what was published as Doyle's work. Robinson (born August 22, 1870, died January 21, 1907) was himself an author, responsible for travel and sports writing as well as many short stories and several novels. His greatest contribution to posterity, apart from whatever he did to help give birth to *The Hound*, was *The Chronicles of Addington Peace*, a set of detective stories (1905). It is clear that he visited Dartmoor with Doyle in the spring of 1901, and the dedications variously credit him with "help" in "the general plot," "the local details," "all the details," and the "evolution" of the story. Exactly what that involved is now unclear, despite careful teasing out of the available biographical evidence. Robin Paige presented one theory in the form of a light-hearted novel, *Death at Dartmoor* (2002). At about the same time, the question became fodder for the newspapers when a Devon man named Rodger Garrick-Steele called for the exhumation of Fletcher Robinson's body in order to determine whether he had been poisoned by Doyle. Not only did Doyle steal the plot of *The Hound* from Fletcher Robinson, Garrick-Steele charged, he may also have had an affair with his friend's wife, then murdered him to conceal his double offence. The charges were elaborated in a rambling, ill-punctuated six-hundred-page book, *House of the Baskervilles* (2003). Scholars have laughed Garrick-Steele's claims out of court, and church authorities rejected the request for exhumation.

The Hound was first published as a serial in the *Strand*, between August 1901 and April 1902 (in the American edition, September through May). Chapters I–II appeared together; Chapters III–IV; Chapters V–VI; Chapters VII–VIII; Chapter IX alone; Chapters X–XI; Chapter XII alone; Chapter XIII; and part of XIV; the remainder of XIV with XV. As soon as the final installment had appeared, book editions were ready, from George Newnes, Ltd., in England and from McClure, Phillips & Co. in the United States. They were best sellers, particularly after the American publisher obtained the manuscript, broke it into leaves, and distributed it to booksellers across the country as a publicity gesture. *The Hound* was also serialized in several American newspapers during the summer of 1902.

THE RETURN OF SHERLOCK HOLMES

In 1903 Doyle was persuaded to bring Holmes back to life, or rather to invent a way in which his detective might have been alive all the time in spite of the report from Reichenbach. The persuasive influence was money, primarily from the American magazine *Collier's Weekly*, although the stories continued to appear in the British edition of the *Strand* as well. Doyle's own experience, and the emotional complexities he was undergoing during the first decade of the twentieth century, led him to write more realistic, more deeply coloured adventures for Holmes than anything the earlier two series had offered. *The Return of Sherlock Holmes* may be his finest work.

The thirteen stories in this sequence were collected in book form as soon as they had all appeared in magazines, even while they were still being republished in a group of American newspapers. The first edition appeared in the United States, from McClure, Phillips & Co., in February 1905; the rights were soon transferred to Doubleday, Page & Co. for subsequent editions. A British edition from George Newnes, Ltd., appeared in March, but the rights were soon taken over by Smith, Elder & Co. The American book edition was illustrated by Charles Raymond Macauley, and the British once again by Sidney Paget, whose drawings continued to appear in the *Strand* appearances. However, the illustrations most often associated with the stories in *The Return* are those of Frederic Dorr Steele, who drew dramatic covers for *Collier's* as well as black-and-white illustrations to accompany the stories inside that magazine.

THE ADVENTURE OF THE EMPTY HOUSE. This tale is rather a chapter of biography, or autobiography, than a mystery story in the accepted sense, for the mystery Holmes solves is incidental to other matters, and explained in only a few sentences. What matters is the return of Sherlock Holmes to London, and the unsuccessful attempt on his life by Colonel Sebastian Moran, right-hand villain to the late Professor Moriarty. The memorable scenes involve Watson's faint when he is confronted with his friend, whom he has presumed dead, and the vigil in the "empty house" across from 221B Baker Street while Moran tries to shoot the dummy which he supposes to be Holmes. The story first appeared in *Collier's* for September 26, 1903, and the *Strand* for October 1903.

THE ADVENTURE OF THE NORWOOD BUILDER. *Collier's* published this story October 31, 1903, and the *Strand* in November 1903. Its most memorable feature is the use of a thumbprint as a clue; the print never has to be matched with anything, for its very presence is sufficient to tell Holmes that something is wrong, but any reference to the uniqueness of fingerprints marks the story as modern (fingerprinting, developed for police use in India, was introduced in England in a paper given to the British Association in 1899, and adopted by Scotland Yard in 1901). In other respects the story is of interest for its plot of sexual revenge, and for the device Holmes uses (an echo of what he tried in "A Scandal in Bohemia") of enticing a fugitive out of his hiding place by raising an alarm of fire.

THE ADVENTURE OF THE DANCING MEN. With this story Doyle returns to themes of adultery and love gone wrong, which evidently obsessed him during the early years of the century, while his own emotions were painfully divided. The "child's scrawl" that proves to be an underworld cipher, and the clue in a gory murder, makes this story one of the most memorable in the Canon, and one of the most frequently dramatized (although solving such a cipher is ordinarily a far simpler matter than Holmes, or the author, makes out). Much attention has been given to Doyle's possible sources for the dancing men, and to the genuine existence of an ancient Cubitt family in Norfolk. For the first time since "The Five Orange Pips," Doyle uses an American background in this story, reasonably enough since he now had a major American audience. It appeared in *Collier's Weekly* for December 5, 1903, and in the *Strand* for December 1903.

THE ADVENTURE OF THE SOLITARY CYCLIST. Violet Smith (who is not herself the solitary cyclist of Charlington; that was her pursuer) is the distressed damsel in this dramatic story, and the second of the four Canonical Violets. Like Violet Hunter in "The Copper Beeches," she is a career woman making her way in the world, and finding the atmosphere at a remote country house threatening. In short, the tale is as much a Gothic work as it is a detective story. The dramatic wedding scene at the end is among the most exciting passages in the Canon. This story was first published in *Collier's* for December 26, 1903, and the *Strand* for January 1904.

THE ADVENTURE OF THE PRIORY SCHOOL. A lonely little boy from a broken home runs away from school: the plot of this story must reflect Doyle's childhood fears. Its concluding scene, in which Holmes patronizes and swindles the rich and powerful Duke of Holdernesse, gives a convincing picture of the detective as iconoclast; the scene in which he arranges crumbs on the tablecloth to show Watson how the cow-tracks on the moor were arranged is a classic of detection, explication, and dramatic sense. The story was first published in *Collier's* for January 30, 1904, and the *Strand* for February 1904.

THE ADVENTURE OF BLACK PETER. Not, please, "the" Black Peter: the title indicates a person's name. The story appeared first in *Collier's* for February 27, 1904, and in the *Strand* for March 1904, and deals with a particularly violent murder — Holmes is first seen returning from an attempt to drive a spear through a pig's carcass, to estimate the force involved in the harpooning of Peter Carey. The whaling background doubtless owes something to Doyle's youthful experience in that industry.

THE ADVENTURE OF CHARLES AUGUSTUS MILVERTON. Holmes has not much to detect in this case; he is employed instead as an agent to recover papers from Milverton the society blackmailer. To do so, he resorts to wooing Milverton's housemaid (a sordid episode which has led to much Sherlockian speculation and sniggering) and, in Watson's company, to burglary; in his presence, Milverton is shot dead by an unidentified woman who has been dubbed "Lady X." The case thus has much colour and action, as well as moral satisfaction, the noble Holmes vanquishing the snakelike Milverton. The tale was first published in *Collier's* for March 26, 1904, and the *Strand* for April 1904.

THE ADVENTURE OF THE SIX NAPOLEONS. The British fear of Napoleon, emperor of France, even eight decades after his death, figures large in this story, though ultimately only as a red herring: the gem might have been hidden in busts of anyone, but Napoleon is a plausible subject for monomania, on which everyone except Holmes blames the curious incidents of vandalism. The tale gives an opportunity for Holmes to display his clear reasoning and, in the scene at the end where he triumphantly produces the pearl, his flair for drama as well. "The Six Napoleons" was first published in *Collier's Weekly* for April 30, 1904, and the *Strand* for May 1904.

THE ADVENTURE OF THE THREE STUDENTS. Improbable details abound in this story of a student who cheats on a university exam; the very procedure used to unmask the cheater, in which the don responsible calls in Holmes privately, is alien from the way a university would deal with such an incident. But as a logic puzzle the tale is splendid, giving Holmes the opportunity to choose from among three young men, the only possible suspects. At last he confronts the culprit, who confesses in a burst of emotion. The story first appeared in the *Strand* for June 1904 and *Collier's* for September 24, 1904.

THE ADVENTURE OF THE GOLDEN PINCE-NEZ. Holmes is made to appear politically somewhat retrograde in this tale of Russian nihilists, exiled revolutionaries of the kind much feared in the England of that generation. The story is not of the first rank, despite Holmes's perception in understanding the dying words of the murdered secretary — "The professor, it was she" — and his ingenuity in scattering cigarette ashes so that the concealed murderess would leave footprints when she emerged. It was first published in the *Strand* for July 1904 and *Collier's Weekly* for October 29, 1904.

THE ADVENTURE OF THE MISSING THREE-QUARTER. Doyle's beloved world of amateur sport (with which Holmes ostentatiously denies any familiarity) provides the background for this pathetic tale, in which mystery proves to be domestic tragedy. The comic portrait of the miser, Lord Mount-James, is hardly enough to make the tale a success. It appeared first in the *Strand* for August 1904 and *Collier's* for November 26, 1904.

THE ADVENTURE OF THE ABBEY GRANGE. By 1904, Doyle had spent almost a decade tending to a dying wife, while he was in love with another woman. Two years later he would become president of the Divorce Law Reform Union. Thoughts on such matters clearly lay behind the writing of this story, about a brave woman who helps her lover kill her aristocratic but drunken husband. The story is also notable for its picture of Holmes seeing more than the official police can see as he inspects the bloody room at the Abbey Grange, and for its juxtaposition of free-minded Australians with decadent English. "The Abbey Grange" was first published in the *Strand* for September 1904 and *Collier's* for December 31, 1904.

THE ADVENTURE OF THE SECOND STAIN. The title of this story is as intriguing as the story itself; its resonance can be seen in its mention in "The Naval Treaty," along with the untold "Adventure of the Tired Captain." The second stain is a clue that helps Holmes solve his case, which involves not the usual murder but a matter of espionage and statecraft, again recalling "The Naval Treaty." By far the most interesting feature of the case is the beautiful Lady Hilda Trelawney Hope, who is faithful to her high-placed husband after her fashion. The story was first published in the *Strand* for December 1904 and *Collier's* for January 28, 1905.

THE VALLEY OF FEAR

This novel may just be Doyle's masterpiece; it may even be two masterpieces, for it consists of two almost entirely separate mystery novels, and the second of them, "The Scowrers," is if anything more successful than the first, "The

Tragedy of Birlstone," which involves Sherlock Holmes in a way the second does not. J. Bliss Austin, prominent collector and scholar in Pittsburgh, felt such an affinity for the second book that he managed to become owner of the entire manuscript of *The Valley of Fear* — but then he was a vice-president of United States Steel, a company whose shadow can easily be felt in "The Scowrers," a tale of the Pennsylvania coal and iron fields.

"The Scowrers" is set in the 1870s, in a time of technological and social change, and hence of conflict between the mostly Irish miners and labourers and their American-English bosses. One flower in the carbonized soil of the Shenandoah Valley (a metaphor repeatedly used in *The Valley of Fear*) was a fraternal and, eventually, terrorist group called the Mollie Maguires, largely a perversion of the otherwise legitimate Ancient Order of Hibernians. It has been the subject of several books, variously historical and fanciful, and of a 1969 film (*The Molly Maguires*, starring Sean Connery). The Mollies were eventually infiltrated by the new Pinkerton detective agency, in the person of agent James McParlan, and a number of them hanged for murder, including Jack Kehoe, the most prominent leader or "bodymaster." Doyle learned the story of the Mollies from a somewhat partial source, Allan Pinkerton's book *The Molly Maguires and the Detectives* (1877), and while *The Valley of Fear* is not precisely a *roman à clef*, it follows the Pinkerton version of the story closely. Sherlockians have enjoyed speculating about which of the coalfield towns — Tamaqua, Pottsville, Mauch Chunk (now Jim Thorpe) or Mahanoy City — is the original of "Vermissa." Bruce Kennedy and Robert Watson Douty explore such questions, and recreate the grim atmosphere of the Valley in those days, in their chapbook *In the Footsteps of Birdy Edwards* (1980). The Baker Street Irregulars carried out further inquiries during a weekend excursion to the area in 2004, resulting in the publication of an anthology, *Murderland*, the following year.

But none of this background is apparent in the first half of *The Valley of Fear*, which begins as a country-house murder mystery with Professor Moriarty lurking in the background. The seven chapters of "The Tragedy of Birlstone" give some scope for a mystery and its solution to develop, and for personal touches of a kind impossible in a short story, such as the curious behaviour of the late John Douglas's devoted wife. The clue of the missing dumb bell is one of the most amusing, and hence unforgettable, in the whole Canon. Eventually, after the seven "Scowrer" chapters, an "Epilogue" returns the scene to England, and Holmes is seen brooding when — astonishingly — Moriarty is victorious after all.

The Valley of Fear was serialized in the *Strand* magazine from September 1914 through May 1915, after most of the tales that would later appear in

His Last Bow. In the United States it was not carried by Collier's, but instead appeared in the "Associated Sunday Magazines," a group of newspaper supplements, beginning on September 20, 1914, and concluding on November 22. In book form it appeared in February in the United States (from George H. Doran Co.), and in June in England (from Smith, Elder & Co.). As Gibson and Green note in their *Bibliography*, there are a number of deliberate textual variations, some caused by the war with Germany, in which Britain (but not America) was engaged beginning late in 1914, some "for greater accuracy" in the American details.

HIS LAST BOW

This fourth collection of Canonical short stories is the smallest of all, containing but eight tales — and that figure includes "The Cardboard Box," originally published as one of *The Memoirs* but suppressed from 1894 until this volume appeared in 1917. The stories were somewhat rearranged from the order in which they had been originally published. The British edition was published by John Murray, apparently because Smith, Elder & Co. thought seven or eight stories too few to make a worthwhile book. The American edition appeared simultaneously, from George H. Doran Co. The subtitles of the two editions differ slightly: in Britain it was *Some Reminiscences of Sherlock Holmes*, and in the United States *A Reminiscence of Sherlock Holmes*. Many editions (but not, for example, the John Murray *Short Stories*) include a one-paragraph Preface signed by Watson: "The friends of Mr. Sherlock Holmes will be glad to learn that he is still alive and well...."

Shortly after *His Last Bow* was published, Doyle wrote an article, "Some Personalia about Mr. Sherlock Holmes," which appeared in the *Strand* for December 1917. It was later revised as a chapter in his autobiography, *Memories and Adventures* (1924). Clearly intended as an epilogue to the entire Canon, the existence of this article makes it clear that *His Last Bow* was intended to be, indeed, Holmes's *last* bow. It leaves open, however, the question of which sort of "bow" the author had in mind: the kind an actor takes at a curtain call, or the kind the dying Robin Hood drew to shoot an arrow to his final resting place.

THE ADVENTURE OF WISTERIA LODGE. Like "The Naval Treaty," the only Canonical short story that is longer, this one was first published in the *Strand* in two parts: "The Singular Experience of Mr. John Scott Eccles," September 1908, and "The Tiger of San Pedro," October 1908. *Collier's*

Weekly published the two parts August 15, 1908, under the title "The Singular Experience of Mr. John Scott Eccles." The titles for the two parts survive in modern editions; the title "Wisteria Lodge" for the full story was first used when *His Last Bow* was published in book form. This tale was "a difficult story to write," Gibson and Green say *obiter* in their book *Bibliography*, and it shows, being long and confusing. The horrible face at the window and the shocking relics of voodoo that serve as clues along the way are hardly sufficient to redeem the story, nor is the sudden appearance of "Don Murillo," the deposed Latin American dictator.

THE ADVENTURE OF THE RED CIRCLE. A background of Italian-American mafia activity makes this story a favourite with many readers, though its early pages, in which Holmes reassures a distressed landlady and puzzles over the identity of her mysterious lodger, is in fact more typical of the Canon. The "cipher" which proves to be Italian has excited much commentary; whichever way Holmes counted the letters, they don't seem to come out right. The story was first published in the *Strand* in two parts, in March and April 1911 (a month later in the American edition), and retains a division into Parts I and II.

THE ADVENTURE OF THE BRUCE-PARTINGTON PLANS. Mycroft Holmes, last seen in "The Greek Interpreter," returns in this story, bringing his brother a case which, like two or three others, involves espionage and international intrigue rather than domestic crime. Apart from its supposed political importance, the case is of interest chiefly for the ingenious disposal of a body atop an Underground train — and of course for the presence of the dead man's fiancée, one of the four Canonical Violets. "The Bruce-Partington Plans" (the title referring to the blueprints for the Bruce-Partington submarine, a thoroughly up-to-date invention in 1908) appeared first in the *Strand* for December 1908 and *Collier's* for December 12 of the same year.

THE ADVENTURE OF THE DYING DETECTIVE. The title is sensational; the story is a splendid one, drawing on Doyle's medical background (and drawing on Watson's medical mediocrity) to present a Holmes who is feigning fatal illness to ensnare a clever adversary. Such detail is given about the ruse that there is hardly room for the mystery itself, and it is not even quite clear who Victor Savage was or why he was killed. "The Dying Detective" was first published in *Collier's* for November 22, 1913, and immediately off printed as a Christmas greeting pamphlet from the advertising department of *Collier's*. It also appeared in the December 1913 issue of the *Strand*.

THE DISAPPEARANCE OF LADY FRANCES CARFAX. Comedy and Gothic melodrama figure more in this story than in most other Canonical tales — the comedy in Watson's clumsy attempts to play detective, acting on Holmes's behalf in Montpellier; the melodrama in Holmes's frantic prying open of the coffin in which the missing lady is about to be buried alive. The story comes nearer than any other in the Canon to being about rape, rather than murder or theft. Its unusual title (without "The Adventure of") is no excuse for the faux pas that was made when it first appeared in the United States, in the *American Magazine* for December 1911; there it was headed "The Disappearance of Lady Carfax." Under its right name it appeared in the *Strand*, also for December 1911.

THE ADVENTURE OF THE DEVIL'S FOOT. As in "The Reigate Squires," Holmes in this case is taking a medically imposed vacation, this time in Cornwall, and conveniently finds himself in proximity to a mystery. Murder is not at first suspected in "the Cornish horror," a phenomenon that rather reminds one of a spiritualist seance gone wildly wrong (but Doyle in 1910 was not yet active as a spiritualist). The most memorable aspect of the story may be the hideously contorted faces of the victims of *radix pedis diaboli*, a root hitherto unknown to science, but its most important feature is the scene in which Holmes holds justice higher than law and lets the culprit go. "The Devil's Foot" was originally published in the *Strand* — in December 1910 in the British edition, in January and February 1911 in the American edition. (The first of those two episodes ended with "Hurry — hurry, before things get disarranged.")

HIS LAST BOW. This story, which gives its title to the collection in which it later appeared, represents a departure from the style of all the previous Holmes tales. It is narrated in the third person, rather than by Watson; it introduces Holmes as a surprise, far into the narrative; it presents not the London-based consulting detective but a Holmes come out of retirement in Sussex; it is a story not of crime but of international espionage, with Holmes acting as a double agent on the eve of World War I. It takes place August 2, 1914, during the hours when the war was actually beginning, and it takes a jingoistic tone, having undeniably been written as war propaganda. One can hear Doyle's voice from the beginning ("the most terrible August in the history of the world") through the slurs on Germany, Irish separatists, and suffragist "Furies," to the peroration about a cleansing "east wind." Holmes as spy, under the pseudonym of Altamont, is little more convincing than Holmes as goateed American, but readers in 1917 may have been grateful for whatever they might get. The tale was subtitled "The War Service of Sherlock Holmes" when it appeared in the *Strand* for September 1917 and *Collier's* for September 22, 1917, but became "An Epilogue of Sherlock Holmes" when *His Last*

Bow appeared in book form. Doyle was indicating once again that he had had enough of him.

THE CASE-BOOK OF SHERLOCK HOLMES

The title is admirable, and Doyle may be given the credit for introducing the term *case book* in the context of a detective (it had previously been used chiefly for medical cases). Two or three of the stories are also first-rate, but in general this final collection is acknowledged to be weaker than the books that preceded it. Gibson and Green in their *Bibliography* say that Doyle was encouraged to write more about Holmes when he saw the early films that starred Eille Norwood as the detective, released beginning in 1921. "Norwood's disguises were remarkable," they say, "and his sphinx-like countenance suggested the idea for *The Crown Diamond*," which was first a play and then the first of this final dozen stories to see print.

The tales — written, or at least published, over a much briefer period than those in *The Return* and *His Last Bow* — were completely rearranged for book publication. They were introduced with a preface, this time in Doyle's voice rather than Watson's, which first appeared in the *Strand* for March 1927, announcing a contest that invited readers to rank the stories and match Doyle's own assessment. It survives as the lovely brief essay that assigns Holmes to "some fantastic limbo for the children of imagination, some strange, impossible place" and yet fixes him firmly in history:

> He began his adventures in the very heart of the later Victorian Era, carried it through the all-too-short reign of Edward, and has managed to hold his own little niche even in these feverish days.

The first edition of *The Case-Book* was published in Britain by John Murray, and in America by George H. Doran Co., in the middle of 1927.

THE ADVENTURE OF THE ILLUSTRIOUS CLIENT. Sex (indeed, probably, prostitution) is the atmosphere and motivation in this tale, which takes its name not from any element of the plot but from the (unidentified) noble party who asks Holmes to take the case. It is a matter outside his usual range, for there is no mystery to solve. Rather, Holmes is supposed to persuade a well-to-do young lady that Baron Gruner, with whom she is infatuated, is a cad and worse. She will have none of his reasoning (he carries it off with dignity, despite his inexperience in such affairs), but violence intervenes, in the nasty old-fashioned form of vitriol-throwing: Gruner is marked for life by the attack of the wild Kitty Winter. This racy fare first appeared in *Collier's* for November 8, 1924, and the *Strand* for February and March 1925 (the first part ending with the dramatic words "Murderous Attack Upon Sherlock Holmes").

THE ADVENTURE OF THE BLANCHED SOLDIER. Current affairs find their way into the Canon more directly than usual in this tale. It deals with a consequence of the Boer War, specifically a medical matter, having its origin in a field hospital much like the one Doyle himself managed during that conflict twenty-five years earlier. Its strength is as a medical tale rather than an instance of detection, as there is little for Holmes to do save to discern the anti-climactic truth and arrange a happy ending for the family of the ex-soldier who believed him to have a dread disease. "The Blanched Soldier" first appeared in *Liberty*, a New York magazine, for October 16, 1926, and in the *Strand* for November 1926.

THE ADVENTURE OF THE MAZARIN STONE. The first words of this story make it distinctive: it is written in the third person, not with Watson as narrator. It is in fact an adaptation of *The Crown Diamond*, a play by Doyle about Sherlock Holmes that was first produced in May 1921. The story saw print in the *Strand* that October, and in *Hearst's International Magazine* in New York in November 1921. Both because of its awkward style (rigidly observing the dramatic unities, it simply describes what might be seen on a stage set), and because of its lack of originality in plot or circumstantial detail, the story is widely recognized as probably the weakest of all the Holmes tales. Nevertheless, it deserves some acclaim as the first new tale to be published since "His Last Bow" four years previously.

THE ADVENTURE OF THE THREE GABLES. Unhealthy sexuality (a young man becomes fascinated by an older woman) and the misuse of wealth make the atmosphere of this story distasteful, and there is little detecting for Holmes to do. The issue in this affair, as in "A Scandal in Bohemia," is blackmail at the point where relationships and money meet. The unusual character of Isadora Klein is probably the story's strongest feature, though there is also some interest in the way Holmes examines the attempt to buy Mrs. Maberley's house, contents and all, eventually realizing that a tell-tale manuscript is what the buyer was after. "The Three Gables" was first published in *Liberty*, New York, for September 18, 1926, and in the *Strand* for October 1926.

THE ADVENTURE OF THE SUSSEX VAMPIRE. Written during Doyle's years as an advocate of spiritualism, this tale nevertheless presents a firmly materialist Holmes: "No ghosts need apply." Among the *Case-Book* stories it is unusually strong and memorable, reminiscent of Holmes's early adventures, although the title is deliberately lurid, the story something of a trick, for Holmes finds that the woman who has been sucking blood from her stepson's neck is no sort of monster. "The Sussex Vampire" was first published in the January 1924 issues of both the *Strand* and (in New York) *Hearst's International Magazine.*

THE ADVENTURE OF THE THREE GARRIDEBS. The appeal of this story depends heavily on the novelty of the grotesque surname "Garrideb." Holmes is called in not to solve a crime but to render advice in the search for men of that name; when three of them stand in a row, a fortune is theirs to divide. Of course he finds the whole business to be a fraud, rather as was the League of the Red-Headed Men in a story written thirty years earlier, a story whose plot is largely borrowed for this one. The dramatic scene in which Watson is wounded is among the high emotional moments of the Canon. This tale was first published in *Collier's* for October 25, 1924, and in the *Strand* for January 1925.

THE PROBLEM OF THOR BRIDGE. This story (which departs from the "Adventure of" style of title) presents a classic piece of deduction by Holmes, in which he works out from a chip on a stone bridge the true explanation for the death of Maria Gibson. It has to do with a gritty love triangle, a plot that seems unmistakably of the 1920s. The story also offers the Sherlockian one of the Canon's finest paragraphs about other cases which Holmes addressed, but for which the world is not yet prepared. "Thor Bridge" was first published in the *Strand* and in *Hearst's International Magazine*, both in the February and March issues of 1922; the first part ends with "We come at once upon a most fruitful line of inquiry."

THE ADVENTURE OF THE CREEPING MAN. Holmes makes his nearest approach to science fiction in this story, in which the unusual behaviour of a professor proves to be caused by a "serum" extracted from langur monkeys. Experiments with such injections of testicular extract began in the 1880s and attracted much attention in the 1920s, but they seem somehow too modern for Holmes's attention, in a case that requires little action from him but does lead him to some philosophizing, and a hint that he might soon retire. The story was first published in the *Strand* and in *Hearst's International Magazine*, both for March 1923.

THE ADVENTURE OF THE LION'S MANE. Sherlock Holmes himself is the narrator of this tale (his prose style is, however, revealingly similar to Watson's). Its events take place on the Sussex coastline, after Holmes's retirement to a "villa," and involve the strange death of Fitzroy McPherson, which proves to be the result of a natural phenomenon rather than of human violence. The story has novelty (not least, the absence of Watson) to distinguish it, as well as the portrait of that "most complete and remarkable woman," Maud Bellamy. "The Lion's Mane" first appeared in *Liberty* for November 27, 1926, and in the *Strand* for December 1926.

THE ADVENTURE OF THE VEILED LODGER. Holmes waxes philosophical in this sad tale, as does Doyle, who wrote it near the end of his life (it was published in *Liberty* for January 22, 1927, and the *Strand* for February 1927). Readers might reasonably feel a little cheated, for Holmes is called on to do no detecting at all, only a little speculating and a good deal of listening as Eugenia Ronder tells the dramatic story of how her face was ruined, so that she now lives behind a veil.

THE ADVENTURE OF SHOSCOMBE OLD PLACE. Original publication of the Canon came to an end with this story, appearing in *Liberty* for March 5, 1927, and the *Strand* for April 1927. It is a story of degeneration, death, and old bones, with the suspected murder proving to be nothing more serious than a fraud born of desperation. Still, its final paragraph tries to offer hope, speaking of "a happier note than Sir Robert's actions deserved ... an honoured old age." It harks back to *The Hound of the Baskervilles*, with the association of mysterious dogs and spooky death, and its highlight is the brief exciting scene in which Holmes lets a spaniel loose to bark at the mysterious occupant of a carriage. (The story was originally announced as "The Adventure of the Black Spaniel," but never published under that title.) A return to the horse-racing milieu that gave "Silver Blaze" much of its novelty also adds interest to this story.

THE ADVENTURE OF THE RETIRED COLOURMAN. Perhaps because of the word "retired" in the title, and because its theme is the hopelessness of old age, this story was put last in *The Case-Book*, although there were two tales still to come when it was first published in *Liberty* for December 18, 1926, and the *Strand* for January 1927. Doyle returns to his frequent theme of a love triangle, includes his only mention of chess ("one mark of a scheming mind"), makes Sherlock Holmes conduct one of his most clever, if inconsiderate, ruses, and offers perhaps the most chilling image in the entire Canon, the incomplete phrase scrawled on the wall of the death chamber by the two murder victims. The seven-word question with which Holmes nails the unsuspecting killer is a splendidly dramatic note for the story which a cover-to-cover reader of the Canon will encounter last.

II
CHARACTERS
AND ADVENTURES

IN WRITING THE SHERLOCK HOLMES tales, Arthur Conan Doyle invented the valuable literary genre of "linked" short stories: their plots are independent (so that they can be read in any order) but the central characters and settings continue. A detective is the perfect figure to appear in such a structure, for he remains unchanged while a succession of clients bring their various problems to him.

Because Holmes appears in all the stories, Watson in all but two, and several other characters repeatedly, it is easy for the reader to see the tales as fragments of biography. Enthusiasts, either believing or pretending to believe, have speculated and written endlessly about Holmes's accomplishments and character, and about the deeds he may have performed which Doyle (or Watson) unaccountably failed to record. In addition, it is easy to see themes and characteristics that appear in story after story, some with gradual changes over the decades from *A Study in Scarlet* to the final, sad tales published in 1927.

Readers who see the Canon as a unit, rather than as unconnected stories, have felt the need for reference books that help them trace the developments and locate specific names or incidents. An early alphabetical guide of this kind was Jay Finley Christ's *An Irregular Guide to Sherlock Holmes of Baker Street* (1947). It was valuable, but idiosyncratic and, even with two supplements, inadequate. A modern successor is *Good Old Index* (1987), by William D. Goodrich. Both are keyed to the Doubleday *Complete Sherlock Holmes*. Some devotees prefer *The Canonical Compendium* (1999) by Stephen Clarkson, with references to several editions of the Canon. Rather different, and enjoyable as well as useful, is Jack Tracy's *Encyclopaedia Sherlockiana*

(1977), which concentrates on proper names and some matters of Victorian daily life, defining them and indicating the story (but not the precise page) that gives each its interest to a reader of the Canon.

SHERLOCK HOLMES

"What is it that we love in Sherlock Holmes?" asked Edgar W. Smith in his first essay as editor of the *Baker Street Journal* (1946). His answer began with discussion not so much of Holmes as of Holmes's time, but then it turned to the figure of the great detective himself:

> Not only there and then, but here and now, he stands before us as a symbol — a symbol, if you please, of all that we are not, but ever would be. His figure is sufficiently remote to make our secret aspirations for transference seem unshameful, yet close enough to give them plausibility. We see him as the fine expression of our urge to trample evil and to set aright the wrongs with which the world is plagued.

That is a lot to ask of a human being, or even of a literary approximation of a human being, and yet enthusiasts continue to ask it. Perhaps it would be better first to take the measure of Holmes as a man — "the best and wisest man whom I have ever known," Watson is made to call him, borrowing a phrase first used by Plato about Socrates.

Holmes reports that his ancestors were "country squires" and that a grandmother was a sister of "Vernet, the French artist" (presumably Émile Jean Horace Vernet, 1789–1863). His older brother Mycroft appears significantly in two of the stories, and is glimpsed in a third. Otherwise, the reader knows nothing of Holmes's family or background beyond vague hints about his university education. The Canon provides an outline of his career, from his early cases as an amateur ("The 'Gloria Scott'" and "The Musgrave Ritual") through his establishment in London as a consulting detective; his meeting with Watson in (probably) January 1881; ten years of professional success; his encounter with Professor Moriarty at the Reichenbach in 1891; his return from supposed death three years later; a further nine years of professional work; his retirement to Sussex, from which he emerged for counter-espionage work ("His Last Bow") in 1912–14. During his active career he is said to have handled thousands of cases, only a handful of which are chronicled. The great stretches of time unaccounted for — if one accepts Holmes as a historical figure, and the tales as fragments of his biography — are an immense temptation to the tale-spinner and the scholar alike.

HIS LIMITATIONS. Sherlock Holmes is first presented in *A Study in Scarlet* as a tall, thin, flamboyant, and eccentric student in the pathology laboratory of St. Bartholomew's Hospital, London, where he is developing a practical test for bloodstains. By Chapter II he is rooming with Watson at 221B Baker Street, and before long Watson, puzzled about his companion, tries to set out his "limits" in a famous chart:

> 1. Knowledge of Literature. — Nil.
> 2.   "   " Philosophy. — Nil.
> 3.   "   " Astronomy. — Nil.

And so on. Eventually he discovers that Holmes is "a consulting detective," who believes in keeping in the "lumber-room" of his brain only such information as he is likely to need. As the acquaintance deepens, however, it becomes clear that Holmes is by no means so utilitarian in his thoughts, or so innocent of literature, philosophy, astronomy, and the rest. Indeed, by the time of "The Lion's Mane" late in the Canon, the reader is not surprised to hear Holmes himself speaking of the vague and half-remembered information stored somewhere in the "box-room" that his mind has become.

Holmes's intellectual limits extend at least to these distances:

- A vast knowledge of (non-fictional) criminal literature and the history of crime and strange occurrences, which he is wont to cite for the bewilderment of professional detectives.
- Technical knowledge of tobacco ash, footprints, tattoos, ciphers, manuscript dating, and other such subjects, on all of which he claimed to have written monographs — to say nothing of "the influence of a trade upon the form of the hand." At the end of his career he prepared *The Whole Art of Detection*.
- A detailed knowledge of London, including its geography and an extraordinary number of its people among all classes.
- An enjoyment of serious music and at least a superficial acquaintance with composers and performers, although it appears that he attended concerts as a means of relaxation rather than to be stimulated through

close attention as a genuine musical aficionado might. He also showed the ability to play the violin passably, and the flexibility to extract noises from it while it was flung carelessly across his knee rather than held in the usual position.

- An acquaintance, perhaps broad rather than deep, with literature in a number of languages; he refers to Hafiz, Horace, Gustave Flaubert, George Sand, Goethe, and even the occasional English author, and claims at one point to be carrying "my pocket Petrarch."

- "A good practical knowledge of British law," as Watson puts it — the sort of familiarity that bred contempt, judging from a number of incidents in which Holmes lets malefactors go free, breaks into dwelling-houses in the nighttime, extorts evidence in defiance of the Judges' Rules, and otherwise comports himself outside the law.

- Considerable knowledge of chemistry, to the point that he spent months (at least) conducting researches at Montpellier shortly before the affair of "The Empty House." He used chemistry in his professional work at times, probably chiefly to detect poisons, but also apparently did experiments to occupy his mind in the intervals between cases. He was frequently unable, however, to explain his work clearly to Watson, who reports him attempting to "dissolve" a hydrocarbon as though that were a difficult achievement.

- An unparalleled ability to observe trifles about a person, room, or road and to apply logic and a knowledge of daily life in order to reconstruct the events of the past.

HOLMES THE MAN. But there is more to Sherlock Holmes than this intellectual catalogue; there remain the traits that caused Watson to label him "best and wisest." Such traits are not so easily listed, for they are conveyed to the reader — as they were to Watson — through long acquaintance and leisurely intercourse.

Christopher Morley, selecting episodes from the Canon and preparing a school edition of them in 1944, called his volume *Sherlock Holmes and Dr. Watson: A Textbook of Friendship.* The modern reader may snicker at the portrayal of a close, emotional friendship between two adult men, and certainly at such sentiments as Holmes and Watson express about one another in "The Three Garridebs" at the dreadful moment when Watson is wounded. Are they lovers? one may wish to ask. They are not, although one or two pornographers have chosen to interpret them that way. They are simply close friends, demonstrating a kind of relationship that was common both in the literature and in the real life of the 1890s. It was an era when friendship between men and women on equal terms was virtually impossible, and when the bonds one might associate with soldiers under fire could also be formed between men in the world of London clubs and flats. The picture of it seen in Holmes and Watson appears wholesome indeed beside the male relationships in, say, George du Maurier's *Trilby* (1894).

Holmes evidently has some of the qualities one might want most in a friend, the right combination of loyalty (emphasized in "The Dying Detective" when Holmes is obliged to pretend betrayal) and independence. The mutual affection of Holmes and Watson is understated, both as a demonstration of the friendship's firmness and as a natural consequence of Victorian formality. "My dear Watson," and "My dear Doctor," Holmes still calls his colleague after twenty years of shared danger. He is obeying the conventions of his time and place, but no doubt the stress was all on the "dear."

How tolerable Holmes may have been as a companion is another question altogether. His "cat-like love of personal cleanliness" is balanced by a pack-rat love of clutter, an indifference to the proper places for household objects, a taste for strong tobacco to the point of filling his rooms with a thick blue haze of smoke. He is demanding, both of Watson and of strangers; he is secretive, preferring to spring surprises rather than take a companion into his confidence. He is also a captive of many Victorian prejudices, seen in their ugliest form in his baiting of a black man in "The Three Gables" and one or two remarks that may be anti-Semitic. At times he fawns on the rich and aristocratic, although he can be contemptuous of those, such as the King of Bohemia, who do not live up to *noblesse oblige*, and he can occasionally be very gentle with the lowly.

Most notably, Holmes is moody, alternating periods of energy, enthusiasm, and prodigious work with periods of languor, inactivity, and apparent depression. Alan Bradley and William Sarjeant in *Ms. Holmes of Baker Street* (1989), affecting to believe that the detective was secretly a woman, attribute this alternation of moods to the influence of a strong menstrual cycle. Most other commentators have unhesitatingly seen it as a manic-depressive personality at work. Holmes could be arrogant (though rarely as disagreeable to Watson as Basil Rathbone makes him in his films of the 1940s) and nervous (though not nearly so full of tics, shrill cries, and mindless movement as Jeremy Brett makes him in the television series of the 1980s).

In the early stories, most explicitly *The Sign of the Four*, Holmes is seen as a user of drugs, "a seven-per-cent solution" of cocaine, which is a stimulant and anti-depressant. Watson scolds him for this abuse of his body, but seems resigned to it. Use of such drugs was legal in the England of the 1890s, and is used to emphasize Holmes's mercurial personality and his pose of sophisticated eccentricity. Many details are elucidated by Jack Tracy and Jim Berkey in *Subcutaneously, My Dear Watson* (1978):

Holmes's cocaine habit was in no way unlawful. . . . Not until 1916 was the sale of cocaine restricted to a doctor's prescription. . . . If Holmes made use of a 10- to 20-mg. dose in each of his three-times-daily injections, then his habit was costing him between 2¢. and 4¢ a day. . . . 10 percent became the official strength of solution in the *British Pharmacopœia* in 1898. . . . One grain, or 65 mg. — legally purchased from the neighbourhood chemist — would then provide three ample doses, one day's supply, and a grain a day was often mentioned in the literature of the time as a recommended dosage for the treatment of melancholia.

The horrified reaction of modern readers, aware of contemporary drug abuse, is a misunderstanding of the character as Doyle was drawing him and his habits.

HOLMES AND WOMEN. "Women have seldom been an attraction to me," Holmes says in "The Lion's Mane," "for my brain has always governed my heart." But the converse is far from true; something in Holmes's character has attracted the opposite sex since the days when the first stories were being published, and Doyle received proposals of marriage on his character's behalf. One contemporary woman has observed that "I feel sorry for men Sherlockians, because they don't have Sherlock Holmes to fall in love with." Even within the Canon, such women as Violet Hunter ("The Copper Beeches") and Mary Morstan (who eventually marries Watson) show some attraction to Holmes. He does not reciprocate, making a number of derogatory remarks about women, although he does demonstrate an expert knowledge of perfumes and millinery when they are relevant to his investigation. The apparent exception, on which many Sherlockians have written at length, is Irene Adler of "A Scandal in Bohemia," significantly a story written before Holmes's character was fully formed and demonstrated. He calls Irene Adler *the* woman," giving a lasting impression of infatuation even though Watson assures the reader that there was nothing emotional in Holmes's admiration of her. She is an extraordinary woman compared to the damsels in distress who populate many of the other tales, and those who insist that Holmes should have a mate could do worse than settle for her.

"May I marry Holmes?" William Gillette is said to have telegraphed to Doyle when he was writing his play *Sherlock Holmes* at the turn of the century, meaning that he felt the need to introduce a love interest. Doyle's response: "You may marry him or murder him or do what you like with him." Gillette did, and numerous dramatizers and authors have followed suit, including Jerome Coopersmith, who explained what he had done in the musical *Baker Street* (1965): "I gave Sherlock Holmes a girl friend, and that is as it should be." Novelist Laurie R. King has gone farther, giving Holmes a wife, a far younger woman named Mary Russell who is a theology student and apprentice detective, in a series of novels that began with *The Beekeeper's Apprentice* (1994). They have attracted a large coterie of (mostly female) fans with an online presence (*www.rj-anderson.com/russell*), although many sober Sherlockians have trouble recognizing the Holmes they portray. In the Canon itself, the fair sex is, as Holmes says, Watson's department. (Holmes's love life, and related issues, are treated at length in my book *In Bed with Sherlock Holmes*, 1984.)

THE GREAT HIATUS. No aspect of Holmes's life is odder than the three years that are said to have elapsed between May 1891 and April 1894, that is, between the events of "The Final Problem" and those of "The Empty House." The latter story offers Holmes's brief narrative: after escaping Professor Moriarty at the Falls of the Reichenbach, he travelled to Tibet, conducted explorations under the name of Sigerson, visited such exotic sites as Mecca (where non-Muslims are not welcome) and Khartoum (capital of the Sudan, during an interlude between bitter wars against Britain), and spent time at Montpellier in France doing laboratory research into "the coal-tar derivatives."

The reader who sees the stories as biography demands a better truth, an explanation that adds something to the understanding of Holmes's personality. The fascination with the Great Hiatus (a term for this three-year interlude apparently coined by Edgar W. Smith in a 1946 article in the *Baker Street Journal*) may also proceed from a wish to know exactly why and how Holmes changed — why, as folklore insists that a contemporary reader told Doyle, "Sherlock Holmes may not have died when he fell down that waterfall, but he was never the same man afterwards." Jack Tracy, in his *Encyclopaedia Sherlockiana* (1977), says quite truthfully: "In the absence of supporting evidence, an enormous number of alternate theories have been formed to account for Holmes's activities during this period, each more outrageous than the others." For example, the story of his involvement in the August 4, 1892, murders at Fall River, Massachusetts, in which Lizzie Borden was acquitted, has yet to be told. The events of "Wisteria Lodge" are alleged to have taken place in 1892, clearly an impossibility.

A FIGURE OF REAL LIFE. William S. Baring-Gould's *Sherlock Holmes of Baker Street* (1962) is a full-length "biography," with this significant authorial note: "No characters in this book are fictional, although the author should very much like to meet any who claim to be." He thus takes to its extreme the Sherlockian game of treating Holmes as a historical figure, skillfully blending inferences from the Canon with information from more conventional historical sources. He begins with Holmes's birth, continues with his hypothetical education and his known early cases, and goes through the dramatic points of his career as narrated in most of the sixty stories. Final chapters deal with his retirement and with his imagined death on January 6, 1957, on a cliff top in Sussex.

Along the way, Baring-Gould introduces a number of ideas that are sometimes accepted by Sherlockians as authentic parts of Holmes's life, although they are best classified as folklore:

- That Professor Moriarty was his mathematics tutor in his youth.
- That Holmes had a second brother, Sherrinford (a name taken from Doyle's earliest notes for *A Study in Scarlet*, which used the name "Sherrinford Holmes" for the detective himself, and "Ormond Sacker" for Watson).
- That Holmes toured America as a young actor in 1879–81.
- That he assisted in the solution of the Jack the Ripper murders in London in 1888.
- That he enjoyed a dalliance with Irene Adler in Montenegro shortly after his supposed death at the Reichenbach Falls.

At the same time, he gives the status of history to speculations that have been vaguely accepted by Sherlockians, such as a birth date for Holmes of January 6, 1854. The year seems plausible from several Canonical references. The month and date are attributed to Christopher Morley, who apparently chose them to match those of his brother Frank, and to refer to *Twelfth Night*, a play which Holmes twice quotes. A later scholar has seen significance in Holmes's behaviour on a January 7 in *The Valley of Fear*: he shows signs of suffering from a hangover.

More recent "biographies" of Holmes are the work of June Thomson (*Holmes and Watson*, 1995) and Nick Rennison (*Sherlock Holmes: The Unauthorized Biography*, 2005). In addition, a number of novelists have imagined or reimagined parts of Holmes's life, from Michael Harrison (*I, Sherlock Holmes*, 1977) to countless authors of pastiches. Doyle might well have been astonished by such detailed attention to his creation, although he saw something of Holmes's power in the indignant letters he received after "The Final Problem" killed off the detective, as well as the proposals of marriage that arrived for Holmes at other times in his career. Letters in fact still are directed to Holmes at his address of 221B Baker Street, and through the latter half of the twentieth century were answered by a staff member at the Abbey National Building Society, which happened to occupy that address. A selection of them was published as *Letters to Sherlock Holmes* (1985). More recently, correspondence addressed to 221B is delivered to the Sherlock Holmes Museum nearby at 239 Baker Street. The existence of such letters is a tribute to the plausibility of the figure Doyle originally created, although the image of Holmes that now lives in the public mind is much less subtle and complex than the one that lives in the pages of the Canon.

JOHN H. WATSON

The Canon, save for four short stories and a few other passages, is presented as memoirs by John H. Watson, a former army doctor who was the companion of Sherlock Holmes for most of his working life. Indeed, the first half of *A Study in Scarlet* is subtitled as "a reprint from the reminiscences" of the good doctor, leading playful bibliographers to speculate about the very limited press run those *Reminiscences* must have had. Watson thus must be considered first as an "author" (in which case Arthur Conan Doyle is relegated to the status of Literary Agent, a title some Sherlockians have been happy to give him) and then as a character.

As author — biographer, one might say — Watson is a trifle self-conscious; several Canonical stories mention exchanges between him and Holmes about the narratives he has published, which Holmes says are full of "romanticism" and empty of detective logic. "I could not tamper with the facts," Watson indignantly replies in *The Sign of the Four*. But there is much evidence that he does tamper with them, both deliberately and accidentally. "The Second Stain," for example, acknowledges the need to be "vague in certain details," to avoid betraying state secrets. The frequent references to towns and streets that do not exist, politicians who did not hold office, and weather that does not match the records in *The Times*, all suggest similar concealment. Other inconsistencies, such as the jump from June to September within a few hours in *The Sign of the Four*, can be attributed to carelessness. Sherlockians have taken joy for several decades in identifying and explaining such little errors, often blaming them on a medical man's dreadful penmanship. Late in the Canon, Watson is very bold about addressing his audience directly, as when he uses the introductory paragraph of "The Veiled Lodger" to announce that a certain story will be made public if illicit attempts to get at his papers are not abandoned. By that time, the relationship between Holmes and Watson is one of equals, the author having an established position just as the detective has. Holmes himself observes that "I am lost without my Boswell," alluding to James Boswell, the companion and biographer of the eighteenth-century figure Dr. Samuel Johnson. Certainly Holmes without Watson is far different, far less comprehensible, the forlorn eccentric of "The Lion's Mane" with no one to narrate the tales — and, more important, no one to serve as reliable setting for his sparkling gem.

Watson has been called "boobus Britannicus," a phrase originated by Edmund Pearson (in *The Bookman*, 1932), who blamed illustrator Arthur Keller for making Watson look truly stupid. That was before Nigel Bruce's bumbling portrayal in the 1940s films where he is made a constant fool, the better to set off Basil Rathbone's Holmes. But the original Watson is no boob. Holmes is perhaps generous in telling Watson that "though you are not yourself luminous, you are a conductor of light," but beyond doubt Watson is a man of common sense — as a physician, and certainly an army doctor, must be — and of courage as well as other good qualities which Holmes often recognizes. He may patronize Watson for lacking intellect to match his own, sometimes descending to cruelty, but it seems clear in most of the stories that he also respects Watson's judgement. A passage in *The Valley of Fear* is particularly telling. Holmes has spun an elaborate web of speculation about the case, and Watson is doubtful:

> "We have only their word for that."
>   Holmes looked thoughtful. "I see, Watson. You are sketching out a theory by which everything they say from the beginning is false.... Well, that is a good sweeping generalization. Let us see what that brings us to...."

Watson proves to be wrong and Holmes right, of course, but the mutual respect remains. Holmes also finds his companion valuable as a reliable ally in time of emergency, the man who carries the gun in several crises and who will keep his wits about him. Indeed, there is more. At the end of "The Abbey Grange" he addresses his friend: "Watson, you are a British jury, and I never met a man who was more eminently fitted to represent one." Readers of the stories have generally agreed, as did Edgar W. Smith in one of his eloquent editorials in the *Baker Street Journal* (1955), observing that it is the admirable

Watson, rather than the unpredictable Holmes, who would make the more welcome friend. He may be ancestor of a hundred foolish companions to brilliant detectives (a cliché which also owes something to early Westerns), but he is himself an very fine fellow.

Biographical details about Watson are few. Of his family, the reader hears only about the "unhappy brother" whose alcoholism and death are chronicled in the early pages of *The Sign of the Four*. Watson took his medical degree in 1878 from the University of London (which validated credentials earned through hospital study, rather than providing medical instruction of its own), entered the army, and served in the Second Afghan War. British troops were in Afghanistan for the defence and consolidation of the Empire, and in particular to deter Russia from menacing India through the mountains. A treaty signed in 1879 with local puppet rulers got little respect from the heavily armed populace, and a powerful force massed in the spring of 1880. As Watson reports in *A Study in Scarlet*, he was wounded at the Battle of Maiwand, which took place July 27, 1880, about fifty miles northwest of Kandahar. It was an utter rout for the British; he was unusually lucky to survive in the slaughter and terrible heat, and to be carried to Kandahar in safety and eventually returned to England. *Maiwand* (2008) by Richard J. Stackpoole Ryding tells the story of the battle but somehow omits any reliable explanation of how Watson was injured. Although he claims that the Jezail bullet which hit him struck his shoulder and grazed the subclavian artery, there are references in later Canonical tales to a wound in his leg, or in one instance to an injured Achilles tendon. A number of Sherlockians have tried to reconcile all those references, suggesting two wounds, a faulty memory, malingering, or a bullet with an ingeniously complicated trajectory.

Repatriated to England, Watson soon met Holmes (on January 1, 1881, according to at least some scholars) and took up residence with him at 221B Baker Street. He remained there, apparently, for about seven years, until his marriage to Mary Morstan, at the end of *The Sign of the Four*. Thereafter, in several cases that are part of *The Adventures*, Watson is clearly living with a long-suffering wife, presumably Mary, and has entered private medical practice. Repeatedly he leaves Mary (and turns over the practice to an accommodating colleague, Jackson or Anstruther) briefly to accompany Holmes on some adventure. But by the time of "The Empty House," which takes place in 1894, Watson has suffered a bereavement, and is free to move into the old rooms again, abandoning medicine for biography, when Holmes returns to London after a three-year absence. Still later, in "The Blanched Soldier," Holmes speaks of Watson having "deserted me for a wife," and one infers a second marriage. Sherlockians traditionally drink a toast to "Dr. Watson's second wife," and a number of them have tried to identify her. The chronology is impossibly complicated, with inconsistencies that can be attributed to Watson's muddled thinking or, more realistically, to Doyle's complete indifference to such details. Of course it is more fun for Sherlockians to speculate that, as one of them has put it, "Watson had as many wives as Henry VIII."

The fair sex is his department, as Holmes says; but he is chivalrous about it, and decent in every way. (Rex Stout's article "Watson Was a Woman," in the *Saturday Review of Literature* in 1941 and the anthology *Profile by Gaslight* three years later, was only a joke.) He seems to be the ideal Britisher, whom the author holds up to the reader as the measure of the less conventional Holmes. Indeed, one might say, he seems to be the author's representative. Says Peter Costello in *The Real World of Sherlock Holmes* (1991): "Dr. Watson, whatever other models he may have had in real life, such as Conan Doyle's own secretary Major Wood, is largely drawn from Doyle himself. For a start both are medical men of much the same age with sporting interests. Both have a bluff, hearty appearance. Both seem conventional, Imperialist in politics, non-intellectual men of action. Dr. Watson even shares Conan Doyle's love for Southsea, and his literary tastes." If Holmes is Arthur Conan Doyle's mentor, Joseph Bell, surely Watson is Doyle himself.

THE SUPPORTING ACTORS

PROFESSOR JAMES MORIARTY. For all the reputation he has developed as Holmes's arch-enemy, Professor James (if that was in fact his given name) Moriarty figures in only three stories — in "The Final Problem" and "The Empty House," with complementary narratives of the events surrounding his death, and briefly in *The Valley of Fear*. Countless cartoonists and parodists have drawn Moriarty into their creations; such respectable Holmesians as the producers of the Granada television series of the 1980s have succumbed to the temptation to expand his role, for example making Moriarty the genius behind the events of "The Red-Headed League," an idea for which there is no justification in the original story.

Moriarty is presented, in "The Final Problem" and the second chapter of *The Valley of Fear*, as the master-criminal behind "half that is evil and ... nearly all that is undetected" in London:

He sits motionless, like a spider in the centre of its web, but that web has a thousand radiations, and he knows well every quiver of each of them. He does little himself. He only plans. But his agents are numerous and splendidly organized. Is there a crime to be done, a paper to be abstracted, we will say, a house to be rifled, a man to be removed — the word is passed to the professor, the matter is organized and carried out.

In short, Moriarty is the modern Jonathan Wild, a successor to the criminal leader who operated in London at the beginning of the eighteenth century (born in 1683, he was hanged in 1725) and is known chiefly from Henry Fielding's 1743 satire *The Life and Death of Jonathan Wild the Great*. Alec MacDonald, the Scotland Yard inspector in *The Valley of Fear*, vaguely dismisses Wild as "someone in a novel." Holmes, of course, noting that Wild was real, adds that "The old wheel turns, and the same spoke comes up." In "The Final Problem" he calls Moriarty "the Napoleon of crime." The title is apparently borrowed from the sobriquet of another real-life criminal, Adam Worth (1844–1902), best known for the 1876 theft of a portrait of the Duchess of Devonshire by Thomas Gainsborough from a London gallery. His story is told in *The Napoleon of Crime* by Ben Macintyre (1997).

Moriarty is presented as a professor of mathematics, formerly of "one of our smaller universities," dismissed as the result of "hereditary tendencies" which led him into unspecified wickedness. "At the age of twenty-one he wrote a treatise upon the binomial theorem which has had a European vogue," Holmes says, referring to one of the basic principles of algebra. More ominously, he elsewhere refers to Moriarty's work on *The Dynamics of an Asteroid*, which has been interpreted as having to do with space travel or even atomic energy (and may in fact be a study of the notoriously complicated three-body problem of gravitational attraction). Sherlockians have sometimes compared his academic career with that of Simon Newcomb (1835–1909), an astronomer and author in other fields who worked at the Johns Hopkins University and elsewhere and is known as the rival of logician Charles Sanders Peirce. Of Moriarty's personal life the only information provided in the Canon is that one brother was "a station master in the west of England" and another, also named James, a colonel. The professor's physique was remarkable, as Holmes describes it in "The Final Problem," as he was "extremely tall and thin," with a great domed forehead, rounded shoulders, and a habit of oscillating his face "from side to side in a curiously reptilian fashion."

Some close readers of the text have suggested that Moriarty never existed — that he was a fantasy of a drug-addicted Holmes, or at least that he was an innocent man, all his crimes imagined by Holmes in some paranoid delusion. Nicholas Meyer used that idea to good advantage in his highly successful novel *The Seven-Per-Cent Solution* (1974), and Jeremy Brett's play *The Secret of Sherlock Holmes* (1989) offers a variation on it. That extreme is no more reasonable than the popular Sherlockian belief that everything evil has Moriarty behind it, and the vague impression among the public that the Holmes stories are about one struggle after another between the detective and the professor, rather as Denis Nayland Smith endlessly battles Fu Manchu in the writings of Sax Rohmer. A particularly well-rounded picture of Moriarty the master criminal is provided in a trilogy of novels by John Gardner: *The Return of Moriarty* (1974), *The Revenge of Moriarty* (1975), and, much delayed, *Moriarty* (2008).

IRENE ADLER. "She is the daintiest thing under a bonnet on this planet," Holmes reports in "A Scandal in Bohemia," before setting eyes on Irene Adler. No matter: the description has been generally accepted, as has Watson's report that Holmes characterized her as "*the* woman." She is mentioned in one or two other stories, but only in reference to the adventure of which she is the central figure, "A Scandal in Bohemia."

Early in that story, Holmes looks her up in a reference book and reports that she is an operatic contralto, born in New Jersey and now retired from the international stage. He patronizingly calls her a "young person"; the King of Bohemia, who feels the threat of blackmail from her, calls her a "well-known adventuress." Holmes is engaged to recover the compromising papers from her clutches, and quite fails to do so. By the end of the tale, having seen the lady in person, he is so impressed — perhaps with her courage and intelligence, perhaps with her beauty — that he asks for her photograph as a souvenir, and allows Watson to record that he had been "beaten by a woman's wit."

Irene Adler lives in St. John's Wood, the fashionable London neighbourhood in which wealthy men did typically install their mistresses. She is presumably modelled on the women known as adventuresses, *grandes horizontales*, or "pretty horsebreakers" — courtesans more realistically associated with the 1860s, such as Laura Bell, Cora Pearl, Catherine Walters, and Caroline Otero. *Fanfare of Strumpets* (1971), a non-Sherlockian book by that venerable Sherlockian Michael Harrison, is full of anecdotes about them. In Irene Adler there may also be a whiff of the scandalous Sarah Bernhardt (1844–1923) and of Lillie Langtry (1852–1929), "the Jersey Lily" who became a mistress of Edward, Prince of Wales. Yet another original is clearly Lola Montez (1818–61), whose intrigues with Louis of Bavaria had been notorious five decades earlier. At a less exalted level, Sherlockians associate Irene Adler with "Aunt Clara," the spoilt heroine of a 1940s comic song, the full story of which is told in *We Always Mention Aunt Clara* (1990) by W.T. Rabe.

There is little in the text of the story to justify attaching to Irene Adler either the social standing or the morals of such women. A feminist interpretation of her life (as put forward, not surprisingly, by some of the Adventuresses of Sherlock Holmes) makes her an early career woman, misused and cast aside by a snob of a Bohemian prince. The American mystery novelist Carole Nelson Douglas interprets her in that way with particular sensitivity and conviction in a series of eight books:

- *Good Night, Mr. Holmes* (1990)
- *Good Morning, Irene* (1991), also published as *The Adventuress*
- *Irene at Large* (1992), also published as *A Soul of Steel*
- *Irene's Last Waltz* (1994), also published as *Another Scandal in Bohemia*
- *Chapel Noir* (2001)
- *Castle Rouge* (2002)
- *Femme Fatale* (2003)
- *Spider Dance* (2004)

But most readers, it seems, have preferred to see her as the woman Sherlock Holmes loved and lost (or, in a minority view, loved and later won). Belden Wigglesworth celebrated her in a poem in the *Baker Street Journal* in 1946, one of many such apostrophes:

> I wonder what your thoughts have been,
> Your inmost thoughts of him, Irene,
> Across the years?....
> Did you forget?
> Did Baker Street *quite* lack a Queen?
> I wonder.

These and other imaginings are discussed at length, as are all aspects of Irene Adler, in chapters of my book *In Bed with Sherlock Holmes* (1984).

There is much to say about her, and much that has already been said, but the Canon provides little basis for either sentimental or prurient speculation about a Holmes-Adler connection.

MYCROFT HOLMES. The brother of Sherlock Holmes, older than he by seven years, figures in two cases, both of which he brings to the detective's attention. One is "The Greek Interpreter," in which the client, Mr. Melas, happens to lodge in the same building as Mycroft. The other is "The Bruce-Partington Plans," a government affair in which Mycroft, on behalf of the highest authorities, demands his brother's assistance — for Mycroft, who "audits the books in some of the government departments" in the first case, turns out in this later one to have a much more crucial position. "Occasionally he *is* the British government," Holmes tells an astonished Watson:

> We will suppose that a minister needs information as to a point which involves the Navy, India, Canada and the bimetallic question; he could get his separate advices from various departments upon each, but only Mycroft can focus them all, and say offhand how each factor would affect the other.... Again and again his word has decided the national policy.

Such a description foreshadows the computerized "expert systems" of modern times, and indeed Robert A. Heinlein (in *The Moon Is a Harsh Mistress*, 1966) found it appropriate to name an omniscient computer Mycroft. In more recent years the name has been borrowed for a number of software projects, including "a network that allows thousands of people to collaborate on large, complex jobs" developed at the University of California at Berkeley.

Watson describes Mycroft's body as "gross," his fat hand "like the flipper of a seal." His habits are unvarying and unathletic — "Jupiter is descending," says Holmes when his brother condescends to call. Otherwise, "Mycroft has his rails and he runs on them. His Pall Mall lodgings, the Diogenes Club, Whitehall — that is his cycle." (The Diogenes Club, described in "The Greek Interpreter," is a club — which Sherlock Holmes finds "soothing" at times — for unclubbable men, forbidden by by-law to take any notice of one another, or to talk, save in the Strangers' Room.) But his detective powers are immense. "It was Adams, of course," he says to his more active brother about a case the latter has been working to solve. Action, of course, is "not my *métier*," but theorizing and thought from an armchair — in that, Mycroft Holmes excels. The passage from "The Greek Interpreter" in which the brothers compete in deductions about a stranger on the street is a classic, so much so that Doyle used it as one of his "readings" when he lectured in North America in 1894:

> "An old soldier, I perceive," said Sherlock.
> "And very recently discharged," remarked the brother.
> "Served in India, I see."
> "And a non-commissioned officer."

And so on. Not for nothing has it been suggested that Nero Wolfe, the corpulent, chair-bound detective created by Rex Stout in *Fer-de-Lance* (1934), *The Doorbell Rang* (1965), and several dozen other novels, is a relative of Mycroft Holmes.

MRS. HUDSON. The best appreciation of Holmes's landlady, Mrs. Hudson, is an article by Vincent Starrett that appeared in the 1944 anthology *Profile by Gaslight*. He writes of her possible background, her management of the house at 221B Baker Street, her staff, and her loyalty to Holmes, shown particularly in her patience with his foibles. Other writings about her have interpreted her relationship with the detective in various ways, some suggesting that it was peculiarly personal. Certainly the kind of devotion seen in "The Empty House," in which she repeatedly crawls to Holmes's wax bust "on my knees" and in danger of her life to adjust its position, suggests something more than the usual relationship between tenant and landlady.

But "landlady" may be slightly misleading. In story after story, Mrs. Hudson is presented as the "housekeeper," and it seems possible that rather than owning the house outright, she had it on a long-term lease and proceeded to rent rooms to gentlemen. Watson does speak, in "The Dying Detective," of Holmes's "princely" rental payments to her. On the other hand Holmes frequently treats her as an employee, demanding refreshment and ignoring scheduled mealtimes, and abuses the fabric of the building when it suits him. The most famous instance is his indoor target practice, in which he shoots the initials V.R. (for Victoria Regina) into the wall — an activity which must at least have filled the house with plaster-dust.

There may well have been a housemaid at 221B, although she is never mentioned, and certainly there was Billy the pageboy, at least during some periods. Other staff are uncertain; Holmes in "Thor Bridge" speaks of a "new cook," which may imply that there had been a former cook, or may mean that Mrs. Hudson had finally delegated the kitchen duties to an employee. Breakfast may have been her forte, for it is mentioned in story after story, and in "The Naval

Treaty" Holmes offers the high praise that Mrs. Hudson has "as good an idea of breakfast as a Scotchwoman," a comment that has led to the general impression that she was in fact Scots. Then there is the famous reference in "A Scandal in Bohemia" to "Mrs. Turner," one of those cruxes that Sherlockians love; it has been variously interpreted as meaning a cook, a temporary replacement while Mrs. Hudson was holidaying or unwell, or simply absent-mindedness on someone's part.

Of the woman herself we know little, not even her first name, although without evidence she has been identified with the "Martha" who is the housekeeper in "His Last Bow." Holmes once speaks of her cronies, but their identity is as unknown as Mrs. Hudson's taste in amusement, food, or furnishings. Even her physique can only be inferred from a reference to her "stately tread." What matters to the reader of the Sherlock Holmes tales is her reliable maintenance of the house in Baker Street, and her presence (in only fourteen of the sixty stories) as the motherly figure without whom the sometimes childlike Holmes would be lost in London. For that role, readers remember and honour her. Vincent Starrett again: "It is proverbial that landladies never die."

BILLY. The pageboy of 221B Baker Street appears in ten of the stories, only three times by name. The "Billy" who ushers in visitors in *The Valley of Fear*, *circa* 1889, can hardly be the same boy who is there for "Thor Bridge" and "The Mazarin Stone" more than a decade later. A succession of boys is the obvious explanation, and it may be as few as two of them, since the appearances are clustered, most in stories that take place in the 1880s, two in the early 1900s. Among the latter is the passage in "The Mazarin Stone" that has made Billy the object of great affection among readers:

> It was pleasant to Dr. Watson to find himself once more in the untidy room of the first floor in Baker Street.... Finally, his eyes came round to the fresh and smiling face of Billy, the young but very wise and tactful page, who had helped a little to fill up the gap of loneliness and isolation which surrounded the saturnine figure of the great detective.
> "It all seems very unchanged, Billy. You don't change, either...."

A mythical character can remain unchanged for a quarter of a century; perhaps Billy now deserves that title.

THE BAKER STREET IRREGULARS. The youngsters who helped Holmes in a few cases would be of the smallest importance to modern readers had not the American Sherlockians of the 1930s chosen the name "Baker Street Irregulars" for their organization. They might almost have been the same people, for the children of (say) 1890 were middle-aged folks in 1934, when the American BSI had its beginning.

But the original Irregulars were Londoners (one presumes Cockney accents), urchins or "street arabs" in the contemporary phrase. They are seen in *A Study in Scarlet* and *The Sign of the Four*, where their wages are fixed at one shilling a day (around $5 in modern buying power), and their leader is Wiggins. After these two early cases they return only in "The Crooked Man," when the leader is Simpson, the earlier generation of boys having presumably grown past the age when they could be of use to Holmes as unobtrusive spies. In one other case, *The Hound of the Baskervilles*, Holmes uses a boy (Cartwright), but as a lone agent on Dartmoor rather than as the leader of a London gang.

"Irregulars" are combatants not from the regular army (George Washington used the word about his own ragged troops). Applying it to the boys of Baker Street (and there may have been girls too; the text is indefinite), Holmes means investigators who are independent of the police. He uses the same word in "Lady Frances Carfax" to mean himself and Watson.

THE UNPUBLISHED CASES

Throughout the tales, Watson is made to drop hints about other cases in which Sherlock Holmes was engaged. Usually he makes mention of the other business that was under way at the time, but sometimes he compares the current case to some other, and on several occasions Holmes does the same thing, drawing both on his direct experience and on his reading.

Such allusions range from the generic ("a very commonplace little murder," Holmes calls his current business in "The Naval Treaty") to the memorable:

> As I turn over the pages, I see my notes upon the repulsive story
> of the red leech and the terrible death of Crosby, the banker.
> Here also I find an account of the Addleton tragedy, and the
> singular contents of the ancient British barrow. The famous
> Smith-Mortimer succession case comes also within this period,
> and so does the tracking and arrest of Huret, the Boulevard
> assassin — an exploit which won for Holmes an autograph

letter of thanks from the French President and the Order of the
Legion of Honour. ["The Golden Pince-Nez"]

Listing the unpublished cases in *The Tin Dispatch-Box* (1965, reprinted
1994), I defined them as "any criminal investigation or professional business in
which Holmes was involved or took a particular contemporary interest. Using
this definition, there are altogether 111 cases." (The listing which led to that
total has a few omissions.) Such cases are of interest to the would-be biographer as clues to filling in the great stretches of Holmes's career not covered in
the published stories, and as instances in which he made use of his powers to
solve mysteries about which the reader would love to hear.

The unpublished cases have provided motifs for a number of "pastiches,"
or imitations of the original tales, including several of the *Exploits of Sherlock
Holmes* (1952–53) by Adrian Conan Doyle and John Dickson Carr. They were
also the basis of many scripts by Edith Meiser and her successors for a long-
running series of American radio dramatizations (1932–43). For such purposes the unpublished cases are ideal, since generally there is merely a thought-
provoking phrase, rather than a plot to which the writer must stick.

A surprising amount can, however, sometimes be deduced about an unpublished case. Edward F. Clark, Jr., in the *Baker Street Journal* in 1963 offered
a careful exegesis of a few words in "The Final Problem": "I knew in the
papers that [Holmes] had been engaged by the French republic upon a matter
of supreme importance." A number of scholars have toyed with "the papers of
ex-President Murillo," mentioned in "The Norwood Builder," identifying that
gentleman with various former South American leaders. Exploration of what
Watson meant to say begins to overlap with investigation of Doyle's sources, as
when "the peculiar persecution of John Vincent Harden" is said to have been
suggested to the author's mind by his reading about Texas bandit John Wesley
Hardin. Some of the unpublished cases refer to historical people, including the
Pope (presumably Leo XIII) and Vanderbilt (one of the New York railroad
clan). Others contain intriguing but inexplicable names, personal or geographi-
cal, including "Isadora Persano" and "the island of Uffa." In a class by itself is
"the giant rat of Sumatra," a phrase that has intrigued not only pasticheurs and
scholars but also the designers of new hazards in the popular game "Dungeons
and Dragons."

THE ROOMS AT 221B BAKER STREET

The arrangement of Holmes's (and, in some of the stories but not all, Watson's) rooms is unclear, and in any case may have changed over the years. "The Mazarin Stone," a story that is a one-act play lightly rewritten, contains what amount to stage directions, calling for exits and entrances hardly compatible with a conventional suite in Baker Street. It is more satisfactory to build up the lodgings — and particularly the sitting room, where most of the action takes place — in the mind's eye. Still, a creditable job has been done by the proprietors of several restorations, particularly the one at the "Sherlock Holmes" public-house in Northumberland Street, London. Some enthusiasts have 221B rooms in their own homes; one created by the late Allen Mackler is now housed at the Wilson Library of the University of Minnesota at Minneapolis. Illustrators, stage designers, and television producers have faced the same challenges as creators of the full-scale article, generally emphasizing whichever features of the room, authentic or otherwise, are needed for their immediate purposes.

A monstrous amount of furniture must be fitted into the room if every sentence in the Canon is to be taken as true. The chairs on either side of the fire, in which one imagines Holmes and Watson sitting to chat, are a bare beginning: Don MacLachlan, writing in *Canadian Holmes* in 1989, includes in the inventory "12 chairs, two stools, one sofa, and something sittable-on by the window. Enough seating for at least 17 people." But there are many other objects in the room as well, from the dining table to the workbench with Holmes's chemicals, not to mention a bearskin rug, a safe, a sideboard, and the coal-scuttle in which Holmes kept his cigars. A plausible floor plan was drawn by Julian Wolff to accompany his analysis of the rooms in the *Baker Street Journal* in 1946. He includes a bathroom adjacent to the sitting room — a facility that may have amounted to a luxury in 1895. He also puts Holmes's bedroom (which figures in "The Dying Detective" in particular) adjacent to the sitting room, relegating Watson to an upper storey (British "second," American "third," floor).

The dominant feature of the suite at 221B must have been clutter. Holmes had "a horror of destroying documents," Watson reports, and attached his unanswered letters to the mantelpiece with his jackknife. Chemical experiments were often in progress, discarded newspapers and telegrams littered the floor, and relics of cases were, Watson says, wont to turn up in the butter dish. There may have been a little space left for Watson's cherished portrait of General "Chinese" Gordon, but the conventional decorations of a Victorian sitting room, the antimacassars and ostrich eggs, must have been almost entirely absent. For it is probably a mistake to imagine a spacious room; the chamber of a pair of bachelors was surely rather cosy than elegant.

HOLMES'S METHODS

"You know my methods," Holmes repeatedly told his companion. If the reader does not know them — as sometimes, it seems, Watson did not — they are evident in passages throughout the Canon, or systematically set out in Brad Keefauver's book *The Elementary Methods of Sherlock Holmes* (1987). Keefauver considers Holmes's immense general knowledge, his reference library, his readiness to compare the present case to precedents in criminal activity, his use of disguise, and other stratagems and resources. But the essence of Holmes's detective ability lay in the data he was able to collect and the reasoning in which he engaged.

Chiefly, Holmes worked from facts. "I cannot make bricks without clay," he said once; and over and over again, "It is a capital mistake to theorize in advance of the facts." And for him facts were usually tiny things — a burnt match in the mud, the torn and ink-stained finger of a glove:

> I can never bring you to realize the importance of sleeves, the suggestiveness of thumb-nails, or the great issues that may hang from a bootlace.... Never trust to general impressions, my boy, but concentrate yourself upon details. My first glance is always at a woman's sleeve. In a man it is perhaps better first to take the knee of the trouser. ["A Case of Identity"]

In using such a procedure to size up a client or a suspicious character, Holmes is following the example of Doyle's medical mentor, Joseph Bell. It is a technique exactly suited to the Victorian age, a period of many specialized trades, and to the British multiplicity of social classes and local customs. In a modern, homogenized North America, where all classes dress alike and only a few people work in trades that leave such marks as the weaver's tooth or the compositor's left thumb, a Sherlock Holmes might have a much more difficult task.

The observation of trifles is not limited to assessing profession and character. Holmes uses it particularly in examining the scene of a crime, engaging in the famous "floor-walk" with his "powerful convex lens" in search of tiny objects: a pill in *A Study in Scarlet*, "what seemed to me to be dust" (but was tobacco ash) in "The Boscombe Valley Mystery." Footprints and other traces are a specialty. The ability to see details, rather than "general impressions," makes it possible for Holmes to understand the significance of a chip on a railing in "Thor Bridge," and of beeswing in a wineglass in "The Abbey Grange."

Writing in the journal *Endeavour* in 2004, Laura Snyder, a specialist in the history and philosophy of science, assesses whether Holmes can fairly be called a pioneering "scientific detective." She concludes in part:

> Rather than inventing forensic science, the Holmes stories instead presented the "science of criminal detection" in a positive light in Britain. This was particularly important after the 1859 Smethurst case, in which a leading toxicologist had been forced to admit that his earlier findings ... had been mistaken.... Sherlock Holmes did not invent forensic science, but he probably did more than any other person, fictional or not, to portray it as a valuable tool.

Sir Bernard Spilsbury (1877–1947), dubbed by one biographer "the father of forensics," will be disappointed to hear it.

Finally, of course, Holmes has the knowledge of previous cases, and his general knowledge of society, to help him focus his attention:

> "How did you see that?"
> "Because I looked for it." ["The Dancing Men"]

What he does not have is the improbable, detailed knowledge of every science, craft, and art seen in such later detectives as R. Austin Freeman's Dr. Thorndyke. Holmes is widely read and experienced, but chiefly in the areas that he knows will come in handy. His methods strongly resemble those of the physician, writes Kathryn Montgomery Hunter in *Doctors' Stories* (1991): he compares the symptoms of his current case to those of many previous cases, his own and those of other investigators, before making a diagnosis and prescribing treatment. Chapter V of the present work includes some consideration of the state of science in Holmes's time.

The form of reasoning Holmes uses, which he variously calls "deduction," "logical synthesis," and "inference," is certainly not the same as the traditional formal logic, which is a form of mathematics developed in the middle ages, concerned not with truth but with consistency. The simplest example of a "syllogism," the form into which logic casts its ideas, is this:

> All dogs are mortal.
> The Hound of the Baskervilles is a dog.
> Therefore the Hound of the Baskervilles is mortal.

The first two statements, or "premises," lead to the conclusion; thus the syllogism is logically sound. A second syllogism,

> Scotland Yard inspectors are detectives.
> Sherlock Holmes is a detective.
> Therefore Sherlock Holmes is a Scotland Yard inspector.

is unsound because of what logic calls "the fallacy of the undistributed middle." The premises may or may not be true, but either way they do not prove the conclusion. On the other hand, a logically sound syllogism can have wildly untrue premises, and thus demonstrate nothing about the truth of the conclusion.

Holmes rarely works in this way, although he speaks of it: "From a drop of water, a logician could infer the possibility of an Atlantic or a Niagara." If traditional logic is "deduction," a moving from the general to the specific, from cause to effect, then Holmes's method is really "induction," moving from the specific to the general, from effect to cause. ("The grand thing is to be able to reason backwards," he says in *A Study in Scarlet*.) The nineteenth-century American philosopher Charles Sanders Peirce spoke of induction as moving from "case" and "result" to "rule": "These beans are from this bag. These beans are white. [Therefore,] all the beans from this bag are white." Peirce also offered a third form of logic, abduction: "All the beans from this bag are white. These beans are white. These beans are from this bag." As philosophers Umberto Eco and Thomas A. Sebeok, along with colleagues, explain in *The Sign of Three: Dupin, Holmes, Peirce* (1983), Holmes is strongly inclined to that sort of logic, as in "The Second Stain":

> Here is one of the three men whom we had named as possible actors in this drama, and he meets a violent death during the very hours when we know that that drama was being enacted. The odds are enormous against its being coincidence.

No figures could express them. No, my dear Watson, the two
events are connected.

But neither induction nor abduction is rigorously valid: the process is prone
to error, coincidences do happen, and an effect can have many causes.

As Keefauver demonstrates, Holmes frequently works through "deduction"
in a different sense: imagining as many explanations for the facts as possible,
then deducting (eliminating) the less promising. In his most famous dictum
("The Beryl Coronet") he alludes to this process: "When you have excluded
the impossible, whatever remains, however improbable, must be the truth."
The danger of course is deeming something "impossible" when it is not. Holmes often does that, but such is the art of the detective story that he never goes
wrong in his leaps.

OVERTONES IN THE STORIES

THE MYTH AND THE HERO. To call Sherlock Holmes the "hero" of the
Canonical stories is more than simply to observe that he is the central figure. A
hero is someone who acts in a cause, such as freedom or justice, and according to certain conventions. One classic statement of the hero "pattern" is that
of Lord Raglan (in *The Hero*, 1936), who finds twenty-two common features
in the stories of figures from Oedipus to King Arthur. Holmes can be seen to
have about thirteen of those features, a higher score than Siegfried's, and equal
to that of Robin Hood. He "prescribes laws," for example (*The Whole Art of
Detection*), nothing is known of his childhood, nothing is known of his death.

Many of Raglan's "heroes" are supposed gods. Holmes is not presented
as a god (although G.K. Chesterton wrote about his apotheosis in "Sherlock
Holmes the God" as early as 1935), or even as a king, but merely as "the
head of his profession." However, it is hard to deny that some of his appeal
derives from his conformity to the classic pattern. Most important is his
"death" at the Reichenbach and his "resurrection" three years later. (A fall
from grace and a mysterious death at the top of a hill are involved in several
of Raglan's points.) The spring dates of Holmes's death and resurrection, and
the name of the adversary whom he conquers (Moriarty, suggesting *moriar*,
"I shall die"), remind the attentive reader of Easter, and the Christian story of
the death and resurrection of Jesus (who incidentally scores at least sixteen
points on Raglan's scale). Springtime resurrection is of course not unique to

Christianity, for most religions include some hint of it, based on the natural cycle of vegetation.

Holmes's heroic qualities are such that enthusiasts have tried to associate him with practically every known hero and other prominent figure, pretending that he is the descendant of Shakespeare, the colleague of Marconi, the lover of Sarah Bernhardt, the antagonist of Hitler, the father of Nero Wolfe, the grandson of Horatio Hornblower, and the near relative of Mr. Spock of "Star Trek." Science fiction master Philip José Farmer connected many heroic figures of popular literature, including Holmes, in his hypothetical "Wold Newton Universe," first revealed in *Tarzan Alive* (1972). All such speculations are feeble attempts at describing the emotional, even spiritual, significance of a figure like Sherlock Holmes, who bestrides his world, and the world of the imagination, like a colossus.

There are various short catalogues of the figures who, though fictional or nearly so, have become universally known; they may perhaps include Santa Claus, Robinson Crusoe, Romeo, and Ronald McDonald, but there is no doubt whatsoever that they include Holmes. It is also said that only two characters from literature regularly receive mail. One is Juliet, whose correspondents are lovelorn teenage girls, and the other is Sherlock Holmes.

SEXUAL IMPLICATIONS. Although one might expect a "detective story" to be concerned only with crime and adventure, in fact the Sherlock Holmes tales are rich in love and sexual elements as well. They can be seen from the earliest tales to the latest: *A Study in Scarlet* is about a murder prompted by sexual jealousy, as is "The Retired Colourman," the last story in *The Case-Book*.

Holmes's own love life receives much attention, chiefly through attempts to read more into his relationship with Irene Adler than the text warrants. Some Sherlockians have also attempted to link him with Violet Hunter of "The Copper Beeches," largely through such paragraphs as this one, identified by David Hammer in *Baker Street Miscellanea* (1991):

> I remember nothing until I found myself lying on my bed trembling all over. Then I thought of you, Mr. Holmes.

Taking sentences out of context can, of course, be a delight — John Bennett Shaw, the master of that craft, collected many examples in a paper he titled "To Shelve or to Censor" (1971). A classic is Holmes's remark in "The Speckled Band" that "Mrs. Hudson has been knocked up," an idiom with quite different meanings in America and England.

Legitimate romance plays an important part in *The Sign of the Four*, in which Watson's love affair with Mary Morstan alternates with Holmes's detective work as the plot develops, and in such short stories as "The Noble Bachelor." Less proper relationships drive the plots of "A Case of Identity," "The Crooked Man," and "The Cardboard Box." In *The Hound of the Baskervilles*, much of the dramatic complexity comes from the relations between the sexes: the apparently wholesome attraction between Sir Henry Baskerville and Beryl Stapleton, the sadomasochistic relationship between Beryl and Jack Stapleton, the sad if not scarlet past of Laura Lyons. Then there are any number of stories in which romance provides a subplot, a "love interest" to vary the pace, from Arthur Cadogan West's desertion of his fiancée in "The Bruce-Partington Plans" to Violet Smith's engagement in "The Solitary Cyclist" (a matter which leads Holmes to make a remark that makes the lady blush coyly).

Not surprisingly, traces of the author's own life and relationships can be seen in all these features. Mary Morstan in *The Sign of the Four* is in many respects a portrait of his first wife, Louise. The solid bonds of love between John and Ivy Douglas in *The Valley of Fear* strongly suggest those between Doyle and his second wife, Jean, to whom he had been married seven years when the book was published. Most important in reflecting the author's experience and feelings, however, are a cluster of stories published in the first decade of the twentieth century, during and just after a difficult period in his life, while he was married to the dying Louise but already in love with Jean. In these tales — "The Norwood Builder," "The Solitary Cyclist," "The Devil's Foot," and others — sex is a source of trouble, and repeatedly there are men obliged to choose between two women, or women obliged to choose between two men. In the most dramatic example, "The Abbey Grange" (published in 1904, two years before Louise's death), Doyle puts in the mouths of his characters eloquent arguments for divorce-law reform. Such motifs appear in his stories as late as 1922, when he published "Thor Bridge" and pictured the illicit lady-love of Holmes's client, Neil Gibson, as a woman much like Jean, and every bit as acceptable for him as his true wife.

Sexual motifs have been examined by a number of Sherlockian writers, but chiefly for prurient effect, or as a way of demonstrating that Victorian life was by no means sexless. The latter point should hardly need making again, after demonstration in such non-Sherlockian volumes as *The Worm in the Bud* (1969) by Ronald Pearsall and *The Other Victorians* (1974) by Stephen Marcus. It was an era of fashionable mistresses and *grandes horizontales*, pervasive street prostitution and some white slavery, and lavish pornography. That sexual enthusiasm prevailed, but public discussion of sexual matters was impossible, goes far to explain the origins of the kinds of crime Holmes is seen investigating. Sex in the Sherlockian Canon is discussed at full length in my book *In Bed with Sherlock Holmes* (1984).

OTHER THEMES. Literary theorists and indeed ordinary readers have spotted a number of other themes running through the stories, such as these:

- The conflict between reason (enlightenment, science, civilization, urbanization) and superstition (the ignorant, the supernatural, the primitive, the countryside) as represented, for example, by the contrast between Holmes and such antagonists as Tonga in *The Sign of the Four*, the Hound of the Baskervilles, and Dr. Grimesby Roylott with his cheetah, his baboon, and his "speckled band."

- The nature of masculinity, as seen in a society dominated by men and indeed, so far as the events of the Holmes stories are concerned, populated mostly by men, and represented by a figure whose primary relationship is with another man and who veers from decisive, even violent action, including boxing and swordsmanship, to idleness, "catlike" neatness and a "dreamy" enjoyment of violin music.

- Holmes's ambivalent attitude to the established social order, which he expresses sometimes as fawning on the upper classes and sometimes as undisguised contempt, although he almost always works to enforce the law in the interest of the established authorities and the middle class.

Such topics lie just beneath the surface of stories that are considerably more than puzzles to be solved or adventures to provide thrills.

III

SHERLOCK HOLMES
IN PRINT

THE PUBLISHING OF SHERLOCK HOLMES has been a substantial industry for a hundred years. Each of the sixty stories, though it may appear fixed and inevitable on the printed page, finds its present form — its content, its text, its typography, its illustration — as the result of choices and chances not only on the part of Doyle but on the part of publishers, editors, typographers, and readers over the decades.

An understanding of the stories' origins, the circumstances of their writing, and the details of their transmission from the author's pen to the modern printed page is valuable in understanding their intentions and their ingenuity. The reader must sometimes be a bibliographer, sometimes a critic, and sometimes a connoisseur of language and of art.

There is no complete bibliographical listing of editions of the Canon. Some editions, especially early ones, appear in Green and Gibson's *Bibliography of A. Conan Doyle* (1983) and other works on Doyle. Ronald B. DeWaal's *World Bibliography of Sherlock Holmes* (1974), *International Sherlock Holmes* (1980), and *Universal Sherlock Holmes* (1994, now online at *special.lib. umn.edu/rare/ush/ush.html*) include hundreds of versions of the stories separately and in collections, but the descriptions provided are sparse and often unhelpful, and editions frequently surface that were unknown to this award-winning bibliographer.

SOURCES

A direct source for *The Hound of the Baskervilles* is generally believed to exist, in a "west country legend" told to Doyle (for so he himself says) by a friend, Bertram Fletcher Robinson. At best, however, he worked from a complex of "black-dog" legends associated with unpopulated parts of England, including Dartmoor. Janice McNabb explores those sources in *The Curious Incident of the Hound on Dartmoor* (1984). In *A Study in Surmise* (1984), Michael Harrison sets out in detail what he previously argued elsewhere: that *A Study in Scarlet* is extensively based — indeed, that the existence of Sherlock Holmes is based — on "the vanishing, from his shop in the St. Luke's district of London, of a German baker, Urban Napoleon Stanger. This was in 1881." Indisputably, *The Valley of Fear* is largely based on the doings of the "Mollie Maguires" in the coal country of Pennsylvania in the 1870s. A few other direct sources for large portions of Doyle's plots can be identified.

It has become clear that Doyle not only read voraciously but stored what he read, at least half consciously, to reuse and recombine names and details years later. Donald Redmond has written extensively on specific sources as they can be unearthed:

> Holmes "spoke [in *The Sign of the Four*] on a quick succession of subjects" including the Buddhism of Ceylon and miracle plays. In fact, it seems that he was only relating what he had read in the papers. For *The Times* (London) had on 15 June 1888 reported upon the Congress of Protestant Foreign Missions, then in session, with a long account: "Wednesday afternoon's conference ... subject was 'Buddhism and other kindred heathen systems; their character and influence compared with those of Christianity'.... Sir Monier Monier-Williams [the president of the conference] at once proceeded to place in contrast the Bible of Christianity and the Bible of the Buddhists." Among other matters in the account, evident anti-Catholic accounts would have attracted Conan Doyle's attention. As to miracle plays, Geoffrey S. Stavert, in his recent *A Study in Southsea*, points out that the Rev. H. Shaen Solly of Southampton spoke to the Portsmouth Literary and Scientific Society (in which Conan Doyle was very active) on this exact subject....

After Mary Morstan had left their sitting-room, Sherlock Holmes was probably striving for effect when he "smiled gently" at Watson's shocked reaction to Holmes's languid put-down, and cried, "I assure you that the most winning woman I ever knew was hanged for poisoning three little children for their insurance-money...." In the *Sherlock Holmes Journal* (vol. 11, Summer 1973, pp. 58–63) I looked at this remark, with instances.

Many such connections are of course conjectural. In the absence of a full reading of everything Doyle can have read over a period of several decades, much will emerge only by chance. And it is often unclear whether a correspondence between something in the news, or in an earlier author, and something in Doyle is deliberate allusion, unconscious repetition, or pure coincidence. The researcher can easily be tempted to substitute wishful thinking for evidence. Patterns do, however, emerge. Donald Redmond reports in *Sherlock Holmes: A Study in Sources* (1982) that at least eight of the Scowrers, and some twenty-three other characters in *The Valley of Fear*, appear to be named after medical acquaintances of Doyle. Many characters in *A Study in Scarlet* share surnames with neighbours of Doyle in Southsea and Portsmouth, where he lived when he wrote that book. Often, it appears, a character is named for more than one original, or takes a name from one and an attribute ("club foot" or "tiger hunter") from another.

Sherlock Holmes's own name has been the subject of much interest, especially in the light of his first incarnation as "Sherrinford Holmes" in a page of Doyle's handwritten notes. The author claimed that he had taken the "Sherlock" from a bowler of the Marylebone Cricket Club against whom he once had a run of luck — although the eighteenth-century theologian Thomas Sherlock lurks in the background, and James McCord revealed in the *Baker Street Journal* in 1992 that Jane Sherlock Ball was the mother of one of Doyle's aunts. "Holmes," meanwhile, is popularly assumed to come from Oliver Wendell Holmes the elder, the American doctor and author, whom Doyle much admired. Another possibility is a physician friend and neighbour of Doyle's. Dr. John H. Watson probably takes his name from Dr. James Watson, a medical colleague of Doyle's in Southsea; the first Moriarty ever encountered by Doyle was a master at his school, Stonyhurst College.

JOSEPH BELL. Doyle always maintained that Sherlock Holmes was modelled on Dr. Joseph Bell (born December 2, 1837, died October 4, 1911), professor of surgery in Edinburgh, and the teacher who impressed the young Doyle most. He wrote in his autobiography, *Memories and Adventures*, that when he came to create Holmes, "I thought of my old teacher Joe Bell, of his eagle face, of his curious ways, of his eerie trick of spotting details." Elsewhere in the same book, he tells an anecdote or two about Bell the master of diagnosis, including the famous exchange, quoted in many writings about Doyle, in which Bell begins by greeting a patient: "Well, my man, you've served in the army... Not long discharged?... A Highland regiment?" And so on.

Ely M. Liebow accepts that attribution in his biography *Dr. Joe Bell: Model for Sherlock Holmes* (1982), although he acknowledges that Holmes had other origins as well. ("His importance can be exaggerated," Richard Lancelyn Green agrees in his Introduction to the *Adventures* volume of the *Oxford Sherlock Holmes*.) Bell was editor of the *Edinburgh Medical Journal* from 1873, and a teacher from 1878, as well as an expert consulted by the police in forensic matters, but it was as a practising surgeon that he was best known. Says Liebow:

> Joe Bell was an operator, a great one. He was in all probability better than Syme, better than Lister or Annandale, or any other contemporary, with the exception of the great-but-silent Patrick Heron Watson. While he was in the post-Listerian age, and the post-Simpson age, he would be operating many times in his life without anesthesia and when septicemia still plagued the hospitals. "Rapidity," writes a colleague, "was his keynote, swiftness in operating."

His textbook, *A Manual of the Operations of Surgery* (1866 and subsequent editions), is available in modern facsimile. Doyle, as a medical student, was chosen to be clerk for Bell's clinics at the Royal Infirmary, and heard the great man assess patients with rapid perceptions that he would later put into Holmes's mouth: "This man's limp is not from his hip but from his foot. Were you to observe closely, you would see there are slits, cut by a knife, in those parts of the shoe where the pressure of the shoe is greatest against the foot. The man is a sufferer from corns, gentlemen." Such flashes of insight made an impression, and when Doyle created Holmes he wrote to Bell, "I do not think that his analytical work is in the least an exaggeration of some effects which I have seen you produce in the out-patient ward." Bell's compassion, and his thirst for justice, may also be reflected in Sherlock Holmes.

MANUSCRIPTS

Doyle wrote his stories in longhand, in a firm, squat, generally legible script but with apparent disdain for the rules of punctuation and capitalization. ("For a medical man, Conan Doyle's handwriting was commendably legible, though his o could look like an 'a'," Owen Dudley Edwards wrote in 1993. For that matter, the o could pass for an s on occasion, and vice versa.) There is evidence in the known manuscripts that his first draft was also generally his last; on occasion he left a space in which he would later fill in a name or phrase. It is generally assumed that at least in later years, the text was then typewritten for attention by editors and printers, but no such typescripts seem to survive.

The manuscripts have been thoroughly dispersed by the publishers or by the author's heirs, and the whereabouts of some is unknown. A number, including *The Sign of the Four* and *The Valley of Fear*, are in private hands. Others are in public collections — "The Red Circle" at Indiana University, "The Three Students" at Harvard, three short stories and a chapter of *The Hound of the Baskervilles* at the New York Public Library. A census of the manuscripts by Peter E. Blau can be found, amid many other useful resources, through Randall Stock's web site *www.bestofsherlock.com*.

Portions of many manuscripts have been reproduced in facsimile in Sherlockian journals, and several complete manuscripts have been published in book form, including "The Priory School," "The Dying Detective," "The Lion's Mane," "The Six Napoleons," and "Shoscombe Old Place" (under what appears to have been its original title, "The Adventure of Shoscombe Abbey").

PUBLISHING AND TEXTUAL TRANSMISSION

A publisher is someone, an individual or more commonly a firm, who takes on the responsibility for having an author's book printed and distributed. The usual arrangement is that the author receives "royalties," a percentage of the sale price of the book, often with a minimum payment represented by an "advance" or cash payment when the manuscript is submitted. A 10 percent royalty is a rule of thumb, but the figure can vary: in 1902 Doyle was receiving 25 percent of the sale price on copies of his best-selling *The Hound of the Baskervilles* in Canada. In some cases — rarely today, but more commonly in the nineteenth century — the publisher buys the book outright. The publishers of *Beeton's Christmas Annual* paid Doyle £25 (a not ungenerous $2,000

Study in Scarlet

Ormond Sacker - ~~from~~ ~~Soudan~~ from Afghanistan

Lived at 221 B Upper Baker Street

with

J Sherrinford Holmes -

The Laws of Evidence

Reserved -

Sleepy eyed young man - philosopher - Collector of rare Violins
An Amati -   Chemical laboratory

I have four hundred a year -

I am a Consulting detective   -

What rot this is" I cried - throwing the volume
petulantly aside " I must say that I have no
patience with people who build up fine theories in their
own armchairs which can never be reduced to
practice -   Lecoq was a bungler -
Dupin was better. Dupin was decidedly smart —
His trick of following a train of thought was more
sensational than clever   but still he had analytical

It was "Sherrinford" Holmes, not yet Sherlock, when Arthur Conan Doyle first sketched out his character in 1886. The single page of notes has been reproduced publicly many times (first in Vincent Starrett's The Private Life of Sherlock Holmes *in 1934) but the original is thought to remain in the hands of lawyers for one of the Doyle family estates.*

in today's currency) for the ownership of *A Study in Scarlet*. The author may choose to sell only certain "rights" to a publisher, restricted by geography ("North American rights") or limited to a period of time. Whatever the exact terms of the contract, it becomes the publisher's obligation to pay for the printing of the book, and the publisher makes a profit or takes a loss depending on how well the book sells. A publisher employs editors who do their best to improve the text of the book before it is printed, and staff whose job is to send copies to reviewers, encourage booksellers to stock the book, and so on.

Doyle dealt with several publishers in the course of his career, some briefly and others over long periods. Among the latter were George Newnes, whose interests included book publishing as well as the *Strand*, and the great family firm of Lippincott in Philadelphia, who also published both books and magazines. Much information about the publishing and distribution of Doyle's works is found in the fine print of Green and Gibson's *Bibliography of A. Conan Doyle* (1983). Much, however, is not known, for publishers do not necessarily keep the records of their former projects. By the early 1890s, Doyle was conducting financial negotiations with his publishers through the intermediary of A.P. Watt, a professional literary agent, and it was to Watt that (for example) the Toronto publisher George N. Morang & Co. sent substantial sums as royalties. (Records of those are in the Berg Collection of the New York Public Library.)

Most of the Sherlock Holmes stories were published first in magazines; the author would have sold "serial rights," for magazine publication, before the "book rights." The manuscripts went first to an editor, such as Greenhough Smith of the *Strand*, and from the editor to a typesetter, whose mercy and competence largely determine the text known to succeeding generations. There is evidence, as from the manuscript of "The Three Students," that the typesetter was given much latitude for making sense out of Doyle's erratic punctuation and capitalization. Negative evidence, such as the survival of many inconsistencies in the stories, as well as the lack of markings on them, suggests that an editor's hand touched the manuscripts little or not at all.

The mechanics of printing were little different in the 1890s from what they had been in Shakespeare's day. Machinery was now powered by steam rather than by muscle, but type was for the most part still set by hand, letter by letter, allowing full scope for typographical errors of a kind now extinct, such as "wrong font" and inverted characters. The detailed study of these mechanics, as described in the definitive *An Introduction to Bibliography for Literary Students* by Ronald B. McKerrow (1962), is applied to portions of the Sherlockian Canon by Donald Redmond in *Sherlock Holmes Among the Pirates* (1990). A typographical error, unless very obvious, could easily be perpetuated in subsequent editions of the same text, as the new typesetter might well work from a previous printed page rather than from a reliable manuscript. The consequence is that mistakes and variations throughout the Canon survive to bedevil researchers; and a new generation of such errors has been created when the text is "scanned" into computer memory, with technology that is still somewhat fallible.

THE STRAND MAGAZINE. All the Sherlock Holmes stories except the first two novels had their first British publication in the *Strand*, a monthly magazine founded at the beginning of 1891 by George Newnes (1851–1910). Newnes, originally a Manchester merchant, had become a publisher in 1881 with the creation of *Tit-Bits*, a weekly paper of entertainment and miscellaneous information for the lower middle class, which was becoming steadily more literate after the reforms of the 1870 Education Act. He introduced the *Strand* as a more respectable product, with a title taken from a fashionable West End street just around the corner from the magazine's offices. It boasted modern-looking typography and an illustration on every double page (a policy from the beginning), and it quickly became enormously successful, reaching a circulation of half a million. In its heyday, it sold a hundred pages of advertising every month. George Newnes Ltd. went on to publish dozens of other periodicals, and briefly an American edition of the *Strand*. The British magazine survived until 1951, when it became a victim of financial losses and a change in public reading habits.

Although Newnes (later Sir George for his contributions to journalism) was nominally editor of the *Strand*, its day-to-day manager was H. Greenhough Smith (1855–1935), the "literary editor" from the magazine's beginnings, who continued at its helm until 1930. Reginald Pound in *Mirror of the Century: The Strand Magazine 1891–1950* (1966) describes him:

> Tall, lean, sandy-moustached, with freckles to match on a pallid expressionless face, he surveyed the world with kindly scrutineering eyes through rimless *pince-nez*. His distrust of emotion gave an impression of a temperament that did not fully warrant the nickname by which he was known to his fellow clubmen, "Calamity" Smith.... Wary of originality, he was prepared to encourage it but not at the expense of readability or of the reputation of the magazine.

He encouraged H.G. Wells, Grant Allen, E. Nesbit, Rudyard Kipling, E.W. Hornung, W. Somerset Maugham, and countless other important figures of Victorian writing; the *Strand* was noted for good story telling rather than for ground-breaking literature. It carried articles about travel, science, the aristocracy, and public affairs as well, and deferential interviews with prominent persons, all in a generally complacent tone but without entirely concealing the problems of British society. Newnes, always insisting that he represented "the common man" but resplendent in the snug waistcoat of the successful businessman, cultivated — and received — the approval of prominent figures, including Queen Victoria, who more than once gave the magazine access to the royal apartments and scrapbooks.

A story by Arthur Conan Doyle, "The Voice of Science," appeared in the first volume of the *Strand*, but his importance to the magazine — and its to him — began in Volume 2 no. 1, July 1891, when Smith received the first episodes of what became *The Adventures of Sherlock Holmes* and called them "a gift from Heaven." At first Doyle was paid £5 per thousand words for the stories of Sherlock Holmes; by the end, nearly forty years later, he received £648 14s just for "Shoscombe Old Place." Doyle also wrote dozens of non-Sherlockian tales for the *Strand*, and his credibility with the magazine was such that when he appeared in 1921 with an article maintaining that two little girls' photographs of fairies in their garden were authentic, Smith swallowed hard and published it. A collection of letters from Doyle to Smith, now at the Toronto Reference Library, was discussed by Cameron Hollyer in *Baker Street Miscellanea* in 1985.

The *Strand* is of more than bibliographical interest for students of Sherlock Holmes, for it perfectly reflects his Victorian and Edwardian times, in its fiction, its articles, and even its advertisements. It seems likely that Doyle read it closely, and even alluded to it, as when Watson in "The Five Orange Pips" speaks of "Clark Russell's fine sea stories"; he may have been thinking of "Captain Jones of the 'Rose'," which the *Strand* had published in May 1891. *An Index to the Strand Magazine, 1891–1950*, compiled by Geraldine Beare, was published in 1982.

THE AMERICAN MAGAZINES. The stories of *The Adventures* and *The Memoirs*, and *The Hound of the Baskervilles*, were first published in the American edition of the *Strand* magazine, which was begun along with the British *Strand* in 1891 and was discontinued in 1916. When "The Empty House" appeared in 1903, however, and was followed by the other stories that would soon make up *The Return*, they appeared not in the *Strand* but in *Collier's*

Weekly, which was one of the two leading magazines in the United States (the other, about equally popular, being the *Saturday Evening Post*).

It had been founded in 1888 by Peter Fenelon Collier, as a weekly in the nineteenth-century tradition of *Frank Leslie's*, and from 1898 was managed by his son, Robert J. Collier, fresh from Harvard College and keen to give American journalism "a little true literary flavor." He commissioned stories by Henry James but also by Rudyard Kipling and Hall Caine as well as Doyle, and he paid Charles Dana Gibson $1,000 apiece for a hundred of his double-page "Gibson girl" drawings. He also, in 1902, hired Norman Hapgood to be the editor, chiefly to take charge of the editorial page and to direct the magazine's muck-raking coverage of public affairs. Its war coverage, its articles on labour problems, and its exposés of patent medicines gave *Collier's* much of its popularity. In 1904 it changed its title from *Collier's Weekly, An Illustrated Journal* to *Collier's, The National Weekly*.

When the stories of *His Last Bow* began to appear in 1908, *Collier's* published the first two ("Wisteria Lodge" and "The Bruce-Partington Plans"). But the magazine's interest in fiction was fading, as were its fortunes in general after the death of Peter Collier in 1909, and for the next couple of stories Doyle's agent returned to the American edition of the *Strand*: "The Devil's Foot" and "The Red Circle" in 1911. Later that year one story, "Lady Frances Carfax," appeared in the *American Magazine*. Holmes returned to *Collier's* for "The Dying Detective" in 1913, "His Last Bow" in 1917, and "The Three Garridebs" and "The Illustrious Client" in 1924. They would be the last of Holmes's adventures to appear there. The magazine was sold in 1919, suffered financial and production difficulties, but recovered in the 1920s to have reasonable influence in public affairs and reasonable success in publishing such stories as Sax Rohmer's adventures of Fu Manchu. In 1952–53 it would publish the stories by Adrian Conan Doyle and John Dickson Carr that became the *Exploits of Sherlock Holmes*. *Collier's* ceased publication in 1957.

The stories of *The Case-Book*, apart from those two in 1924 that were claimed by *Collier's*, appeared in two American magazines: four in *Hearst's International* from 1921 through 1924, and six in *Liberty* in 1926 and 1927. *Hearst's International* was originally an educational journal (*Current Encyclopedia*, founded in 1901), and in 1911 was taken over by William Randolph Hearst, who turned it into a public-affairs monthly. Before long it became clear that there was more money in fiction, and the magazine published prominent authors, both American and European. At first it was *Hearst's Magazine*, then simply *Hearst's*, and from 1921 *Hearst's International*. In 1925 it was merged into *Cosmopolitan*, another title in the Hearst publishing empire (and ancestor of the racy modern magazine for single women).

Liberty, having begun publication in May 1924, was only two years old when it began carrying Canonical stories. Already it was among the three leading weeklies in the United States, having joined *Collier's* and the *Saturday Evening Post* in selling more than a million copies of each issue. What it did not do was make money for its proprietors, Robert McCormick of the Chicago *Tribune* and Joseph Patterson of the New York *Daily News*. They sold it in 1931; successors kept trying to make it profitable, but gave up and closed the magazine in 1951.

COPYRIGHT

Copyright is literally the right (owned by an author unless it is specifically assigned or sold to someone else) to copy — that is, to publish — an author's written words. The law of copyright is byzantine and, to most lay people, dull, but even an amateur can learn not to violate copyrights simply by not copying and distributing someone else's work. The chief exception to copyright protection is known as "fair use" in the United States, "fair dealing" in Britain and Canada. The limits on this exception are complicated and subject to litigation, but it might, for example, allow making a single photocopy of something for private use, or quoting a reasonable passage (300 words is often cited) in an article or book.

In Canada, copyright generally expires 50 years after the author's death; Doyle's stories thus were free of copyright in 1980. The same rule formerly applied in Britain, so that his writings were copyright-free ("in the public domain") from 1980 until 1996. At that time, to harmonize British law with European law, the term was lengthened to 70 years, with the result that Doyle's work was protected by copyright again from 1996 until 2000.

In the United States, foreign authors, such as Doyle, were unable to claim copyright protection until changes to the law were made in 1891. At that time the term of copyright was 28 years from first publication, renewable for another 14 years. In 1909 the renewal term was extended to 28 years, and there have been several subsequent extensions. For newly published works copyright now lasts until 70 years after the death of the author. However, the Copyright Term Extension Act of 1998 had special provisions for works that had first appeared between 1923 and 1978: if they had not already fallen into the public domain, their term of protection was extended to 95 years from first publication. That category includes ten of the twelve stories in *The Case-Book of Sherlock Holmes*, and the collection as a whole, which was published in 1927 and so will not enter the public domain until the end of 2022. The result has been that while *The Adventures*, *The Hound of the Baskervilles*, and other earlier works are available in dozens of editions — anyone can legally publish them — there continues to be a monopoly on the final stories and therefore on any edition that contains the entire Canon. They can be published only by a company licensed by the copyright owners.

Copyright in most of Doyle's stories was originally owned by the author and, after his death in 1930, by his estate, which licensed or sold them in various ways. After American copyright law reform in 1976, it became possible for an author's surviving spouse or children to "recapture" copyrights that had been sold, and in November 1981 Dame Jean Conan Doyle, the only surviving member of Doyle's family, did that. Since Dame Jean Conan Doyle's death in 1997, the American copyright in those writings that are not yet in the public domain, including the *Case-Book* stories, has been the property of her estate. The estate has been managed by Jon L. Lellenberg of Chicago, who reports that as of early 2009, steps are under way to wind up that legal entity and assign the American rights to a new organization to be called the Conan Doyle Estate Ltd. To be based in Britain, it will also control some British rights to Doyle's work, such as copyrights in texts that have never been published. The agent for the Conan Doyle Estate Ltd. is to be United Agents (*unitedagents.co.uk*) of London.

Through the second half of the twentieth century, the copyright owners licensed the firm of Doubleday (also variously known as Doubleday Doran and Garden City Publishing; it is now a division of Random House) to publish *The Complete Sherlock Holmes*. In recent years several other editions have also been licensed. In addition, Dame Jean also asserted a right to control the use of the characters and names of Sherlock Holmes and Dr. Watson both in print and in other media such as film. Such a right would be based indirectly on common law, intellectual property (copyright and trademark), and unfair competition laws, since a character itself cannot be trademarked. The extent to which such a right is enforceable, allowing the owner to control the writing of new tales using the characters, is legally unclear, but American publishers typically continue to seek permission and pay fees to the estate, and most books that feature "Sherlock Holmes" include a fine-print acknowledgement to that effect.

Meanwhile, the estate of Sir Arthur Conan Doyle himself had been tangled in litigation among his children and their heirs for decades beginning in the 1950s. A settlement was at last reached shortly before Dame Jean's death, and by 2004 the assets of that estate had been distributed. There remains, however, "the Sir Arthur Conan Doyle Literary Estate," operated by Andrea Plunket, the former wife of television producer Sheldon Reynolds. He had first been involved with the use of the Sherlock Holmes characters in the 1950s, and acquired the copyrights from a receiver in bankruptcy in 1974, shortly before their 1980 expiry in Britain and Dame Jean's "recapture" in the United States. The estate headed by Plunket now maintains a web site (*www.sherlockholmesonline.org*) and has lawyers who maintain that it owns the American rights to the Sherlock Holmes stories. Such claims have been repeatedly rejected in U.S. federal court decisions in favour of the estate of Dame Jean.

EDITIONS OF THE STORIES

The original magazine publication, and the newspaper syndication that followed in most cases, did not exhaust publishers' interest in the Canonical stories, as they were republished in American and British newspapers from the early 1890s through the early years of the twentieth century. The *New York World* Sunday magazine rediscovered *The Adventures of Sherlock Holmes* in 1905, for example; the *Boston Sunday Post* published the stories of *The Return* as "Masterpieces of Sherlock Holmes" in 1911.

Authorized publishers continued to bring out the books in full. Some of the Sherlock Holmes tales appear in the official "Author's Edition" of Doyle's works (1903). All are among the twenty-four volumes of the "Crowborough Edition," begun before Doyle's death in 1930 and published posthumously in a limited edition of 760 sets; many copies include signatures which the author affixed to pre-publication sheets. *The Complete Sherlock Holmes* was published in eight volumes by P.F. Collier & Son in 1928, and a six-volume edition followed in 1936. A ten-volume "Literary Guild" edition was produced by Doubleday in 1933.

In addition there were many piracies, that is, books published without the author's approval. In the 1890s in particular, *The Sign of the Four* (in more than two hundred unauthorized editions) and *A Study in Scarlet* were extensively pirated by American publishers operating in a free-for-all atmosphere. Donald Redmond in *Sherlock Holmes Among the Pirates* (1990) identifies and classifies many of those early volumes, but a full bibliographical listing of them will probably never be compiled.

Partial collections of Canonical stories have appeared over the decades with such titles as *Conan Doyle's Stories for Boys* (1938), *Famous Tales of Sherlock*

Holmes (1958), and *Sherlock Holmes' Greatest Cases* (1966). In addition, a few stories were published yet again in periodical format, the oddest examples being an excerpt from *The Sign of the Four* and the full texts of "A Scandal in Bohemia" and "The Copper Beeches," which graced the first three issues of *Playboy* magazine (1954). Many of the stories have been used in anthologies, from "The Dancing Men" in *Famous Stories of Code and Cipher* (1947) and "A Scandal in Bohemia" in *With All My Love: An Anthology* (1945) to "The Five Orange Pips" in *Masterpieces of Mystery & Detection* (1965). Unusual publications also include *Sherlock Holmes and Dr. Watson: A Textbook of Friendship* (1944), edited by Christopher Morley and including two novels (one abridged), five short stories, and extensive notes. A little later came *The Blue Carbuncle* (1948), a slipcased collector's item published by the Baker Street Irregulars.

Over the decades, by far the most commonly available version of the stories in North America has been *The Complete Sherlock Holmes*, published by Doubleday. The first of several Doubleday *Completes* was the "Memorial Edition," shortly after Doyle's death in 1930, which had erratic and repetitive pagination because it was printed from the plates previously used for separate volumes of the various tales. It also presented "In Memoriam Sherlock Holmes," an eloquent if maudlin introduction by Christopher Morley, which has been a fixture ever since. A one-volume edition of *The Complete* followed in 1936. Early Sherlockian writings frequently refer to its 1,323-page layout, also published (from the same printing plates) as "the Literary Guild Edition" and "the De Luxe Edition" in two-volume and one-volume formats. One-volume and two-volume editions in a new format of 1,122 pages were introduced in 1960 and remain standard, in part because over several decades the Book-of-the-Month Club distributed many thousands of whatever was the most recent impression.

The one-volume Doubleday edition has also appeared as a Penguin paperback. These editions, widely and inexpensively available, have been the standard to which reference works have generally been keyed. In recent years, however, the Doubleday edition has had rivals, including two-volume paperback editions from Bantam Classics and Barnes & Noble, as well as innumerable editions of the earlier volumes of the Canon that are no longer protected by copyright. The word *piracy* no longer strictly applies, but contemporary paperback collections are often as cheap in every way as were the piracies of the 1890s.

The Doubleday edition suffers from a good deal of textual corruption — a famous example is "Somomy" for the historical racehorse Isonomy mentioned in "Silver Blaze" — and when he undertook to edit the entire Canon for the Limited Editions Club in the early 1940s, Edgar W. Smith laboured to correct errors and misapprehensions, eventually producing what is still widely thought to be the best text available. The original idea had been to bring out all the stories with illustrations by Frederic Dorr Steele, who had already created the art for about half of them. George Macy of the Limited Editions Club commissioned him to do the other half, but Steele died in 1944 with little of the work completed. Other artists filled the breach, and the edition finally appeared as *The Adventures* (three volumes, 1950), *The Later Adventures* (three volumes, 1952), and *The Final Adventures* (two volumes, 1952) with introductions and notes by several scholars. Jon L. Lellenberg in *Irregular Crises of the Late 'Forties* (1999) tells the story of the delays and difficulties that lay behind the project, particularly resistance from Adrian Conan Doyle, who was then managing his father's estate. Lellenberg writes that the Limited Editions Club achievement deserves, for the efforts of Smith and others and the joy with which it was received, to be remembered as "the Baker Street Irregulars edition" of the Canon. It was republished in 1952–57 as a three-volume edition from the Heritage Club, and facsimiles were issued by Easton Press in 1987 and 1996.

In Britain, the standard edition for many years was a two-volume set from the old publishing firm of John Murray: *The Complete Sherlock Holmes: Long Stories* and *Short Stories*, cited as "S" and "L" with a page number by some British commentators. John Murray is now part of a conglomerate, and its Sherlock Holmes is no longer to be found in bookshops. In its place there are hardback volumes, both titled *The Complete Sherlock Holmes*, from Wordsworth and CRW Publishing; a six-volume hardback set also from CRW; and multi-volume paperback editions from Wordsworth and Headline Review. All these choices provide a British text of the stories — that is, for example, one of the stories is titled "The Reigate Squires," not "The Reigate Puzzle," and the textual errors introduced in the Doubleday on the other side of the Atlantic do not appear. British readers can, however, get the Doubleday text if they like, as the Penguin paperback *Complete* is also easily available.

There is a frequent desire among Sherlockians for facsimile editions in which the original *Strand* appearance of the stories, including Sidney Paget illustrations, is reproduced. The most satisfactory of these is a heavy volume of 1,126 pages, *The Original Illustrated 'Strand' Sherlock Holmes*, with the *Strand* pages enlarged from their original size (and *A Study in Scarlet* and *The Sign of the Four*, which never appeared in the *Strand*, set in a similar typeface and format). Unlike some earlier facsimiles, this one manages clear and bright reproduction of the drawings by Paget and his successors. The British edition appeared from Wordsworth in 1989, the American from Mallard Press in 1990. The price of its elegance is a weight that makes the book impractical for, say, reading in bed without the aid of hydraulic equipment. There is, however, a paperback edition, less hefty and correspondingly less legible. Several other facsimiles have smaller pages and, frequently, thinner paper, with the predictable disadvantages.

ANNOTATED EDITIONS

The complete Canon was published with a vast apparatus of notes under the title *The Annotated Sherlock Holmes* (Clarkson N. Potter, 1967; a British edition followed in 1968 from John Murray, and there is also a one-volume reprint). Its editor was William S. Baring-Gould (1913–67), whose death while the book was still in proof prevented the correction of some errors and imperfections. Its two volumes (688 pages in the first, 824 pages in the second) provide hundreds of illustrations from many sources — often murkily reproduced — and marginal notes explaining Victorian terms, pointing the reader to related passages in other stories, and providing a wealth of background and enrichment. In addition, there are nineteen chapters on general subjects, all the editor's work: on Sherlockian parodies, on films, on Watson, on the snake in "The Speckled Band," on Watson's wounds, on Watson's marriages, on the Great Hiatus, and so on. These chapters are interspersed with the stories, in facsimile from the John Murray collected edition, arranged in the order in which Baring-Gould deemed them to have taken place. Thus "The 'Gloria Scott'" comes first and "His Last Bow" last; the first volume goes as far as *The Sign of the Four*. Constant recourse to the table of contents is unavoidable.

The *Annotated* holds unswervingly to the pretense that what Sherlockians do when they exercise their imaginations about Holmes is sober biographical scholarship. Baring-Gould also included, without distinguishing it from other kinds of knowledge, biographical detail that he had invented for Holmes in his own *Sherlock Holmes of Baker Street*, published five years earlier. The result can be cloying; the pervasive fiction slights Doyle and limits the book's use for some kinds of study. Nevertheless, for almost forty years Baring-Gould's enormous industry and range of knowledge were agreed to more than compensate for his quirks. The *Annotated* had an enormous influence on the spread of interest in Sherlock Holmes in the 1970s, and was indispensable for a generation of Sherlockian scholars.

A very different annotated edition appeared in 1993 from Oxford University Press: *The Oxford Sherlock Holmes* in nine volumes, under the general editorship of Owen Dudley Edwards, a professor of history at the University of Edinburgh. "Given Conan Doyle's general lack of close supervision of the Holmes texts, it is not always easy to determine his final wishes," he wrote in the "General Introduction." Edwards edited three of the nine volumes himself; two were done by Christopher Roden, two by Richard Lancelyn Green, and two by W.W. Robson. In each case the editor of a volume contributed a solid introduction, with context and detail about how the stories came to be written; provided explanatory notes; and, most important, edited the text, making changes to produce a readable but also authoritative version. Some of the alterations are mildly surprising (moving "The Cardboard Box" out of *His Last Bow*, where it has traditionally sat, and into *The Memoirs*, where it made its brief first bow in 1893). Others are positively startling, as when Edwards turns the familiar if puzzling reference to "the Long Island cave mystery" in "The Red Circle" into "the Long Island cove mystery" on the grounds that there are no caves on Long Island, New York, and Doyle's handwriting was ambiguous anyway. Whether or not one applauds all the editors' decisions, the Oxford edition is enormously useful as a reference about textual variations and similar matters. Many of its notes also illuminate connections between Doyle's own life and allusions that he drops into the stories. It can be tediously exhaustive ("Hampshire: a southern English county much loved by ACD") but it can also be quickly helpful. Although some notes do address the lives of the characters, such as speculation about whether Watson had returned to medical practice at the time of "The Illustrious Client," the *Oxford* editors do not indulge in make-believe biography as Baring-Gould had done. They are literary critics writing about literary characters and the author who created them, rather as one would expect from such a publisher. Also as one would expect, the books are clear and comfortable to read. The editorial notes are at the end of the volume rather than on the same pages as the text, and are signalled by modest asterisks. And each volume is compact, little larger than pocket-sized. (A paperback edition followed the original hardbacks, and Oxford is in the process of reissuing all nine volumes in its *World's Classics* paperback series.) If there was one criticism generally agreed on by early users of the *Oxford Sherlock Holmes*, it was that it appeared entirely without illustrations.

The *Sherlock Holmes Reference Library*, edited by Los Angeles lawyer Leslie S. Klinger, took a very different attitude and addressed a very different audience, being intended mostly for dedicated Sherlockians and published in small quantities by a specialized firm, Gasogene Books of Indianapolis. Its ten paperback volumes — nine for the usual nine volumes of the Canon and a tenth for the "Apocrypha," writings by Arthur Conan Doyle with a less authoritative connection to Sherlock Holmes — appeared over more than a decade, the first being dated 1998 and the last 2009. They include only a small number of illustrations, but in other respects the *Reference Library* has everything for which readers had come to rely on the Baring-Gould *Annotated*, with the further merit of presenting the stories in a conventional order. Klinger uses some of Baring-Gould's notes and adds hundreds referring to other sources, including the thirty years' worth of Sherlockian scholarship that had intervened as well as the ninth edition (1875–89) of the *Encyclopaedia Britannica* and a library full of other reference works. Although quoting at length from such works, Klinger frequently adds his own perceptions as well. He was more interested than Baring-Gould had been in the possibilities opened by textual criticism; he presents what he called "my own version" of the text, based primarily on what had appeared in the *Strand*, and includes many notes about variant readings and the known manuscripts. The books are not good as reading copies, their pages dense with small type, but for scholars in search of Sherlockian understanding they are indispensable, and have largely rendered Baring-Gould obsolete.

A landmark in Sherlockian publishing came in 2005 with the appearance of *The New Annotated Sherlock Holmes*, volumes I and II, slipcased together and weighing nearly as much as a piece of furniture. The two blue-bound volumes dealt with the fifty-six Holmes short stories, with a red-bound volume III following in 2006 and addressing the four novels. These too were the work of Leslie S. Klinger, whose *Reference Library* was almost complete by the time the *New Annotated* appeared.

"There are significant differences between this edition and Baring-Gould's classic *Annotated Sherlock Holmes*," Klinger insisted in a note that begins on page 1841 of his volume II. "Baring-Gould emphasized the 'chronology' of the stories," he points out, whereas Klinger relegates most questions of what happened when to a chronological table, "The Life and Times of Sherlock Holmes," appended to volume I (and including year-by-year highlights of Arthur Conan Doyle's life and historical events as well as the cases and happenings in Holmes's career). In keeping with his lack of interest in chronological puzzles, Klinger again keeps the stories in a predictable order. Large numbers of his notes reproduce material from the *Reference Library* word for word, but for the convenience of a larger and more general readership, he cuts out a great deal of specialized Sherlockian material and emphasizes Victorian life, geography, and technical terms. "The Golden Pince-Nez," for example, has forty notes in the *Reference Library* volume for *The Return of Sherlock Holmes* and just twenty-one in the *New Annotated*. Sherlockian readers of the former are given three technical paragraphs about the likelihood and identity of a "red leech"; general readers of the latter get three brief sentences. They are altogether spared a note listing possible identifications of Yoxley Old Place with several existing houses in Suffolk, and also do not get to read Klinger's three paragraphs about the availability of a "spirit-lamp" at 221B Baker Street.

The *New Annotated* follows the layout introduced by Baring-Gould, with notes in the outer margins of the pages (and long white spaces where nothing strikes the editor as worthy of annotation). For many of the stories there are separate brief essays on contentious or interesting topics, such as "The Rules of Rugby" to clarify "The Missing Three-Quarter," but one thirty-page introductory essay, "The World of Sherlock Holmes," takes the place of Baring-Gould's many introductory chapters about Doyle, Holmes, actors, and other general topics. The *New Annotated* offers many illustrations taken from early editions of the Canon, and although the volumes are much too heavy for recreational reading, the typography is easy on the eye.

ILLUSTRATION

It is difficult to think of Sherlock Holmes without his deerstalker hat, which is never mentioned in the Canon, but was the inspiration of an early illustrator. That lasting gift from artist to character is one example of how important illustration has been in establishing the myth of Sherlock Holmes, and in making the stories successful and memorable. No wonder, then, that Walter Klinefelter found it easy to devote a full volume to Sherlockian illustration: *Sherlock Holmes in Portrait and Profile* (1963). Admirable so far as he goes, he only scratches the surface, for there have been dozens of illustrators whom he has no room to mention.

Unless one is merely a cartoonist, there is more to illustrating Holmes than the presence of the deerstalker hat and its usual companions the magnifying glass, the curved pipe, and the Inverness cape. Still, some modern illustrators do no more than that when they try to interpret Holmes visually. One expects from an illustrator the discernment of an artist, revealed in features, expressions, and gestures that match the Holmes described in the text. It is for achieving those expressions and gestures, in particular, that two early artists — Paget and Frederic Dorr Steele — are acknowledged to be great interpreters of Holmes, while others are nearly forgotten. In addition, the reader deserves authenticity in Victorian clothing and furnishings; the scenes illustrated should be ones that are not merely exciting and action filled but significant to the progress of the story; the illustrations should be placed on the page or in the volume in such a way that the story is not spoiled for the first-time reader; and their reproduction should be clean and clear.

The first person to draw Sherlock Holmes for print was D.H. Friston, whose illustrations for *A Study in Scarlet* appeared in *Beeton's Christmas Annual* for 1887. (It is not clear that the often-reproduced cover of *Beeton's* is intended to represent Holmes or have anything to do with *A Study in Scarlet*.) Klinefelter is critical of Friston's Holmes, calling it "a travesty," not so much in physiognomy as in clothing and headgear. Those illustrations were abandoned when *A Study in Scarlet* was republished, and in Friston's place stood the author's father, Charles Doyle, by 1888 confined to a mental institution and exercising his talent rather for therapy than professionally. Gibson and Green, in their *Bibliography of A. Conan Doyle*, observe that "The six frail drawings bear no relation to later conceptions of the subject but are of interest none the less." Later illustrators for the same novel included George Hutchinson.

SIDNEY PAGET. Always admired, the drawings of Sidney Paget for the original publication of about half the Canon have been more widely known since facsimile editions became available. One or two of them, such as a drawing for "Silver Blaze" of Holmes and Watson together in a railway carriage, and one for "The Naval Treaty" of Holmes sniffing a rose in a moment of ecstasy, have become virtual icons. Others, less often reproduced, still capture moments of characteristic action, or aspects of Holmes's milieu, as no other illustrations have been able to do. It can be seen as a tribute to Paget's mastery of his medium, and of his Victorian subject as well, that selected illustrations have twice been reproduced by the spicy British magazine *Mayfair* with off-colour captions replacing the original Canonical ones.

Gibson and Green in their *Bibliography* explain the conjunction of Paget and the Canon thus: "George Newnes wanted the [*Strand*] magazine to have a picture at every opening, and to achieve this appointed W.H. Boot as the art editor. He in turn chose one of the Paget brothers for this series, intending it to be Walter Paget, though in fact the offer went to Sidney Paget. The choice was a good one and met with the author's approval, though he had envisaged a 'more beaky nosed, hawk-faced man'." Tradition says that Walter Paget became, rather than the artist, the model for Holmes.

It was Paget who attached the deerstalker hat to Sherlock Holmes, identifying the detective's "travelling cap" as the headgear he himself favoured: a cloth

"I found Sherlock Holmes half asleep": a corner of the Baker Street suite, with chemical laboratory, as drawn by Sidney Paget for "A Case of Identity" when it appeared in the Strand *magazine in September 1891, early in the sequence of stories. The soft edge and complex shape of this illustration are characteristic of Paget's work.*

cap in plain or (often) houndstooth fabric, with fore-and-aft peaks and with earflaps that could be tied up or down. He first drew such a hat in a picture to go with "The Boscombe Valley Mystery" when it appeared in 1891. (However, researchers have found a deerstalker in drawings that appeared in the *Bristol Observer* newspaper when it published *The Sign of the Four* as a serial in 1890; the artist is unknown.) Paget drew it only four more times, but that was enough, especially as one of the five deerstalkers is seen falling from Holmes's head into the gorge of the Reichenbach in an illustration for "The Final Problem." Other artifacts of the Paget household can also be identified in some of the illustrations.

Sidney Paget did a total of 356 illustrations for the Canon, to accompany the magazine publication of *The Adventures*, *The Memoirs*, *The Hound of the Baskervilles*, and *The Return*. (Many of them were carried along when those texts were published in book form.) Ann Byerly, writing in *Baker Street Miscellanea* in 1983, described his technique:

> Employing the black-and-white watercolor technique, he worked [the illustrations] up on a kind of cardboard about 6" X 8" in size, first pencilling in his composition, next filling in the background with a light wash, then applying black watercolor paint to dark areas in the picture, and finally, filling in the details with black and white after that had dried.... Much more of his draftsmanship is evident when an original is tilted to the light to catch the glint of the pencilling than is apparent in the reproductions.

(Still less, of course, can be seen in most modern facsimiles.) Some of the drawings were reproduced from engravings, others from (cruder) woodcuts. Warren Scheideman, writing in the same issue of *BSM*, notes that some of Paget's genius resides in the "creative rather than formal" shape of his drawings, which lack hard edges: "The lines drift into the text, sometimes like smoke, clouds, dreams, or thoughts, often in physical conjunction with the words they illustrate."

Sidney Paget was born October 4, 1860, and was a young painter and newspaper artist when he was accidentally chosen to illustrate "A Scandal in Bohemia" and the stories that followed it. He went on to produce drawings for many other stories by Doyle, and for other authors' works in the *Strand* and elsewhere. In October 1897, it is reported, he painted Doyle's portrait. He suffered from a "chest complaint" in the early years of the twentieth century, gradually doing less and less work, and died January 28, 1908. He and his wife,

Edith Hounsfield, whose wedding-present from Doyle was a silver cigarette-case inscribed "From Sherlock Holmes," had six children; one of them, Winifred, has written about her father and was a member of the Sherlock Holmes Society of London from its founding until her death in 1978. "Only a handful" of his original drawings are known to exist, Ann Byerly reported in 1983.

FREDERIC DORR STEELE. The leading American illustrator of the Canon was in fact its illustrator only for the final three volumes of short stories. Walter Klinefelter, in *Sherlock Holmes in Portrait and Profile* (1963), introduces the contributions of Frederic Dorr Steele thus:

> For the text of the stories of *The Return*, which made its first American appearances in various numbers of *Collier's Weekly* from September 26, 1903, to January 28, 1905, Steele drew forty-six illustrations. The master detective's visage appears in twenty-six of them. For each story Steele also provided individual headpieces and decorative initials. But at the most these drawings, though of very special merit, comprise the lesser part of this artist's contribution to the embellishment of *The Return*. The choicest of his drawings for this section of the canon consist of the ten gorgeous portraits which he executed in color for the front covers of a like number of the issues of *Collier's* in which Watson's stories appeared. These portraits were the finest of Holmes done up to that time, perhaps the finest that ever were or ever will be done of him.

Steele went on to do similar work for most of the stories that would make up *His Last Bow*, and for two of the *Case-Book* stories. He later illustrated one story (with cover) for the *American Magazine*, four (without covers) for *Hearst's International*, and six (again without covers) for *Liberty*. A number of newspaper illustrations were also his work.

The cover illustrations are, indeed, Steele's most important Sherlockian work, from the deerstalkered figure at the Reichenbach for "The Empty House" to his gaunt, bedridden Holmes for "The Dying Detective" and the aging figure of Holmes in retirement for "His Last Bow." For "The Norwood Builder," Steele drew Holmes looking not at a thumb-print but at an entire bloody handprint on the wall, perhaps his only concession to melodrama; for a pamphlet edition of "The Dying Detective" some years later, the same drawing was used, with a sketched portrait of Doyle replacing the handprint on the wall under Holmes's piercing

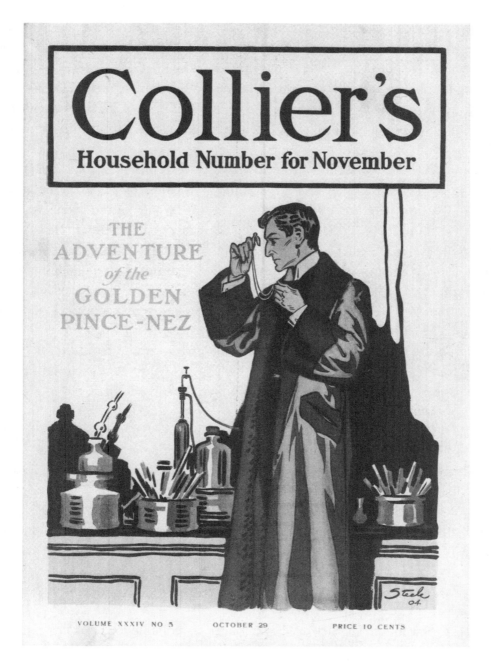

Frederic Dorr Steele's drawing of Holmes in his Baker Street laboratory was one of eleven spectacular covers he created for Collier's *magazine. Done in black and bronze, it appeared October 29, 1904, when "The Golden Pince-Nez" was first published as part of* The Return of Sherlock Holmes. *The story makes no mention of test tubes, but Holmes does use "my spirit-lamp," perhaps a feature of the laboratory, to make coffee.*

scrutiny. It seems clear that the model Steele used for Holmes was William Gillette, who toured America through the early decades of the century presenting the great detective on stage. Walter Klinefelter identifies the *Collier's* cover for "The Priory School" as being the most like Gillette; indeed, that picture of Holmes staring away across the moor does bear a striking resemblance to pictures of Gillette that appeared on publicity material for his play and also as a frontispiece in some contemporary editions of the Canon.

Frederic Dorr Steele, born August 6, 1873, was primarily a book illustrator, having worked with texts by such authors as Richard Harding Davis, Mark Twain, Rudyard Kipling and O. Henry. He was winner of the bronze medal at the St. Louis Exposition of 1904, and spent his working life in New York, where he was a member of the elite Players Club. His obituary in *The New York Times* said he was also a member of the Baker Street Irregulars, but that does not seem to have been the case in any formal way, although he certainly was a friend of such early Sherlockians as Vincent Starrett and Gray Chandler Briggs. The *Times* also mentioned that shortly before his death (July 5, 1944) he had been working on illustrations for the projected Limited Editions Club version of the Canon. He was survived by his wife, Mary. A collection of anecdotes about Steele and appreciations of him and his work appeared in a 1991 issue of *Baker Street Miscellanea*.

LATER ILLUSTRATORS. American magazines which published the stories in the early years of the century, but did not accompany them with Steele's drawings, used such other illustrators as Arthur I. Keller, G. Patrick Nelson, W.T. Benda and John Richard Flanagan. The American book edition of *The Return* was illustrated not by Steele but by Charles Raymond Macauley. As for British editions after Paget, the editors of the *Strand* had similarly played the field, entrusting the illustration to Arthur Twidle, Gilbert Holiday, Joseph Simpson, H.M. Brock, Frank Wiles, Howard Elcock, Alec Ball, A. Gilbert, and even Paget's brother Walter, who had been intended as the original illustrator two decades earlier.

By the twentieth century it was no longer fashionable for books to contain illustrations. *The Valley of Fear* had only a frontispiece (by Wiles) in England, although the American edition had a few Keller drawings scattered through the text. *His Last Bow* and *The Case-Book* had no illustrations at all in either American or British editions. The collected editions of the Canon, the Doubleday *Complete Sherlock Holmes*, and the *Long Stories* and *Short Stories* published by John Murray, do not have illustrations, nor do most of the paperback volumes available.

There has been no well-known illustrator of the Canon since Paget and Steele; images of the detective since the 1920s have been based on the faces and postures of actors, primarily (at least in North America) Basil Rathbone. The Paget illustrations, little-known in the United States until the appearance of *The Annotated Sherlock Holmes* with its many reproductions, are now often seen. A number of undistinguished illustrators have made attempts at Holmes for various post-copyright editions of the stories, often not rising above the deerstalker-and-calabash level of caricature also seen in countless cartoons and advertisements. Perhaps the most successful Sherlockian artist in recent decades has been Dan Day, whose work in the 1980s was not for book illustration but for comics.

TRANSLATIONS AND TRANSCRIPTIONS

The stories of Sherlock Holmes have appeared in languages from French and German to Sinhalese and Urdu, despite the vast difficulties in conveying the nuances of British life and the subtleties of Holmes's work to readers in far different cultures. It is said — although such statements are difficult to verify — that portions of the Canon have been put into more tongues than any other work save the Bible. There is also a persistent story that in some language, in some country (Egypt?), the Canon has been used as a textbook for detectives, but the facts have never been demonstrated. Certainly the Canon has often been a textbook for the learning of English; student editions with notes and apparatus in French, Russian, Swedish, and other languages are known.

Translation into French began before the turn of the century, with *The Sign of the Four* appearing from Hachette in 1896 as *La Marque des Quatre: Roman Anglais*. The bibliographical record is nearly as confused as its English-language counterpart, with partial, probably unauthorized translations appearing frequently. There is the further complication of variant titles: *A Study in Scarlet* is found both as *Une Etude en Rouge* and as *Les Débuts de Sherlock Holmes*. The full Canon appears along with other works of Doyle in his *Oeuvres Complètes* from Robert Laffont (1956–58) and subsequent collected editions.

German translations and adaptations began in 1894, according to *A Centenary Bibliography of German Sherlockiana* published by enthusiasts in 1993. Further afield, *A Study in Scarlet* and *The Sign of the Four* in the German language are known from Milwaukee newspaper serializations in 1903, under the titles *Späte Rache* ("Belated Revenge") and *Das Zeichen der Vier*. Milwaukee and Pittsburgh also saw early publications of *Der Hund von Baskerville*. Publishers in Germany, particularly Robert Lutz of Stuttgart, were bringing out portions of the Canon between 1906 and 1910, and many editions followed, leading to the *Sämtliche Romane* and *Sämtliche Stories* in the 1960s.

The earliest Japanese translations date from the 1890s; more appeared in the 1920s (*Shinku No Isshi* is a 1923 version of *A Study in Scarlet*), and they became numerous after World War II. A complete Canon in thirteen volumes, *Sherlock Holmes Zenshû*, appeared in 1951–52 from Getsuyô-shobô in Tokyo.

Russian is a special case. The first translations came early, about 1903, as Anatole Chujoy recalled in the *Baker Street Journal* in 1953. But they were less than perfect:

> In *A Study in Scarlet*, for instance, Dr. Watson's jezail bullet became a piece of shrapnel, and the valiant Murray's name is changed to Miurrai. The providential meeting between Watson and young Stamford takes place not at the Criterion Bar, as we have always believed, but in the street. The reason for this is perhaps that the institution we know under the appellation "bar" was foreign to Russians, and the paraphrast probably could not find a suitable definition for "bar" in the dictionary.

Multiple editions in Russian appeared in later decades, including an eight-volume edition in 1966 (Ogonyok Library) and a 1945 edition of "The Man With the Twisted Lip" as part of The Little Library of the Journal of the Red Army Soldier. It was said that 11 million volumes of the Canon had been sold in the two years before a 1959 lawsuit in which Doyle's estate asked a Soviet court to award it royalties on those books. The suit was unsuccessful because the Soviet Union, unlike most other countries, was not then party to any of the international copyright conventions.

Most European languages had accepted Holmes early: *Le Avventure di Sherlock Holmes* (Milan) dates from 1895, *De Fires Tegn* (Christiania, i.e. Oslo) from 1891. The full history of translation remains to be unearthed, as many items are doubtless unknown to bibliographers, and many items that have been listed are undated or only vaguely described. Translation remains an area where collectors can specialize, explore, and point to novelties — a Ukrainian edition of *A Study in Scarlet* published not in Ukraine but in Edmonton, Alberta; Hebrew editions of the Canon (mostly published in Tel Aviv in the 1950s) in which, for lack of the initial letter *H*, the great detective is named Golmes.

Some collectors have a special enthusiasm for translated editions because the possibilities have been so incompletely explored. One specialist, Don Hobbs (*221b@verizon.net*), produces a bibliography of translations (with reproductions of many covers, and other associated material) under the title *The Galactic Sherlock Holmes*; it is distributed in CD-ROM format and updated two or three times a year as new material reaches him.

OTHER FORMATS. Apart from conventional print, portions of the Canon have been commercially published in Braille (*The Adventures* in Britain in 1920, selected *Cases of Sherlock Holmes* in the United States in 1965). A more common novelty on collectors' shelves is an edition in shorthand, either Gregg or Pitman. Several have been produced for practice by novice stenographers; the earliest Pitman version, of *The Sign of the Four*, appeared in England shortly after the original book's first edition.

Sound recordings of the stories began as a service to blind readers and were provided on audiotape; in recent years the medium is CD-ROM and the audience is chiefly commuters who listen as they drive. Various companies have produced and distributed readings done by such actors as Basil Rathbone, John Brewster, Robert Hardy, Douglas Wilmer, Christopher Lee, Michael York, and Edward Hardwicke. In addition, complete readings of the sixty stories have been issued by Worldtainment (*www.decklinsdomain.com*), read by Patrick Horgan; by One Voice Recordings (*www.onevoicerecordings.com*), read by David Ian Davies; by Naxos AudioBooks (*www.naxosaudiobooks.com*), read by David Timson; and by Audible (*www.audible.com*), read by Walter Covell. Getting through the complete Canon takes about three days around the clock: in the Naxos version, seventy-two hours and fifty-seven minutes. Some of this material is also available in the older format of audiotape cassettes, and some is available for download through iTunes or on the web (AudiobookStandDL at *www.audiobookstanddl.com* is one commercial site) for enjoyment on an iPod or similar device. Readings by a number of amateur volunteers are available through the web site LibriVox (*www.librivox.org*). Recordings of complete stories, read by a narrator, should not be confused with tapes of dramatizations, chiefly from radio broadcasts, which are also widely available.

ELECTRONIC TEXT. The text of the Canon has doubtless existed in computer-readable form, in some publisher's typesetting machinery, for half a century, but there was a time not so long ago when enthusiasts who wanted to perform computer analysis on the Canon, search for elusive phrases, or even compile a concordance were faced with the prospect of typing its more than four million characters themselves. In 1987, however, PsyLogic Systems of Connecticut began to distribute *An Electronic Holmes Companion*, a Canonical text on diskettes, along with documentation and a number of programs for text analysis. The text was created by optical character scanning, a process with a notoriously high error rate. This single source has been used for most, if not all, subsequent electronic products, probably including the CD-ROMs offered by Creative Multimedia (Portland, Oregon), Pencil Productions (Denver), and The Battered Silicon Dispatch-Box (Shelburne, Ontario; *www.batteredbox.com*). Even more extensive is *The Works of Sir Arthur Conan Doyle*, a CD-ROM of everything from Sherlock Holmes to Doyle's spiritualist works, from Insight Engineering (Franconia, Virginia).

The Canon in this portable form is in less demand than it was a decade ago, however, as the stories are now available at a number of Internet sites. Such locations can come and go without warning, but reliable sources, as of early 2009, include Project Gutenberg (*www.gutenberg.org*), Scribd (*www.scribd. com*), the University of Virginia (*etext.lib.virginia.edu*), the University of Adelaide (*ebooks.adelaide.edu.au*), Trit (*www.trit.org*), and a particularly elegant site maintained in Germany by Christoph Ender (*spellbreaker.org/~chrender/*). Because of copyright considerations, servers based in the United States may not include the *Case-Book* stories. The web site Sherlockian.Net (*www.sherlockian. net/canon*) includes links to a number of online sites for each of the sixty tales.

IV

ARTHUR CONAN DOYLE

FOR SEVENTY YEARS SHERLOCKIANS have dismissed Arthur Conan
Doyle half seriously as "the Literary Agent," but acknowledging his authorship, and the life behind it, does give the stories of the Canon an additional
richness. Even outside Sherlockian circles, he is chiefly known only for Sherlock Holmes, to the point that the detective's name almost invariably appears
in the titles of books about Doyle. But there is more to him than his nine volumes of Holmes — more even than all his literary writings, models though they
are of English prose. Doyle is of importance as a social reformer, a religious
leader, and a public figure generally.

Academic scholars of course acknowledge the author when they write
about the works, and Doyle does have his fans among a wider public. In 1989
an Arthur Conan Doyle Society was founded in Britain, though it is now based
in Canada (*www.ash-tree.bc.ca/acdsocy.html*); its president is Christopher
Roden. The society's twice-yearly *Journal* and occasional newsletter, *The
Parish Magazine*, dedicated to scholarship about Doyle and news about
activities in his memory, have not been published in recent years but have
not officially been suspended. Other web sites also exist to pay tribute and
provide information, such as The Chronicles of Sir Arthur Conan Doyle (*www.
siracd.com*). The Conan Doyle (Crowborough) Establishment (*www.the-
conan-doyle-crowborough-establishment.com*), founded by Malcolm Payne,
is based near Doyle's home in Sussex and is now headed by Brian W. Pugh.
It holds occasional events and issues publications as well as maintaining a
Doyle collection at Groombridge Place, a nearby stately home that has been
postulated as the original of Birlstone in *The Valley of Fear*.

Arthur Conan Doyle in early middle age, from an engraving used as the frontispiece to an edition of The Refugees *published in 1900 by Harper & Brothers. According to his daughter, Doyle stood six feet, one and a half inches tall. A recording betrays more than a hint of a Scots burr in his speaking voice even in later life.*

There is a persistent difference of opinion about the preferable form of the great man's name. He always signed himself "A. Conan Doyle," which leaves doubt whether he considered "Conan" a given name or the first part of a compound surname. His father was simply "Doyle," but his children have been determinedly "Conan Doyle." Cataloguers for the Library of Congress and the British Library have chosen "Doyle" to stand alone as the surname.

LIFE AND MEDICAL CAREER

Arthur Conan Doyle was born May 22, 1859, at 11 Picardy Place, Edinburgh, a lower-middle-class row house in the capital city of Scotland. The family were Roman Catholics, members of a not insignificant minority in Presbyterian Scotland. Doyle's father was an Englishman: Charles Doyle, youngest son of the prominent cartoonist John Doyle — an artist himself, but unsuccessful, whose work was as a draftsman in the Scottish Office of Works. His mother was Mary, née Foley, a strong-minded Irishwoman with a strong, even imaginative, sense of family tradition. They had ten children:

- Anne Mary Frances (Annette), born 1856, who became a governess (in Portugal for one period) and probably gave Doyle the sympathetic interest in governesses reflected in "The Copper Beeches." She died, unmarried, in 1889.
- Catherine, born 1858, died in infancy.
- Arthur, born 1859.
- Mary, born 1861, died in 1863.
- Caroline (Lottie), born 1866. In 1900 she married Leslie Oldham, a military man who became a major in the Royal Engineers and was killed in World War I. She died in 1941.
- Constance, born 1868, also worked as a governess for a time. In 1893 she married Ernest William Hornung, who went on to create A.J. Raffles, the celebrated gentleman-burglar, in *The Amateur Cracksman* (1899) and to elaborate him in *The Black Mask* (1901), *A Thief in the Night* (1905), and *Mr. Justice Raffles* (1909). She died in 1924.
- Innes Hay, born March 31, 1873, who lived with Doyle when he was a young doctor in Southsea. Innes entered the army and rose during World War I to be a brigadier-general; he died in February 1919. Innes married Clara Schwensen. Their son, John Doyle, also became a

brigadier-general, and a keeper of Doyle memorabilia; he died in 1990, survived by his third wife, Georgina, who has become a Doyle biographer and custodian of family traditions.

- Jane Adelaide (Ida), born 1875, married Nelson Foley, died in 1937.
- Bryan Mary ("Dodo"), born 1877. In 1899 she married the Reverend Cyril Angell, who officiated at Doyle's second wedding. Dodo, who wrote two novels under the pen name of H. Ripley Cromarsh, died in 1927.
- A final child whose name and sex are not known and who apparently died in infancy.

These details have been quarried from official and unofficial records with a good deal of difficulty. Doyle scholars are much indebted to Minnesota scholar Phillip G. Bergem, who collected them, and much more, in his privately published *The Family and Residences of Arthur Conan Doyle* (2003).

The Doyles' genteel poverty became something worse as Charles Doyle became unable to work. He was both epileptic (a condition poorly understood in the middle of the nineteenth century) and, from some point during Arthur's childhood, alcoholic. Although there are no first-hand descriptions of life in the Doyle home in the 1870s, one may see reflections of it in some of the tales in which Doyle, as an adult, wrote with horror about the effects of drink (including "The Abbey Grange"). Charles Doyle was finally institutionalized in 1883; the story of his descent was revealed by Michael Baker in the Introduction to *The Doyle Diary* (1978), a facsimile of a sketchbook dating from Charles Doyle's years of confinement. He died October 10, 1893.

Arthur's mother, Mary (Foley) Doyle, held the family together and became, by general consent, the dominant figure in his life, even if John Dickson Carr (in *The Life of Sir Arthur Conan Doyle*, 1947) exaggerates the relationship and invents out of whole cloth the title "the Ma'am" for her. Irish by extraction, she was rigid in moral and social standards, and mindful of a proud ancestry which most researchers now think she largely imagined. Doyle wrote to her constantly ("Dearest Mam," the letters often began) until her death December 30, 1920, only ten years before his own death. Hundreds of those letters survive, and many have been published for attentive scholars in *Arthur Conan Doyle: A Life in Letters*, edited by Jon Lellenberg, Daniel Stashower, and Charles Foley (2007). Doyle's mother was unquestionably the chief source of his life-long interest in history, as well as of his character and chivalric standards. Bryan Charles Waller

(1853–1932), a family friend who was a few years ahead of Doyle at medical school, influenced him both towards medicine and towards literature, and apparently contributed to supporting the family after Charles Doyle was incapacitated; Mary Doyle spent her later years living on Waller's estate at Masongill, Yorkshire. The exact nature of the relationship between Waller and Mary Doyle is often mentioned as one of the important unanswered questions in Doyle biography.

After early schooling in Edinburgh, Doyle was sent to prominent Roman Catholic "public" (boarding) schools in Lancashire: to Hodder School in 1868, to nearby Stonyhurst College in 1870. There he survived physical abuse, played sports with determination, read adventure stories voraciously, and perhaps learned a little of what the Jesuit masters sought to teach him — enough, anyway, that they sent him to their school at Feldkirch, Austria, for a year (1875–76). He returned to Edinburgh to begin medical studies at the age of seventeen, at what was probably the leading medical school in Europe. Ely M. Liebow, in *Dr. Joe Bell: Model for Sherlock Holmes* (1982), gives a picture of life at the University of Edinburgh:

> One had to learn much self-discipline, Doyle noted, for once the timid young freshman turned over his £1 note to the bursar he was practically on his own. While there certainly was a number of required courses in the arts as well as in medical school, the students were free to attend what lectures they pleased (text books, especially in the medical school, were practically non-existent until the 1880s).... Doyle, who was trying to compress five years' study into four to save money, admits quite readily that he was "always one of the ruck, neither lingering nor gaining — a 60 per cent man at examinations."... Doyle, like many a student in the 1870s, not only took courses from University professors, but often took classes on the same subject from an extra-curricular lecturer.

The most famous "extra-curricular lecturer" to instruct Doyle was Dr. Joseph Bell, to whom (Liebow reports) Doyle paid £4.4s for surgical teaching at Edinburgh's new Infirmary, where Bell became senior surgeon in 1878. Other professors, at the university or the surrounding hospitals, who made an impression on Doyle included Dr. Patrick Heron Watson, Bell's senior and a brilliant surgeon, and Dr. William Rutherford, whose voice and physique provided the model for Professor Challenger in stories Doyle would write decades later.

LITERARY WORK

Sherlockians affect to say that the tales of Sherlock Holmes are history, not fiction. Even if one accepts that postulate, it is still reasonable to describe Doyle as a prominent author of fiction, for the sake of his many other writings. Apart from the Canon, only *The White Company* and (intermittently) the stories of Brigadier Gerard are generally in print, but when antiquarian editions can be found, nearly all his books are worth the reading. Not only are they of interest for plot and character; Doyle's prose is clear and workmanlike, its effects coming from the marshalling of ordinary, mostly short, concrete words. Occasional descriptive passages provide relief from the brisk progress of a tale through dialogue, and the names of people and streets, specific numbers and dates, keep the narratives anchored in everyday reality. Charles Press discusses his skills as an author in a small 2004 book under the title *Looking Over Sir Arthur's Shoulder*.

Following is a list of Doyle's fiction, plays, and poetry with the heading numbers assigned by Green and Gibson in their 1983 *Bibliography of A. Conan Doyle*.

A1. *A Study in Scarlet,* 1887.

A2. *The Mystery of Cloomber,* 1888.

A3. *Micah Clarke,* 1889.

A4. *Mysteries and Adventures,* 1889 (also published as *My Friend the Murderer and Other Stories, The Gully of Bluemansdyke and Other Stories*).

A5. *The Captain of the Polestar and Other Tales,* 1890.

A6. *The Firm of Girdlestone,* 1890.

A7. *The Sign of Four,* 1890.

A8. *The White Company,* 1891.

A9. *The Doings of Raffles Haw,* 1892.

A10. *The Adventures of Sherlock Holmes,* 1892.

A11. *The Great Shadow,* 1892.

A12. *The Refugees,* 1893.

A13. *The Great Shadow and Beyond the City,* 1893.

A14. *The Memoirs of Sherlock Holmes,* 1893.

A15. *An Actor's Duel and The Winning Shot,* 1894.

A16. *Round the Red Lamp,* 1894.

A17. *The Parasite,* 1894.

A18. *The Stark Munro Letters*, 1895.

A19. *The Exploits of Brigadier Gerard*, 1896.

A20. *Rodney Stone*, 1896.

A21. *Uncle Bernac*, 1897.

A22. *The Tragedy of the Korosko*, 1898 (also published as *A Desert Drama*).

A23. *Songs of Action*, 1898 (poetry).

A24. *A Duet with an Occasional Chorus*, 1899.

A25. *The Green Flag and Other Stories of War and Sport*, 1900.

A26. *The Hound of the Baskervilles*, 1902.

A27. *Adventures of Gerard*, 1903.

A28. *A Duet*, 1903 (drama).

A29. *The Return of Sherlock Holmes*, 1905.

A30. *Sir Nigel*, 1906.

A31. *The Croxley Master*, 1907.

A32. *Waterloo*, 1907 (drama).

A33. *Round the Fire Stories*, 1908.

A34. *Songs of the Road*, 1911 (poetry).

A35. *The Last Galley*, 1911.

A36. *The Speckled Band*, 1912 (drama).

A37. *The Lost World*, 1912.

A38. *The Poison Belt*, 1913.

A39. *The Valley of Fear*, 1915.

A40. *His Last Bow*, 1917.

A41. *Danger! and Other Stories*, 1918.

A42. *The Guards Came Through and Other Poems*, 1919.

A43. *The Poems of Arthur Conan Doyle — Collected Edition*, 1922.

A44. *Three of Them*, 1923.

A45. *The Land of Mist*, 1926.

A46. *The Case-Book of Sherlock Holmes*, 1927.

A47. *The Maracot Deep and Other Stories*, 1929.

(Gibson and Green continue the listing with posthumously published books and re-collected stories.) These titles include the nine volumes of Sherlock Holmes, four books of poetry, and three plays, one of them the 1912 *Speckled Band*. Those aside, there are thirty-one books of fiction, chiefly novels. There is some repetition as tales were published in more than one collection.

GENERAL FICTION. Doyle's first published novel was *A Study in Scarlet* (1887), but it was not the first written. Of his surviving work, the earliest is *The Firm of Girdlestone*, written in 1884–85 but published only in 1890. Like most writings by young novelists, it is somewhat autobiographical, drawing on Doyle's Edinburgh background. The same might be said for some of his later, more substantial novels: *The Stark Munro Letters* draws on his experiences as a young doctor, *A Duet with an Occasional Chorus* on his courtship of his first wife. Both combine corroborative detail — pictures, presumably accurate, of middle-class life in the 1890s — with frequent flashes of humour. In the same category is the much later *Three of Them*, a barely fictionalized description of the childhood of Denis, Adrian, and Jean.

Middle-class life is also portrayed in *Beyond the City*, which is of special interest for its early picture of an unconventional, self-supporting professional woman. Doyle, though never a sympathizer with feminists (he opposed extension of the vote to women), had a life-long admiration for strong women, presumably because of his mother's influence. (Biographer Owen Dudley Edwards deals with this point in "The Hero as Woman," second chapter of *The Quest for Sherlock Holmes* [1983].) He makes an admiring point about women in his own profession, medicine, in "The Doctors of Hoyland," an 1894 short story.

The medical short stories that appeared in *Round the Red Lamp*, along with a few others, reveal so much about Doyle — and about the medicine of the later Victorian era — that they were given elaborate attention in an annotated version, *Conan Doyle's Tales of Medical Humanism and Values* (1992), by Alvin E. Rodin and Jack D. Key, who had already collaborated on other analyses of Doyle and medicine. Their volume *Medical Casebook of Doctor Arthur Conan Doyle* (1984) includes a detailed discussion of these stories, which range from the gentle to the chilling. Doyle's medical background is evident in many of his other writings as well, including several of the Holmes tales ("The Resident Patient" most obviously). One can also see, in all his fiction, a preoccupation — verging on the morbid — with injured or amputated legs and with scarred or mutilated faces; surely his tolerance for descriptions that distress some squeamish readers was a result of his experiences in medical school and professional practice.

Not all Doyle's early writings were about the experiences of people like himself, however. There is a strong element of sensation, seen also in the early Holmes tales. *The Mystery of Cloomber*, probably written early although not published until 1888, reflects the author's interest in blood revenge, mysticism, and exotic India. "It was not among the author's favourite works," Green and Gibson note in their *Bibliography*, "as he considered it very immature." Most commentators have concurred. *The Parasite* is also sensational, although scientific hypnotism takes the place of eastern religion, and is one of the most overtly sexual of Doyle's writings. That by no means makes it unique; he returns again and again to themes of obsession and jealousy, and to motifs of the supernatural, eerie, and inexplicable, with a strong presence of evil. "The best of [Doyle's stories]," biographer Charles Higham wrote in 1976, "are poetic evocations of sexual obsession." The comment may say as much about Higham's imagination as about Doyle's, but it is not entirely untrue.

A more masculine aspect appears in such books as *Rodney Stone*, a tale, perhaps unjustly neglected, of boxing in the Regency era — a period Doyle clearly enjoyed. He returned to the same background in *The Croxley Master*. Dozens of his short stories, many of them collected in such books as *The Captain of the Polestar*, *The Green Flag*, and *The Last Galley*, are about swashbuckling adventure. He did well to have many of them reissued late in his life (1922) as *Tales of Pirates and Blue Water*, *Tales of Terror and Mystery*, *Tales of Twilight and the Unseen*, *Tales of Adventure and Medical Life*, *Tales of Long Ago*. These tales include such classics as "A Straggler of '15," about a survivor of the Battle of Waterloo; "J. Habakuk Jephson's Statement," about a ship which is found abandoned, a tale that was widely taken as non-fiction when it first appeared in 1884; and "The Man from Archangel," a reflection of his youthful experiences in Arctic waters that does also have that undertone of sexual obsession.

Stories that did not appear in collected form have been searched out by Doyle's admirers in recent years, and many became available for the first time in a century in the pages of *Uncollected Stories* (1982), edited by Gibson and Green as a byproduct of their *Bibliography*. Adventure at novel length is found in such books as *The Tragedy of the Korostko*, about a party of English men and women in dire straits in the Egyptian desert; strikingly, the one character who emerges well from the ordeal does so by drawing on a Roman Catholic faith, the religion in which Doyle was raised but which he abandoned.

NAPOLEONIC WORKS. Repeatedly Doyle wrote about the era of Napoléon Bonaparte (1769–1821), Emperor of France. Napoléon conquered most of Europe between 1800 and 1814, was defeated in that year and forced to abdicate, but returned from his exile on Elba to rally his army; he was finally defeated at Waterloo June 18, 1815. The fifteen years of the Napoleonic wars against France were stressful and memorable for England, and the figure of Napoléon — "Boney" — was still a bogeyman eighty years later. It is thus no surprise that Doyle made those wars the subject of several pieces of writing.

He was, however, sufficiently sympathetic to France, if not to Napoléon, that he treats the wars as much from the French point of view as from the English, and that his central Napoleonic figure, Brigadier Etienne Gerard, attracts the reader's admiration and affection. Doyle's Napoleonic fiction is discussed in detail in *The Great Shadow* (1997) by Clifford S. Goldfarb.

Doyle's first work set in this era was a short story, "A Straggler of '15," about the aftermath of the Battle of Waterloo. Published in 1891, that tale led to the one-act play *Waterloo*, which opened September 21, 1894, with Henry (later Sir Henry) Irving in the principal role. Then came *The Great Shadow*, set chiefly in Scotland but with its climax on the battlefield of Waterloo. Yet another novel with a Napoleonic background was *Uncle Bernac*, this one interpreting the emperor and his era in a comic tone.

But by far the most important of Doyle's Napoleonic work are his stories of Brigadier Gerard — seventeen short stories altogether, eight that were quickly collected in *The Exploits of Brigadier Gerard*, eight more in *Adventures of Gerard*, and a seventeenth, "The Marriage of the Brigadier," eventually appearing in *The Last Galley*. The tales are based more or less on the memoirs of Jean Baptiste de Marbot (1782–1854), a genuine Napoleonic general and baron. (Gerard never achieves either rank, although the emperor does decorate him for valour, if not for brains.) Marbot's memoirs were published in French in 1891 and in English the following year, and signalled an avalanche of military reminiscences and history, as well as such Napoleonic fiction as Doyle's. Gerard is given more bluster and more heroism than the blustering, heroic Marbot, whose experiences the tales follow with a wry fidelity that makes them read better in fiction than they do in sober history. Many readers think the stories of Gerard are, in fact, Doyle's finest work, their strength being in the use of irony (shading into comedy), the depiction of a larger-than-life personality, the choice of the perfect detail to illuminate a man, an event, and an age.

HISTORICAL NOVELS. Doyle believed that his reputation would rest on his four major historical novels, above all on *The White Company*, which is rich in historical detail about English and French life of the fourteenth century. He read exhaustively, exhaustingly, to collect the material for it, drawing also on the stories of chivalry his mother had told him in childhood:

> I had recourse to the study of 115 books before I could put a pen to paper. It was very much as Charles Reade had said of *The Cloister and the Hearth*: "I milked three hundred cows into my pail, but the butter was my own for all that."

106

Doyle is supposed to have added that when he wrote the book's final words he cried "That's done it!" and flung his pen across the room, staining the blue wallpaper of his study. The final words are a hymn of praise to England, in which the author escapes from narrative to say (rather self-consciously, the modern reader may think) what noble meanings he attaches to English virtue:

> The sky may darken, and the clouds may gather, and again the day may come when Britain may have sore need of her children, on whatever shore of the sea they be found. Shall they not muster at her call?

Writing in 1948, Doyle's biographer, John Dickson Carr, was thrilled by *The White Company*, and saw it above all as honest: "What his characters would have done, *he* would have done. And did do, until the end of his life."

But the book has weaknesses, so that it has largely fallen out of favour. Its plot is weak; it follows young Alleyne Edricson from the abbey of Beaulieu (in the New Forest, where all his life Doyle longed to live) into worldly life, to the wars in France under the banner of Sir Nigel Loring, and home again to success in love. The climax is a minor battle in Spain, in which the "white company" of archers in which Alleyne has enlisted is gloriously annihilated. Most of the characters are cartoons, and the language is cloying, with voices crying "Nay!" and "By the rood!" However, the author displays an intimate, or at least convincing, knowledge of mediaeval archery, heraldry, underclothing, horsemanship, politics, stained glass, social hierarchy, medicine, and bad language, and misses no opportunity to demonstrate his versatility with them all. The most interesting figure in *The White Company* is Sir Nigel Loring, who became the central figure in another novel in which Doyle tried to repeat his success. *Sir Nigel*, published fifteen years later, shows Nigel Loring as a younger man, not yet with the bald head he boasts in *The White Company*. A second well-drawn figure joins him in this book — his grandmother, Dame Ermyntrude, generally considered to be a portrait of the author's mother, Mary Foley Doyle.

Doyle's earliest historical novel was given a pseudo-antique title which at least indicates its subject well:

> *Micah Clarke His Statement as Made to His Three Grand-Children Joseph, Gervas & Reuben During the Hard Winter of 1734 Wherein is Contained a Full Report of Certain Passages in His Early Life Together with Some Account of His Journey*

from Havant to Taunton with Decimus Saxon in the Summer of 1685. Also of the Adventures that Befell Them During the Western Rebellion, & of their Intercourse with James Duke of Monmouth, Lord Grey, & Other Persons of Quality Compiled Day by Day, from His Own Narration, by Joseph Clarke, & Never Previously Set Forth in Print. Now for the First Time Collected, Corrected, & Re-Arranged from the Original Manuscripts by A. Conan Doyle.

The book is, of course, entirely fiction, set in the tumultuous period (much less well known than the English Civil War forty years earlier) of Monmouth's rebellion, crushed by James II, who thus managed to reign four more years before the "Glorious Revolution" saw him deposed. Monmouth and his followers were Puritans, close kin to the Presbyterians of the Scotland in which Doyle grew up; James and his followers were Roman Catholics, competing with the Puritans for control of the Church of England. So it is fitting that the most dramatic battle in *Micah Clarke* takes place inside the thirteenth-century cathedral at Wells. *Micah Clarke* contains the same balance of character, compulsive historical detail, and episodic adventure as Doyle's later historical novels, and is as rarely read today.

The fourth of those major historical books is *The Refugees*, set at exactly the same date as *Micah Clarke*, but this time in France (chiefly at the court of Louis XIV) and in America, both in Québec and in the forests of what is now northern New York. The plot, more suited to a serial, with repeated cliffhangers, than to a novel, deals with Huguenot (Protestant) lovers escaping from Roman Catholic oppression. Doyle gives himself the opportunity to describe every class of society, as well as the excitement of ocean travel, the baseness and nobility of various parts of the church, love and lust, and the drama of the frontier. His Iroquois are bloodthirsty torturers (the book includes mutilation scenes of a kind that were always dear to Doyle) and his whole picture of America is drawn, none too reliably, from the early historian Francis Parkman, whose books were among his youthful enthusiasms.

SCIENCE FICTION. Educated to be a doctor, Doyle had something of the scientific temperament as well as some scientific knowledge. Medicine figures in many of his stories, but so do other sciences and technologies, particularly electricity, with which he seems to have been fascinated. As early as 1891 he wrote the short story "The Voice of Science," about the gramophone, invented just a decade before. "The Japanned Box" (1899) returns to the subject of sound recording, which was still new enough to amuse readers of Sherlock Holmes in "The Mazarin Stone" in 1921. The titles of other short stories indicate the range of the sciences on which they touch: "An Exciting Christmas Eve, or, My Lecture on Dynamite"; "The Great Keinplatz Experiment" (hypnotism); "The Beetle-Hunter"; "The Great Brown-Pericord Motor." Of special interest is "The Horror of the Heights" (1913), a story about aircraft pilots who find more at high altitudes than they had bargained for. Doyle had his one and only experience of airplane flight in 1911, at Hendon, and was exhilarated but terrified; he also had some experiences of ballooning.

The Best Science Fiction of Arthur Conan Doyle (1981), edited by Charles G. Waugh and Martin H. Greenberg, reprints some of these stories as well as others, including two from the Sherlock Holmes Canon: "The Devil's Foot" and "The Creeping Man." Both are about the effects of chemicals on human behaviour. The editors might have included "The Lion's Mane" as well, and there is a modern flavour to "The Bruce-Partington Plans," with its talk of double valves with automatic self-adjusting slots.

Much the most important of Doyle's science fiction, however, is the little body of material — three novels and two short stories — about Professor George Edward Challenger. The greatest of these is *The Lost World*, the story of an expedition to South America, where dinosaurs prove to have survived into modern times on an isolated plateau. Two young and practical men (Edward Malone, the newspaperman narrator, and adventurer Lord John Roxton) are juxtaposed with two elderly scientists — Professor Summerlee and the incomparable Challenger. The name of the latter is presumably taken from HMS *Challenger*, the ship that had spent 1872–76 circumnavigating the world and collecting data about the ocean bed and its inhabitants. The physique (short, broad, with "the face and beard of an Assyrian bull") and to some extent the personality are taken from William Rutherford, one of Doyle's professors at Edinburgh. But no medical professor abused his wife, bit his housekeeper, broke a newspaperman's skull, interrupted public meetings, boasted, bellowed, dared, and discovered as Challenger does. He is, if not the most realistic character in Doyle's writings, the most memorable after Sherlock Holmes himself.

The Lost World, says Charles Higham in his biography of Doyle, "is a masterpiece of imaginative fiction, reminiscent of Jules Verne but not suffering from the comparison." (Verne [1828–1905] was the author of, among other works, *Twenty Thousand Leagues Under the Sea* [1869].) Doyle based it on anthropological and travel writings of the time — South American exploration was fashionable — and his own keen interest in evolution. That interest has led to accusations that he was the originator of the Piltdown Man hoax, fabricator of the skull and jaw bones discovered near Doyle's Sussex home in the same year in which *The Lost World* was published. Although the Piltdown hoaxer has never been identified, Doyle is definitively acquitted in *The Curious Incident of the Missing Link* (1988) by Douglas Elliott. Whether the science in *The Lost World* is any more authentic than that of Piltdown, or that in Verne, is questionable, but the adventure story is first-rate (the love story rather less so), and the book was a success. A verse by Doyle that is sometimes quoted as if it were about Holmes was in fact the epigraph for *The Lost World*:

> I have wrought my simple plan
> If I give one hour of joy
> To the boy who's half a man,
> Or the man who's half a boy.

To add to the fun, Doyle costumed himself as Challenger to pose for a photograph that appeared as frontispiece to the book's *Strand Magazine* serialization (April–November 1912) and first British edition. The photograph is revived opposite the title page of *The Annotated Lost World*, edited by Roy Pilot and Alvin Rodin, published in 1996 and offering dozens of clarifying notes as well as reproductions of early illustrations.

A year after *The Lost World*, Doyle brought Challenger back in *The Poison Belt*, this time proclaiming a theory in astronomy rather than in palaeontology. The world is about to pass through a belt of poison in the "ether," with disastrous consequences expressed in rather the same tones as modern warnings about the ozone layer and global climate change. Challenger and a few friends seal themselves in a cozy room (the story may owe a little to Poe's "The Masque of the Red Death") in order to survive. The professor is also the central character of a third novel, *The Land of Mist*, which, though it may be classed as science fiction, is really an apologia for the beliefs of spiritualism, to which Doyle adhered in the 1920s. In that 1926 book, the iconoclastic and ultra-rational Challenger is converted to spiritualism — a conversion which, strikingly, Doyle never attempted to force on Sherlock Holmes. Finally, "When the World Screamed" (1928) and "The Disintegration Machine" (1929) are short stories also involving Challenger.

The Lost World has survived better, and had more influence on popular culture, than any of Doyle's other work apart from Holmes himself. It was first filmed in 1925 by First National, with Wallace Beery as Challenger, and can claim to be the first stop-motion animated film ever produced, with creaky animated dinosaurs created by Willis O'Brien, the technician who was later responsible for King Kong. Much of the original film has not survived, but a painstaking reconstruction was issued on DVD in 2001. A 1960 remake starred, rather oddly, Claude Rains; further versions came in 1992 (with John Rhys-Davies), 1998 (with Patrick Bergin), and 2001 (with Bob Hoskins). A television series, "Sir Arthur Conan Doyle's The Lost World," ran in syndication for three years starting in the spring of 1999. It starred Peter McCauley as Challenger, and attracted viewers with plot and visual elements not found in the original, such as the skimpy costumes of Jennifer O'Dell as jungle girl Veronica.

In 1995 came Michael Crichton's best-selling novel *The Lost World*, a sequel to *Jurassic Park* (1990). Though the background is genetic engineering rather than a survival of dinosaurs in a remote region, Crichton's stories deal, like Doyle's, with humans encountering prehistoric beasts. The novelist was a candid admirer of his predecessor, and had dedicated an earlier book, *The Andromeda Strain*, to Doyle, acknowledging that it was based on *The Poison Belt*. "Conan Doyle," he once wrote, "recognized the limitations of Verne's simple narrative structure, which quickly devolves into a mere survival story, a search for water in passages beneath a volcano. For *The Lost World*, Conan Doyle establishes a more complex plot, with more intriguing characters." He wrote an introduction for a 2003 edition of Doyle's book. Both Crichton's novels became highly successful films directed by Steven Spielberg, which have contributed to the survival of the "Lost World" meme independent of its 1912 creator. More direct descendants of the original also exist, such as Greg Bear's 1998 novel *Dinosaur Summer*.

Novel-length science-fiction works by Doyle which do not use Professor Challenger as their protagonist include *The Doings of Raffles Haw*, a slight story of chemistry and social climbing; *The Parasite*, an early and rather creepy novel about hypnotism and sexual obsession; and his last published work of fiction, *The Maracot Deep*, a feeble adventure in which a party of explorers finds the advanced civilization of Atlantis. The idea is by no means original, and the purpose of the book seems to be to preach spiritualism (a belief whose truth the Atlanteans are able to demonstrate) rather than to entertain.

Doyle's science fiction is discussed in detail in *Lost Worlds in Time, Space and Medicine* (1988) by Alvin E. Rodin and Jack D. Key. They divide his stories in this genre according to the sort of science involved: Electrical Energy, Alien Creatures, Geographic, and of course Medical. They also suggest that science fiction is a reasonable product for an author who also excelled in mystery writing: "Both genres have in common the elements of adventure, danger, suspense, heroes and villains." It could also be said that a great deal of Doyle's writing is, if marginal as science fiction, unquestionably about the occult, for ghosts, mummies, uncanny influences, and other such phenomena abound.

DRAMA AND POETRY. Doyle's three principal plays are all reworkings of his fiction — *A Duet*, "A Straggler of '15" (a major success in 1894–95 and several subsequent productions, starring Henry Irving), and "The Speckled Band." He was also author of several unpublished plays of the same kind, including "Brigadier Gerard," performed in London in the spring and summer of 1906, with a brief run in New York that autumn. The Green and Gibson *Bibliography* mentions a dozen plays that were performed in Doyle's lifetime, and another half-dozen that were unfinished or never produced. One play of some historical interest is "Jane Annie, or, The Good Conduct Prize," a comic opera jointly by Doyle and J.M. (later Sir James) Barrie, produced in London and Newcastle in 1893 (text published the same year).

Doyle's four volumes of poetry — three significant collections and a "collected edition" with a little new material — are among his least-known work, and rightly so. Says biographer and critic Pierre Nordon in *Conan Doyle* (1966): "Anecdotes, ballads, odes, comic verse or doggerel, their unpretentiousness charmingly excuses their insignificance. But if they mark the lowest level of Conan Doyle's inspiration, they also stress the diversity of his ambitions and literary activities." The poems include "The Song of the Bow" (originally from *The White Company*), "The Storming Party," "A Ballad of the Ranks," "The Guns in Sussex" (reflecting the martial mood of 1917), "The Wreck on Loch McGarry," and other such topics, as well as a few more philosophic verses. Only one poem is quoted with any frequency, and that is "The Inner Room," dating at least from 1898, when it first appeared in *Songs of Action*. Its significance for understanding Doyle, or understanding Doyle's image of himself, is greater than its poetic virtues:

> It is mine — the little chamber,
>   Mine alone.
> I had it from my forbears
>   Years agone.
> Yet within its walls I see
> A most motley company,
> And they one and all claim me
>   As their own.

There's one who is a soldier
  Bluff and keen;
Single-minded, heavy-fisted,
  Rude of mien.
He would gain a purse or stake it,
He would win a heart or break it,
He would give a life or take it,
  Conscience-clean.

And near him is a priest
  Still schism-whole;
He loves the censer-reek
  And organ roll....

If the stark-faced fellow win,
  All is o'er!
If the priest should gain his will,
  I doubt no more!
But if each shall have his day,
I shall swing and I shall sway
In the same old weary way
  As before.

PERIPHERAL WORKS ABOUT HOLMES. The Sherlockian Canon of novels and short stories might seem complete and self-contained, but other fragments about Sherlock Holmes also came from Doyle's pen. They appear, with slightly different inventories, in four modern collections: *Sherlock Holmes: The Published Apocrypha* (1980), edited by Jack Tracy; *The Final Adventures of Sherlock Holmes* (1981), edited by Peter Haining; *The Uncollected Sherlock Holmes* (1983), edited by Richard Lancelyn Green, whose well-informed 140-page Introduction to the volume is a sympathetic and valuable biographical study of Doyle; and most recently *The Apocrypha of Sherlock Holmes*, edited by Leslie S. Klinger (2009). These are the most important "apocrypha" from Doyle's pen:

- "The Field Bazaar," a parody of a Baker Street breakfast scene, written in 1896 to help raise funds for a sports field at his old university. It was published in a special issue of the *Student* magazine.

- "How Watson Learned the Trick," another breakfast parody, written for a dollhouse created for Queen Mary in the 1920s, and published in 1924 in *The Book of the Queen's Dolls' House Library*.
- *The Speckled Band*, a play first produced at London's Adelphi Theatre on June 4, 1910, based on the short story of some eighteen years earlier. The best-known difference between story and play is in the proper names: Dr. Roylott becomes Rylott, and Helen Stoner becomes Enid Stonor; her deceased sister, Julia, now bears that favourite Doylean name Violet. The play was originally to be titled "The Stonor Case," research has revealed. Holmes, appropriately, has the curtain line at the end of the second act:

  > Watson *(looking at snake)*: The brute is dead.
  > Holmes *(looking at Dr. Rylott)*: So is the other. *(They both run to support the fainting lady.)* Miss Stonor, there is no more danger for you under this roof.
  > *Curtain.*

- *The Crown Diamond*, a one-act play first produced in the spring of 1921. Its plot is that of the short story "The Mazarin Stone," published later in that year, and the stagelike quality of the story strongly suggests that it was adapted from the script rather than the other way around. The most striking difference is that the villain is not Count Negretto Sylvius, as in print, but Colonel Sebastian Moran, already familiar from "The Empty House," which shares an essential plot feature — the wax bust — with "The Mazarin Stone."
- "The Man with the Watches" and "The Lost Special," a pair of short stories first published in the *Strand Magazine* for July and August 1898, respectively, and later included in *Round the Fire Stories*. Both are mysteries that baffle the authorities but are addressed, in letters to the newspapers, by an "amateur reasoner of some celebrity" whose style makes clear that he must be Sherlock Holmes. Writes Jack Tracy, introducing the stories in his anthology: "Nearly five years after ... the supposed death of his detective creation, Conan Doyle could still neither forget Sherlock Holmes nor even resist the urge to write about him."
- "Angels of Darkness," a play that substantially overlaps with the second part of *A Study in Scarlet*. In this interpretation, Holmes is not involved in the case, but Watson is, and has a serious romantic interlude

in America. After decades of rumour about its content, the text was published in 2001 (by the Baker Street Irregulars) to a general reception of disappointment at cheap humour and what would now be interpreted as racist stereotyping. Subsequent publication of Doyle's letters has made it clear that *Angels* was not a source of *A Study in Scarlet* but was written subsequently; it was never produced.

In addition to such apocrypha, Doyle wrote about Holmes a number of times in his own person. The most important such piece is "Some Personalia about Mr. Sherlock Holmes," published in the *Strand Magazine* in December 1917. There is also a plot for a Holmes story Doyle never wrote, involving a man who proves to have committed his crime with the help of stilts. Finally, there is a verse, "To an Undiscerning Critic," first published in the magazine *London Opinion* for December 28, 1912:

> Have you not learned, my esteemed commentator,
> That the created is not the creator? ...
>
> He, the created, the puppet of fiction,
> Would not brook rivals nor stand contradiction.
>
> He, the created, would scoff and would sneer,
> Where I, the Creator, would bow and revere.

GENERAL INTERESTS

To describe Doyle as an author is to neglect his many other activities and contributions to the public good — although, to be sure, he carried on many of them through the written word, not only in books but in pamphlets, letters to the newspapers, and a heavy private correspondence. *Letters to the Press* (1986), edited by John Michael Gibson and Richard Lancelyn Green, gives glimpses of a Doyle who was as interested in rifle shooting, retail closing hours, photography, inoculation, divorce law, cricket, income tax, war, motor-cars, prostitution, and the Olympic Games as he was in conventional literary work.

His interest in literary topics led him to take a prominent part in the Society of Authors and to appear on public occasions of a literary kind. He spoke on "the literature of the Scottish border" at a banquet of the London Scottish Border Counties Association in 1904, and took the chair at a dinner honouring the 1909 centenary of Edgar Allan Poe. In 1899 he was in print in the *Daily Chronicle* on "The Ethics of Criticism," and in 1911 in the *Bookman* about bogus literary agents. And repeatedly he wrote about other authors and their works, both his contemporaries and those who had influenced him in his early years. *Through the Magic Door* (1907), based on a series of 1894 magazine articles that had been titled "Before My Bookcase," is an appreciation of such writers as Scott, Carlyle, Macaulay, Parkman, and Poe — his childhood favourites.

Late in his life he wrote not only an autobiography (*Memories and Adventures* [1924, revised edition 1930) but several books of travel and commentary: *Our American Adventure* (1923), *Our Second American Adventure* (1924), *Our African Winter* (1929). The latter books also include long defences of spiritualism, to which he had by that time been converted. The autobiography includes many of Doyle's opinions and experiences, but is markedly lacking in personal insight and in reference to his emotional or private life. It shows him as clearly a public man — a role he played for some forty years.

SPORTS. Every form of sport was of interest to Doyle, and often as a participant, though he also became known as that vaguely defined thing, "a sportsman." At the 1908 Olympic Games, held in London, he was on hand to report for the *Daily Mail* at the finish line of the marathon race (the first race to use the now standard marathon distance of 26 miles 385 yards). When the Italian competitor, Dorando Pietri, who had led most of the way, collapsed just short of the finish line, was helped up by officials and was dragged across the line, but disqualified after a protest, Doyle immediately led a movement to present him with a cash purse (which reached £308) to honour his courage. A few years later he was in the newspapers repeatedly as Britain debated the merits of participation in the projected 1916 Olympics and the best way of organizing a team. A chapter entitled "Some Recollections of Sport" in Doyle's 1924 autobiography *Memories and Adventures* ranges from fishing to billiards, to say nothing of the Prince Henry International Road Competition in 1911, in which Doyle was one of nearly a hundred drivers who spent three weeks touring Germany, Scotland and, England.

The major sports in England were and are cricket, a bat-and-ball game, and football, of the kinds known in North America as rugby and soccer. Doyle played all three. Cricket, he wrote in the autobiography, has on the whole given me more pleasure during my life than any other branch of sport. I have ended by being its victim, for a fast bowler some years ago happened to hit me twice in the same place under my left knee, which has left a permanent weakness.... I fulfilled a secret ambition by getting into the fringe of first-class cricket, though rather, perhaps, through the good nature of others than my own merits. However, I can truly say that in the last season when I played some first-class cricket, including matches against Kent, Derbyshire, and the London County, I had an average of thirty-two for those games.... I was more useful, however, in an amateur team, for I was a fairly steady and reliable bowler.

He once performed a hat trick, that is, bowled three "clean" wickets in a row; he bowled the great W.G. Grace, equivalent to striking out Ted Williams in baseball; he hit a century (one hundred runs) at Lord's, the shrine of cricket grounds. As an amateur he was a member of a team of literary and artistic men organized by J.M. Barrie: the Allahakbarries, or Gawd-help-us-es, whose style on the playing field seems to have reflected their name.

Oddly, there is nothing of cricket in the Sherlockian Canon, save a mention that young Gilchrist of "The Three Students" played the game. That is hardly surprising, for Gilchrist was an all-round athlete, whose visits to the clay-bottomed jumping pit helped lead to his undoing. Football, on the other hand, figures importantly in one story, "The Missing Three-Quarter." Its plot has to do with the disappearance of a star player on the Cambridge University team just before a big game.

> My ramifications stretch out into many sections of society [says Holmes], but never, I am happy to say, into amateur sport, which is the best and soundest thing in England. However, your unexpected visit this morning shows me that even in that world of fresh air and fair play, there may be work for me to do.

That is Doyle speaking, about the game he played as a young man at Edinburgh, his position being forward. This football is rugby, the collegiate game of the time and still frequently played by amateurs in England, though there is also a professional league playing a slightly different game. The major form of professional football is "association," or soccer, so called for the governing body established for it as a new sport in 1863. In Portsmouth, Doyle helped organize a new club for association football, and played for several seasons as a fullback and occasionally goalkeeper (usually under the discreet nom-de-plume of Smith). His autobiography deals with football in complimentary terms:

> If boxing is the finest single man sport, I think that Rugby football is the best collective one. Strength, courage, speed and resource are great qualities to include in a single game. I have always wished that it had come more my way in life....
>
> I took to Association, and played first goal and then back for Portsmouth, when that famous club was an amateur organization. Even then, we could put a very fair team in the field, and were runners-up for the County Cup the last season that I played. In the same season I was invited to play for the county. I was always too slow, however, to be a really good back, though I was a long and safe kick. After a long hiatus I took up football again in South Africa and organized a series of inter-hospital matches in Bloemfontein.

Many other sports are reflected in the Canon, with only eleven of the sixty stories lacking some reference to a sport or athletic activity, according to Mark Alberstat in an unpublished study of *Sherlock Holmes, the Canon and Sports*. Most dramatically there is racing in "Silver Blaze," a sport of which Doyle confessed that he knew little (an ignorance confirmed by the story's many solecisms). "I never could look upon flat-racing as a true sport," he wrote in *Memories and Adventures*. "Sport is what a man does, not what a horse does."

He is equally critical of hunting ("I cannot persuade myself that we are justified in taking life as a pleasure"), and there is little of hunting in the Canon. Fishing does figure here and there, to the point that Donald G. Jewell was able to find material for a monograph about it: *A Trout in the Milk: A Monograph on Fish and Fishing in the Time of Sherlock Holmes* (1991), and Doyle did occasionally indulge in that form of killing. He also voyaged to the Arctic on a whaling ship in his youth.

The greatest sport, in his estimation, was boxing, which had been reorganized by the introduction of the Marquess of Queensberry rules (1867) and the foundation of the Amateur Boxing Association (1884). With these innovations boxing became less deadly than it had been, not only because of a spirit of fair play but because padded gloves were now required. Doyle boxed himself (as a "fair average amateur," he wrote) and loved to watch boxing; in 1909 an American promoter invited him to referee a heavyweight championship bout between Jack Johnson and James J. Jeffries, but he had to decline. (Johnson knocked out Jeffries in fifteen rounds July 4, 1910.) Doyle wrote about boxing in his novel *Rodney Stone*, set in the bare-knuckle days of the late eighteenth century, and in the novelette *The Croxley Master*, with a contemporary setting (the Queensberry Rules are mentioned). There is also a play, "The House of Temperley," performed in 1910 but never fully published; it is vaguely based on *Rodney Stone*. Boxing plays no large role in the Sherlockian Canon, but Holmes is described by Watson as an "expert" boxer, and on a few occasions he has to apply his pugilistic skill in situations much removed from sport.

Among Doyle's many other sporting interests was rifle-shooting. The Conan Doyle Cup is an event held annually as part of the National Rifle Association's meeting; a friend of Doyle's donated the prize in 1906. He was also associated with skiing:

> I can claim to have been the first to introduce skis into the Grisons division of Switzerland, or at least to demonstrate their practical utility as a means of getting across in winter from one valley to another. It was in 1894 that I read Nansen's account of his crossing of Greenland, and thus became interested in the subject of ski-ing. It chanced that I was compelled to spend that winter in the Davos valley, and I spoke about the matter to Tobias Branger, a sporting tradesman in the village, who in turn interested his father. We sent for skis from Norway, and for some weeks afforded innocent amusement to a large number of people who watched our awkward movements and complex tumbles.

That experience may have prepared him for the hilarity with which the folk of Brattleboro, Vermont, received him and Rudyard Kipling when they tried golfing near Kipling's home there in November 1894. The two of them took eighty-four strokes over nine holes, and Doyle recorded later that he had never become much of a golfer.

THE PURSUIT OF JUSTICE. Biographers have been fond of describing Doyle's intervention in two prominent criminal cases, those against George Edalji and Oscar Slater. But a remarkable book by Peter Costello, *The Real World of Sherlock Holmes* (1991), second edition titled *Conan Doyle, Detective* (2006), reports dozens of crimes in which Doyle took an interest, and sometimes an active role. Costello manages to include the affair of Jack the Ripper in this category, on the strength of an investigation carried out in 1905 — seventeen years after the murders took place — by the Crimes Club, a private group of connoisseurs of which Doyle was a member. Beyond doubt, Doyle was interested in crime, and occasionally intervened casually in a case, as in an 1896 letter to *The Times*:

> Apart from the evidence of medical experts, it is inconceivable that any woman in her position in her sane senses would steal duplicates and triplicates — four toast-racks, if I remember right. Small articles of silver, with the hotel mark upon them, so that they could neither be sold nor used, were among the objects which she had packed away in her trunk. It can surely not be denied that there is at least a doubt as to her moral responsibility.

As Doyle became famous for creating a detective, he was in demand for such opinions; Costello discusses the Frank Westwood murder in Toronto in 1894, noting that Doyle gave it passing attention because he was badgered into doing so by reporters while he was visiting Toronto that year.

Although he deprecated his own detective skills, he could demonstrate vigorous common sense in attacking the salient points of a problem. More important, he was tireless, and applied his energy fearlessly to what he thought was right. In the Edalji and Slater cases, he was the chief advocate of men wrongly accused, and in each case he managed to earn something like justice for them after long periods of effort.

- George Edalji was a young solicitor in Birmingham who had served part of a seven-year prison sentence after being convicted in a series of knife attacks on farm animals near his home village of Great Wyrley, Staffordshire, in 1903. He maintained his innocence, and Doyle realized as soon as he met Edalji that the young man, being nearly blind, could not have committed the outrages under cover of rural darkness. Doyle easily uncovered an ugly tale of anonymous letters and decades-long harassment: Edalji's father, the vicar of the little community, was a Parsee, so that race prejudice lay at the root of the affair. After investigating, he wrote a pair of articles which appeared in *The Daily Telegraph* January 11 and 12, 1907 (and in *The New York Times* February 2 and 3); they were quickly republished in pamphlet form as *The Story of Mr. George Edalji.* He reported that the police and Home Office had been unsympathetic to requests that the case be reopened, and declared that he was now taking it to "a tribunal that never errs," namely public opinion. Immense excitement and controversy followed, and a government investigation led to a pardon for Edalji in May 1907. But Doyle was not satisfied — the real mutilator, and author of the nasty letters, remained to be found. Later that year he submitted a detailed accusation of the man he believed guilty; it was never acted upon.

There has been a revival of interest in the Edalji case in recent years, largely because the story, including Doyle's involvement, provided the theme for Julian Barnes's novel *Arthur & George*, which was shortlisted for the 2005 Man Booker Prize for Fiction. The case is analyzed at great length in *Conan Doyle and the Parson's Son* (2006) by Gordon Weaver and, along with the Slater case, provides the material for *The True Crime Files of Sir Arthur Conan Doyle* (2001) by Stephen Hines.

- Oscar Slater had served more than three years of a life sentence for murder when his case came to Doyle's attention in 1912. The victim was Marion Gilchrist, an elderly woman in Glasgow, who was beaten to death in her flat December 21, 1908; a diamond brooch was apparently stolen, but other valuable jewellery left behind. Slater, a shady gem dealer, was arrested in New York. The case against him was built on a diamond brooch he had pawned in Glasgow (which was eventually proven not to have been the missing item), on identifications by unreliable witnesses, and on his general shady reputation as a crook and pimp (as well as on his German-Jewish origins). After the conviction there was an outcry, leading to the publication of a book by William Roughead, *The Trial of Oscar Slater.* Doyle's interest was attracted, and he contributed a pamphlet, *The Case of Oscar Slater* (1912). Two years later new information surfaced, with a hint that Marion Gilchrist's downstairs neighbour had suppressed the identity of a man who had been seen in the hallway just after the murder. Doyle and others pressed for official action, but nothing was done. As late as 1927 the case was still open; in that year Doyle wrote a preface for a new book, *The Truth about Oscar Slater,* by William Park, and had it published by the Psychic Press, which he was managing. At last, in the fall of 1927, Slater was released from prison, and a pardon and compensation followed. No one else was ever convicted, although researchers have blamed Francis Charteris, a relative of the victim.

MILITARY AFFAIRS. Doyle never held a commission in the armed forces. During World War I he did insist on enlisting as a private in the Volunteer Battalion of the Royal Sussex Regiment, which drilled near his home at Crowborough, but otherwise his longstanding interest in military matters found expression through unofficial channels.

Most of his experience of warfare came in South Africa, during the curious conflict known to history as the Boer War, 1899–1902. The black population of what is now South Africa was almost incidental to this war, fought between British troops and the British settlers of the Cape Colony and Natal on the one hand, the Dutch ("Boer," i.e. farmer) settlers of the Transvaal and the Orange Free State on the other. The most dramatic events of that war included the siege of Mafeking, which led to wild excitement in the streets of London on "Mafeking Night," May 17, 1900, when the news came that British troops had reached the city, and a similar siege at Ladysmith. Its less savoury contributions to civilization included the first modern concentration camps, into which British troops under Lord Kitchener (Horatio Baron Kitchener) herded some of their Boer prisoners.

Doyle saw the war as a noble enterprise and was determined to serve in it somehow, but the army would not accept him, and he volunteered instead to serve as a doctor with a private field hospital. The war had been going badly for Britain, and Doyle was interested in studying the military situation and writing about the war, as well as rendering medical help. He sailed for South Africa on the day of the relief of Ladysmith (February 28, 1900), and spent five months in hard work at the temporary hospital in Bloemfontein, chiefly battling enteric fever (typhoid) rather than battle wounds. It was a filthy, hellish experience. But he found time to observe the strategy of the war as well, and when he returned to England got them into print as *The Great Boer War* (first published in October 1900, with many subsequent editions). His suggestions were shocking, as John Dickson Carr observes in *The Life of Sir Arthur Conan Doyle*:

> First, the artillery. British guns must be concealed, as the Boers' were....
>
> Second, the cavalry. The cavalry must cease to be armed with swords or lances, which belonged only in a museum. What good were swords or lances against Mauser rifles sighted up to two thousand yards? Equip your cavalry with rifles.
>
> (Here the military experts and the old gentlemen in clubs really did have an apoplectic fit.)

> Third and most important, the infantry. They must learn to
> dig trenches.... Teach your infantry to shoot; and for the love
> of heaven give them some ammunition with which to practise.

And in letters to the newspapers, Doyle called for army reform: "roughly halving their numbers, doubling their pay, and keeping them entirely for the foreign service of the Empire." Home defence would be the duty of a home guard, "civilian riflemen."

Once the war had ended, stories of the concentration camps and other alleged British atrocities swept Europe. In response, Doyle wrote a pamphlet, *The War in South Africa — Its Cause and Conduct*, which had a huge sale in England and was distributed across Europe in many translations. This propaganda service earned him a knighthood (on the day of Edward VII's coronation, August 9, 1902), making him *Sir* Arthur, although it is possible that the publication of *The Hound of the Baskervilles* eleven weeks after that of *The War*, reviving Sherlock Holmes, helped to gain him that honour.

For the rest of his life he broke into print at intervals on military subjects — suggesting in 1906 that motor-car owners sign up to transport riflemen to where they were needed in case of invasion, arguing in 1910 for the use of bicyclists in warfare, suggesting in 1913 and many times thereafter that a tunnel under the English Channel would protect Britain against blockade in time of war. The short story "Danger!", published in July 1914, warned of the dangers of submarines if a tunnel were not put in place, and many of its predictions came true during World War I. Once the war began (on August 3, 1914), Doyle followed it keenly and wrote constantly about it, suggesting the use of inflatable lifebelts on transport ships, calling for energetic recruitment, urging the use of body-armour, and discussing air raids and ways of keeping soldiers from frequenting prostitutes.

The war, fought by Britain and France (joined in 1917 by the United States) against Germany and its eastern European allies, including Turkey, lasted four years and changed Britain's history, killing a generation of young men and destroying its class system. Most of the warfare, which killed an estimated 10 million soldiers, took place in trenches in Belgium and northern France, where shooting continued across a sea of mud and barbed wire. But it touched everyone at home. The sound of the big guns could sometimes be heard at Doyle's home on the south coast of England. Malcolm Leckie, brother of Lady Doyle, was an army doctor, killed at Mons in August 1914. Kingsley, Doyle's oldest son, was in the Royal Army Medical Corps as well; Innes, Doyle's beloved younger brother, was a lieutenant-colonel at the battlefront, then a colonel, by war's end a brigadier-general. At home, Doyle's daughter Mary did volunteer work, and he and Lady Doyle entertained Canadian troops when they had leave from their nearby camps.

Letters from the front came not only from relatives but from the generals directing the mostly ineffective British fighting. The government sent him on a tour of the battlefields in the spring of 1916, just before the terrible battle of the Somme; on his return he wrote reports in the *Daily Chronicle* that were collected as the little book *A Visit to Three Fronts*. There had been other war writing as well, and that fall appeared the first volume of *The British Campaign in France and Flanders*, which would run to six volumes, the last appearing in January 1920. *The British Campaign* is immensely detailed about tactics ("Meanwhile the enemy had made a spirited attempt to push through between the Seventh Corps and the Fifth"). The author gives credit in it to the "innumerable correspondents" who provided information for him and in some cases made suggestions about what he had drafted. The work was published in chapters in the *Strand Magazine* before appearing in book form: "I was really the only public source of supply of accurate and detailed information," Doyle said later about this project. But his work lacks historical perspective on the war, having been written while the fighting was continuing, and often omits information which later historians, drawing on official secrets, were able to use.

PUBLIC AFFAIRS. Although he twice ran for Parliament, Doyle was not generally active in party politics, except apparently during his early years in Portsmouth, when he helped to organize a local association for Liberal-Unionists — a political group favouring most of the platform of the then ruling Liberal Party, but opposing the Liberal policy of "Home Rule" for Ireland. In later years, save for those two unsuccessful appearances on the ballot, his involvement in public affairs was through pamphleteering and the newspapers, where his courteous letters were frequently to be seen.

Aside from crime and, in his later years, spiritualism, the domestic issue that occupied him the most was reform of the laws governing divorce. By 1904, when he published "The Abbey Grange," the problem of intolerable but indissoluble marriages was clearly on his mind, probably in part because of his personal position, married to the invalid Louise while in love with Jean Leckie. In 1906 the Divorce Law Reform Union was formed; Doyle served as its president. His pamphlet *Divorce Law Reform* was published by the Union in 1909, and many letters and articles followed, as he argued that England should not "lag behind every other Protestant country in the world, and even behind Scotland, so that unions which are obviously disgusting and degrading are maintained." In Doyle's lifetime the only ground for divorce was adultery, and only a man could claim that as the sole ground; a woman had to claim something like physical abuse as well. Further, the expense of a divorce was estimated at about £700, a sum very few could find.

The atrocities practised in the Congo region in the first decade of the twentieth century enraged Doyle perhaps more than any other injustice to which he turned his attention. A huge region of central Africa, nominally independent as the Congo Free State, was in effect the private property of Leopold II, King of the Belgians, who with his associates exploited it for the rubber trade, with slavery and dreadful cruelties. A Congo Reform Association was founded in Britain in 1904, and Doyle became involved in 1909. Within weeks he had *The Crime of the Congo* in print, exposing the atrocities; a frontispiece showed photographs of nine Congolese whose hands had been cut off as part of the campaign of terror that had been going on for years. Later that year Doyle was lecturing on the subject, and as late as 1912 he was still writing to the newspapers about it. Much of the information about the Congo came from Roger Casement, the British consul in the area. A few years later, at the beginning of World War I, Doyle found himself defending Casement in vain after the young adventurer, having tried to make terms with Germany on behalf of his native Ireland, was charged with treason. Casement, who may have been mentally ill and was certainly indiscreet in what he put in writing about his homosexual affairs, was hanged.

Doyle was keenly interested in Irish affairs. Proposals for "Home Rule" in Ireland were the central issue of British politics for much of his lifetime; he had been opposed to the idea, but by 1911 was grudgingly in favour. "There is no possible reason," he wrote in one letter, "why a man should not be a loyal Irishman and a loyal Imperialist also." He stressed his own "Irish extraction" in arguing the close ties between Ireland and the rest of the Empire. When Home Rule was finally granted, after World War I, Doyle opposed division between Ulster (northern Ireland) and the southern three-quarters of the country; he did not live to see the south become fully independent in 1937.

The word *Imperialist,* which Doyle used to describe his own position, meant not loyalty to England but loyalty to a worldwide empire, which had already come to embrace a more or less independent Canada and South Africa as well as the motherland and her colonies. Australia had followed in 1901, and Ireland could become an adult member of that family, he suggested in the later years of his life. His dreams were still larger; he sympathized with, though he did not actively campaign for, the movement towards "Anglo-American Union," an eventual alliance between the British Empire and the United States. He put that idea in the mouth of Sherlock Holmes in "The Noble Bachelor" (1892), he spoke feelingly on the subject during and after his American tour of 1894, and less idealistically he speculates in *Our American Adventure* (1923) about a world in which the American Revolution had not taken place:

> Then, as the most populous must always govern in any democratic system, America would quite naturally and peacefully have become the centre and chief guide to all the scattered English-speaking nations, with the four home countries as part of the huge, world-wide confederation which might have stopped all war and ushered in the millennium.

SPIRITUALIST INTERESTS

Enthusiasts and even biographers have been a little embarrassed by the last dozen years of Doyle's life, which he devoted to preaching the doctrine of spiritualism. How, they have asked, can the rational doctor, the practical man of public affairs, and the creator of the purely intellectual Sherlock Holmes have let himself fall into a belief in communication with the dead, and make a laughing-stock of himself on four continents as he argued that fraudulent "mediums" were channels for communicating a vital divine message to humanity? The usual explanation is that he was somehow unhinged by the terrible experiences of World War I, in which family members and friends died so senselessly. The carnage of the war did predispose England to look for some new religious comfort and explanation, and may have directed Doyle's attention more closely to spiritualism, but in fact he was interested in the subject long before the deaths of his brother, son, and brothers-in-law during and shortly after the war.

Doyle's life-long interest in psychic matters, as they were often called, is helpfully traced in *Conan Doyle and the Spirits* (1989) by Kelvin I. Jones. He begins with a discussion of the Roman Catholicism in which Doyle was raised as a child. The young Jesuit-educated doctor rejected that church, and all organized Christianity, but clearly never lost his interest in God, in the meaning of life, and in supernatural phenomena. Many of his early short stories (Jones instances "Lot No. 249") deal with the occult, often edging into the horrible. As early as the fall of 1893, he joined the Society for Psychical

Research, a body which existed to investigate unexplained phenomena ranging from "automatic writing" to the manifestation of spirits at seances. Some members of the SPR (founded 1882) were convinced spiritualists; others were rationalists, interested rather in finding a scientific explanation for hypnotism, clairvoyance, and the like. The times were good for a rich variety of philosophies and practices that in a later generation would come to be loosely grouped as "the new age movement."

Spiritualism itself is frequently dated from March 31, 1848, when remarkable events took place in Hydesville, New York, a village in the so-called "burnt-over district" from which a series of religious revivals and creations, including the birth of Mormonism, had sprung through the early nineteenth century. On that day Kate Fox, an adolescent girl in Hydesville, established apparent contact with some entity that lived in her house. Through "rappings" the being identified itself as the spirit of a murdered man, who soon also communicated with Kate's older sister, Margaret. Interest in such communication spread; by the fall of 1849 there were enough people in touch with other spirits that a mass meeting was held in nearby Rochester. In 1852 a Mrs. Hayden brought the rapidly growing movement to England, and a British National Association of Spiritualists was organized in 1873. Among its members from an early date was Major-General Alfred W. Drayson, an astronomer and author as well as military officer, who had retired to Southsea and was a major influence on Doyle through the Portsmouth Literary and Scientific Society in the 1880s. After Doyle moved to London he continued his interest in spiritualism, and continued to write fiction that reflected a preoccupation with the occult, although its echoes in the Sherlockian Canon are very limited. *The Hound of the Baskervilles*, seeming to promise the supernatural, proves to involve fakery instead, and "The Sussex Vampire" is almost mocking in its attitude to "ghosts."

The theory of spiritualism took time to develop. A milestone was the 1903 publication of *Human Personality and Its Survival of Bodily Death*, by Frederick Myers, one of the founders of the SPR. This volume greatly influenced Doyle, who continued to read up on psychic subjects, and to act occasionally as a member of SPR investigative teams looking at mediums or visiting allegedly haunted houses. The range of phenomena being observed by spiritualists — or, as they put it, the range of messages being delivered to the living by spirits — now extended far beyond rapping noises. Mediums (unusually sensitive people who were able, sometimes in trances, to get in touch with spirits) often spoke with the voices of spirits, moved objects about the room without touching them, materialized unexpected items or "apports" such as foreign

127

coins, and secreted "ectoplasm," a spirit substance that could form itself into the faces or bodies of spirit figures. Communication from the world of spirits might also come through writing, dictated to the hand of a medium, or photography, with faces that had been invisible to the human eye appearing when a picture was developed on film.

Doyle came to believe in the authenticity of these messages: not all of them, for he accepted that there were charlatans, particularly among mediums who were paid for their services, but enough of them to provide the basis for religious conviction. He made his conversion to spiritualism public November 4, 1916, in a letter to the journal *Light*, and in 1918 he amplified his beliefs in *The New Revelation*, a little book in which he not only declared his acceptance of spiritualist communication but set out a description of the new life in which the spirits of the dead find themselves:

> The reports from the other world are all agreed as to the pleasant conditions of life in the beyond.... Life is full of interest and of occupation.... People live in communities, as one would expect if like attracts like, and the male spirit still finds his true mate though there is no sexuality in the grosser sense.... We catch dim glimpses of endless circles below descending into gloom and endless circles above, ascending into glory, all improving, all purposeful, all intensely alive.

Certainly, he said, there was no hell, and this was a conception of heaven much modified from the traditional picture.

The New Revelation was followed in 1919 by *The Vital Message*, with new arguments and detailed replies to critics. Both books made a number of references to the recent war, which "brought earnestness into all our souls" and prepared the world for direct contact with the spirit messengers. In these two early books Doyle made it clear that he saw no necessary conflict between spiritualism and Christianity, although the new revelation would compel many changes in the system taught by the traditional churches. The "great Christ spirit," he wrote, clearly guides and directs the spirit world. "It is only the occultist who can possibly understand the Scriptures as being a real exact record of events," and he explained Jesus as a moral teacher and a powerful psychic medium — "a supreme character in the world's history who obviously stands nearer to the Highest than any other." But for organized Christianity he had chiefly contempt.

Is it not time, then, for the religious bodies to discourage their own bigots and sectarians, and to seriously consider, if only for self-preservation, how they can get into line once more with that general level of human thought which is now so far in front of them?... They must gather fresh strength by drawing in all the new truth and all the new power which are afforded by this new wave of inspiration which has been sent into the world by God.

For the rest of his life Doyle would continue to write about his new beliefs, in countless letters, articles, and pamphlets, and in several books, including *The Case for Spirit Photography* (1922) and *The Edge of the Unknown* (1930). The unusual book *Pheneas Speaks* (1927) was a report of the messages Doyle and his family received from their designated spirit guide over a period of several years. Doyle's largest book on the subject is the two-volume *History of Spiritualism* (1926), written with the assistance of Leslie Curnow, a researcher and expert. As well as history, it describes spiritualist thought and practice, and includes a strong chapter on the compatibility of spiritualism and Christianity, especially in the belief in life after death that the two systems share. *The History of Spiritualism* was dedicated to Sir Oliver Lodge (1851–1940), a friend and prominent physicist who was keenly interested in psychic research.

Doyle travelled extensively in England and repeatedly in Europe, addressing crowds about spiritualism whenever he could find an audience. He also made trips to Australia (1920–21), America (1922 and again 1923), and South Africa (1928–29) to spread his message, and wrote four books that discussed both his travels and his spiritualist insights: *The Wanderings of a Spiritualist* (1921), *Our American Adventure* (1923), *Our Second American Adventure* (1924), *Our African Winter* (1929). In 1925 he opened a Psychic Bookshop, Library and Museum in Victoria Street, London (cables: *Ectoplasm*). He devoted much of his energy and fortune in the last five years of his life to subsidizing its work. Doyle became the world's best-known spiritualist, and was honoured in the movement with such titles as Honorary President of the International Spiritualist Congress. A sour note came in March 1930 when he resigned from his life-long membership in the Society for Psychical Research, crying that it had become closed-minded and hostile to genuine psychic phenomena.

In the course of his spiritualist work Doyle came to know Harry Houdini, the noted American conjurer and escape artist (real name Erich Weiss, 1873–1926). Conjurers were often called in to help psychic investigators detect trickery in the work of suspect mediums, and Houdini prided himself on being able to detect such fraud. He observed some mediums during a tour of England in 1920, and formed a friendship with Doyle despite their diametrically opposed views of spiritualism. When Doyle went to America in 1922 they met for a seance in Atlantic City. Doyle believed that they had been visited by the spirit of Houdini's dead mother; Houdini thought, and wrote, that the phenomena he had seen through the mediumship of Lady Doyle were spurious. The friendship did not survive the resulting recriminations, although Doyle spoke not unkindly of Houdini in *The Edge of the Unknown*. First-hand material about the relationship appeared in *Houdini and Conan Doyle: The Story of a Strange Friendship* (1932), by Bernard Ernst and Hereward Carrington. More recently there has been *The Final Séance: The Strange Friendship Between Houdini and Conan Doyle* (2001) by Massimo Polidoro.

The oddest aspect of Doyle's psychic work is certainly the episode of the Cottingley fairies. Two girls — Elsie Wright, age fifteen, and Frances Griffiths, age ten — reported in 1917 that they had seen fairies in their garden and been able to take photographs of them. The pictures came to Doyle's attention three years later; he accepted them as genuine, and made the news public in the December 1920 issue of the *Strand Magazine*, and more fully in a brief book, *The Coming of the Fairies* (1922). As early as 1921 there were plausible claims that the photographs had been faked, but a confession from the perpetrators came only in 1983. In old age they said they had always felt somewhat guilty for fooling Doyle and holding him up to the ridicule he suffered. The quality of the deceptive photographs (which were reproduced in Doyle's book, and frequently since) must have been very high to fool a man who was a keen amateur photographer and had written a series of essays for the *British Journal of Photography* in the 1880s (collected as *Essays on Photography*, 1982). The whole affair, including Doyle's role, is discussed in *The Case of the Cottingley Fairies* (1990) by Joe Cooper. It formed the background for the novel *Photographing Fairies* (1992) by Steve Szilyagi, which was made into a feature film (1997) with Edward Hardwicke as Doyle. The same year saw a second film on the topic, the improbably named "Fairy Tale: A True Story," with Peter O'Toole as an improbable Doyle.

POSTERITY

Lady Doyle (née Jean Leckie) continued some of Doyle's spiritualist work after his death; she herself died June 27, 1940, still a believer, and was buried beside

Sir Arthur in the grounds at Windlesham. (When the property was sold in 1955, the bodies were reburied in the churchyard at Minstead, Sussex, where Doyle lies under a headstone with the famous inscription "Steel True, Blade Straight.") Doyle had been heard from in a number of seances, some of his messages being published in *Thy Kingdom Come* (1933), edited by Ivan Cooke (later reissued as *The Return of Arthur Conan Doyle*). Doyle's eldest son, Kingsley, had died October 28, 1918, a victim of the 1918–19 influenza epidemic. His daughter by his first marriage, Mary, long survived him, dying June 12, 1976.

Doyle was also survived by all three children of his second marriage: Denis, Adrian (known in his earlier years as Malcolm), and Jean. Denis and Adrian pursued a variety of their father's interests, including spiritualism, sport, and literature. Adrian published a few books, including *Tales of Love and Hate* (1960), much in the style of his father, and was co-author with John Dickson Carr of *The Exploits of Sherlock Holmes* (1954), a collection of well-received pastiches. After Lady Doyle's death, Denis and Adrian also inherited responsibility for their father's properties, including the copyrights and papers of "the Doyle estate." Through the 1940s and 1950s, the estate was managed with vigour, if eccentricity; it licensed the use of Sherlock Holmes in the Basil Rathbone films of the 1940s and the Ronald Howard television series of the early 1950s, for example. Denis, who headed the estate, attended at least one dinner of the Baker Street Irregulars, and spoke movingly on "My Father's Friend, Mr. Sherlock Holmes," but never truly understood the Sherlockian movement. Matters worsened after Denis's death on March 9, 1955, when control of the estate passed to the temperamental Adrian (dubbed "the man with the twisted lip" by Edgar W. Smith of the BSI), and Sherlockian activities were carried on for a spell entirely without reference to the Doyle family or, for the most part, to the memory of Doyle himself.

Adrian had already made himself conspicuous by an unpleasant reaction to Hesketh Pearson's biography of his father, *Conan Doyle, His Life and Art* (1943), and wrote a tract to contradict it, *The True Conan Doyle* (1945). Fourteen years later, he had the opportunity to edit a sort of scrapbook about his father: *Sir Arthur Conan Doyle Centenary, 1859–1959*. In 1965 Adrian, who was living in Switzerland for tax reasons, opened an Arthur Conan Doyle Museum, housing many of his father's papers, curios, and works of art, in a twelfth-century castle, the Château de Lucens. Within a few years, however, he began steps to sell many of the papers and manuscripts, through the New York rare-book dealer Lew David Feldman (the House of El Dieff). In the early stages of legal proceedings involving Adrian, the Swiss government, the

University of Texas (which had hoped to buy the Château with its contents), and other parties, Adrian died, on June 3, 1970.

Two of the remaining heirs were Adrian's widow, Anna (married 1938) and Denis's widow, Nina Mdivani (married 1936), eldest daughter of an allegedly royal family from Asian Georgia, who was now remarried and surnamed Harwood. The third was Doyle's daughter Jean, who meanwhile had pursued the military career her father had always half-envied, reaching the rank of Director of the Women's Royal Air Force, with the rank of Air Commandant; she was given the title Dame, equivalent to a knighthood, for her work. In 1965 she married Air Vice-Marshal Sir Geoffrey Bromet, thus acquiring the alternative title of Lady Bromet. He died in 1983. After Adrian's death, Nina and her husband bought the copyrights in Doyle's published works and went into business as Baskervilles Investments Ltd. That corporation was subsequently taken over by the Royal Bank of Scotland when it ran into financial difficulties, and the rights were sold to Swiss financier Andre Milos. In the late 1970s they were managed by Sheldon Reynolds of New York, who had produced the Ronald Howard television series twenty-five years earlier.

When British and worldwide copyrights on Doyle's work expired in 1980, the position also changed in the United States; remaining copyrights there (those on stories that have been published for less than seventy-five years) passed into the control of Dame Jean, rather than of the "Estate," and in old age she took an active interest in seeing that Sherlock Holmes was presented with restraint and dignity. Meanwhile, both the management of the Doyle Estate and the extent of its remaining assets were less than clear. Its properties included both the copyrights in unpublished writings by Doyle, and the physical manuscripts that were owned by Doyle at his death, ranging from originals of the Sherlock Holmes stories to hundreds of letters to his mother. These materials continue to be sequestered while litigation involving the three heirs ground on, but with the deaths of Nina in 1987 and Anna in 1990 a settlement seemed closer. Meanwhile, some previously unknown Doyle material, including his diaries from his early years of authorship, was gradually being cited by researchers as they became available from unexplained sources.

Dame Jean Conan Doyle died November 18, 1997, leaving the American copyrights to the Royal National Institute for the Blind; a settlement was reached that returned them to the ownership of her estate. The many manuscripts and documents that she had owned, in her own right or as survivor of the three last heirs to her father's estate, were left to benefit various institutions. Some controversy resulted when it became known that the papers were not, as many had hoped, necessarily going to find a resting-place in a major library where they would be available to the public. The apparent suicide of prominent scholar Richard Lancelyn Green came a few weeks before a historic sale at Christie's auction rooms in London May 19, 2004, in which some 3,000 items that had once been Doyle's, including the notebook in which he first sketched out his idea for Sherlock Holmes, raised a total of £948,000 for Dame Jean's estate. Hundreds of items were bought by the British Library, some by other institutions, and some by private collectors. A handsome catalogue of the sale was produced, with many items reproduced in colour.

What remains of Doyle's own estate is controlled by Charles Foley, an entrepreneur who resides in Hove, Sussex, and is a great-nephew of the author by descent from his sister Jane. With two American scholars, Jon Lellenberg and Daniel Stashower, he edited *Arthur Conan Doyle: A Life in Letters* (2007), revealing more than six hundred pages of text selected from Doyle's letters to (primarily) his mother, documents that scholars had longed to see for decades. The remaining assets of both father's and daughter's estates are being finally wrapped into a new entity, the Conan Doyle Estate Ltd., being organized in 2009.

A rival point of view on many issues, however, comes from Georgina Doyle, widow of the author's nephew John (son of Innes Hay Doyle). She resides in a village in Hampshire's New Forest, owns many documents and souvenirs of Doyle and the family, and has contributed to the reassessment of his reputation with a long book published in 2004: *Out of the Shadows: The Untold Story of Arthur Conan Doyle's First Family*. It seeks to redress most biographers' emphasis on the period in which he was married to Jean Leckie, by looking closely at his life with his earlier wife, Louise Hawkins, and the lives of their children: Kingsley, who died young, and Mary, who was never fully successful in life and who through quirks in her father's will was financially much less secure than her half-siblings from the "second family." The book implies a less benign influence exerted by the second Lady Doyle than has previously been generally assumed.

BIOGRAPHICAL WRITINGS

Fifteen years ago it could be said that there was not only no definitive biography of Arthur Conan Doyle, but no really satisfactory one. That is no longer the case, with the recent publication of several sophisticated full-length studies. However, the best known biography, and the one most likely to be found on library shelves, is a much earlier and less authoritative one: *The Life of Sir Arthur Conan Doyle* (1949) by mystery writer John Dickson Carr (1905–77). Carr, unlike most subsequent scholars, had access to Doyle's papers (then under the control of Adrian, with whom he would later collaborate on *The Exploits*). His *Life of Doyle* is excitingly written, with long passages of conversation, including many encounters that can have had no witnesses, and the colourful language of a novel. Carr's Doyle is a chivalric hero much like Sir Nigel, and just a little like Sherlock Holmes, from a childhood under the nobility-minded tutelage of the Ma'am (a title Carr seems to have invented) to his defences of George Edalji and Oscar Slater. Here is Carr describing Doyle's spiritualist campaigns:

> For eleven years his sword did not sleep. For eleven years, through a changed post-war world, all that incredible energy poured into going anywhere, speaking anywhere, challenging any opponent, working with scarcely any rest, seeming charged with an inexhaustible force and light.
>
> "This can't go on forever," his medical advisers told him again and again. "A man at your age —"
>
> At his age? To him, who somehow combined the mellowness and kindliness of a sixth decade with the driving-power of his thirties, it was not a question of his age. It was a question of what had to be done.

Carr presents a Doyle that his children could be proud to acknowledge, and a Doyle whom sixty years of readers have been happy to admire. He omits the dark side of his subject: his sexual tensions, the life-long effect of watching his father's descent into alcoholism, the touchiness that led to his quarrel with Houdini. He also frequently omits dates and details, adding to his book's effectiveness as entertainment but devaluing it as a basis for further research.

A thought-provoking overview of Doyle's life and work can be found in *The Quest for Sir Arthur Conan Doyle: Thirteen Biographers in Search of a Life*, edited by Jon Lellenberg, which is a collection of essays about the many biographical works that had appeared by the time of its publication (1987). It begins with consideration of Doyle's own autobiographical *Memories and Adventures* (1924, second edition 1930). This valuable basic work for an understanding of Doyle provides classic anecdotes and the author's own summary of the public side of his life, though it glosses over controversial topics, ignores most parts of his private life, and omits much that scholars have wished to know about the development of his religious thought. *The Quest* then continues with an overview of his minor works about his travels, and his several quasi-biographical novels, before turning to the biographies that have appeared from other hands. In the course of the reports and analysis, which discuss each book in turn, most of the available interpretations of Doyle's life are considered, and the story is told in greater — more balanced — detail than any single biography had at that time managed to do.

After Doyle's death the first work about him to appear was *Arthur Conan Doyle: A Memoir* (1931) by John Lamond, a clergyman and spiritualist colleague, who wrote an appreciation rather than a scholarly biography. Even more extreme in its hagiography is Adrian Conan Doyle's *The True Conan Doyle*, written in response to Hesketh Pearson's *Conan Doyle* (1943), which treated Doyle without the habitual respect, in particular labelling him (with no great justification) "the man in the street." Next in the series of books about Doyle came *Sir Arthur Conan Doyle, l'homme et l'oeuvre*, by Pierre Nordon (1964), with an English translation (*Conan Doyle*, 1966) in which long passages of the French original were omitted. Nordon was a Sorbonne scholar whose work betrays his approach through literary criticism rather than history. Devoted to detail, he drew extensively from the Doyle papers (and was the last researcher for several decades to have access to them). Unlike the majority of other biographers, he gives ample attention to Doyle's non-Sherlockian writings, and he makes a serious attempt to investigate and describe Doyle's personality, something much more complex than Pearson or Carr had acknowledged.

Other biographies followed: *The Man Who Was Sherlock Holmes* (1964), by Michael and Mollie Hardwick, is a brief narrative emphasizing the ways in which Holmes resembles his creator. *The Real Sherlock Holmes* (1965), by Mary Hoehling, is a brief biography for young people. *The Man Who Hated Sherlock Holmes* (1965), by James Playsted Wood, is also for young people, but with greater attention to Doyle's fiction than to his life in general. *Conan Doyle* (1972), by Ivor Brown, is a general book that breaks little new ground. Then came the highly successful *The Adventures of Conan Doyle* (1976), by Charles Higham, a lively book emphasizing the excitement of Doyle's life, with enthusiastic, if not always convincing, attention to psychological and sexual matters. The book contains vast numbers of factual errors that lead the wise reader to treat its every statement with the greatest suspicion.

The succession of biographies continued. *Conan Doyle: A Biographical Solution* (1977), by Ronald Pearsall, is a readable book with few new insights, but with some attempt to put Doyle into his historical and cultural context.

Conan Doyle: Portrait of an Artist (1979), by Julian Symons, himself a mystery author, is a brief and derivative book that provides a good general picture of Doyle. Its most useful feature is a chronological appendix, convenient for quick reference. *Arthur Conan Doyle* (1985), by Don Richard Cox, is chiefly a report of Doyle's fiction, set briefly into biographical context.

Biographical study of Doyle was changed dramatically by the last work to appear in time for consideration in the Lellenberg anthology. *The Quest for Sherlock Holmes* (1983) applies a historical rather than literary lens, as Owen Dudley Edwards, a historian at the University of Edinburgh, used his professional expertise and his access to Edinburgh sources to explore Doyle's early years in detail. Despite many references to the works of his later life, Doyle reaches only his early twenties in this volume. But Edwards delves deep, discussing the influences of Mary Foley Doyle, Charles Doyle, Bryan Charles Waller, and other important figures on Doyle's formative period. The writing is dense and the speculation sometimes seems daring to the non-academic reader, but the amount of information unearthed by Edwards is overwhelming. For the first time a reader can be reasonably confident that at least one period of Doyle's life has been fully explored.

In the next few years came other books: *Arthur Conan Doyle* (1987), by Jacqueline A. Jaffe, concentrates on describing the fiction, and acknowledges that Carr's book has been its chief source for biographical information. *Arthur Conan Doyle* (1988) by James McCearney, a biography in French, focuses on Doyle's historical and literary context. Michael Coren's *Conan Doyle* (1995) had been awaited as the long-desired definitive biography, but proved to be considerably less, a short book without depth and without new insights. Two years later came *The Doctor, the Detective and Arthur Conan Doyle* (1997) by novelist Martin Booth, a solid narrative bolstered with some details that had not been used by earlier writers ("he was a prime activist behind the movement to ban the fashionable use of exotic birds' feathers in women's couture"). *Arthur Conan Doyle: Beyond Baker Street* (2000) by Janet B. Pascal is a slim volume evidently aimed at a younger audience. *Arthur Conan Doyle: Beyond Sherlock Holmes* (2007) by Andrew Norman puts its emphasis on medical matters and on how Doyle must have been affected by his father's illnesses and breakdown.

Recent years have brought three more full-length biographies:

- *Teller of Tales: The Life of Arthur Conan Doyle* (1999) by Daniel Stashower, mystery novelist and popular historian.

- *Conan Doyle: The Man Who Created Sherlock Holmes* (2007) by Andrew Lycett, biographer of Rudyard Kipling and Dylan Thomas.
- *The Adventures of Arthur Conan Doyle* (2008) by journalist and war historian Russell Miller.

All three are substantial brick-like tomes with glossy illustrations, indexes, and bibliographies; Miller has some source notes and Lycett has more than thirty pages of them. All take seriously the many different phases of Doyle's life, not just his creation of Sherlock Holmes but his childhood and education, his two marriages, his diverse writings and his spiritualist crusade. All have been favourably reviewed and are reliable sources for both general and scholarly readers. Lycett and Miller were both able to draw on the Doyle letters that had been kept from the public eye for decades because of litigation among the heirs to Doyle's estate, and came into public view following the death of Dame Jean Conan Doyle in 1997. Stashower was not, though a few years later he served one of the three editors (together with Jon Lellenberg and Charles Foley) when a selection of those papers was published in 2007 as *Arthur Conan Doyle: A Life in Letters* (2007). Interpolations by the editors bring the book almost to the status of a biography in itself, but reviewers have detected few explosive revelations or important new interpretations in it.

In addition to all these general biographies, over the years several studies have appeared concentrating on limited aspects of Doyle's life. Among them are *Sherlock Slept Here* (1985), by Howard Lachtman, a quick report of Doyle's American tours of 1894, 1914, 1922, and 1923; *A Study in Southsea* (1987), by Geoffrey Stavert, in which a prominent British Sherlockian uses his easy access to local records to reveal the details of Doyle's years as a physician in Southsea; my own book *Welcome to America, Mr. Sherlock Holmes* (1987), a day-by-day study of Doyle's 1894 tour of America. *Sir Arthur Conan Doyle: Interviews and Recollections* (1991), edited by Harold Orel, is a collection of contemporary documents and reminiscences. Although not separately published, a good general biography of Doyle is the 140-page Introduction to Richard Lancelyn Green's *The Uncollected Sherlock Holmes* (1983). A valuable reference for day-to-day work is *A Chronology of the Life of Sir Arthur Conan Doyle* (2009), compiled by Brian W. Pugh of the Conan Doyle (Crowborough) Establishment.

BIBLIOGRAPHIES. *A Bibliography of A. Conan Doyle* by Richard Lancelyn Green and John Michael Gibson (1983) is definitive so far as it goes, listing first and other early editions of Doyle's books, together with a vast number of periodical articles by and about him. Extensive notes provide information which either has not been previously brought forward or has not been conveniently gathered. The book can reasonably be called indispensable for any study of Doyle. Inevitably there are errors; there are also omissions, and in particular Green and Gibson make no attempt to list modern editions.

Conan Doyle Bibliography (1977) by Gaby Goldscheider was greeted as a useful checklist before the Green and Gibson bibliography existed. There are other now superseded listings as well. Many editions both early and modern are included, though sometimes with incomplete or unhelpful information, in Ronald B. DeWaal's two large bibliographies of Sherlockiana, *The World Bibliography of Sherlock Holmes and Dr. Watson* (1974) and *The International Sherlock Holmes* (1980). Other bibliographies include Jay Finley Christ's pamphlet *The Fiction of Sir Arthur Conan Doyle* (1959) and the two editions (1973 and 1977) of *A Checklist of the Arthur Conan Doyle Collection* at the Toronto Reference Library, compiled by Donald Redmond. An unpublished Master of Arts thesis from the University of Minnesota (1968) is *Sir Arthur Conan Doyle in America* by Lawrence L. Reed; it lists "first English and subsequent American editions." *The Sign of the Four* has received special attention in *'Signs' of Our Times* by Nathan L. Bengis (1956) and *Sherlock Holmes Among the Pirates: Copyright and Conan Doyle* by Donald Redmond (1990), the latter also giving attention to *A Study in Scarlet*.

In addition to all such material, there are now a number of scholarly books about Doyle's writings, which are discussed in a later chapter.

FICTION. Possibly in reaction to everything that had been done with, and to, Sherlock Holmes in the "pastiches" of the 1970s, a number of authors in recent years have made Arthur Conan Doyle, rather than Holmes, into a character for their novels. Except perhaps for Julian Barnes's *Arthur & George*, such uses tend to be exploitive rather than literary, and Mark Frost's *The List of Seven* (1993) and *The 6 Messiahs* (1995) are distinctly creepy. More than one author has seized on Doyle's connection with Houdini; other writers have juxtaposed Doyle with Oscar Wilde, Lewis Carroll, the Piltdown affair, events on Dartmoor as *The Hound of the Baskervilles* was being written, and inevitably the Cottingley fairies. Of special interest are David Pirie's *The Patient's Eyes* (2002), *The Night Calls* (2003), and *The Dark Water* (2004). Those three books are novelizations of the BBC television series "Murder Rooms: The Dark Beginnings of Sherlock Holmes," which aired in 2000 starring Robin Laing as Doyle and Ian Richardson as his mentor Joseph Bell.

V

THE VICTORIAN BACKGROUND

THE STORIES OF SHERLOCK HOLMES were published as late as 1927, but their setting is late Victorian and early Edwardian, the years from 1881 to about 1904. It was part of Doyle's genius that he exactly reflected his period in his writings: both its general concerns, justice, and order for example, and its everyday details. Unlike many previous writers of detective fiction, he gave specific dates and referred, always plausibly, to real places and persons, from Regent Street to George Wombwell the circus proprietor. But many such allusions, and much of that atmosphere, are unfamiliar to a modern North American reader, who finds it difficult to judge whether what is strange in the world of Sherlock Holmes is so because of the century that has elapsed or because of the ocean that lies between America and Britain. Frequently the answer is that both reasons apply.

"The truth is that the Victorians had almost nothing in common with us," writes Jack Tracy in the admirable Introduction to his *Encyclopaedia Sherlockiana* (1977, already more than thirty years ago). He provides a brief essay about the dangers of misunderstanding the lost civilization of London *circa* 1895. Differences are many, from the state of technology (Victorian Britain was the great optimistic age of engineering) to the class-bound social structure. Sherlock Holmes needed precisely the environment he found, in which most men had trades, so that he could spot the weaver's tooth, the cork-cutter's hand; in which a lock could not be opened without the right key, made perhaps from an illicit wax impression; in which letters were delivered reliably enough to be, as in "The Man with the Twisted Lip," evidence.

Britain in the 1890s was still, in the satirists' phrase, Top Nation, hub of a worldwide Empire that was maintained through a vast civil service and an invincible Navy. But British domination was economic as well as political — British exports were valued at £309 million in 1891, compared to £182 million for the United States (with more than double Britain's population). Above all, however, Britons felt themselves superior in a cultural and moral sense, evident both in Holmes's amusement at his American clients and in the confidence with which British missionaries set out to civilize India and China. "Take up the White Man's burden," Kipling wrote in 1899, "Send forth the best ye breed." Britain was, and was meant to be, as Benson wrote in 1902, "mother of the free." At home, meanwhile, it was a good life for the optimistic middle classes, and a world of unsurpassed glory and delight for the rich.

So elusive is the political and social system in which Sherlock Holmes lived that it is not even easy to name his country. "England" is just one of three units that make up "Britain," the others being Scotland and Wales. In turn, Britain together with Ireland made the United Kingdom (which survives today though three-quarters of Ireland became independent in 1937). Holmes was an Englishman, though Doyle, born a Scotsman (of Irish descent), was not; both were British, but would have looked askance at being called "citizens" of anything. They were "subjects" of Her Majesty the Queen, who was not "Queen of England" but Queen of the United Kingdom of Great Britain and Ireland.

Almost all of Holmes's cases are set in England, and the majority of them in London, the capital and greatest city, although Britain in the 1890s was still largely a rural nation. The population of England and Wales in 1891 was altogether 29.0 million; a further 4.0 million people lived in Scotland and 4.7 million in Ireland. London had some 4.3 million people; Glasgow in Scotland fewer than 700,000; Liverpool and Manchester in the industrialized north each about 500,000, with nearby Birmingham a few thousand people behind.

England, Wales, Scotland, and Ireland are divided into counties, which are both geographic terms and divisions of local government. The historic counties of England are as follows, grouped unofficially by regions:

> **The home counties:** Middlesex, Surrey, Kent, and Essex, surrounding London, which itself became a county, severed from Middlesex, during Holmes's active years.
> **East and southeast:** Norfolk, Suffolk, Cambridgeshire, Sussex (where Holmes retired), Berkshire, Buckinghamshire, Oxfordshire, Doyle's beloved Hampshire, and the Isle of Wight.
> **Southwest:** Cornwall, Devon (where Dartmoor is located), Dorset, Somerset, and Wiltshire.

The Midlands: Derbyshire, Gloucestershire, Herefordshire, Leicestershire, Northamptonshire, Nottinghamshire, Rutland, Shropshire, Staffordshire, Warwickshire (includes Birmingham) and Worcestershire.

The north: Yorkshire (largest county in England by far), Lancashire (includes Manchester and Liverpool), Cheshire, Lincolnshire, Westmorland, Cumberland, Durham, and Northumbria. The notional "Hallamshire" of "The Priory School" would also be in this region.

In modern times the boundaries and names have been considerably altered, and county governments are "local authorities."

TRAVEL. It is hard to think of Holmes's England without thinking of trains. The first steam railway was built in Britain in 1825; by Holmes's time railways were the universally accepted way of travelling from one town to another (and of shipping goods, unless it was possible to send them by one of the country's many canals). Trains were frequent, fast by modern standards, and punctual most of the time. The large railway companies competed over some principal lines, with constant service between important cities, but there was less competition in the provision of periodic service to an enormous number of villages — such as Little Purlington in "The Retired Colourman." Although it was possible to make journeys in the Midlands, or along the south coast, without reference to London, much of the British network of tracks radiated from the metropolis. Each railway company had built its own station, or stations, as close to the centre of London as it could get, providing service outward in one or two directions. Stations north of the river were (and are) Cannon Street, Charing Cross, Victoria, Paddington, Euston, St. Pancras, King's Cross, and Liverpool Street; south of the river are London Bridge and Waterloo.

The Sherlockian today retracing Holmes's journeys outside London may go by rail or by car. Books discussing the location of Sherlockian sites include *Adventuring in England with Doctor Arthur Conan Doyle* (1986), by Alvin E. Rodin and Jack D. Key, and two by David L. Hammer: *The Game Is Afoot* (1983) and *For the Sake of the Game* (1986). Hammer subsequently extended his range to North America (*To Play the Game*, 1991) and Europe (*A Dangerous Game*, 1997). A landmark volume is *Holmes & Watson Country: Travels in Search of Solutions* (2008) by Bernard Davies of the Sherlock Holmes Society of London, gathering up a lifetime of scholarship about exact locations across England where Holmes's adventures might have taken place.

LONDON

Samuel Johnson in 1777 is supposed to have said that "When a man is tired of London, he is tired of life; for there is in London all that life can afford." That diversity and the city's very size make nonsense of Sherlock Holmes's assertion a century later that it was his "hobby ... to have an exact knowledge of London." It is so vast (690 square miles within the 1890s boundaries of the Metropolitan Police District) and so densely developed that one can know only selected regions of it, and even a map, or the tourist's inevitable *A to Z Atlas*, is of limited help. Certainly a Sherlockian or other scholar needs both a general map for orientation and a detailed one for close study. A reproduction of a Victorian-era street map is a virtual necessity. (Some of the small-scale Ordnance Survey maps have been reproduced in modern facsimile; an original, larger-scale one is far more useful.) Much of London has changed out of all recognition since 1895, through growth and development, and in key districts also through the destruction of the 1940–41 Blitz.

Whole libraries of books have been written about London, including several specifically for Sherlockians, such as *On the Scent: A Visitor's Guide to Sherlock Holmes' London*, by Arthur M. Alexander (1984); *A Tourist Guide to the London of Sherlock Holmes*, by Charles O. Merriman (originally published in the *Sherlock Holmes Journal*, 1970–73, and reprinted in pamphlet form); *Sherlock's London Today* by Gunnar Sundin (1985); *Five Sherlockian Walks in London*, by William S. Dorn (1996); *Finding Sherlock's London* by Thomas B. Wheeler (2003, 2009); and *Close to Holmes* (2009) by Alistair Duncan. *Sherlock Holmes in London* (1989) by Charles Viney is an exquisite collection of photographs of the city in which Holmes lived; *Sherlock Holmes's London* (1986, based on a 1984 edition in Japanese) by Tsukasa Kobayashi *et al.* chiefly pictures the city as it is today.

Unusual among capital cities, London is the principal commercial city of its nation as well as the seat of government. Also unusual among capitals, London is built on an estuary — the tidal section of the Thames — and in the nineteenth century the constant maritime traffic brought the world's products, people, and news to its heart day and night. The docklands fell into disrepute and some decay in the twentieth century (only to be revived as the home of high-tech industry at century's end), but in 1895 the warrens of streets, alleys, buildings, and docks along the Thames were central to London metaphorically as well as geographically. The Canon reflects the littoral nature of London. That can be seen most graphically in *The Sign of the Four*, with its climactic

Baker Street looking northward from Oxford Street to Regent's Park. The Metropolitan Railway station at the corner of Marylebone Road, near the top of Baker Street, made the neighbourhood accessible and popular. The engraving appears in various editions of London: Illustrated *by Herbert Fry, published through the 1880s and 1890s. Which house was 221B? Probably one of those on the west (left) side just south of Marylebone Road.*

scene of a boat chase down the Thames, but the river and the sea figure also in such tales as "The Man with the Twisted Lip" and "Black Peter." And constantly there are reminders of London as a city divided by water: the better-established regions north of the Thames, the Southwark slums and the new suburbs on "the Surrey shore" to the south of it.

The easternmost crossings of the Thames now are expressway tunnels and bridges. In Holmes's early years there was no crossing downstream of the ancient London Bridge, which spans the Thames at a narrow point where some nine hundred feet separate the City of London from Southwark. In 1894 Tower Bridge was opened, the picturesque crossing further downstream which most people think is "London Bridge." Below Tower Bridge are the entrance to the Grand Union Canal (a major commercial waterway from London north to the Midlands), the docks, Woolwich, Tilbury, Southend, and the North Sea. Blackwall Tunnel, in the dock area, was opened in 1897. Upstream of London Bridge are half a dozen crossings, including Waterloo, Westminster, and Vauxhall Bridges.

Says a guidebook prepared for the Franco-British Exhibition of 1908: "The Metropolis, as we know it, is almost entirely a creation of the Victorian Age, most of the leading thoroughfares having been widened and improved — many of them actually constructed — and the bulk of the chief public edifices remodelled, if not built, during that period." But there remained much that was very old. London became (and remains) a nineteenth-century city superimposed on a cluster of longstanding villages and two larger centres, the original City of London and the City of Westminster. Besides those two, the most important communities that became part of London by 1900 included Chelsea, Kensington, Paddington, and Hampstead north of the Thames; Lambeth, Southwark ("the Borough") and Camberwell south of it. Further out lie regions that were suburban or still rural in 1895 but have since become absolutely part of the metropolis, including a few mentioned in the Canon — Norwood, Croydon, Harrow.

Most of the places known to today's tourists or would-be tourists are in either Westminster or the City of London. In Westminster are the Houses of Parliament (properly, "the Palace of Westminster") and the government offices in Whitehall and Downing Street, as well as Westminster Abbey, Trafalgar Square, Buckingham Palace and Piccadilly Circus. To the east, in the City, are the Tower of London, St. Paul's Cathedral, the Bank of England, and the Old Bailey (Central Criminal Court). Most of these places are ancient; most of them are within a short stroll of the Thames. Not far away are such neighbourhoods as Mayfair (the "West End"), Soho and Bloomsbury, just north of Westminster, and Whitechapel (the old, sordid East End) east of the City.

It is just a little further out, to the north and west, that Sherlock Holmes country chiefly lies: in St. Marylebone, Paddington, Bayswater and Kensington, areas developed in Victorian times and demarcated by the great green stretches of Regent's Park, Hyde Park and Kensington Gardens. The principal thoroughfares here include Oxford Street, Edgware Road, Park Lane, Euston Road, Kensington High Street, Maida Vale, Regent Street, and a name that thrills every Sherlockian: Baker Street.

London roads twist, turn, and change their names at every opportunity, and in Holmes's day there was no thought of "motorways" such as those that now encircle London and in some places tunnel underground. Driving from west to east in a virtually straight line, one can travel in turn along Holland Park Avenue, Notting Hill Gate, Bayswater Road, Oxford Street, New Oxford Street, High Holborn, Holborn Viaduct, Newgate Street, Cheapside, Poultry, Cornhill and Leadenhall Street, within six miles. Those are major streets; most London streets are short and small, and it is no accident that the British idiom is to live "in" a street, rather than "on" it, for residential streets or squares often have a sense of enclosure. There were few detached houses in Victorian London; the "houses" in which middle-class people lived were what would today be called "terraced houses," or in North America "townhouses" or row houses: narrow segments of a uniform three- or four-storey structure that might stretch for a full block. Individual "freehold" ownership of such houses was rare. More common was "leasehold," by which the householder leased the land for a long period and built or bought the house standing on it. Rental was still more common: whole districts of London, recently developed from great landowners' estates, were enriching a few families through rental of street after street. Even in the suburbs rental was the norm, as shown by Grant Munro of "The Yellow Face," who proudly acquired a "villa" at Norbury for the characteristically modest sum of £80 a year, about $650 a month in today's currency. Mansions such as Pondicherry Lodge did exist, but were hardly typical of living conditions in London. At the other extreme were the squalid rooms in which whole families lived in Whitechapel and Southwark.

BAKER STREET. In the mind's eye of any reader of the Canon, Baker Street shines as if it were built of gold. For the most part, in Holmes's time the street was occupied by residences and small businesses; the streetscape is of four-storey houses (of the attached kind typical of London) built in the early decades of the nineteenth century, in "Georgian" style and largely of brown sandstone. Michael Harrison in *In the Footsteps of Sherlock Holmes* (revised edition, 1971) sets the home of Holmes in context:

> Baker Street dates from the last quarter of the eighteenth century, being named after a friend and Dorset neighbour of the Mr. Portman who developed this part of London: Sir Edward Baker, of Ranston. At the beginning, Baker Street was a fashionable street indeed, and many years were to pass before it lost its fashionable character, though it is fair to say that it has never lost its respectability. The change in character has come about through the introduction of commerce into the street: a change due principally to the building of Baker Street station in the early 1860s....
>
> In 1881, Baker Street's transition from Residential to Commercial was but half-way achieved: if there were many shopfronts carved out of the rusticated lower-courses of the tall houses... there were not so many shop-fronts as there are today, and quite half of the upper portions of the houses were in private occupation: some tenanted by the shop-keepers themselves, others by lodgers of that quiet, permanent type. . . .
>
> One feels that the eminent respectability of Baker Street, no less than its convenient proximity to rail- and bus-routes, was in Holmes's mind when he picked on rooms in Baker Street.

Baker Street today is about two-thirds of a mile long, and runs north-south in the district of London known as St. Marylebone. It begins at Wigmore Street, in an intersection called Portman Square, and extends north just past Marylebone Road to merge with Park Road at the southwest corner of Regent's Park. Until after World War I this section north of Marylebone Road was "York Place" and "Upper Baker Street"; eventually it became part of Baker Street proper, and the houses of the entire street were renumbered in 1930. (Nearby York Mews South was renamed Sherlock Mews in 1936.) At the south end of Baker Street is Orchard Street, a brief extension reaching down to busy Oxford Street. Marble Arch, a principal London landmark, is a few yards away along Oxford Street; to the north, Madame Tussaud's waxworks and the Planetarium are in Marylebone Road just around the corner from Baker Street.

As Harrison notes, a principal influence on the street was (and is) Baker Street station. It serves not a main-line railway but the Metropolitan Line, a commuter railway which today is part of London's Underground (subway or "tube") system, and it can claim to be the oldest subway station in the world, dating from 1863. Travellers from east and west of the city would connect at Baker Street to underground trains bound for other parts of the metropolis. The Baker Street & Waterloo Railway, now the Bakerloo line of the Underground, was not opened until 1906, just after Holmes's time. Other connections have also been added, and the decor of the station now includes tile work with a silhouette of Holmes. A statue of him stands just outside the Marylebone Road exit from the station. In the nineteenth century, visitors seeking Holmes and Watson would probably go by Metropolitan or tube train to Baker Street station, then walk or take a cab.

Other landmarks of Baker Street, in the seven blocks (as a North American would express it) from Wigmore Street to Marylebone Road, included a post office, about halfway along the west side of the street; the Portman Rooms, a well-known place of entertainment; and the Baker Street Bazaar, an indoor shopping district with something of a reputation as a place for scandalous behaviour. The entrance to Madame Tussaud's had been at the Bazaar until the museum moved to the Marylebone Road in 1884.

THE LOCATION OF 221B. Tourists frequently wish to see the house in which Holmes lived, and Sherlockians dream of identifying it. Having learned that the B is a suffix indicating upstairs rooms ("first-floor" in British parlance, "second-floor" in North American), if it is not simply affectation, they go in search of a house numbered 221, and find none. The modern 221 is included in the large building at the northern end of Baker Street that for many years was the headquarters of the Abbey National Building Society, a major financial institution. Its public relations department famously took responsibility for answering the many letters that come addressed to Holmes. The company, now Abbey National plc, has moved elsewhere in London, and its building has been redeveloped for residential space.

The search quickly changes direction: which house on Baker Street did Watson or Doyle "disguise" with the number 221, or 221B? The classic answer was determined in the 1930s by Dr. Gray Chandler Briggs of St. Louis, who first looked for the "empty house" that stood opposite 221B, as described in the story of that title. His success was reported by his friend Vincent Starrett in *The Private Life of Sherlock Holmes* (1933, 1960):

> Like Holmes himself he had approached the empty dwelling
> from the rear. He had turned into a narrow alley and passed
> through a wooden gate into a yard, to find himself at the rear

door which had admitted the detective. Peering in, he saw the long straight hall extending through the house to a front door of solid wood, above which was a fan-shaped transom. Conclusive all of it — for already over the front door he had read the surviving placard: *Camden House....*

Since Camden House stood opposite the famous lodgings, the rooms of Sherlock Holmes in Baker Street were, of necessity, those upon the second story of the building numbered 111.

Camden House survived into recent decades, and the house now numbered 111 is today a post office. It is important to note that it was in Holmes's day not in Baker Street at all; it was 30 York Place.

Gavin Brend in *My Dear Holmes* (1951) considers 111 to be too close to the railway station for plausibility (no one would take a cab for that short distance, as clients of Holmes sometimes did), and by examining other evidence carefully concludes that 61 Baker Street is the most likely candidate, with 59 and 63 also quite possible. Also suggested as the original of 221B have been such other Baker Street houses as 19, 21, 22, 27, 49, 66, 77, and 109.

Because of the "Empty House" description, it seems reasonably certain that the house was on the west side of the street. Arthur M. Axelrad in *On the Scent* (1984) shows a nice appreciation of how a candidate for the correct house might be evaluated:

> The building at 109 Baker Street, one-half block south of Marylebone Road, is certainly the most appealing choice among the traditional candidates. Expertly reconstructed by Haslemere Estates, it has what appears to be the only intact ground floor along the entire street, surmounted by three upper stories and an attic of beautiful gray-black brick. Relief is provided by three fine white-framed windows on each floor as well as the fanlighted front door painted a brilliant red and set off by a pair of slim white columns. There is also a small iron balcony across the first-floor level — very pretty but non-Canonical. The railinged area, as elsewhere on Baker Street, has been built over.

No known building meets all the criteria — bow windows are unknown in Baker Street, for example — but in any case the real location of 221B is in the mind's eye.

CITY TRANSPORTATION. Holmes and Watson are often seen walking through London — still, many experts say, the best way to see the city and the speediest way of making many trips. For longer trips the choice lay between "Underground" trains and cabs, notably the one-horse hansom cabs that are familiar to readers of the Canon. (London's speedy hansoms — named after their inventor, Joseph Aloysius Hansom — charged a shilling for the first two miles of travel.) There were also horse-drawn omnibuses, such as the Brixton bus mentioned in "The Red Circle," and the "Baker Street and Pimlico" bus, which could have taken Holmes and Watson conveniently to Victoria Station.

To travel by Underground, they would have walked the short distance to Baker Street station, where the regular trains of the Metropolitan Railway travelled clockwise and counter-clockwise around the "inner circle." The Circle Line is still an important feature of the system, which has expanded hugely since Holmes's time, although trains still operate on many of the same tracks. The Metropolitan Railway, operating the northern half of the circle, is now part of the Metropolitan Line, one of eleven lines operated by London Underground Limited. The southern half is part of the District Line, successor to the District Railway that Holmes knew. On these tracks, a passenger from Baker Street could (and can) travel through Euston, King's Cross, Liverpool Street, Cannon Street, Charing Cross, Victoria, and Paddington before returning to Baker Street — touching, that is, most of the major railway stations, and making a twelve-mile circuit of the city. Attached to the inner circle were two extensions, one dubbed the "middle circle," to the westward, and the other dubbed the "outer circle," across north London. Both were branches of the Metropolitan Railway; the middle circle now forms small parts of the Metropolitan and District lines, while the outer circle is part of the British Rail commuter system rather than of the Underground. A third important underground line in Holmes's time was the City and South London Electric Railway, which now forms part of the Northern Line, running north-south across the circle.

The most famous Underground passenger in the Canon is Arthur Cadogan West of "The Bruce-Partington Plans," whose body is found lying beside the Metropolitan tracks near Aldgate station. In the course of the investigation Holmes displays familiarity with the Underground — "According to my experience it is not possible to reach the platform of a Metropolitan train without exhibiting one's ticket" — and eventually finds that rather than being a legitimate passenger while alive, West was deposited, after death, on the roof of a train. It is taken for granted that the reader will understand: at various places in London the Underground actually runs through cuttings open to the sky, rather than in tunnels, and a house window could easily overlook the tracks.

PUBLIC AFFAIRS

Government and politics touched the ordinary person less in the Victorian era than they do today. For all the growth of inspectorates during the late nineteenth century, little of daily life was subject to regulation; most of the public were hardly even touched by taxation. Income tax in the 1890s was set at sixpence in the pound, or 2.5 percent, with incomes of less than £150 exempt. When Holmes spoke in "The Second Stain" of "another penny on the income tax," he meant an increase that would add more than £2 million (perhaps $200 million in today's buying power) to the annual collections of only £13 million, out of a total public revenue of £100 million. Ordinary people's taxation was chiefly indirect, in their contribution to the licence fees paid by publicans, tobacco manufacturers, and many other merchants, and to the customs duties paid on imported goods.

It would be untrue to say that politicians attracted great respect, but Victorian society was based heavily on deference to those in positions of authority, including government. Britain is a constitutional monarchy, governed by machinery developed slowly over the centuries, with occasional discontinuities such as the "glorious revolution" of 1688, in which Parliament established its supremacy by deposing one King and choosing another. Victoria, Queen from 1837 to 1901, could trace her ancestry to Alfred the Great, not to mention bad King John, but she had considerably less power than those earlier monarchs had enjoyed. Although she retained some discretion in making government appointments, power lay chiefly with Parliament during Victoria's reign.

PARLIAMENT AND GOVERNMENT. Approval of the House of Commons, which in the twentieth century is effectively supreme, had to be coupled with that of the House of Lords and with the Queen's signature (which could not be refused, although Victoria occasionally came close), for a bill to become law. The upper house, or Lords, consisted of the entire English peerage, some 470 members from dukes to barons, as well as some bishops and Scottish and Irish peers. The lower house, or Commons, had 670 elected members. After the reform bills of 1868 and 1885, all adult men — though not women — could vote, and the old "rotten boroughs" containing only a few voters had been eliminated in favour of roughly equal constituencies.

While most peers served for life, members of the House of Commons were elected for each Parliament. The leader of whichever political party had the strongest representation in Parliament became prime minister, and could form a cabinet that might serve as long as it had the confidence of the Commons. Members of the "cabinet," frequently called "the government," today come almost entirely from the Commons, but in Victorian times they could come from either Lords or Commons. Several Canonical stories refer to members of the government. In "The Second Stain," Holmes is visited by the prime minister, Lord Bellinger, and by the "Secretary of State for European Affairs," whose title does not correspond to reality; substitute "Foreign" for "European," however, and one has the Foreign Secretary. Lord Holdhurst in "The Naval Treaty" holds the same office. In "The Mazarin Stone," the prime minister and the Home Secretary appeal to Holmes; the latter is the cabinet officer in charge of internal affairs, particularly the police. Other leading members of the cabinet included the Chancellor of the Exchequer, in charge of finances, and the Colonial Secretary.

There is no appeal from the decisions of Parliament, which are, so long as the government maintains confidence, really the decisions of the prime minister and cabinet. Britain still has no written bill of rights, and no judicial review by which laws can be set aside as unconstitutional. A respectable middle-class Briton of the Victorian era might, however, have felt well armed with what are now called civil rights, for unwritten provisions of the constitution clearly protect freedom of speech and other such activities. A prohibition against unreasonable search and seizure is expressed in the ancient saying that "An Englishman's home is his castle." Such rights were less reliably applied to members of the lower classes, against whom abuses were not unknown.

Local government depended on a mixture of tradition and centrally managed bureaucracy. Many local matters were in the hands of "vestry councils," still not fully divorced from the local parish churches. (Holmes refers to a vestry council with some amusement in *The Hound of the Baskervilles*.) Cities and boroughs were individually incorporated, with responsibilities conferred on councillors and mayors; the office of Lord Mayor of London had existed since 1189. The entire country was divided into counties, each headed by a Lord-Lieutenant and other officers (Arthur Conan Doyle was Deputy-Lieutenant of Surrey from 1902 to 1921). The vast area surrounding London became an "administrative county," governed by a London County Council, in 1888, in a change which nearly obliterated the old county of Middlesex. The ancient City of London, though geographically a mere district of the metropolis, retained its historic self-government.

POLITICAL HISTORY. "From 1868 to 1881 English politics were dominated by the rivalry between Disraeli and Gladstone," says R.J. Evans, introducing a chapter of his handy book *The Victorian Age 1815–1914*. Disraeli (later Lord Beaconsfield) was the leader of the Conservative Party; Gladstone, "the Grand Old Man," was leader of the Liberal Party. Both parties had been lately formed, from the old "Tories" and "Whigs," after a Reform Bill in 1866 which greatly expanded the number of voters, and it would be dangerous to assume that they had rigid principles or the sort of structure associated with modern political parties. They did have general philosophies — the Liberals emphasizing social reform and meritocratic institutions on behalf of the middle classes, the Conservatives extolling the benefits of tradition for the squires and landowners, but also for the working classes. Such politics are entertainingly reflected in the novels of Anthony Trollope (1815–82), including *The Prime Minister* (1876). But, as Evans points out, the rivalry between Gladstone and Disraeli was as much personal, or a consequence of social origins, as political.

The parties alternated in office: Gladstone came into office in 1868; Disraeli in 1874; Gladstone again in 1880. Disraeli died in 1881 and Lord Salisbury succeeded him as Conservative leader, becoming prime minister in 1885. Gladstone returned to office for a few months in 1886, to be followed by Salisbury again until 1892. Gladstone's final turn in office ran from August 1892 to his death in March 1894. He was succeeded by Lord Rosebery, who was promptly defeated by Salisbury's Conservatives in 1895 and again in 1900. Salisbury retired in 1902, to be succeeded by Arthur Balfour. The parties continued to alternate, but within a few years, the Liberals would be in difficulties, eventually to be eclipsed by the Labour Party further to the political left, which was not even imagined in Holmes's time.

The public issues of the Victorian era are often incomprehensible to modern readers. But many dramatic changes, now seen as inevitable steps forward, had been introduced in the 1870s, chiefly by Gladstone: reform of the notoriously corrupt and disorganized army; an overhaul of the ancient, complicated judicial system; the Trade Unions Act of 1875, which gave such organizations their rights and legalized collective bargaining; a Public Health Act to provide for "drains" (sewers, a British fascination ever since) and water supply; perhaps most important, the Education Act of 1870, which established across England the "board schools" which Holmes praises in "The Naval Treaty." Until that time, such elementary education as existed had been in private hands or those of the Church of England. Gladstone had also made unsuccessful attempts to regulate licensing hours (the times when pubs could be open) and the liquor trade. But after 1880, through his second and subsequent governments, alternating with those of Salisbury, little was done save for the 1888 reform of local governments. There was considerable social unrest, reflected in the Trafalgar Square riots of 1887 and the London dockers' strike of 1889, during the depressions of the 1880s and 1893, but in the later 1890s the economy was healthier again. It was another age of optimism.

The chief issue of the period, however, was the complicated and tragic question of Ireland, which had been an organic part of the United Kingdom since 1800, electing Members of Parliament just as England, Scotland, and Wales did, although local laws and customs were different. From time to time attempts were made to introduce reforms in Ireland, particularly to change the rules under which landlords (often living in England) were able to oppress their tenants. Sir Robert Peel, prime minister 1834–35 and 1841–46, was a leader in promoting such reforms, and Gladstone, his disciple, continued in the same direction, but gradually came to recognize that reforms (the Irish Church Act of 1869, the Land Act of 1870) were not working.

While England was almost entirely Anglican (in nineteenth-century terms, Protestant), Ireland had a Roman Catholic majority. The census of 1861 reported an Irish population of 5.8 million; twenty years earlier, before the massive starvation and emigration prompted by the potato famine of 1845–47, it had been more than 8 million. The number continued to fall, reaching 4.6 million by the turn of the century. The census also revealed, to some astonishment in England, that three-quarters of the population of Ireland were Roman Catholic, a fraction that was not falling. This anomaly, in a supposedly united country with an active and legally "established" Anglican church, led to tensions, particularly as the Roman Catholic Church sought greater control of educational and social institutions. As concessions and reforms were introduced, more were demanded; Ireland was, says historian D. G. Boyce, "handed over to the priest and the farmer." Inevitably there were proposals for self-government, known in the language of the day as Home Rule.

By 1885 a Home Rule party led by Charles Stewart Parnell (1846–91) was able to win a sizeable number of parliamentary seats. After some wavering, Parnell chose to support the Liberals, and in April 1886 Gladstone, accepting the inevitable, introduced a Home Rule bill. By a narrow margin it failed, largely because it was not seen to provide adequate protection for the Protestant minority in Ireland, concentrated in the northern province of Ulster. From that point positions hardened, the Protestant "Unionists," as they became called, forming a long-lasting alliance with the Conservatives.

A second Home Rule bill in February 1892 was also defeated, and thereafter there was as little progress on the "Irish Question" as on any other important issue during the 1890s. It returned to the agenda in the tumultuous first decade of the twentieth century, and a tentative Home Rule bill was finally approved, but its implementation was delayed by World War I. Von Bork speaks in "His Last Bow" about "Irish civil war," something of an exaggeration by 1914, although there had been isolated outbreaks of violence; his suggestion of a close connection between Irish agitation and German subversion seems authentic. The Easter Rising of 1916 was a more serious affair, and finally, after the war, a Liberal coalition government under David Lloyd George passed the Government of Ireland Act of 1920. It was a compromise that pleased neither the Home Rule faction under John Redmond nor the Ulster Unionists, but after a fashion it worked, conceding autonomy separately to a six-county region in Ulster and to the remainder of Ireland. The southern, chiefly Roman Catholic region quickly moved from Home Rule to independence as the Irish Free State (later Eire or simply "Ireland"). After a condition approaching civil war in the early 1920s, relations between Eire and a self-governing Ulster were stable for a generation. The Ulster violence of the late twentieth century can be seen as a continuation of the Irish unrest that delighted Von Bork as a destabilizing influence in Victorian and Edwardian England.

Of politics in the usual sense, there is nothing in the Sherlock Holmes stories. Leaders of the government are seen a few times, in connection with international crises, and the occasional Member of Parliament is mentioned, including Reginald Musgrave. In "The Bruce-Partington Plans," Watson reads in the newspaper of "an impending change of government," probably the 1895 cataclysm in which the Liberals, split over Home Rule, lost power to Salisbury's Conservatives; but there is no hint of how (or whether) Watson and Holmes intended to vote. Five years later, Arthur Conan Doyle was in no doubt, standing for an Edinburgh seat in Parliament on the ticket of the "Liberal-Unionists," a splinter group supporting the Conservatives. He lost narrowly to a Liberal, but Salisbury's Conservatives were returned to office. In 1906, when Sir Henry Campbell-Bannerman led the Liberals to a landslide victory, Doyle tried again, this time in a rural district of Scotland, and lost decisively.

MONEY AND SOCIAL CLASS

Holmes, visiting the Queen in one story, is able to pass as a young plumber in another; the unique profession of consulting detective made him as nearly classless, it seems, as any man in Victorian England. His finances are similarly indeterminate, and it is not even clear whether he earned enough by his profession to support himself. But the society in which he moves is depicted with deadly accuracy in terms of its wealth or poverty and its exact gradations of status.

MONEY. The British unit of currency is the pound, or pound sterling, so called because its value was once based on the weight of silver; its symbol is £. The pound was divided into twenty shillings and the shilling (symbol s) into twelve pence (symbol d); shillings were abolished in 1971 and the pound re-divided into one hundred new pence, so that 5p corresponds to one shilling. Paper money was rare in the Victorian era, and began with the £5 note — a single pound was represented by a gold coin called a sovereign. Silver coins in general use included the half-crown (2/6, that is, two shillings and sixpence), the florin (two shillings), the shilling, the sixpence (half a shilling), and the threepenny bit; bronze coins were the penny (a giant coin weighing one-third of an ounce), the halfpenny, and the farthing (a quarter of a penny). Other coins, such as the crown, existed but were less often used. The "guinea" of twenty-one shillings (one pound and one shilling) was mentioned in some business transactions, but there was no coin corresponding to it.

International exchange rates, based on silver and gold, valued the pound at $4.87 American, not far from the old rule of thumb that £1 was five dollars, and thus a shilling equalled a quarter. More important as a measure of the currency, however, was its buying power, enormously greater than twentieth-century inflation has left it. There was no net inflation in Britain from 1815, when the Napoleonic Wars ended, until World War I. The 3 percent interest typically paid on solid investments was thus a fair return, and Mary Sutherland in "A Case of Identity" was doing exceptionally well with 4.5 percent. Judging from prices reported in the Canon and elsewhere, it seems possible to estimate that £1 in 1895 bought about as much as $100 in the North America of 2009. A shilling, the daily wage of a Baker Street Irregular, thus corresponds to $5, and the eightpence for an "expensive" glass of sherry in "The Noble Bachelor" to about $3.35. Henry Baker's goose in "The Blue Carbuncle" cost twelve shillings, which thus amounts to $60 — a plump, pricy bird which would indeed have hampered him as he carried it. Jabez Wilson, earning £4 a week for copying the encyclopaedia, might have been happy indeed with a $400 supplement to his income. The same formula makes it clear that John Clay had his eye on $3 million in gold, and that the cost of going round the world in style (£5,000 in "The Three Gables") was half a million dollars. Less lavishly, the dress John Straker of "Silver Blaze" bought for his mistress was worth $2,300.

This conversion formula is based chiefly on price indices between 1900 and the present. Translations of incomes will tend to look low; in fact, incomes were low, which is to say that the standard of living has risen since 1900. Watson's wound pension of 11/6 a day works out to $21,000 a year; Neville St. Clair of "The Man with the Twisted Lip" earned $200 a week as a journalist, $130 a day as a beggar. The beleaguered St. Clair could not, even in an era without income taxes on the middle class, afford that middle-class villa rented by Grant Munro of "The Yellow Face," but a beggar's life gave him a living wage.

For a few Victorians, of whom the most striking Canonical example is the Duke of Holdernesse in "The Priory School," money was never an issue. He could write a cheque for £6,000 with hardly a wince. The wealthy had their country houses, their tenants (land, not capital, was still the principal form of wealth), and their London clubs — and the less than wealthy often tried to keep up with them; Holmes notes in "The Second Stain" that a prominent politician has "many calls" on his resources and has been forced to get his boots resoled. In an era before credit cards (and when cheques were chiefly a recourse of the rich) nearly everyone lived strictly on a cash basis, a constraint one sees in — for example — Henry Baker's difficulty: when he lost his hat, he had to make shift, for he had no immediate funds to buy a new one.

SOCIAL CLASSES. "Class" in Britain in Victorian times was not chiefly a matter of wealth. More important for many purposes was "birth" or ancestry, and there were also such factors as education, the experience of an elite public (boarding) school and perhaps university days at Oxford or Cambridge. For gentlemen and ladies thus defined, expectations could be rigid. Karl Krejci-Graf, writing in the *Sherlock Holmes Journal* in 1973, explained some of the constraints, citing Canonical stories by their four-letter abbreviations:

> A nobleman might discard a mistress when about to marry money (Nobl), but he might not wear ostentatious clothes or jewels (Scan). A foreigner could be a lady (Houn, Danc, Suss) or become one by marriage (Nobl), but a man would remain a foreigner, whether he was well liked (Gold) or not (Thor). A gentleman might become a burglar (Reig, Seco, Chas, Bruc, Vall, Illu, Last ...) or a murderer (Abbe, Devi); as might a lady (Chas). A nobleman might shield a criminal (Prio); there was respect even for a noble spy (Last). But a man who had been a criminal was left in the lurch even if innocent (Blue), unless he

had become wealthy and a member of society in the meantime (Glor, Bosc, Illu).

A full analysis of class-bound Britain, in the Victorian period or today, is work for a sociologist, but one can at least define some of the categories of "gentlemen" and "ladies" with whom Holmes came into contact — and can note that those terms may, by and large, define their manners, but say nothing about their morals.

At the peak of society came royalty, the large family of Victoria, who had been Queen since 1837. She figures indirectly in the Canon as "a certain gracious lady" honouring Holmes after his success in "The Bruce-Partington Plans." Her oldest son, "Bertie" — more formally Edward, Prince of Wales, later to be Edward VII — may have been the "illustrious" client in the story of that name. About Victoria's eight other children, the Canon is silent. Royal families of several other nations — Scandinavia and the Netherlands, in particular — do figure, however. European royalty was heavily interrelated at the end of the nineteenth century, members of all its families tracing their ancestry to the aged Victoria and to Christian IX of Denmark.

"Nobility" means the members of the House of Lords, or "peers" — dukes, marquesses, earls, viscounts and barons — and their families. The Canon presents a few dukes, such as the Duke of Holdernesse in "The Priory School," and a number of noblemen with the title "Lord," usually attached to marquesses and earls. The etiquette of such matters is complicated (and well set out in Jack Tracy's *Encyclopaedia Sherlockiana*). It is helpful to know, for example, that "The Noble Bachelor" commits a solecism in identifying Lord Robert St. Simon as "Lord St. Simon"; the first form suggests correctly that he is the son or grandson of a peer, the second form suggesting incorrectly that he is a peer himself. "Lady" indicates the wife or daughter of a peer, but it may also indicate the wife of a knight, such as Arthur Conan Doyle, and knights are not peers but commoners. (Doyle's wife was Lady Doyle; his daughter was Dame Jean Conan Doyle not because of her relationship to him but to honour her own military career, "Dame" being the female equivalent of "Sir" as a knight's title.)

Ranking below the nobility were, and are, the aristocracy, a less rigidly defined category of distinguished persons who might be knights or baronets (holders, like the Baskervilles, of a hereditary but not noble title) or merely members of what were recognized as "good families." This stratum of society is seen occasionally in Holmes's cases, though aristocratic clients are less conspicuous than the few who came from the nobility. Reginald Musgrave perhaps qualifies, as does Lady Brackenstall of "The Abbey Grange"; their cases are both set in the ancient, sprawling country houses one identifies with the propertied English classes. But the likes of Hilton Cubitt in "The Dancing Men" and Dr. Grimesby Roylott in "The Speckled Band" are, at best, gentry, respectable persons with country property but hardly aristocratic. Professors — Coram in "The Golden Pince-Nez," Presbury in "The Creeping Man" — barely qualify even for that category, having achieved their reputations through merit rather than social origins.

All these distinctions were of great importance to those who held them, or aspired to them, at the turn of the century, and studied *Debrett's Peerage* or *Burke's Peerage, Baronetage and Knightage* assiduously. Some social mobility was possible, but within limits of the kind shown in Gilbert and Sullivan's 1878 satire *H.M.S Pinafore*: a rear-admiral earning as much as £2,737 did not associate with an able seaman making £18 to £29 a year. The riches Nathan Garrideb saw within his grasp would have bought him treasures, but not social acceptance, and even Neil Gibson of "Thor Bridge," probably the richest man in the Canon, was not the social equal of someone with "Lord" in front of his name. Of course, Gibson was an American, and thus condemned to be an outsider in a generally closed social system; entry to it was chiefly, as in "The Noble Bachelor," through marriage.

Holmes moved only rarely in such circles, despite his own descent from "country squires," that is, landed (land-owning) gentry. The majority of his cases involve him with the middle classes of professional, commercial and trading people, for whom money was indeed, the paramount source of position. One sees in *Whitaker's Almanack*, which published pages of government appointments and salaries, the range of their incomes, from £2,000 for the President of the Board of Agriculture (a Member of Parliament) to £150 for his private secretary, £700 for the Chief Inspector and £400 for his deputy, to "£70 to £250" for the second-division clerks. That at least was secure income, enough to permit luxuries like magazines, travel, and antimacassars in the parlour. More than one case mentions the new and glamorous profession of engineering; other cases involve lawyers, doctors, clerks, civil servants of varying status, military officers, a tea merchant, a schoolmaster, and a newspaperman. Such people were the readers of the Holmes stories as well as their characters; they were a new phenomenon in England with the nineteenth century increase in literacy, and they made the *Strand Magazine* possible and necessary. Lower on the social scale, in turn, come such clients as landladies, governesses (though they might move, on carefully limited terms, in the households of the gentry and even nobility), pawnbrokers and policemen.

But many in Victorian England were much poorer, although the desperately poor and the underclass are seldom seen in the Canon; it is a novelty when Henry Baker falls among "a little knot of roughs" in the Tottenham Court Road. Donald Rumbelow, setting the social stage for the strange crimes of Jack the Ripper, describes how people lived in the poorer districts, as analyzed by a contemporary, Charles Booth:

> At the bottom were the occasional labourers, loafers and semi-criminals. Above them were the "very poor" and the "poor". The word "poor" he defined as those who had a meagre but regular income of between 18 shillings and 21 shillings a week, and the "very poor" were those whose income fell below this level. The former struggled to make both ends meet and the latter lived in a state of chronic want. The condition of the lowest class of all, which doesn't get a rating, can be imagined. At a rough guess there were about 11,000 of them....This figure includes the "dossers" and the homeless outcasts who slept on staircases, in doorways and even in dustbins and lavatories for warmth. Their lives, Booth said, were the lives of savages, "with vicissitudes of extreme hardship and the occasional excess."

And about the slightly less desperate classes:

> The commonest work was sweat shop tailoring. For trouser finishing (sewing) linings, making button holes and stitching on the buttons a woman might get twopence ha'penny a pair and have to buy her own thread.... Fifty-five per cent of East End children died before they were five.... *The Lancet* ... had estimated that in 1857 one house in every sixty in London was a brothel and one woman in every sixteen a whore.... [In lodging-houses] a double bed was eightpence a night and a single bed fourpence.
>
> After the horribly cold winter of 1886–87 came massive demonstrations about dockyard pay and standards of living in general, leading to riots in Trafalgar Square in November 1887; but little changed. Steps to introduce any form of relief for the poor were not quick in coming.

It perhaps goes without saying that women's class was determined by that of their fathers or husbands, save for the few (Irene Adler, Mrs. Hudson) who managed to make independent lives. The Canon presents a number of them, again representing the middle class: Mary Sutherland with her £100 a year from blue-chip investments (more than enough for a single lady living at home), Violet Hunter unsure why an employer should offer her £100 in addition to room and board, and Mrs. Warren for whom 50s. (two and a half pounds a week, or $250 in today's money) would have been generous for board and lodging, although her mysterious lodger was willing to pay twice that.

Complicating these many social gradations are considerations of race, ethnicity, religion, and national origin — concepts that were less distinct to Victorian thinking than they are today. Not only Italians ("The Six Napoleons") but Irish, Welsh, and Scots were frequently looked down upon by the English of all classes. Catholics, the object of suspicion since Tudor times, were freed from many official disqualifications by a law passed in 1829. Jews, despite a similar emancipation in 1858, were unwelcome in many parts of society, and it is possible to detect anti-Semitism in several brief passages in the Canon. Nonwhites were still seen as outsiders, although two natives of India were elected to Parliament, both from London constituencies, in the 1890s. North Americans frequently think of racial issues as largely involving whites and blacks, but Britain had few black people in the nineteenth century. The two stories in the Canon where blacks play a noticeable role present very different pictures: "The Yellow Face," with its touching but improbable intermarriage, and "The Three Gables," with Holmes's distasteful baiting of Steve Dixie. As Bruce Aikin wrote in an article in *Canadian Holmes* in 1998, the latter story "contains the most blatant examples of racism and class prejudice in the Sherlockian Canon, but they are far from isolated incidents."

SERVANTS. The modern impression of domestic servants in the Victorian period depends heavily on the picture given in *Upstairs, Downstairs* on television in the 1970s (a serial largely written by those good Sherlockians Michael and Mollie Hardwick). There, one saw an affluent upper-class household with a large staff of servants, headed by a strict, efficient butler and a jolly, competent cook. Such establishments are found in a few places in the Canon — Reginald Musgrave, living at Hurlstone, kept thirteen servants, and Charles Augustus Milverton at Appledore Towers probably had a similar number.

But less ambitious households are far more common in the Canon, and they too had their servants — eight at Birlstone in *The Valley of Fear*, four maids and presumably a few other servants in Alexander Holder's house in "The

Beryl Coronet." Smaller households might have only a single servant, generally a maid ("housemaid" or "maid-of-all-work"). Hilton and Elsie Cubitt had but one maid, as did Grant and Effie Munro in their far from ostentatious suburban cottage. Watson himself, in his married days, had a maid, Mary Jane. Still less impressive was the household of Jabez Wilson, the pawnbroker in "The Red-Headed League": he had "a girl of fourteen" to do a little of the domestic work.

The Canon is, in fact, pervaded by servants; Jack Tracy's *Encyclopaedia Sherlockiana* devotes six columns to listing them in their various categories. "Domestic service" is a calling now almost extinct, but in Victorian England it was both universal and respectable, if hardly enviable. Vast numbers of people earned their living in that way, being sometimes little better than slaves, sometimes virtually members of the family that employed them, albeit members who knew and kept their place. Far more women than men were in service; there were a few positions for gardeners and grooms (those in charge of horses), and the wealthiest households needed butlers and footmen, but every respectable household needed its maid, or maids. Their brothers and suitors were likely to be labourers ("navvies"), although a maid like Agatha, in Charles Augustus Milverton's household, would naturally choose Escott, the rising young plumber, as a suitor if she could get one. The soldiers "flirting with a nurse-girl" in "A Scandal in Bohemia" are similarly very plausible. A maid, certainly in a less wealthy household, would be presumed to be as uncouth as Isadora Klein's Susan in "The Three Gables." More intelligent and skillful maids naturally looked to places in more comfortable households, where nevertheless they might be exploited economically and even sexually. Enoch Drebber made himself "disgustingly free and familiar" with the maids in his boarding house, *A Study in Scarlet* notes.

In a quite different category from housemaids came ladies' maids such as Theresa Wright, who attended Lady Brackenstall in "The Abbey Grange." The status of Irene Adler's maid is unclear, but a maid who travelled with the mistress, as one did with Lady Frances Carfax, was an assistant whose functions involved clothes, toilette, and correspondence rather than the stereotypical feather duster. Maids in large households did not cook, although the single maid in a smaller household (to say nothing of Jabez Wilson's "girl") probably had kitchen duties as well as the responsibilities of serving meals, sweeping, answering the door, and building the parlour fire. Other miscellaneous categories of servant ranged from gardeners through coachmen to pageboys.

Governesses were different altogether. They were employees rather than servants, and ate their meals with the children in the "nursery" rather than with the servants (in the kitchen or, in grander houses, the "servants' hall"). Such Canonical stories as "The Copper Beeches" deal touchingly with the position of governesses, dependent on the income they could earn with "a little French, a little German, music, and drawing." Those were middle-class, even upper-class, achievements, but the governess's sex and financial need condemned her to precarious social position and vulnerability to every sort of danger. A "nurse," or nanny to younger children, had still lower status.

DAILY LIFE

The popular idea of the "Victorian" period as dull, stifling, and prudish is hardly borne out by the Canon, which shows people engaging in a full range of normal human activity — bicycling, attending the theatre, buying children's toys, drinking in pubs, collecting butterflies, betting on horse races. No doubt Mary Sutherland of "A Case of Identity" spent many hours in a narrow drawing room, pasting cuttings in an album and singing to the piano, but she escaped by taking paid work as a "type-writer" and attending the gas-fitters' ball so she could show off her purple plush dress. On every page of the Canon are people whose lives are full and complicated. In the case of the aristocracy who populate a few of the stories, that richness is perhaps not surprising, but the fact is that the reader will find it also in the majority of stories that are about the middle classes.

Of course it is true that the Victorian period gave far more liberty to men than to women. The Canon shows a few women earning their living as governesses (like Arthur Conan Doyle's sisters), a couple of type-writers, and a few landladies, but otherwise women confine their activity to the household circle or, like Nancy Barclay in "The Crooked Man," to charitable activity. The Canon hardly deals with the immense lower class, in which women, like men, had to earn a living or starve: as factory operatives, in piece-work manufacture of matchboxes and other little articles, or as prostitutes. Women of the classes chiefly encountered by Sherlock Holmes function primarily as wives, mothers, and sisters. Watson gives some loving descriptions of the elaborate clothes they wore about their daily activities, but of course does not refer to that unmentionable and ambiguous garment the corset, somewhere underneath the mousseline-de-soie, a garment at once confining (it is impossible to slouch, and hard to breathe, in a corset) and provocative (giving Mrs. St. Clair of "The Man with the Twisted Lip," for example, her notable "figure"). The corset is also a more likely cause than modesty for the fainting spells that characterized Victorian women at moments of stress.

The legendary sexual repression that required Victorians to veil the legs of their pianos, and to refer to men's trousers as "inexpressibles," is a feature not of the 1890s but of two generations earlier. Even by the 1860s, English society enjoyed a good deal of sexual freedom, and the "pretty horse-breakers," or high-society prostitutes, attracted great admiration in the press and imitation in their style and fashion. (Michael Harrison, well known as a Sherlockian author, deals with them at length in *Fanfare of Strumpets*, 1971.) Prostitution was commonplace at less exalted social levels as well, and there were, quite apart from brothels, many places of amusement where men and women mixed familiarly, including the Portman Rooms in Baker Street. This of course is not to say that everyone engaged in lascivious behaviour, but the possibility was certainly there. Pornography, too, was a sizeable industry throughout the Victorian period. Repression, indeed prudery, returned somewhat in the latter part of the century; in 1877 the closing of the merry and notorious Cremorne Gardens amusement-rooms in London marked the end of an era. The "social evil" that was lower-class prostitution continued, providing the context for Jack the Ripper's bloody work in 1888, but the newspapers spoke more about the need for social reform, and less about the stylish carriages of aristocratic men's mistresses. Middle-class late Victorians were supposed to be respectable, although there were fewer constraints on their daily and hourly behaviour than their grandparents had known.

The crinoline that was fashionable in the 1860s, a rigid framework giving support and shape to a woman's petticoats, was a coquettish rather than modest garment, for it allowed glimpses of the "ankle" — a Victorian enthusiasm — and frequently revealed a great deal more. Extremely low necklines were also in fashion at that period. In the 1870s, the crinoline having passed out of fashion, women wore bustles, an artificial augmentation of the derrière, and longer skirts. By the 1890s, the fashion was for an hourglass figure, with wide shoulders, puffed sleeves and, long flared skirts, supported by multiple petticoats. There was plenty of lace, and there was plenty of variety, as a woman of the upper classes might change her costume several times in a day: breakfast-gown, morning dress, walking costume, at-home dress, tea-gown, and finally dinner dress (much barer, especially about the shoulders, than anything worn during daylight hours). Men wore narrow, tight trousers, and shirts with detachable, starched, upright collars. Hats were essential for both sexes when out of doors: elaborate millinery for women, bowlers or top

hats for men (certainly not, except in the countryside, deerstalkers). Sherlockians occasionally plan costume parties that, at their best, involve impassioned
hunting through Victorian magazines for the details of clothing appropriate to
an exact social station and circumstance.

Many attempts to imitate the Watsonian (or Doylean) style have come to
grief over details of daily life and etiquette. It is useful, for example, to understand the Victorian obsession with death — hardly surprising in an era before
antibiotics, when women often died in childbirth and children did not survive
infancy. The annual death rate in London was about twenty-nine per thousand,
four times the modern figure. The Canon makes casual mention of mourning-
stationery with its black border, mourning-bands on men's arms, black veils,
and undertakers' wreaths; the proper use of these articles amounted to a cult.
Less concretely, one has to understand the degree to which social respectability depended on an arbitrary conception of "honour," involving not so much
morality as responsibility for one's debts. Such considerations lie behind the
seriousness of "the Tankerville Club scandal" and other incidents throughout
the Canon. One might rise above many kinds of misbehaviour, but money was
of central importance to Victorian society.

Lacking television, Victorians entertained themselves, and if the results
could be ghastly hours of parlour games, it could also be a level of articu-
late conversation that sounds artificial to the modern ear, although the Canon
may well be reporting it accurately. Lacking the telephone, they relied on frequent postal service, and wrote readable, grammatical letters with pens that
had to be dipped in liquid ink. Lacking airplanes (or funds) to take them to
distant holiday destinations, they made occasional excursions by rail to see
the sights of London or to attend the races at Winchester. Lacking movie stars
to admire, they bought souvenir photographs (like the one Watson spots in
"Charles Augustus Milverton") of society beauties, and they read with interest
about the doings of royalty. Lacking citrus fruit and, for part of the year, green
vegetables, they ate meat and potatoes, and made much of green peas when
spring provided them. Lacking the disillusionment and disorientation that
would come with the World Wars of the twentieth century, and be expressed
by its philosophers and artists, they lived (if one overlooks the desperation of
the poorest classes) a comfortable and satisfied life.

Many books describe life in Holmes's day, especially in bustling London
and among the wealthier classes. For Sherlockians a particularly useful volume is *Oscar Wilde's London* (1987), by Wolf Von Eckardt and others, which
begins with Wilde and his literary circle but extends to every aspect of life in

the great city between 1880 and 1900. A popular reference work for readers and authors is *What Jane Austen Ate and Charles Dickens Knew* (1993) by Daniel Pool. One author in the field strongly recommends *Victorian London, the Tale of a City 1840–1870* by Liza Picard (2006) and *Daily Life in Victorian England* by Sally Mitchell (1996). Books about life as it was during Holmes's later years include *The Edwardians: The Remaking of British Society* (1975) by Paul Thompson, and *Edwardian Life and Leisure* (1973) by Ronald Pearsall. Of course many nineteenth-century novelists picture their own era with insight and accuracy, but it is important to remember that some important figures were working long before Doyle. Dickens, for example, wrote his major works between 1837 and 1861, and Anthony Trollope wrote his between 1855 and 1875. Thomas Hardy (1840–1928) was a contemporary of Doyle, but his fiction is set in a rural area distant in every sense from London.

NEWSPAPERS. Local and regional newspapers existed throughout England — in *The Hound of the Baskervilles,* Holmes speaks of the *Leeds Mercury* and the *Western Morning News* — but the more important part of the press for Holmes was the London newspapers. He read them chiefly for the crime news and the "agony column," more formally known as the personal advertisements. The papers varied in social standing, political position (many of them regularly conducting crusades for reforms of one kind or another), and quality, descending to the "garbage papers" for which Langdale Pike of "The Three Gables" wrote.

The morning papers of London were, and are to this day, "national," being distributed throughout England, as one sees for example in "The Stock-Broker's Clerk." Most famous of these is *The Times*, founded in 1788, known for its extensive political coverage (in Victorian times it published virtually verbatim reports of parliamentary proceedings) and for its role as a newspaper of record, with the Court Circular detailing the engagements of royalty, and its Births column listing the offspring of everyone of importance across the land. *The Times*, however, is a minority, highbrow taste, the general reading public being catered to by other newspapers. "The Blue Carbuncle" provides a nice illustration: the Countess of Morcar advertised for her missing gem in *The Times*, which cost 3d when most of the other morning newspapers (*Daily Telegraph, Standard, Morning Post, Daily Mirror* and others) were a penny or a halfpenny. In the same case Holmes advertises the hat and goose in the evening papers, which were more local (and which are now extinct): "the *Globe, Star, Pall Mall, St. James's Gazette, Evening News, Standard, Echo,* and any others that occur to you." In addition to the daily papers there were weeklies that ranged from the political and satirical *Punch* to *The Sporting Times*, known as "the Pink 'Un" for the distinctive colour of its paper, and the *Illustrated London News*.

TELEGRAPH AND POSTS. A telegram is a message put in writing by its sender, transmitted over wires in an electrical code, and reduced to writing again at the other end of the wire, where a messenger from a telegraph office delivers it to the recipient. Introduced in the 1840s, telegrams became the first means of communication that eliminated distance as a consideration; the Post Office could deliver a message from London to Edinburgh as quickly as from one part of London to another, and for the same basic charge of sixpence for the first twelve words and a halfpenny for each additional word. To France the charge was 2d a word; to Canada one shilling. Telegrams pervade the Canon as an idiosyncrasy of the nervous and impulsive Holmes, who can be terse ("telegraphic") in one message, and be expensively chatty in another, such as the two-shilling-and-threepence telegram that introduces "The Boscombe Valley Mystery." Telegrams serve also as a device to emphasize the period quality of the tales, for Holmes is seen to use the telegraph even when telephones (introduced in London in the early 1880s) would have served better. He does have a telephone by the turn of the century, but it seems an anomaly.

Watson observes that Holmes "never wrote when he could telegraph," but he did frequently write, as did everyone who wanted to communicate in Victorian England. A one-penny postage stamp would take a letter (weighing up to one ounce) anywhere in the United Kingdom, while the parcel Holmes examines in "The Cardboard Box" probably cost 3d to convey from Belfast to Croydon. At these prices a vast number of items passed through the post office: some 1.8 billion letters, and 50 million parcels, each year. Modern North Americans accustomed to thinking of the mail as a leisurely means of communication must remember that it was both reliable and rapid in Victorian England. Says *Whitaker's Almanack*:

> In the E.C. or City district [of London] there are twelve deliveries daily.... In the other districts there are from six to eleven collections and deliveries. Letters properly directed, and properly posted, should be delivered within from two to four hours.

Still more urgent messages could be designated for "express delivery" at an additional 2d, or the "district messenger service" for 3d per half-mile. For letters outside London, overnight delivery was the standard.

HIGHER PURSUITS

LITERATURE. To posterity, the chief Victorian writers are Charles Dickens (who died when Doyle was a child) and Alfred Lord Tennyson (whose important work had all been written by the 1870s, though he lived to 1892). The writers Doyle loved best were similarly out of date by the 1890s: Sir Walter Scott (1771–1832) and James Fenimore Cooper (1789–1851), whose historical novels Doyle tried to emulate. Of the authors who were his contemporaries, he probably admired Robert Louis Stevenson (1850–94) the most. Stevenson was in the Scott and Cooper tradition, and so was Rudyard Kipling, whose friendship Doyle acquired in 1894. The Canon never mentions Kipling, or another author of romantic adventures, H. Rider Haggard (1856–1925). But it does portray Watson, the man of action but hardly of intellect, as a reader of the now almost forgotten sea stories of William Clark Russell (1844–1911), whom Doyle also admitted to enjoying. Other objects of his admiration, and also friends, were Robert Barr and Jerome K. Jerome.

Yet Doyle, a more complex man than Watson, also admired Thomas Hardy, whose *Tess of the D'Urbervilles* (1891) and *Jude the Obscure* (1895) are about sex and complex human relationships. Hardy's work is realistic with a grimness that emerges only occasionally in Doyle: "nearer to nature in his writing than any other contemporary writer," Doyle said of him. And he spoke with enthusiasm of a figure now almost forgotten, Olive Schreiner (1855–1920), South African author of *The Story of an African Farm* (1883) and other works about emotion, sex, and progressive social themes. Much better known now, and less understood in his own time, was George Meredith (1828–1909), who by the 1890s had progressed from radical crank to grand old man. Doyle lectured on his work as early as 1888, but confessed that he admired him more for his ideas than for "artificial" characters and "grotesque" language.

By the 1890s, readers were looking for such modern stuff, and finding it in the pages of the *Strand* and competing magazines: stories and novels by H.G. Wells, Grant Allen, and soon W. Somerset Maugham (1874–1965), more readily thought of as a twentieth-century figure. The old-fashioned three-decker novel was dead, and modern novelists were writing slimmer books on racier topics. Doyle complained that too many of them concentrated on love and sex, which indeed was one reason he admired Stevenson: there was only a modest representation of women among his characters. "In British fiction," he once told an audience, "nine books out of ten have held up love and marriage as the be-all and end-all of life. Yet we know in actual practice this is not so."

Still, he admired skill where he found it, even saying complimentary things about Oscar Wilde. For success in presenting male friendship rather than conventional love, Doyle might also have cited George du Maurier (1834–1896), whose *Trilby* (1894) is as much about men's friendship as is Doyle's own saga of Holmes and Watson.

RELIGION. In the Victorian period the majority of the people of England were nominally Anglican — adherents of the "established," or officially endorsed, Church of England — although only a minority attended services regularly. In 1893 it was estimated that in the parishes of England and Wales there was seating-room for 6,255,000 people in Church of England establishments; "the Church population" was estimated at twice that. The Roman Catholic Church had about two million adherents in England, many of them probably of Irish extraction. Methodist bodies accounted for about a million, other Nonconformists such as Presbyterians and Baptists fewer than a million. The rest (with small exceptions such as an estimated 80,000 Jews) clearly had no religion at all.

Since the origin of the Church of England in the well-known sixteenth-century rift between King Henry VIII and the Pope, the buildings, clergy, bishops, and appurtenances of the traditional Roman Catholic establishment were instead "Anglican." The language of the Church of England was English, in which the Bible was read (the King James translation of 1611) and the liturgy was conducted (according to the *Book of Common Prayer*, finally revised in 1662). As a national institution, the Church of England became a "broad church," tolerating considerable variations in belief and practice. In the eighteenth century a liberal Protestant style was dominant, without great rigour in social or moral teaching and also without great elegance in the liturgy. One response to that laxity was an evangelical revival leading to the "Methodist" movement of John Wesley, with its emphasis on individual salvation and social reform, eventually separating from the Church of England altogether. Then in the 1850s came the "Oxford Movement," associated with John Henry Newman, which urged the church in an opposite, Catholic direction, towards formal liturgy and mediaeval piety. Vast numbers of Anglicans stayed somewhere in the middle.

The "supreme governor" of the Church of England was the Queen. Its "primates" were the Archbishop of Canterbury, in southern England, and the Archbishop of York, in the north. But the archbishops had very little authority over the bishops, the unchallenged ecclesiastical rulers of their dioceses. In Victorian times England and Wales were divided into thirty-four dioceses, each divided into parishes in charge of a "rector" or "vicar," who might prefer to be styled "minister" if he were very Protestant in taste, or "priest" if he were very

Catholic. Every person living in England was in a parish, whether the humble Little Purlington, mentioned in "The Retired Colourman," or the elegant St. Monica's, London ("A Scandal in Bohemia"). The parish was still for some purposes a unit of local government, and at least in small communities the vicar was an important figure in local society. Vicars and other clergy were all listed in *Crockford's Clerical Directory*, which Holmes consults in "The Retired Colourman."

SCIENCE. The chief discoveries that are the foundation of modern science had been made before Holmes's time: the second law of thermodynamics was formulated in 1850, the speed of light measured in 1862, Mendel's law of heredity articulated in 1865, the periodic table devised in 1869. Similarly, the great technological innovations had been made: the internal combustion engine was first made to work in 1860 (though it would be decades before it began to supplant steam power), pasteurization (the basis of biotechnology) was introduced in 1864, Bell invented his telephone in 1876. By 1895 there were bicycles, phonographs, vaccines, machine guns, photographs, dynamite, and primitive radio. Bridge building, still seen as the central activity of civil engineering, had achieved such triumphs as the Brooklyn Bridge in 1874 and the enormous Forth Bridge in 1890.

The luckless Victor Hatherley in "The Engineer's Thumb" is a hydraulic engineer; Violet Smith of "The Solitary Cyclist" is engaged to a man with an even more modern profession, an electrical engineer. Pure or applied scientists are thin on the ground in the Canon, however, unless one counts Sherlock Holmes himself, who is first glimpsed conducting research in the pathological laboratory at St. Bartholomew's Hospital. Time and again he is presented as doing chemical work, sometimes for very practical ends ("If this paper turns red, it means a man's life"), sometimes out of sheer curiosity or for recreation. Donald Redmond, writing in the *Baker Street Journal* in 1964, suggested that many of the experiments and analyses Holmes is seen conducting are part of "a consistent pattern of investigation" begun by his work into the chemical definition of bloodstains. At the time of his Great Hiatus he was working in Montpellier on "the coal-tar derivatives," as he says in "The Empty House." Jack Crelling noted in the Sherlockian newsletter *Camden House Journal* in 2001 that "during this entire half-century coal-tar research was the cutting edge of chemistry," with dyes, flavourings, and medications being developed, but largely in Germany rather than in Britain. Somewhat oddly, the Canon, for all its Violets, makes no mention of mauve, a colour that had been made possible by the first coal-tar dye and that was the height of fashion in the 1890s.

Amateur scientists, meanwhile, flourished during the Victorian period, and did much to advance knowledge through collection of data and taxonomic work in botany, zoology, and geology. Stapleton in *The Hound of the Baskervilles*, Nathan Garrideb in the story that bears his name, even Holmes himself in "Wisteria Lodge" with "a spud, a tin box, and an elementary book on botany" are, to various degrees, scientists of this kind. J.G. Wood (1827–89), mentioned in "The Lion's Mane," was a clergyman and amateur scientific writer and lecturer; his book *Out of Doors* was published in 1874.

Finally, there were theorists like Dr. Mortimer, again of *The Hound of the Baskervilles*, with a keen interest in what would now be called anthropology — "the comparative anatomy of the Bushman and the Hottentot" and Sherlock Holmes's own skull. One of Mortimer's monographs is titled "Is Disease a Reversion?" a theme that must have drawn interest from Holmes, who also expressed opinions about the relationship between individual development and the evolution of the species. Charles Darwin had published *The Origin of Species* in 1859, four years after the essentials of evolution had been set out in Herbert Spencer's *Principles of Psychology*. The general principle of evolution was accepted by scientists, and indeed by educated people in general, in Holmes's generation, but many of the specifics were matters of debate and uncertainty, and echoes of the issue can be heard whenever men of science get talking as Dr. Mortimer and Sir Charles Baskerville did. Holmes himself seems, like many contemporaries, to have held to the theory of "atavism," defined by Wikipedia as

> the tendency to revert to ancestral type. An atavism is an evolutionary throwback, such as traits reappearing which had disappeared generations ago. Atavisms occur because genes for previously existing phenotypical features are often preserved in DNA, even though the genes are not expressed in some or most of the organisms possessing them.... During the interval between the acceptance of evolution and the rise of modern understanding of genetics, atavism was used to account for the reappearance in an individual of a trait after several generations of absence. Such an individual was sometimes called a "throwback."

Thus Holmes declares that Professor Moriarty had "hereditary tendencies of a most diabolical kind." He endorses atavism even more clearly in "The Empty House," and in the final pages of *The Hound of the Baskervilles*, saying of Stapleton that "it is an interesting instance of a throwback, which appears to be both physical and spiritual. A study of family portraits is enough to convert a man to the doctrine of reincarnation." One wonders why the truth was not glimpsed by Dr. Mortimer, who knew Stapleton well and whose academic writings included an article on "Some Freaks of Atavism."

As distinguished from science, medicine plays a considerable part in the Canon, as one might expect from stories written by an able and curious physician. In Holmes's day medicine had only a modest number of drugs in its armamentarium; anaesthetics were generally used, but antibiotics, to combat infection, were as yet unknown. It was in the early 1880s, exactly while Doyle was in medical school at Edinburgh, that the German researcher Robert Koch made dramatic discoveries of the specific bacteria responsible for two of the most fearful diseases of the time, tuberculosis and cholera. A decade later, Koch proclaimed that he had identified a cure for tuberculosis, and Doyle was among hundreds of physicians (and patients) who flocked to Berlin to find out more. He reported back, in a landmark letter to the *Daily Telegraph*, that Koch's "tuberculin" treatment was far from proven, and later claimed to have been the first observer to sound such a note of caution. By 1913, when he was able to write "The Dying Detective" with a plot revolving around a "horribly contagious" oriental disease, many bacteria had been identified and vaccines against some were in common use; the first major antibiotic, penicillin, would come a decade later.

Medical matters in Doyle's writings are dealt with exhaustively in *Medical Casebook of Doctor Arthur Conan Doyle* (1984) by Alvin E. Rodin and Jack D. Key. In an appendix they classify the diseases that appear in the Canon, including infections, addictions, ear and eye ailments, heart symptoms, nervous diseases, respiratory problems, and so on, to say nothing of "trauma," very much to be expected in detective stories. Medical themes are important not just in "The Dying Detective" but in "The Resident Patient" (catalepsy and what must surely be congestive heart failure) and "The Blanched Soldier" (leprosy and ichthyosis). There are significant medical notes also in *A Study in Scarlet* (aortic aneurysm, probably associated with Marfan's syndrome) and "The Creeping Man" (the improbable results of injecting monkey gland serum), among others. Half a dozen stories deal with alcoholism, and another half-dozen feature that Victorian equivalent of the nervous breakdown, "brain fever." It appears that none of the stories explicitly mentions syphilis, the disease about which Doyle had written his medical thesis, although the ailment (and its dark moral implications) may lurk below the surface in a number of them. One suspects that he was well aware of Salvarsan, the first chemical therapeutic agent (introduced

1910 as a treatment for syphilis), by the time he wrote "The Illustrious Client," with its reference to the "leprous mark" of sin, in 1924.

Throughout the stories the reader is aware of Watson, the narrator and foil for Holmes, who holds the degree of Doctor of Medicine (not the mere bachelor's degree that would have been adequate for general practice at the time). He serves as an army doctor for a time, and at least twice goes into practice in London, though he is generally ready to abandon his patients for the sake of an excursion with Holmes. Readers have been inclined to ask with amusement about his professional skill, citing especially his enthusiastic use of brandy in almost every circumstance, including accidental amputation ("The Engineer's Thumb"). Such a practice should perhaps not be taken as typical of Victorian medicine, which relied strongly on common sense and a belief in cleanliness and fresh air. Though Holmes in "The Dying Detective" calls Watson "a general practitioner with very limited experience and mediocre qualifications," it would seem he is goading him for strategic reasons, not passing a considered judgement.

Two books published in 2006 address issues of science in the Canon. *Sherlock Holmes and a Question of Science* by Christopher Lindsey is essentially a classified list of references ("ballistics and weaponry," "optics and photography" and so on). *The Science of Sherlock Holmes*, by E.J. Wagner, connects techniques demonstrated in a number of the Holmes stories to forensic science as it developed over the years that followed, with descriptions of many authentic cases.

THE EMPIRE AND THE WORLD

Sherlock Holmes's London was not merely the capital of England and of the United Kingdom; by the later Victorian era it had also become the heart of the British Empire, which extended over 9.8 million square miles (about a sixth of the earth's surface) and 305 million people. Territories of the Empire were ruled through the Colonial Office and the India Office, to which local governors reported. Among those territories were Canada, India, Ceylon (now Sri Lanka), Hong Kong, Natal and the Cape Colony (later to be South Africa), the Gold Coast (Ghana), many Caribbean islands, the Australian territories, and New Zealand. Large areas of East Africa which were later to be British colonies, and eventually such independent nations as Zambia, Tanzania, Kenya, and Zimbabwe, were still in the private hands of the Imperial British East Africa Company (chartered 1888, with Cecil Rhodes as its leading figure) and the British South Africa Company (chartered 1889). Canada, an early colony, had achieved a measure of self-government in 1867; Australia acquired a similar status in 1901, and other colonies and territories would follow.

CANADA. Until World War I, when Canadian troops earned national pride with their blood at Vimy and other scenes of carnage, most English-speaking Canadians still thought of themselves as British. The "Union Jack" still waved, despite the one-third of the population who were French-speaking Québecois rather than in any sense English (their representation has fallen to about one-quarter of the population in the late twentieth century), and despite a tide of immigration from eastern Europe into the opening farmlands of the prairies. "Confederation" in 1867 had meant a large measure of self-government for the newly united British colonies in North America, but the government at Ottawa still looked to Britain to conduct its foreign affairs. Full independence came only with the Statute of Westminster, 1931. In Holmes's time Canada was still, in British eyes at least, a colony; young Henry Baskerville went there to farm, but had no hesitation about returning to the motherland when his time came. And British troops were stationed at such garrisons as Halifax, as "The Copper Beeches" reflects.

AMERICA. The United States, on the other hand, was self-consciously independent of Britain, dating its freedom from July 4, 1776, and actively recalling the battles that had been fought to maintain it. Arthur Conan Doyle addressed the subject in a letter to *The Times* in 1896:

> To understand the American's view of Great Britain one must read such an American history as would be used in the schools.... American history, as far as its foreign policy is concerned, resolves itself almost entirely into a series of wrangles with Great Britain, in many of which we must now ourselves confess that we were absolutely in the wrong.... This war of 1812 would possibly only occupy two pages out of 500 in an English history, but it bulks very large in an American one, and has left many bitter memories behind it....
>
> As recently as 1895 there were threats of war over the boundaries of Venezuela, in which both countries had interested themselves.

In the 1890s the United States had not yet become the world's dominant nation economically, although its primacy in the western hemisphere, asserted in the Monroe Doctrine of 1823, was widely accepted. The need to exert force in support of that doctrine produced America's first foreign war, against Spain, in 1898. The country was growing (by some one thousand immigrants every day through New York) and developing its industry and confidence. But in spite of popular resentment against Britain, and in spite of the notoriously high American tariffs, the cultured classes of America looked to the mother country for much of their literature, art, and furnishings. Audiences were eager, even fawning, to hear Doyle speak about authorship when he toured the country's major cities in 1894.

The Canon is thickly sprinkled with Americans who come to England for things they could not find at home, from Hatty Doran of "The Noble Bachelor" in search of a husband to Neil Gibson of "Thor Bridge" looking for respectability on an old-country estate. The presence of so many Americans reveals Doyle's enthusiastic interest in the United States; indeed, he favoured Anglo-American union some day. It reveals, as well, the close links that existed between the two great English-speaking lands regardless of their periodic political differences. Americans were sometimes figures of fun — not least "Altamont," the Irish-American who proves to be Holmes himself in "His Last Bow" — and many of the Canonical allusions suggest a British understanding of America as a place where the inhabitants shot first and asked questions later. But casual references to points from Long Island to Texas, and Holmes's insights into the fraudulent American in "The Three Garridebs," make clear how thoroughly American visitors were a part of the British scene.

American government in the 1890s was weaker than American business; it was the heyday of the "robber barons" and their powerful companies, led by John D. Rockefeller's Standard Oil and (from 1901) Carnegie's United States Steel. Neil Gibson of "Thor Bridge" is in the mould of these industrial giants, at whom the Sherman Antitrust Act of 1890 was aimed. After the Civil War (1861–65) government was in some disrepute, and presidents were weak: Grover Cleveland (served 1885–89 and 1893–97), Benjamin Harrison (1889–93), William McKinley (1897–1901, assassinated at Buffalo). Then came Theodore Roosevelt (born 1858, president 1901–09, died 1919), whose energy as frontiersman and war hero was translated into active public service not just in antitrust efforts but in world affairs, helping to lead the United States into the international community.

EUROPEAN AFFAIRS. "The whole of Europe is an armed camp," says the prime minister to Holmes in "The Second Stain," a story published in 1904 and set in a "nameless" decade slightly earlier. He goes on:

> There is a double league which makes a fair balance of military power. Great Britain holds the scales. If Britain were driven into war with one confederacy, it would assure the supremacy of the other confederacy, whether they joined in the war or not.

That is a fair statement of the position in Europe after 1893, when France and Russia signed a treaty creating the "Dual Alliance" as a counterbalance to the "Triple Alliance," formed in 1882, of Germany, Italy and Austria-Hungary. Britain remained neutral between these two blocs throughout Holmes's day, even seeking, especially under Gladstone, to arrange a solution of the remaining border disputes and irritants. As an island power, Britain felt little threat of the kind of war that had repeatedly swept over continental Europe. Its protection was not an army but its unchallenged Navy ("Britannia rules the waves"), and its chief geopolitical interest was maintenance of communication with such distant points as India. For that reason, if any major power was a threat it was Russia, menacing the Indian sub-continent from the north. Britain had fought the Crimean War of the 1850s against Russia, and Russia was the unseen opponent in what Rudyard Kipling called "the Great Game," Britain's continuing troubles in southern Asia, including the Afghan Wars of the 1870s.

Russia had also done much to weaken Turkey, the dominant power in southeastern Europe, in a war in 1877–78, and Britain was instrumental in arranging a peace settlement that included the loss of many of Turkey's European territories. Bulgaria became largely independent, its Christian population free from the "atrocities" attributed to the rulers of Muslim Turkey; Bosnia and Herzegovina remained officially part of the Turkish empire but were placed under Austro-Hungarian "administration." Other Balkan states — Serbia, Montenegro, and the rest — were similarly unstable, to the point that "the eastern question" was the accepted political name for the uncertainties of power in that whole region of Europe. In that area would begin the conflict that eventually became World War I and that resurfaced, little altered, in the 1990s.

The British tactic was to keep Russia and Austria in balance in the east, as it did with Germany and France in the west. But in the end neutrality proved impossible, as Britain came to recognize German expansionism as the central fact of European politics. By 1891 the population of Germany was 49 million, while France had 38 million, only slightly more than Britain. Bismarck tried in 1889 to bring Britain into the Triple Alliance, but solving the western question without the eastern — that is, holding France in check without protection against Russia as well — was inadequate, and the plan fell through. Eventually

Britain would instead find itself allied with France, and led the combat against Germany when European war came in 1914–18.

These were the principal countries of Europe in the 1890s:

- France had been Britain's historic enemy, against which the long Napoleonic wars (1798–1815) were fought. After those wars France had endured two monarchies, a republic and the Second Empire before the disaster of the Franco-Prussian War, 1870–71. Largely instigated by Germany's "iron chancellor," Otto von Bismarck (1815–98), that war saw the grim siege of Paris and eventually a humiliating treaty of peace under which the rich lands of Alsace and Lorraine were turned over to German control. The Third Republic, which followed, saw France much weakened, but still perceived as a threat by Germany, and also by Britain, especially where colonial claims came into conflict, as in Egypt. Harmony between Britain and France — the liberal powers of Europe, as distinguished from the conservative empires further east — grew only slowly. But numerous references to France in the Canon indicate the close cultural and commercial relations that inevitably existed between the two countries separated only by the narrow strip of water (twenty-one miles at the Strait of Dover) that is the English Channel.

- Germany came into existence in 1871 as a confederation of German-speaking states under the leadership of Prussia, whose king (Wilhelm I 1871–88; briefly Frederick; Wilhelm II 1888–1918) was also Emperor of Germany. The power lay with Bismarck, as chancellor, until his retirement in 1890. Germany at this period was the world's leading industrial nation, drawing on iron and coal resources and the growing chemical industry. At the same time it was developing a huge military machine with the barely disguised purposes of further damaging France in the west and extending its influence in the Balkan countries of southeast Europe.

- Italy was also a new country, a kingdom created in 1870 from a collection of variously ruled little states. Its king (Umberto I from 1878 to 1900) reigned over 30 million people, and had some territorial and naval pretensions; the treaty stolen in the Canonical tale titled "The Naval Treaty" was between Britain and Italy. Surrounded by Italy, but not part of it, was the Vatican State, an enclave in Rome ruled by a Pope who resented the loss of his temporal kingdom, the "Papal States," to a united Italy, and as a result refused to recognize the Italian king. Leo XIII, pope 1878–1903, appears to have consulted Sherlock Holmes professionally more than once.

- Austria-Hungary was a curious hybrid in southeastern Europe: a German-speaking empire and a Hungarian-speaking kingdom united under one ruler, Franz Joseph, who ruled Austria from 1848, added Hungary to his domain in 1867, and continued on the throne to 1916. Its population was some 45 million; its chief political interest was competing with Turkey for influence in the Balkan states. At the other side of the Austro-Hungarian Empire was the German-speaking province of Bohemia; the title "King of Bohemia," assigned in the story "A Scandal in Bohemia" to a flamboyant princeling named Wilhelm, in fact belonged to the Emperor.

- Turkey, or the Ottoman Empire, was the great Muslim power of the world, its domain extending over northwest Asia, Arabia including Mecca, and a corner of Africa, with a total population of 32 million people. A small corner remained of what had once been large Turkish territories in Europe. Abdul Hamid II, sultan 1876–1908, was noted for cleverness and cruelty, shown particularly to the non-Muslim populations of the empire, such as the Armenians (and, earlier, the Bulgarians). For despotism, corruption, and the gradual disintegration of the empire, Turkey became known as "the sick man of Europe." Britain found it difficult to support the sultan, even for the sake of holding Russia at bay, but Holmes was not above accepting a "commission" from him, mentioned in "The Blanched Soldier."

- Russia was a vast empire stretching over half of Europe, the plains where Napoléon's army had come to grief in 1812, and the full width of Asia as well. The Emperor or Czar (Alexander II ruled 1855–81, Alexander III 1881–94, Nicholas II 1894–1917) presided over a court at St. Petersburg with a strongly French flavour, but the population of some 109 million included 17 million Asians. From the 1860s the Russian government had been menaced by the revolutionary "Nihilist" movement, which was responsible for many violent incidents including the assassination of Alexander II in 1881, and paved the way for the Communist-led Russian Revolution of 1917. A Nihilist attempt on the life of military official Theodore Trepov at St. Petersburg in 1878 is echoed in Holmes's "summons to Odessa in the case of the Trepoff murder," mentioned in "A Scandal in Bohemia," and the plot of "The Golden Pince-Nez" draws on a Nihilist background. Meanwhile, Russia had external difficulties as well. While facing Germany, Austria-Hungary, and Turkey in the west, it also had to consider Japan in the east. When war in the Pacific came in 1904–05, Japan was easily victorious (the peace settlement was mediated by Theodore Roosevelt). There remained constant fear of a Russian menace in Europe, and for Britain there was also concern that Russia would menace its Indian territories to the south..

- The Netherlands and Belgium had been a single country until 1830, when a division took place: Belgium, largely Roman Catholic, becoming a kingdom in the southern districts (Leopold II reigned 1865–1909), and the Netherlands, with a Protestant majority, becoming a kingdom in the north (William III reigned 1849–90, Wilhelmina 1890–1948). Belgium had 6 million people, the Netherlands 5 million. Formerly a world power, and indeed a rival to Britain on the seas, the Netherlands maintained large colonies in the East Indies (including Sumatra, presumably the home of the giant rat) and elsewhere. As the Protestant country nearest England, the Netherlands ("Holland") had traditionally had a sizeable population of expatriate English, and close trade links with Britain.

- Norway, one of the two countries making up the peninsula called Scandinavia, had since 1814 been governed in a joint monarchy with its neighbour, Sweden. Oscar II (reigned 1872–1907) is mentioned as "the King of Scandinavia" in two Canonical adventures. Sweden had about 5 million people, Norway 2 million. In 1905 the union was dissolved and a Danish prince became King Haakon VII of an independent Norway. The third Scandinavian country, Denmark, had a population of 2 million; its king was Christian IX, the grand old man of European royalty (reigned 1863–1906).

Relations among these countries — as well as Spain (population 17 million, but much weakened by the loss of its colonies in the course of the nineteenth century) and other nations — were conducted through private diplomacy and secret treaties, of the kind reflected in "The Bruce-Partington Plans," "The Naval Treaty," and other Canonical tales. No country knew exactly what any other country was bound to do by its treaties with third and fourth countries, and diplomatic and military action could be highly arbitrary and dramatic in an age of autocratic governments not directly answerable to the public will. Individual relationships counted for much, not least the family connections formed as the children and grandchildren of Christian IX of Denmark and

Victoria of Britain married and intermarried. Wilhelm II of Germany, who would lead his country to war against Britain in 1914, was Victoria's grandson.

The geopolitics of Europe was the chief consideration for most of the powerful nations. Russia had to consider its Pacific rim, Germany had colonies in Africa, Belgium had the rubber-rich Congo, France had some overseas possessions, but the mother country and the security of borders was in each case the central concern. The case of Britain was more complicated: first because of its ties with the United States, second because of its island position (enabling it to think first of the seas while other nations had to think of land frontiers), and third because of its colonies scattered around the world, above all India.

INDIA. India (also including present-day Pakistan, Burma, Sri Lanka, and Bangladesh) is as large as Europe and had in the 1890s something like 288 million people, all under British rule in a bewildering variety of provinces, native states, princedoms, and other arrangements. The British presence in India had begun as a commercial venture, becoming military and governmental in the course of the eighteenth century. By Holmes's day power was wielded by a huge bureaucracy, headed in Calcutta by the Viceroy and Governor-General, in London by the officials of the India Office. There was also a large military presence. A number of British regiments had a presence in India, under a system by which one battalion of a regiment would be stationed abroad and the other at home in Britain for enlistment and training; on this principle one battalion of Watson's regiment, the Northumberland Fusiliers, was in the 1890s based near Rawalpindi. In addition there was a much larger Indian Army, made up of native soldiers though largely with British officers.

The great traumatic event in the history of British India was the Mutiny by some of the native soldiers, chiefly in Bengal, in the summer months of 1857. Set off by religious passions on top of a general discontent with the changes British rulers were making to Indian customs (a threat to the caste system, in particular), the Mutiny was the occasion for many dramatic incidents of the kind reflected in *The Sign of the Four* and "The Crooked Man," the most famous being the massacre at Cawnpore and the siege of Lucknow. Women as well as men had the opportunity to show heroism or to be butchered, or to experience horrors that were a familiar background for the early readers of the Canon. When order was restored there were ugly reprisals, followed by reforms in the government of the army and of India in general. In 1877 Victoria was proclaimed Empress of India, and gradually some self-government was introduced. (Full independence came in 1947, and the incidents of ninety years before are now sometimes called the First War of Independence.)

Every Victorian knew a good deal about India. Its principal cities (Madras, Bombay, Calcutta — now respectively called Chenai, Mumbai and Kolkata) were well-known names, and a staple of daily life was the tea that was India's most familiar export. Other Indian trade included wheat, rice, cotton, and opium. Tales of rajahs, tiger-shooting and fabulous gems were familiar, so much so that it seems a little odd that a landlady in "The Crooked Man" should have seen a rupee coin and identified it only as "a bad florin." India was a source of drama and colour for the British of the 1890s, and it is little wonder that it appears in the Canon as the source of swamp adders, cheetahs, cigars, and colonels.

WHO'S WHO

Notable people in Holmes's world ranged from Henry Edward (Cardinal) Manning, head of the Roman Catholic Church in England at a time when it was still under popular suspicion, to Beatrice Webb, young socialist agitator and writer who, with her husband Sidney, helped to found the London School of Economics. A modest selection of other names:

Grant Allen (1848–99) was a Canadian-born journalist, as well as an author of philosophy and some thirty novels, the most famous being *The Woman Who Did* (1895). This book shocked many readers with its depiction of a woman who, in protest against the subjection of her sex in conventional marriage, had a child with her lover. He was acquainted with Doyle, and persuaded him to write the final chapters of the novel *Hilda Wade*, then being serialized, when he realized he would not live to complete it.

Sabine Baring-Gould (1834–1924) was both the principal landlord (squire) and, from 1881 to his death, the rector at Lewtrenchard, Devon, as well as a prolific author and a collector of folk songs and other lore. The novel *The Moor* (1998) by Laurie R. King brings Holmes and his supposed wife, Mary Russell, to Devon for a visit with Baring-Gould. A grandson, William S. Baring-Gould, was a noted Sherlockian, whose *Sherlock Holmes of Baker Street* (1962) reconstructs Holmes's early years based in part on the eccentric upbringing of Sabine Baring-Gould, including much European travel.

Robert Barr (1850–1912) was an author with Scots and Canadian roots who by 1892 was well enough established in the English literary world to be co-founder (with Jerome K. Jerome) of *The Idler*. He was at least an acquaintance of Doyle, and wrote an interview profile in that magazine in 1894 which is an important source about the author's literary opinions and style of life at that period.

James M. Barrie (1860–1937), who became Sir James, is best known as the creator of Peter Pan. Like Doyle, he was originally Scots, and some of his important writings deal with village life in Scotland. He collaborated with Doyle on the comic opera "Jane Annie" (1893).

Henry Ward Beecher (1813–87) was the most prominent of the Protestant preachers who were important figures in American cultural and political life in the late nineteenth century. He used his oratory in support of the Union (the North) during the American Civil War, and subsequently became a fashionable Congregational pastor in Brooklyn. In 1874 a scandal and divorce case in which Beecher was cited as co-respondent tarnished his image but did not end his career; surely this incident was not the reason Watson admired Beecher, as "The Cardboard Box" indicates. Beecher's sister, **Harriet Beecher Stowe**, was author of *Uncle Tom's Cabin*.

Isambard Kingdom Brunel (1806–59) was the first of Britain's great engineers, constructing London's Paddington Station, near Baker Street, and much of the Great Western Railway as well as the colossal steamships *Great Eastern* and *Great Britain*.

Lewis Carroll was the penname of Charles Lutwidge Dodgson (1832–98), Oxford mathematician, and in his spare hours author of *Alice's Adventures in Wonderland* (1865) and *Through the Looking-Glass* (1871). Modern commentators have noted with raised eyebrows his hobby of taking photographs of little girls, sometimes unclad, including Alice Liddell, a colleague's daughter and the apparent original of his fictional Alice. Several novels by Roberta Rogow, beginning with *The Problem of the Spiteful Spiritualist* (1999), show Dodgson as a friend and collaborator of Holmes.

Joseph Chamberlain (1836–1914) was a shopkeeper's son who made a fortune in manufacturing and entered municipal politics. In a three-year term as mayor of Birmingham (a large Midland city, grown quickly on the proceeds of the textile industry), he built parks, roads, courts, markets, gas lines, sewers, and water pipes, adopting policies of activism unlike anything Britain had previously seen, including extensive slum clearance. He then became the first of the prominent "radicals" sent to Parliament from the Midlands, and served in important Cabinet posts in the Liberal governments of Gladstone and Balfour. Neville Chamberlain, prime minister in the 1930s, was his son.

Lord Randolph Churchill (1849–95) was a prominent Conservative politician and hot debater in the late 1870s and 1880s, briefly serving as leader of the House of Commons while the prime minister, Lord Salisbury, was in the House of Lords. (His own title was an honorary one, his father being the Duke of Marlborough.) His son **Winston Churchill** (1874–1965), who became Sir Winston, was a soldier and war correspondent in the 1890s, followed him into politics and served as prime minister and Britain's saviour in World War II.

Charles Darwin (1809–82) developed his theory of "evolution through natural selection" as the result of observations, most famously in the Galapagos Islands, during the voyage of the *Beagle* in the early 1830s. *The Origin of Species* (1859), followed by *The Descent of Man* (1871), dealt with physical evolution; their author can hardly be blamed for the "social Darwinism" developed by enthusiasts to justify unrestrained competition, regressive politics, even racism. The belief that Christianity opposed Darwinism is largely untrue for Britain, where religious leaders accepted Darwin's theories within a generation.

Benjamin Disraeli (1804–81), who became Lord Beaconsfield, was a novelist and orator who made a mark as politician and prime minister through flamboyant style as well as reformist policies and adroit diplomacy. Although a Conservative, he was no Tory, believing rather in a traditional England in which all classes would share the benefits. And he was an enthusiastic supporter of the monarchy, as well as a genius at flattering the elderly Victoria and attracting her endorsement and affection.

Charles Dickens (1812–70) was Britain's greatest novelist, the master of satire and emotion-wrenching language. *David Copperfield* and *Oliver Twist* draw on his own wretched boyhood, while other works demonstrate the range of his genius — *A Tale of Two Cities* is about the French revolution, and *A Christmas Carol* is virtually a morality play. All English novelists are influenced by Dickens's candid portraiture, though many, including Doyle, have revolted from his undisciplined wordiness. Dickens left unfinished *The Mystery of Edwin Drood*, an excellent puzzle that has attracted many Sherlockian speculations.

Charles Dilke (1843–1911), who became Sir Charles, was a prominent figure in the "radical" wing of the Liberal party who could well have become prime minister, leading his party from strength to strength and changing the course of history, had he not been accused in 1885 of dalliance in the bed of young Virginia Crawford. The resulting scandal and divorce case destroyed his career.

Edward, Prince of Wales (1841–1910), originally Albert Edward ("Bertie" to intimates), later King Edward VII (reigned 1901–10), was the oldest son of Queen Victoria. Although he became a dignified, popular, and successful king, particularly effective as "Edward the Peacemaker" in managing the squabbles among European nations, his reputation as Prince of Wales (heir to the throne) was for spendthrift luxury, gambling, and womanizing. Occasionally, as in the Tranby Croft gambling scandal of 1891, he came close to serious trouble.

His most prominent mistress was **Lillie Langtry**, "the Jersey Lily"; there were numerous others, probably including the sensational actress **Sarah Bernhardt** (1845–1923). As the host *par excellence* of weekend house parties, he also had many opportunities for dalliance with society ladies. The Prince has been seen as the "illustrious client" who employs Holmes in the story of that title, and his style is well reflected also in the events of "A Scandal in Bohemia."

Sigmund Freud (1856–1939), a physician in Vienna, became the founder of psychoanalysis, which he maintained was an entirely scientific technique for understanding and changing feelings and behaviour. Freud in fact was as much artist as scientist, basing his theories on only a small number of patients. He treated them in the 1880s; *Studies in Hysteria* was published in 1895, to be followed by more speculative works such as *Totem and Taboo* (1913). "In a little-read memoir by Freud's most famous patient — the Wolf Man — we discover," writes psychologist and novelist Frank Tallis, "that Freud was a great fan of Sherlock Holmes and read Conan Doyle with as much careful consideration as he did Dostoevsky." The Freudian ideas that are now part of general knowledge, such as phallic symbolism and the "Oedipus complex," acquired their influence somewhat after Holmes's day. Nicholas Meyer's *The Seven-Per-Cent Solution* (1974) famously brings Holmes face-to-face with Freud, who treats him for cocaine addiction.

William Schwenck Gilbert (1836–1911), who became Sir William, was a dramatic and comic writer whose chief works are the operettas on which he collaborated with **Arthur Sullivan** (1842–1900), who became Sir Arthur. Gilbert wrote the comic, and often satiric, verse and largely devised the plots; Sullivan composed the music (he also achieved some distinction with more serious choral music, operas and even hymns). There were thirteen Gilbert and Sullivan operettas, from *Trial by Jury* (1875) to *The Grand Duke* (1896), with *H. M. S. Pinafore*, *The Pirates of Penzance*, and *The Mikado* the best known, *The Yeomen of the Guard* probably the finest.

William Ewart Gladstone (1809–98) was known as "the Grand Old Man" by the end of his long career as leader of the Liberal Party, and prime minister four times. The social reforms introduced by his first government were not equalled by any later accomplishments, and he was eventually trapped in the quagmire of Irish Home Rule, which he could not get Parliament to approve. One reference work describes Gladstone as "a good classical scholar and an earnest high churchman." His moral uprightness, coupled with personal quirks, gave him a keen interest in the rehabilitation of prostitutes, and he sometimes walked London's streets himself, seeking soiled doves to rescue.

Charles George Gordon (1833–85) served in the army in several parts of the Empire, earning the nickname "Chinese" for his role in suppressing a rebellion in China, and in the 1870s went to Egypt as a colonial governor having reached the rank of major-general. In 1885 he arrived at Khartoum, Sudan, in the course of dealing with another rebellion, this one more substantial, and was killed by the forces of the Mahdi, predecessor of the charismatic Khalifa. His death outraged Britain and made an impression on Dr. Watson, who subsequently displayed his portrait in the Baker Street rooms.

William Gilbert Grace (1848–1915) was the greatest cricket player of all time, as well as a physician. His broad figure and flamboyant beard attracted attention to his skill with the bat (126 times in his career he scored a "century," one hundred runs or more in a match) and he was a hero to children and sportsmen alike, reputedly the best-known man in England in 1895.

Oliver Wendell Holmes (1809–94) was a medical professor at Harvard University for most of his life, and the author of such humane volumes as *The Autocrat of the Breakfast-Table* (1858) and its sequels, as well as poetry and novels. He was much admired by Doyle, who visited his fresh grave when he came to Boston late in 1894, and repeatedly praised him in his writings about literature. Whether he took the genial doctor's surname for that of his great detective seems an unanswerable question. The doctor's son, **Oliver Wendell Holmes Jr.** (1841–1935), became a justice of the United States Supreme Court.

Ernest William Hornung (1866–1921) was a novelist who became Doyle's brother-in-law. Hornung dedicated his book *The Amateur Cracksman* (1899), in which he introduced the "gentleman burglar" A.J. Raffles, "To A.C.D. — this form of flattery."

Harry Houdini (1873–1926), real name Ehrich Weiss, was an American escape artist and conjurer whose flamboyance made him world famous. Having flirted with spiritualism, he chose to devote his energy to exposing fraudulent mediums, of whom there were many; his friendship with Doyle dissolved because of their differences on this issue.

Henry Irving (1838–1905), who became Sir Henry, original name John Henry Brodribb, was a prominent actor who reached fame in *The Bells* in 1871–72 and went on to be the best-known Shakespearean leading man of his period, often playing opposite **Ellen Terry** (1847–1928) at the popular Lyceum Theatre in London. In 1894 Irving performed in Doyle's play "Waterloo" as half of a double bill with a revival of "The Bells"; he played it again from time to time until his 1905 retirement. Irving's secretary was **Bram Stoker** (1847–1912), the author of *Dracula* (1897), a classic novel about vampirism in eastern Europe, Yorkshire and London.

Jerome K. Jerome (1859–1927) was an actor and humourist whose most enduring work is *Three Men in a Boat* (1889). In 1892 he was part of the small group that founded the literary magazine *The Idler*. Jerome was a good friend of Doyle, having courted his sister Connie and shared many literary conversations with him.

Rudyard Kipling (1865–1936) is the poet of Empire, although also well known for children's stories, most importantly *The Jungle Book* (1894). His "Recessional" was published in *The Times* June 22, 1897, the day of Queen Victoria's diamond jubilee, and was hailed by some as the greatest poem in English:

> God of our fathers, known of old,
> Lord of our far-flung battle-line,
> Beneath whose awful Hand we hold
> Dominion over palm and pine —
> Lord God of Hosts, be with us yet,
> Lest we forget — lest we forget!

These sentiments are less jingoistic than they at first appear. But there was a ruthless, even sadistic, tone to Kipling's work, and his patriotism and vulgarity went out of fashion. Doyle visited Kipling in 1894 while the latter was living in Vermont.

William Morris (1834–96) was an artist, designer, writer and socialist thinker, influenced by, but not precisely part of, the Pre-Raphaelite group of artists (his wife, Jane, conducted a long affair with Dante Gabriel Rossetti). He famously designed the Red House south of London ("the home of the Arts and Crafts Movement"), invented the piece of furniture still called a Morris chair, and operated the Kelmscott Press, all in the interest of melding industrious craftsmanship with a mediaeval aesthetic. Morris's name is borrowed as an alias for Duncan Ross in "The Red-Headed League."

Charles Stewart Parnell (1846–91) was a leader of the movement for Irish Home Rule both in Parliament (where he converted Gladstone to the cause) and outside it (inventing the tactic of boycotts, and organizing other forms of pressure). His public career was ruined in 1890 when his private life became an issue for the courts: he had been living for some years with Kitty O'Shea, with whom he had three children, and finally the lady's husband sought a divorce and created a scandal.

Robert Cecil, third **Marquess of Salisbury** (1830–1903), was the last prime minister to be a member of the House of Lords rather than of the Commons. He held that office for some fourteen years, and for much of the time was his own foreign secretary as well, his interests being more in diplomacy than in domestic affairs. Lord Bellinger of "The Second Stain" is in large part a portrait of Salisbury.

Charles Spurgeon (1834–92) was a hugely popular preacher and prolific writer in the Baptist tradition, whose Metropolitan Tabernacle at Southwark, south London, is seen as the prototype of modern megachurches. Wayne Wall in *God and Sherlock Holmes* (1984) has Spurgeon converting Holmes to Christianity.

William T. Stead (1849–1912) was a crusading journalist, most famous for his editorship of the *Pall Mall Gazette* 1883–89. In order to expose the evils of white slavery and child prostitution, he actually arranged the purchase of a thirteen-year-old girl, subsequently reporting on the events in a series titled "The Maiden Tribute of Modern Babylon." In later life he became an exponent of spiritualism. He died in the sinking of *R. M. S. Titanic* April 14–15, 1912.

Leslie Stephen (1832–1904), who became Sir Leslie, was a prominent writer, editor, and biographer. He edited the *Cornhill* magazine (which would later publish some of Doyle's early fiction) in the 1870s, and was creator and editor of the *Dictionary of National Biography*, a landmark of British historical scholarship and self-consciousness, in the following decade. His wife, Harriet, was the daughter of the novelist **William Makepeace Thackeray** (1811–63). His daughter was feminist author **Virginia Woolf** (1882–1941).

Alfred Tennyson (1809–92), who became Lord Tennyson, was the leading poet of the Victorian period. His work first appeared in the 1830s, and in 1850 he became Poet Laureate, an honour that obliged him to write verses for national occasions. His *Idylls of the King*, blank-verse poems of the Arthurian age, which began appearing in 1859, express the nobility of the Victorian age as well. They were much admired by Queen Victoria and Albert, the Prince Consort. Other important works include "Locksley Hall" and "In Memoriam."

Victoria (born May 24, 1819, died January 22, 1901), became Queen on the death of her uncle, William IV. She wore the crown longer than any other British sovereign and gave her name to an age that lasted from the end of the Napoleonic wars in 1815 until the opening of World War I in 1914. Social and economic changes during her reign were accompanied by the development of a constitutional monarchy, made possible by her long stable reign and frequently wise interventions in public affairs. She was stubborn, eccentric, and middle-class in habit, but well aware of her role as mother of her far-flung peoples. She came to be much loved (and by Sherlockians is frequently alluded to as "A Certain Gracious Lady," a phrase borrowed from "The Bruce-Partington Plans"). Through the royal marriages of her nine children, Victoria was also mother of most of Europe's rulers. **Albert** (1819–61), prince of Saxe-Coburg and Gotha, became Prince Consort when he married Victoria in 1840. He took a keen interest in promoting industry and culture, his works including the Exhibition of 1851 with its "Crystal Palace." The Queen never recovered from his death, living in seclusion as "the Widow of Windsor" for most of her last four decades. A Golden Jubilee in 1887 and Diamond Jubilee in 1897 celebrated the fiftieth and sixtieth anniversaries of her accession to the throne on June 20, 1837.

Herbert George Wells (1866–1946) was a struggling teacher, an undoctrinaire socialist, and the author of a vast body of literature, much of it classifiable as science fiction, including *The War of the Worlds* (1898). He also wrote social commentary and the very successful (and weighty) *Outline of History* (1920).

Oscar Wilde (1854–1900) was an Irish-born author who emerged from youthful "aesthetic" posturing to win critical success with plays such as "The Importance of Being Earnest" (1895). His one novel was *The Picture of Dorian Gray* (1890), written as the result of a meal with American publisher J.B. Stoddart that also produced *The Sign of the Four*. Wilde, who was bisexual, conducted a passionate friendship with **Lord Alfred Douglas** (1870–1945), son of the Marquess of Queensberry, leading to a scandal that destroyed the writer. Wilde served two years (1895–97) in prison for violating a clause prohibiting "gross indecency" that had been enacted, almost by accident, in the Criminal Law Amendment Act of 1885.

VI

CRIME AND PUNISHMENT

AS A DETECTIVE, SHERLOCK HOLMES seeks to solve mysteries, which for the most part involve crimes. (A few of the stories present exceptions, puzzles in which no crime has been committed, although it is not always clear until the mystery is cleared up that that is so.) He traces the event to its origin and brings a malefactor to justice.

But of course "justice" is a philosophical, even theological, idea, distinct from "law" as it is, at the other extreme, distinct from revenge. Sherlock Holmes takes pains in more than one story to make clear that he is neither a police agent nor in any sense an officer of the law; on several occasions he lets malefactors go free either because their deeds were justifiable or because, as in "The Blue Carbuncle," pity takes precedence. In "The Abbey Grange" he constitutes himself judge, and appoints Watson jury, to make the acquittal orderly. In "The Blue Carbuncle" he simply flings the door open and throws the criminal out. "I suppose that I am commuting a felony," he tells Watson, "but it is just possible that I am saving a soul." That too is justice.

The earliest forms of law, barely holding private vengeance in check, prescribed terrible punishments for crimes and what would now be called torts. The principle of "an eye for an eye and a tooth for a tooth," associated with the ancient Hebrews, was intended to limit the penalties that could be extracted, and even that stern *lex talionis* has been much limited not only by the mild teachings of Jesus of Nazareth (and the rabbis before him) but by subsequent legal codes. Although the death penalty applied to dozens of crimes in Victorian Britain, it was relatively rarely imposed, as juries refused to convict in cases where hanging seemed disproportionate. More important, however, is the principle that the punishment for crime was being imposed according to written laws, and by an impartial state rather than by representatives of the victim. Such was the system of law under which Holmes, his clients, and the criminals he pursued all lived.

BRITISH LAW

Underlying the specific "laws" or Acts passed by Parliament, and the "by-laws" of cities, was and is a great body of "common law." The term means law in the form of traditions and court judgements (precedents) dating back to the year 1189, and still in use not only in Britain but in the United States, most of Canada, and many other lands. The best-known use of the phrase is in "common-law marriage," the principle that a partner has the rights of a spouse because of cohabitation rather than a marriage certificate. Sherlockians may be less aware of common-law property rights, which for example give a creator some control over invented characters, quite apart from copyright. Similarly there are the common-law rights of way over which old Frankland, in *The Hound of the Baskervilles*, loved to dispute:

> Sometimes he will shut up a right of way and defy the parish
> to make him open it. At others he will with his own hands tear
> down some other man's gate and declare that a path has existed
> there from time immemorial, defying the owner to prosecute him
> for trespass. He is learned in old manorial and communal rights.

Other aspects of the common law deal with contracts and commercial transactions; inheritances; "torts" or personal wrongs such as slander or trespass; civil rights ("an Englishman's home is his castle"); and crime. The common law changes only gradually, through court rulings on specific cases, unless Parliament intervenes. In one example of abrupt change, the ancient distinction between two classes of crime, "felonies" and "misdemeanours," was abolished in 1967 in Britain. Holmes is said (in *A Study in Scarlet*) to have "a good practical knowledge of British law," but he surely did not have time to rival the knowledge of a solicitor (a lawyer who advises a client) or a barrister (one who, having been "briefed" by a solicitor, conducts a case in court). His knowledge was "practical" for the purposes of a detective.

British legal procedure, satirized in Charles Dickens's novels in the middle of the nineteenth century, was being gradually reformed by Holmes's day, although even now the system remains complicated, especially in civil law (matters concerned with contracts or private lawsuits rather than with crime). As a detective Holmes was more concerned with the disposition of accused criminals, who usually came, except in London, to a Justice of the Peace. Minor matters would be handled there; more serious cases would be referred to the "quarter sessions," more formal proceedings under a panel of JP's, or to the Assizes, court sessions held in the chief town of each county. In London, accused criminals came first to a police-court, such as the one at Bow Street, and matters too serious for disposition there would go to the Central Criminal Court at the "Old Bailey," established in 1834.

Its sentences were final, as there was no court of criminal appeal until 1907, when such a body was created, largely because of pressure from Doyle after his investigation of the George Edalji case. In Holmes's day, the verdict of a court could be put immediately into effect, a convicted criminal being carried off to prison. The chief prisons in London were Newgate (the old horror near the Old Bailey), Pentonville, Wandsworth, and Wormwood Scrubs. Elsewhere, there were important prisons at Portsmouth, Portland, and several other places, including the most famous of them all, Dartmoor Prison near Princetown, Devon, built in 1809 for French prisoners of war, which plays an important role in *The Hound of the Baskervilles*. There were also many local prisons, including Reading Gaol, made famous by Oscar Wilde's "Ballad" about his imprisonment there (1895–97). Prison treatment was, by twentieth-century standards, desperately cruel, depending on isolation, boredom, and (frequently) hard labour, to say nothing of deliberate tortures such as whipping or the treadmill which could be part of a man's sentence. The convict uniform made of coarse cloth stamped with the government's "broad arrow" is familiar to readers of the Canon from a Sidney Paget drawing of Jack Prendergast in "The 'Gloria Scott'." Women convicts were sent to Holloway, in London. The criminally insane could be imprisoned at Broadmoor, in Berkshire. Executions (by hanging) took place inside the prisons; public hanging at Tyburn Tree, where London's Marble Arch now stands, had been abolished in 1783, and the last public execution anywhere in London was in 1868.

POLICING AND DETECTION

Police officers are persons who enforce public order. They are usually paid by the government (although there can also be private police, such as the Coal and Iron Police who figure in *The Valley of Fear*), and their character varies with that of the authority they serve. The police in a dictatorship, or "police state," can be cruel, partial, and arbitrary, as the narrative in "The Golden Pince-Nez" suggests. In a relatively free country, such as Britain, the police generally act according to accepted rules of law and decency. There may be individual instances of corruption or brutality, and of course the police cannot do much to make the law they enforce more enlightened than legislators have decreed, but there is a strong tradition of fairness and independence. No one, not even the authorities responsible for prosecuting an alleged criminal, can tell the police what lines of inquiry to pursue or what to overlook when a crime appears to have been committed. British police are under the guidance of government authorities — the county councils, or in the case of London's police the Home Secretary, one of the senior members of the central government. But legislation and tradition give local police officials, and even individual constables, both the right and the duty to proceed as seems best to them. Policing is independent of prosecution — the arm of the government which argues the case against alleged offenders in court — and that in turn is independent of the judges and the prisons. Individuals are traditionally protected against police mistreatment by, among other things, the Judges' Rules, a codification of longstanding prohibitions against torture, trickery, and other improper ways of obtaining evidence. As Britain moves toward a society where ever more is codified, the Judges' Rules were replaced in 1984 by the Police and Criminal Evidence Act, with largely the same provisions.

SCOTLAND YARD. Police headquarters in London has been called "Scotland Yard" since 1829, when the newly established Metropolitan Police built its headquarters in a little street by that name, just off Whitehall. In 1890 the police moved to a nearby site which immediately became "New Scotland Yard." Headquarters was moved again in 1967 (to a nearby street called Broadway), and the building that was Scotland Yard in Holmes's day is now the Norman Shaw Building, still housing police offices.

Policing in London long predates 1829, but consisted chiefly of local constables and "thief-takers," criminals themselves who would finger their associates for money. The Bow Street Runners, created in the middle of the eighteenth century, were the first uniformed force, attached to one busy police court. The Police Act of 1829, creating a Metropolitan Police under the central government's auspices, was the work of Robert Peel, then Home Secretary and later to be prime minister; in his honour constables became known as "Peelers" and later "Bobbies." They were outfitted in understated uniforms, to emphasize

191

their civilian rather than military character, and equipped with truncheons and rattles (replaced by whistles, after earlier experiments, in 1886. London constables did not carry firearms in Holmes's day, and most still do not; police guns were brought out only in case of need, as for the notorious Sidney Street shoot out in 1911. A volume of *General Instruction for the Police*, issued in the early months of the force, remains the basis for its work today. For historical reasons, the Metropolitan Police do not have jurisdiction in the old City of London. It has its own force, which figures in the Canon only once, in "The Stockbroker's Clerk."

Most police work was — and remains — the tedious duty of patrolling the streets, preventing crime rather than investigating offences. But by about 1840 there were officers assigned to the duty of watching "habitual criminals," and in 1842 a Detective Branch was created, with two inspectors and half a dozen sergeants. It took the name Criminal Investigation Department — CID — in 1878, and was the parent of the later anti-terrorist Special Branch and of the famous Flying Squad ("the Sweeney," as in "Sweeney Todd"). Jack Tracy in the *Encyclopaedia Sherlockiana* sums up the workings of the CID as it figures in the Holmes tales:

> Plain-clothes detectives are distributed throughout the divisions ... as well as assigned to the central office at Scotland Yard. The headquarters staff investigate cases of an imperial or national character ...; and cases in which inquiries may have to be pursued in several districts ... or otherwise can best be handled by them ..., including those referred from provincial forces ... or foreign ones ...; and often those involving special investigative expertise, such as murder cases....
>
> While the C.I.D. has no jurisdiction beyond the Metropolitan Police District, upon occasion it may be called upon by the Chief Constable of provincial forces who wish to avail themselves of the Yard's experience and resources in the investigation of certain cases. Such instances are rare and usually involve murder....
>
> The Metropolitan Police Act of 1839 permits the hiring of official police personnel by private firms or individuals, for private purposes, provided the entire cost of the policeman's maintenance is borne.

The Metropolitan Police are headed by a Commissioner. Occupants of that office during Holmes's era were Sir Edmund Henderson (1869–86), Sir Charles Warren (1886–88), James Monro (1888–90), and Sir Edward Bradford (1890–1903), none of them professional police officers.

Many histories of Scotland Yard have been written, including *The Official History of the Metropolitan Police* (2004) by Gary Mason and *Bloody Business* (1992) by H. Paul Jeffers. *The King's Peace* (1895) by F.A. Inderwick remains a classic. Several volumes deal with the pioneering work of Sir Bernard Spilsbury (1877–1947) in forensic pathology, though it came too late to illuminate Holmes's career.

Most of the police with whom Sherlock Holmes came in contact were from the CID, although he also encountered Metropolitan Police constables (such as the luckless John Rance in *A Study in Scarlet*) and representatives of other forces, from the county constabulary in Berkshire, Kent, Hallamshire, and elsewhere to the police in such foreign cities as New York and Cleveland. Most prominent of the Scotland Yard detectives in the Canon is Lestrade (initial G., first name not known), who appears in some fifteen cases and is praised by Holmes as "the pick of a bad lot," for the Baker Street opinion of the professionals was not high. From *A Study in Scarlet* to "The Three Garridebs," he is seen, sometimes consulting Holmes voluntarily (or under pressure to wrap up a case that is baffling him), sometimes being summoned when Holmes needs the resources of the official force or has a criminal to hand over. Second to Lestrade stands Tobias Gregson, who also receives praise from Holmes ("the smartest of the Scotland Yarders") and turns up in five cases. Other CID men in the Canon include Athelney Jones, Gregory, Merivale *et al.* They are generally pictured as well-meaning and energetic, but unimaginative, hence contemptuous of Holmes's theorizing and unorthodox methods.

VICTORIAN CRIME. The police of the nineteenth century struggled to control petty theft (in an era when coins were virtually the only money) and drunken violence, and although proof is near impossible, it seems clear that England, London in particular, became more orderly through the early decades of organized policing. At times the police were also involved in maintaining order against political demonstrations, the most dramatic case being the battle in Trafalgar Square on "Bloody Sunday," November 13, 1887, against a vaguely socialist mob. More interesting to the modern reader than routine police work are the occasional dramatic cases, often of murder, with which the police dealt. A few examples:

- Poisonings in 1856 attributed to Dr. William Palmer of Rugeley. He was hanged for one of them, never tried for the other deaths including that of his wife. Then in 1865 came the poisonings of a wife and mother-in-law by Dr. Edward William Pritchard of Glasgow. Holmes refers to both cases in "The Speckled Band."
- The arrest of Arthur Orton, unsuccessful claimant to the Tichborne fortune, in 1866.
- A murder (1876) and a long series of burglaries committed by a clever little man described by Holmes as "my old friend Charlie Peace." As Peace was hanged in 1879, Holmes must be referring to his reading in criminal literature rather than to a personal encounter.
- The 1876 theft of a portrait of the Duchess of Devonshire by the real-life "Napoleon of Crime," Adam Worth.
- Arrests beginning in 1886 in connection with a male brothel in Cleveland Street, London, where some of the patrons had close connections with aristocracy and royalty.
- A series of strychnine poisonings of women committed by Neill Cream, hanged in 1892.
- The imprisonment of Adolf Beck for fraud in 1896; he was released in 1901 when it became clear that there had been a case of mistaken identity. He was prosecuted again in 1904 but eventually let go.

Continental (and American) crime was also of interest to Holmes. Remarkably, there is no record that he was involved with the murder-suicide of Crown Prince Rudolf of Austria and his mistress, Mary Vetsera, at Meyerling on January 30, 1889, although it is noteworthy that another member of central European royalty, the King of Bohemia, appeared at his Baker Street door only six weeks later. Holmes missed another memorable foreign case, being in Tibet, or perhaps Mecca, while Lizzie Borden was being tried for the August 4, 1892, murders of her father and stepmother in Fall River, Massachusetts (she was acquitted). It is a pity that the theft of the "Mona Lisa" from the Louvre came too late (August 22, 1911) for his professional attention — although Sherlockian authors have been unable to resist making use of it, including John Gardner in *The Revenge of Moriarty* (1981) and, remarkably, the script writers for the Jeremy Brett version of "The Red-Headed League" (1985). The theft of the Irish Crown Jewels from Dublin Castle in July 1907 is also outside the chronological purview of the Canon.

JACK THE RIPPER. Most dramatic of all Victorian crime stories is that of Jack the Ripper. Unlike other monsters of popular culture, the Ripper did exist, though no one was ever identified as the monster ("Saucy Jack," he called himself in one taunting letter to the police) or charged with the killings attributed to him in London in 1888. Five victims — all prostitutes in the East End of London — are definitely considered the Ripper's work:

- Mary Ann (Polly) Nichols — Bucks Row, August 31.
- Eliza Ann Chapman — Hanbury Street, September 8.
- Elizabeth Stride — Berner Street, September 30.
- Catharine Eddowes — Mitre Square, September 30.
- Mary Jeannette Kelly — Dorset Street, November 9.

Several other cases (notably the August 7 murder of Martha Tabram, or Turner, in George Yard Buildings) are sometimes associated with the Ripper, but do not entirely fit the pattern, which included gruesome and increasingly elaborate disembowelling.

Several features of the Ripper case are peculiarly interesting:

- The taunting letters to the police and the press, including one signed "Jack the Ripper" (origin of the enduring name), and one in which the author claimed to have eaten part of the kidney of one victim.
- A chalked message, "The Juwes are not the men who will be blamed for nothing," erased by police commissioner Sir Charles Warren because it might lead to violence against the large Jewish population in the East End. Some later analysts have seen a Masonic meaning in this message and in the details of the atrocities.
- Incompetent police work, under Warren's direction, and general hysteria from the population, leading to many false arrests.
- A plethora of suggestions about the killer's identity, from Prince Albert Victor, Duke of Clarence (who, however, was in Scotland at the time of some of the killings) to barrister Montague John Druitt. The most plausible suggestions involve not celebrities but local residents, such as "Kosminski, a Polish Jew," referred to in contemporary police files.

For the literal-minded Sherlockian, the important question is why Holmes did not solve the Ripper case. Several parodies and films have him doing so, notably *A Study in Terror* (film 1966; novel by Ellery Queen, published in England as *Sherlock Holmes Versus Jack the Ripper*, the same year) and "Murder by Decree" (film 1979). More recent efforts of this kind include *The Whitechapel*

Horrors (1992), a novel by C. Douglas Baker, and *Chapel Noir* (2001) and *Castle Rouge* (2002) by Carole Nelson Douglas. Adrian Nebbett maintains an online bibliography of connections between Holmes and the Ripper (*www.sherlockian.net/england/ripper.html*). The *Baker Street Journal* published a "Ninetieth Anniversary Jack the Ripper Memorial Issue" in 1978, with a number of articles dealing with aspects of the case from a Sherlockian viewpoint, and *Canadian Holmes* had a similar issue in 1988. Other such articles have appeared from time to time. Perhaps inevitably, a computer game, "Sherlock Holmes vs. Jack the Ripper," appeared in 2009.

Devotees provide a market for an unending stream of books about the Ripper case. Among the most useful ones are the classic *The Ripper File* (1975) by Elwyn Jones and John Lloyd; *Jack the Ripper: A Bibliography and Review of the Literature*, by Alexander Kelly (1984); *The Ultimate Jack the Ripper Companion* (2000) by Stewart P. Evans and Keith Skinner; *Portrait of a Killer* (2002) by Patricia Cornwell; *Jack the Ripper, the Definitive History* (2004) by Paul Begg; and *Jack the Ripper: Scotland Yard Investigates* (2006) by Stewart P. Evans and Donald Rumbelow.

FORENSIC SCIENCES. Holmes insisted that his detective work was "scientific," and indeed he is first glimpsed in the pathology laboratory at St. Bartholomew's Hospital, working on a chemical test for bloodstains. "It is the most practical medico-legal discovery for years," he declares — this in a story published in 1887 and supposed to have taken place in 1881. Later he is seen examining metal filings through a microscope as part of one investigation, testing some liquid with litmus-paper in another, and comparing the idiosyncrasies of typewriters, to say nothing of his work with tobacco ashes, footprints, bicycle tires, and anything else that might be examined through a high-powered lens. Meanwhile, not until the 1930s did the Metropolitan Police set up a laboratory, although the police did rely on the borrowed assistance of outside experts for some years before that. Ballistic evidence (the examination of bullets to identify the gun that fired them) came into use in the 1920s.

Of course the most familiar aspect of forensic science (the application of science to legal and police matters) is fingerprinting. It is reflected in the Canon in several references to "thumb-prints," particularly in "The Norwood Builder," where Lestrade over-casually asks Holmes, "You are aware that no two thumb-marks are alike?" He intends to use a bloody print — faked, it later proves — as evidence against Holmes's client. If the story took place in or about 1895, this reference is a slight anachronism; when it was published in 1903, fingerprinting was still novel in Britain. (Its public acceptance followed the dramatic 1905 conviction of the Stratton brothers for a pair of brutal murders.) But the technique had been used elsewhere for decades: it was first introduced in India by Sir William Herschel as a means of proving identity in a largely illiterate society, and had been introduced for law enforcement in the United States in the 1880s. (Mark Twain's *Pudd'nhead Wilson*, 1894, takes the uniqueness of fingerprints for granted.) A Home Office committee struck in 1899 heard about fingerprinting from Herschel's successor in Bengal, Sir Edward Henry. Not only was the system adopted, but Henry was brought home to introduce it, as assistant commissioner of the Metropolitan Police in charge of the CID.

Although modern methods involve lasers and photography, the classic fingerprinting techniques are straightforward: fine powder is scattered across a fingerprint found at the scene of a crime (a black powder such as lampblack for light surfaces, a light powder such as flour for dark surfaces). The print can then be lifted up with transparent sticky tape, and kept for comparison with known prints that have been collected from suspects using a stamp-pad, or filed at police headquarters from previous crimes.

Fingerprinting replaced the earlier technology of "Bertillonnage," or body measurement, developed by the French forensic scientist Alphonse Bertillon. His ingenious idea, which in turn replaced mere verbal descriptions, was first used in France, and adopted at Scotland Yard and British prisons in the 1880s, as Sir Basil Thomson, records:

> The measurements were the length and breadth of the skull, the length of the foot and the cubit, the length of the middle finger. He distributed them as belonging to one or other of three equally numerous classes — small, medium, and large. Each of these primary headings is successively subdivided according to height, span, length and breadth of the ear, height of the bust, and colour of the eyes, this last providing seven divisions.

Although Holmes in "The Naval Treaty" expresses "enthusiastic admiration" for Bertillon, the system was imperfect in practice. As Thomson also notes, "One prison warder would press the caliper closer home than another, and one mistake of this kind threw the system out of gear." There is the further complication that, for example, a tall man is likely to have long feet and fingers. Holmes paid close attention to body shape and measurement (especially, as in "The Cardboard Box," to ears) but, as Steven Jackson noted in the *Sherlock*

Holmes Journal in 1996, if he flirted with Bertillonage in his early years, he became disillusioned. Certainly in *The Hound of the Baskervilles* he had little patience for Dr. Mortimer's suggestion that he ranked as "the second highest expert in Europe" behind Bertillon.

DETECTIVE STORIES

In the words of P.D. James, who ought to know, detective stories are about "the restoration of order out of disorder." More obviously, detective stories are about a detective, someone attempting to identify (and, usually, capture) a criminal. The limits of the genre are not absolutely clear, for all the vast analysis they have received. David Skene Melvin and Ann Skene Melvin compiled a bibliography of such analysis in 1980 — not a bibliography of detective stories themselves, only of the secondary writings about them — and gave it the long but descriptive title *Crime, Detective, Espionage, Mystery, and Thriller Fiction and Film: A Comprehensive Bibliography of Critical Writing through 1979.* Obviously there is much to be said, and scholars and enthusiasts have continued to say it in the ensuing three decades.

PRECURSORS OF SHERLOCK HOLMES. Doyle did not invent the detective story, though he did much to define its form. A number of earlier authors not only anticipated his work, but influenced it. "The puzzle is vital to the detective story but is not a detective story in itself," writes Julian Symons in *Bloody Murder: From the Detective Story to the Crime Novel* (1972), denying that — for example — the Biblical book of *Susanna and the Elders* is a detective story. On the other hand, he continues, not all crime literature can be called detective stories. (One thinks of the "sensational literature" with which Holmes was said to be familiar: writings about real crimes and criminals, however fancifully recorded, as in Henry Fielding's biography of the eighteenth-century master thief Jonathan Wild, or the *Newgate Calendar*, issued in its definitive five-volume form in 1774.) Says Symons: "The characteristic note of crime literature is first struck in *Caleb Williams* by William Godwin (1756–1836), which appeared in 1794."

In the work of Edgar Allan Poe (1809–49), detective stories are of small importance compared to other kinds of horror. But they figure large in the history of crime fiction, and Poe may even be said to have written the first detective story (in 1841). Three of his tales present the work of a Parisian reasoner, C. Auguste Dupin: "The Murders in the rue Morgue," a "locked-room" mystery in which particularly bloody killings are found to be the work of a wild beast; "The Mystery of Marie Roget," based on the actual murder of Mary Rogers in New York in 1841; and "The Purloined Letter," where the brilliantly simple principle is that the safest place to hide an object is in plain sight. Two other Poe stories are also recognizable as detective tales — "The Gold Bug," which offers a cipher suggestive of that in "The Dancing Men," and "Thou Art the Man," a murder story about guilt and vengeance.

Doyle always acknowledged a great debt to Poe, and called him "the world's supreme short story writer." "Mental acuteness," he wrote, "is the one quality which can be ascribed to the ideal detective, and when that has once been admirably done, succeeding writers must necessarily be content for all time to follow in the same track." Besides creating the essentially acute detective in Dupin, Poe created his dull companion, and teams of that kind remained the pattern of detective stories for decades.

A friend of Charles Dickens who wrote somewhat in his style, William Wilkie Collins (1824–89) is lauded by the *Oxford Companion to English Literature* as a highly successful novelist: "Collins wrote the first full-length detective stories in English, and set a mould for the genre which has lasted for a century. He excelled at constructing ingenious and meticulous plots." Of Collins's many novels, the most prominent are *The Woman in White* (1860) and *The Moonstone* (1868). The latter was identified by Dorothy Sayers, no mean Sherlockian, as the finest detective story ever written. It uses a background of Indian idols and intrigue to set a story of jewel theft, drug use, respectable love, and below-stairs intrigue, in which the detective, Sergeant Cuff, is solid, plodding, and more or less plausible. Its complex construction (an example of what the *Oxford* calls "interesting experiments in narrative technique") leads to confusion and inconsistency in details, but the story-telling is first-rate.

A pioneer of what is now recognized as the detective story was Emile Gaboriau (1833–73), author of five novels about Monsieur Lecoq of the Sureté of Paris: *L'Affaire Lerouge* (1866), *Crime d'Orcival* (1867), *Le Dossier no. 113* (1867), *Les Esclaves de Paris* (1868), and *Monsieur Lecoq* (1869). Lecoq is thought to be modelled on François Eugène Vidocq (1775–1857), a former criminal turned investigator and the first leader of the Sureté. (Vidocq also influenced Victor Hugo in his creation of both the principal characters in *Les Miserables*, 1862.) Although Holmes in *A Study in Scarlet* calls Lecoq "a miserable bungler," the insult is mostly for effect — Gaboriau was in fact the first to make his detective a master of disguise, an observer of trifles, a preserver of footprints in plaster of Paris. His achievement is the greater because the police were even less well respected in France than in England at the middle of the nineteenth century, although the achievements of the Sureté soon surpassed those of its British equivalent.

"A curiosity because of the enormous sale it inexplicably achieved," in the words of Julian Symons in *Bloody Murder*, was the 1886 novel *The Mystery of a Hansom Cab*, by Fergus Hume (1859–1932). Symons calls it "a reasonably good imitation of Gaboriau"; it is set in the lower quarters of the then new, teeming city of Melbourne, Australia. Other detective novels were appearing in the decade before Doyle produced *A Study in Scarlet*, including *The Leavenworth Case* (1878) by Anna Katherine Green (1846–1935) of the United States. But they were imperfect, Doyle wrote later (in "The True Story of Sherlock Holmes," 1900):

> It struck me what nonsense they were, to put it mildly, because for getting the solution of the mystery the authors always depended on some coincidence. This struck me as not a fair way of playing the game, becusae the detective ought really to depend for his success on something in his own mind and not on merely adventitious circumstances, which do not, by any means, always occur in real life.... I read half-a-dozen or so detective stories, both in French and English, and they one and all filled me with dissatisfaction and a sort of feeling how much more interesting they might be if one could show that the man deserved his victory over the criminal or the mystery.

Basing his own detective's methods on what he remembered of Joseph Bell at the University of Edinburgh, he managed to turn away from the "sensational" norms of the 1870s to what became the mature form of the detective story, depending largely on character and deductive technique.

HOLMES'S CONTEMPORARIES. As an alternative to "pastiches" in which modern authors use the characters of Holmes and Watson, Sherlockians who want something new to read sometimes turn to authentic Victorian material, exhumed and repackaged under such titles as *The Rivals of Sherlock Holmes* (1970, edited by Hugh Greene) and many sequels and imitators. Here they will find the stories that filled issues of the *Strand* and its various rivals when the real thing, Doyle's own work, was not available. Some of them were even illustrated by Sidney Paget, the artist who made Holmes come to life for *Strand* readers from 1891 to 1904.

Leading detective authors of this period included Arthur Morrison (1863–1945), who created Martin Hewitt and gave him adventures that were collected in four volumes between 1894 and 1904; Thomas W. Hanshew (1857–1914), creator of Hamilton Cleek, known as "the man of the forty faces" for his talent at disguise; Ernest Bramah Smith (1868–1942), creator of the blind detective Max Carrados; and Jacques Futrelle (1875–1912), whose contribution to posterity was "the Thinking Machine," Professor Augustus S.F.X. Van Dusen. In addition there were Doyle's friends Grant Allen and Robert Barr; there was Emmuska, Baroness Orczy (1865–1947), who turned away from her *Scarlet Pimpernel* for long enough to create a detective, "the Old Man in the Corner"; and there was Richard Austin Freeman (1862–1943), who narrated the cases of that humourless polymath Dr. Thorndyke in short stories that appeared in *The Singing Bone* (1912) and other collections. An author not of detective stories but of crime stories in a humorous vein was E. W. Hornung, Arthur Conan Doyle's brother-in-law, who created Raffles, the gentleman burglar.

Outside Britain, and in a class by himself in other ways as well, is Maurice Leblanc (1864–1941), who created Arsène Lupin, gentleman thief and sometimes detective, first in a series of short stories that began in 1905 and subsequently in dozens of novels. As early as 1906, Leblanc wrote Sherlock Holmes into one of his short stories ("Sherlock Holmes arrive trop tard"). The British detective also appears in a couple of other stories, "La Dame blonde" and "La Lampe juive," so that the second collection of Lupin adventures (1906) was titled *Arsène Lupin contre Herlock Sholmès*, the name spoonerized to avoid annoying Doyle's publishers. He turns up again in the novel *L'Aiguille creuse* (1909). These materials have been translated into English under various titles, and the legend of a rivalry between Holmes and the French rascal continues, surfacing in a computer game, "Sherlock Holmes: Nemesis," in 2007.

CLASSIC AUTHORS. The usual discussion of detective stories through most of the twentieth century divides them into two chief kinds: the British, emphasizing reason and plot, and the American, emphasizing violence and often sex. The stereotypes are Michael Innes and Agatha Christie for the British, Dashiell Hammett and Mickey Spillane for the Americans. As a broad generalization it has some truth, but there are plenty of American detective stories that depend on reasoning, and there can hardly be a bloodier, grittier author than the very British P.D. James or Minette Walters. As with any novel, the style and emphasis are up to the author. Only people who have not read detective stories think that they all follow the same formula.

Although Doyle is acknowledged to have set the standard, even invented the genre, one important change came later. He wrote chiefly short stories, and (although there are dissenting opinions) his four detective novels are generally thought to be weaker than the short stories about Holmes. But the novel is now the norm, and while detective novels sell by the millions, short stories are a specialized taste found chiefly in *Ellery Queen's Mystery Magazine*. The development of the detective novel is usually dated from *Trent's Last Case* (1913) by Edmund Clerihew Bentley.

Bibliographies of detective fiction make long and exhausting reading, even if fringe genres such as thrillers and crime novels, as distinguished from true stories of detection, are excluded. Among the most honoured classic authors are these:

- Mary Roberts Rinehart, for *The Circular Staircase* (1908) and similar stories of the had-I-but-known school.
- G.K. Chesterton, for his Father Brown short stories: *The Innocence of Father Brown* (1911) and four subsequent collections.
- Agatha Christie, for dozens of enjoyable but forgettable novels, many of them presenting Hercule Poirot or (Miss) Jane Marple as the detectives. She was first published in *The Mysterious Affair at Styles* (1920). Her most original accomplishments are *The Murder of Roger Ackroyd* (1926) and *Murder in the Calais Coach* (1934).
- S.S. Van Dine (Willard Huntington Wright), for his wordy, affected novels presenting Philo Vance, the earliest detective in this genre to work in New York. Best of the lot is probably *The Canary Murder Case* (1927).
- Ellery Queen (Frederic Dannay and Manfred B. Lee) for many books, in which the detective is also named Ellery Queen: *The Roman Hat Mystery* (1929), *The Glass Village* (1954), and such exceptions to all the rules as *And on the Eighth Day* (1963).
- Erle Stanley Gardner for Perry Mason, in interchangeable mysteries that began with *The Case of the Velvet Claws* (1933).
- Dorothy Sayers (1893–1957), for a series of books presenting Lord Peter Wimsey, notably *Murder Must Advertise* (1933) and *Gaudy Night* (1935). Sayers was also an early scholar of Sherlock Holmes.
- Michael Innes for John Appleby in *Lament for a Murder* (1939), *Appleby's End* (1945) and many other coolly-plotted books.
- Ngaio Marsh, for Roderick Alleyn in *Surfeit of Lampreys* (1941) and other novels.

- Josephine Tey for Alan Grant in *The Franchise Affair* (1947) and her best, quirkiest book, *The Daughter of Time* (1951).
- Margery Allingham, for Albert Campion and later Inspector Charles Luke in such books as *The Tiger in the Smoke* (1952).
- P.D. James, for Adam Dalgliesh in realistic novels that are also detective stories, such as *Shroud for a Nightingale* (1971).

At the other extreme from the amateur reasoners of these tales come the so-called "hard-boiled" detective stories, originating in the 1940s. Prominent in this category are Dashiell Hammett with his "Continental Op" (*Red Harvest* [1929], *The Maltese Falcon* [1930]), and Raymond Chandler with Philip Marlowe (*The Big Sleep* [1939]). There is detection in such books, but primarily there is violence, usually accompanied by sex.

Deserving special attention is Rex Stout (born December 1, 1886; died October 27, 1975), not only a Sherlockian from the earliest days, but creator of Nero Wolfe, the literary detective who most completely follows in Sherlock Holmes's footsteps. Wolfe appeared first in *Fer-de-Lance* (1934) and continued through more than forty books narrated by his smart-aleck Watson, Archie Goodwin. Some readers grumbled that their quality declined over the decades, but the possibility of a late tour de force such as *The Doorbell Rang* (1965), in which J. Edgar Hoover himself is made the goat, kept them turning the pages. Wolfe lives in the heart of New York, in a bachelor establishment where he raises orchids, drinks prodigious quantities of beer, and growls at clients. He rarely leaves the premises himself, sending Goodwin out to do the legwork while he eats, drinks, and cogitates, finally announcing his solution to a gathering of protesting witnesses and skeptical police officers in his study. These eccentricities are enough to suggest a Holmesian influence, but Sherlockians prefer to see more. John D. Clark made it explicit in an article in the *Baker Street Journal* in 1956: Wolfe is the son of Holmes and Irene Adler, conceived in Montenegro in 1892. It is a pleasant enough speculation, given something like definitive status by William S. Baring-Gould in his mock biography *Nero Wolfe of West Thirty-Fifth Street* (1969). Readers without the patience for such fancies may prefer the suggestion of D.F. Rauber in the *Journal of Popular Culture* in 1973: "Because Rex Stout so completely reproduced the Doyle formulas and characteristics, it is possible to claim, with only slight exaggeration, that Wolfe *is* Holmes in modern dress." His fans, including a number of Sherlockians, have organized The Wolfe Pack (*www.nerowolfe.org*), which publishes a journal, the *Gazette*.

RULES AND CONVENTIONS. Classic detective stories are a sort of game, rather like crossword puzzles, as well as a form of literature. Their rules have been set out by several commentators, most famously by Ronald Knox in an introduction to a collection of *Best Detective Stories of the Year* for 1928. Those were short stories, but what he said applies equally to novels:

I.   The criminal must be someone mentioned in the early part of the story, but must not be anyone whose thoughts the reader has been allowed to follow.

II. All supernatural or preternatural agencies are ruled out as a matter of course.

III. Not more than one secret room or passage is allowable.

IV. No hitherto undiscovered poisons may be used, nor any appliance which will need a long scientific explanation at the end.

V.   No Chinaman must figure in the story.

VI. No accident must ever help the detective, nor must he ever have an unaccountable intuition which proves to be right.

VII. The detective must not himself commit the crime.

VIII. The detective must not light on any clues which are not instantly produced for the inspection of the reader.

IX. The stupid friend of the detective, the Watson, must not conceal any thoughts which pass through his mind; his intelligence must be slightly, but very slightly, below that of the average reader.

X.   Twin brothers, and doubles generally, must not appear unless we have been duly prepared for them.

So stylized is the detective story that these edicts seem inevitable. (Number V may appear a little arbitrary, and is perhaps a reaction against the fashions of the 1920s.) Yet most respected authors have violated one or another of the rules now and again, and certainly Doyle did so repeatedly; Sherlock Holmes is a habitual offender as regards rule VIII.

Knox takes for granted the existence of a "Watson," a convention that is still often followed (though less widely than in the era of Hercule Poirot's Captain Hastings, Philo Vance's S.S. Van Dine, and Dr. Thorndyke's Christopher Jervis). A similar innovation on Doyle's part is the amateur status of the detective, who is independent of the official police and frequently in active rivalry with them. That distinction, as commentators on detective stories have pointed out, seems to require that the police be taken for granted as honest, but not bright. It may not transfer well to other cultures — the great detective of French fiction is an official policeman, George Simenon's Inspector Maigret, and in French detective stories are *romans policiers*, police novels. Even in English, an increasing number of detective stories do centre on police detectives, such as the many best-sellers of Ed McBain; such books are often classified as "procedurals" because they emphasize routine procedure, not amateur brilliance. But the classic detective story, directly derived from Doyle, is most often about a detective who seems to be Holmes's descendant.

And yet modern authors have found ways of bending the rules, stretching the limits. Writes Erik Routley in *The Puritan Pleasures of the Detective Story* (1972):

> We have seen the detective story as romantic and thrilling; we have seen it as moralism; we have seen it as a kind of novel, exploring human and social situations and attempting to reveal character as well as solution. We have pursued it to the point at which some of its authors suddenly found that the solution was as unimportant as their literary ancestors had held it to be indispensable.

Perhaps few Sherlockians would want to go that far.

MYSTERY FICTION TODAY. As the twenty-first century begins, mysteries in their various flavours remain a staple of public libraries, to say nothing of book retailers. Few other genres are bought in sufficient numbers to support specialized bookstores, including Sleuth of Baker Street in Toronto and Otto Penzler's famous Mysterious Bookshop in New York's Lower Manhattan.

Sherlockians today may choose to read historical detective stories, especially those set in the Victorian era; there are authors who specialize in such material, such as Anne Perry and Peter Lovesey (the latter having written, among many other books, three novels in which the detective is Albert Edward, Prince of Wales, himself). Mysteries from previous generations, above all Agatha Christie, also continue to have followings. But contemporary authors, with their work set more or less in the present day, are flourishing. Some write police procedurals, such as Peter Robinson (his work is set in Yorkshire) and Laurie R. King (hers, set in San Francisco, presents a lesbian detective, Kate Martinelli). Colin Dexter, creator of the Oxford-based Inspector Morse, has a large following for the television adaptations of his work as well as for the original published version. The unchallenged leader in the procedural genre is Ed McBain (Evan Hunter, died 2005), author of the "87th Precinct" novels set in a thinly disguised New York.

A growing number of mysteries feature women protagonists. Among the authors responsible, besides King, are Patricia Cornwell (her detective is medical examiner Kay Scarpetta); Sara Paretsky (Chicago private investigator V.I. Warshawski); Sue Grafton (California investigator Kinsey Millhone); and Janet Evanovich (Stephanie Plum, a bail enforcement agent in Trenton, New Jersey, who encounters as much romance as mystery, and rather more slapstick comedy than either). Other important contemporary mystery authors include Tony Hillerman, Ruth Rendell, Dick Francis, Kinky Friedman, and Robert B. Parker.

OF GOOD AND EVIL. A detective story is not simply a puzzle, but specifically a puzzle about the commission of a crime. Sherlock Holmes speaks once or twice of "sin," but much more often of "crime," which is more easily identified. Although there are some detective stories from cultures in which it cannot be taken for granted that law is the same thing as justice — one thinks of Joseph Skvorecky's short stories about Lieutenant Boruvka of Communist-ruled Prague — that equation is usually assumed, and most detective fiction does come from the free countries. The detective represents justice (not merely vengeance) in pursuit of offence (not merely nonconformity), or one might even say good in pursuit of evil. The detective story is in this sense utterly moral: the good guy wins, and the wages of sin is death on the gallows. But of course this is a very mechanical morality. Says Erik Routley:

> The reader of detective stories probably does read them partly because of the curious property they have of providing relaxation from anxiety. If the reader identifies himself with the successful detective, and to some extent with the forces of law and order, he gets some satisfaction from seeing crime brought home to the right culprit, honesty vindicated, and the law protecting society, including himself, from the consequences that would come if the crime were allowed to run free. He gets satisfaction from this precisely because he is worried by the extent to which, in real life, crime does run free.

Generally — as frequently in the Holmes tales — the situation is somewhat muddied. The victim may have deserved killing, and the criminal may thus be a hero. Several times Holmes pardons criminals, once (in "Charles Augustus

Milverton") positively glorying in seeing a murder committed. Holmes, the agent of justice, is also the agent of mercy in "The Boscombe Valley Mystery," "The Blue Carbuncle," and several other stories. Sometimes he justifies himself explicitly with reference to a higher law, noting in the latter story that "it is the season of forgiveness" and in "The Abbey Grange" that *vox populi, vox Dei*, the voice of the people (in this case of Dr. Watson) is the voice of God. One does not expect to find God in a detective story, but when extreme moral questions are at issue, the Almighty is apt to be nearby, and to suggest judgements that go beyond simple-minded human justice.

The Valley of Fear illustrates how Doyle was able to transcend the requirements of simple morality, but first he had to meet them. He caused Holmes to investigate a murder, work out the truth, and locate the murderer — not only the murderer, but the mastermind behind him, the incarnated evil that is Professor Moriarty. As the murderer's story is told, it becomes clear that the victim deserved to die, not only because the struggle amounted to self-defence but because of dark deeds some twenty years in the past. Then, in turn, the story of those dark deeds is told, in the second half of the long novel, and the reader loses track of Sherlock Holmes and John Douglas in reading about the wickedness of the Scowrers. It is perhaps easier for a modern reader than it was for the reader of 1915 to wonder whether the Scowrers, or Mollie Maguires as they were really called, were as utterly black as the story paints them. Were they not, in part, defenders of the working man against the institutionalized violence of the Pennsylvania mine owners? The detective story is better designed to raise such uncomfortable questions than to answer them; and yet the final paragraphs of *The Valley of Fear* do bring ambiguities forward, as Moriarty manages to have John Douglas killed after all, and Holmes is left muttering that "You must give me time!"

If Sherlock Holmes can go against the law, or rise above it, he has greater difficulty going against convention, against custom. Sociologist Bonnie Menes:

> Sherlock Holmes is the defender of social norms; he enters a case not when a law, but when a norm, has been broken..... An exorbitant wage is cause for investigation. There should be no secrets between a husband and wife, yet one spouse in a marriage is acting mysteriously. Two people are scheduled to marry, but one fails to show up at the altar. No public crime has been committed, no private transgression even, but an unspoken social rule has been broken.

And much the same is true of other detectives on the printed page; their business is to investigate what seems odd, as well as to take obvious murders in hand. Holmes is in this way, as well as in his defence of the moral law, profoundly conservative. His personal eccentricities hardly cancel that continuing truth. The title of Routley's book, *The Puritan Pleasures of the Detective Story*, has something to do with these traits, which are not so much limitations as accommodations of the hero and his adventures to the needs of the *Strand Magazine*'s readers:

> Holmes satisfied a craving which had emerged from the puritan background.... The positive principle in the English puritan tradition (which is, as I believe, not wholly or even primarily a religious movement) has three basic constituents: intellectualism, moralism, and the acceptance of the values of the city.

In short, Holmes — like other detectives — is a middle-class figure, whatever his individual style. Again and again he is seen acting for the respectable classes and the established authorities — the Queen herself, the "Illustrious Client," the contemptible King of Bohemia, the Czarist authorities in the unpublished "case of the Trepoff murder." He has no sympathy with the Scowrers, none with the revolutionaries of "The Golden Pince-Nez," none even with "the British workman" whom he mentions in tones of contempt. The reader does see him mixing on cordial terms with boxers, publicans, and sinners when it suits him, and he can be scathing about the boring society of the idle rich, but Holmes is a man who clearly likes his comforts and respects the well-established. Such attitudes are in the mainstream of detective stories, which can hardly exist save in the context of a middle-class order waiting to be disrupted by an untidy murder. A long and illuminating article about these points is "Sherlock Holmes, Order, and the Late-Victorian Mind" by Christopher Clausen, published in 1984 in the *Georgia Review* and reprinted in *Baker Street Miscellanea*. David S. Payne in *Myth and Modern Man in Sherlock Holmes* (1992) explores such aspects of Holmes in detail, observing for example that Holmes's solutions are solutions of individual crimes and serve only to restore the imbalance caused by that crime. He never brings the original balance into question.

BIBLIOGRAPHY. Countless books have been written about detective fiction, of which perhaps the most important is *Murder for Pleasure* (1941), by Howard Haycraft (1905–91), himself a Sherlockian. Routley's *The Puritan Pleasures* contains many insights and many facts, as does *Bloody Murder* (1972, third edition 1992) by Julian Symons, also published as *Mortal Consequences*. Holding a special place in the hearts of many mystery readers is *Murder Ink* (1977, 1984) by Dilys Wynn, for all its idiosyncrasies. The definitive reference book in the field has long been the *Encyclopedia of Mystery and Detection* (1976), edited by Chris Steinbrunner and Otto Penzler. A useful brief bibliography of reference works is provided online as part of a handy mystery site from the Springfield, Massachusetts, City Library (*www.springfieldlibrary.org/stacks/*). Substantial web sites about mystery fiction include The Mystery Reader (*themysteryreader.com*), MysteryNet (*mysterynet.com*), and Stop, You're Killing Me! (*www.stopyourekillingme.com*).

VII

HOLMES IN MODERN MEDIA

READING THE ORIGINAL SIXTY STORIES has never been enough for enthusiasts of Sherlock Holmes. From early days, they have insisted on seeing the great detective on the stage or the screen, and to the present day they continue to demand new adventures, although few, if any, can fitly be compared with the originals. A few films and dramas, perhaps, may claim to be works of art in their own right, somehow rising above the taint of being "derivative." Others achieve dignity by making no attempt to be anything but straightforward representations of the Canonical stories.

Other appearances of Holmes in the media, from print to television, are less admirable, including irreverent attempts to put him in contact with Rasputin, portray him as a duck or a dog, give him explicit sexual experiences, or send him travelling through time and hyperspace. Buster Keaton and Harpo Marx have played Holmes (successfully) for laughs; other less-talented artists have been embarrassing failures.

In print, such efforts may deserve the name of "parody." although some are serious and even moderately successful. All new tales of Holmes are known to Sherlockians as "pastiches." They range from commercially published novels with large print runs, through short stories appearing in publications aimed at a specialized audience, to privately published or online "fan fiction." About work of this third kind, Ruth Berman has observed that "a lot of it is amateurish in all the worst senses, but some of it is amateurish in the best senses." That is, it pays loving tribute to a figure who now dominates a larger area of literature and imagination than its creator had time to manage.

PASTICHES AND PARODIES

Sherlock Holmes was being mocked and imitated in print within a year after *The Adventures* first appeared. Robert Barr — who may have been quietly encouraged by Doyle, a personal friend — published "Detective Stories Gone Wrong: The Adventures of Sherlaw Kombs" in *The Idler* in May 1892, and a sequel came in 1894. John Kendrick Bangs in the United States was doing similar things within a few years, and made Holmes a major character in his comic novel *The Pursuit of the House-Boat* (1897). That and other stories by Bangs are surveyed in an article by Jon Lellenberg, published in *Baker Street Miscellanea* in 1984.

Other parodies in the early years appeared as parts of such series as "Lost Diaries" and "As They Would Have Told It." Bret Harte produced one ("The Stolen Cigar Case") as part of his 1902 collection *Condensed Novels*, and other authors did their best to mock Holmes under such names as Shamrock Jolnes, Kerlock Shomes and Oilock Combs. Humour was the intent of all the early parodies, including Stephen Leacock's "Maddened by Mystery" in *Nonsense Novels* (1911):

> The Great Detective sat in his office. He wore a long green gown and half a dozen secret badges pinned to the outside of it.
>
> Three or four pairs of false whiskers hung on a whisker-stand beside him.
>
> Goggles, blue spectacles, and motor glasses lay within easy reach.
>
> He could completely disguise himself at a second's notice.
>
> Half a bucket of cocaine and a dipper stood on a chair at his elbow.

Mark Twain had done much the same thing in "A Double-Barrelled Detective Story" (1902). Nor were these early parodies limited to English. In 1906 Maurice Leblanc perpetrated "Sherlock Holmes arrive trop tard" in his first book about master-criminal Arsène Lupin, and other such stories followed. All these efforts were good fun, and Doyle did not entirely disapprove, for he wrote two pastiches himself — "The Field Bazaar" (1896) and "How Watson Learned the Trick" (1924). He is reported to have said that "The Adventure of the Two Collaborators," by Sir James Barrie, in which one of the collaborators is Barrie and the other is Doyle, was the best pastiche he had ever seen.

Serious attempts to imitate the Canonical stories may have begun with Vincent Starrett, whose sensitive and convincing "Adventure of the Unique *Hamlet*" was privately printed in 1920, but not given general distribution until twenty years later. In 1944 Little, Brown published *The Misadventures of Sherlock Holmes*, an anthology edited by Ellery Queen that included dozens of parodies including works by Barr, Leblanc, Twain, Leacock, O. Henry, and others. Sherlockians greeted it with enthusiasm, but the heirs of Doyle were outraged, and before long the book was withdrawn from circulation. It is a cherished item in many Sherlockian collections, one printing in particular being a rarity.

In a category all its own is *A Taste for Honey* (1941), by H.F. Heard, a gentle and horrifying story about "Mr. Mycroft" the beekeeper. Heard wrote two sequels — *Reply Paid* (1942) and *The Notched Hairpin* (1949).

THE MAN WHO WAS WANTED. A Sherlock Holmes short story entitled "The Case of the Man Who Was Wanted" appeared in *Cosmopolitan* magazine in the United States in August 1948, and in the *Sunday Dispatch* newspaper in England early in 1949, as the work of Doyle, a long-lost sixty-first story for the Canon. It is, as the story suggests, the tale of how Holmes manages to locate a fugitive; the detection is mostly conducted at a distance, for the man himself is aboard a transatlantic liner. Jon Lellenberg in his little book *Nova 57 Minor* (1990), which also contains the full text of "TMWWW," as it has been abbreviated, tells the full story of this tale. He writes:

> In 1942, the typescript of an unpublished Sherlock Holmes story was discovered among Sir Arthur Conan Doyle's papers. Despite statements by his sons Denis and Adrian that the story was not up to their father's standard, there was great clamor to have it published; and no doubt the financial potential of an unpublished Sherlock Holmes story was not lost upon the Conan Doyle Estate. In due course, it did appear — only to have its authorship quickly claimed by an unknown, retired English architect named Arthur Whitaker (born 1882). Whitaker said that he had written it in 1910 and sold it for ten guineas to Sir Arthur, who had declined any collaboration but was willing to pay for the possible use of the story idea. When this claim surfaced, the reaction of the Conan Doyle Estate was immediate, direct, and vitriolic. It was also premature; Whitaker was able to prove that the story was his work. And so it

became known that "The Man Who Was Wanted," instead of being the sixty-first Canonical adventure, was only a pastiche.

It may, however, have introduced the fashion of writing new adventures that would attempt to rival the authentic ones in tone and length; pastiches were becoming imitation rather than parody.

THE EXPLOITS OF SHERLOCK HOLMES. The most successful imitators of the tales were Doyle's son Adrian and a collaborator, John Dickson Carr, who had written many detective stories of his own, as well as the authorized biography of Doyle. In 1952–53 a dozen stories, the first six by the two collaborators, the latter six by Doyle alone, were published in *Collier's* magazine, where many of the original tales had appeared forty years earlier. Book editions appeared in 1954 and several times thereafter, under the title *The Exploits of Sherlock Holmes*.

These are the story titles, in the order in which they appear in the collected edition (slightly rearranged from their magazine publication):

"The Adventure of the Seven Clocks"
"The Adventure of the Gold Hunter"
"The Adventure of the Wax Gamblers"
"The Adventure of the Highgate Miracle"
"The Adventure of the Black Baronet"
"The Adventure of the Sealed Room"
"The Adventure of Foulkes Rath"
"The Adventure of the Abbas Ruby"
"The Adventure of the Two Women"
"The Adventure of the Dark Angels"
    (previously, "Demon Angels")
"The Adventure of the Deptford Horror"
"The Adventure of the Red Widow"

Reaction naturally varied, although it is clear in retrospect that these stories, whether or not of Canonical quality, are much better than most pastiches that have followed them.

AUGUST DERLETH. Shortly after the publication of the Canon came to an end, a student at the University of Wisconsin, August Derleth, wrote to ask Doyle whether there would be more tales. Learning that there were not, he determined to write substitutes himself, and choosing a page at random from his desk calendar, he scribbled the note, "In re: Sherlock Holmes." When the date thus selected arrived, he sat down and wrote "The Adventure of the Black Narcissus," which was subsequently published in *Dragnet* magazine for February 1929. More stories followed, enough to make a book, which was inevitably titled *In Re: Sherlock Holmes* (1945).

Derleth did not venture to use the names of Holmes and Watson in his stories. He called his hero Solar Pons, the companion Dr. Lyndon Parker, the arch-villain Baron Ennesfred Kroll, the venue Praed Street. No reader can be deceived. Wrote Vincent Starrett later: "Solar Pons is not a caricature of Sherlock Holmes. He is, rather, a clever impersonator, with a twinkle in his eye, which tells us that he knows he is not Sherlock Holmes, and knows that *we* know it, but that he hopes we will like him anyway for what he symbolizes."

In Re: Sherlock Holmes was retitled *The Adventures of Solar Pons* in some later editions. It was followed by other collections of stories: *The Memoirs of Solar Pons* (1951), *The Return* (1958), *The Reminiscences* (1961), *The Casebook* (1965), and *The Chronicles* (1973). There is also a novel, *Mr. Fairlie's Final Journey* (1968). Derleth had at one time intended to duplicate the Sherlockian Canon, and ended up with more stories than the sixty required. Miscellaneous Pontine material appeared in *Praed Street Papers* (1965) and *A Praed Street Dossier* (1968). Sherlockians welcomed the tales of Solar Pons with enthusiasm. A society of "Praed Street Irregulars" was organized by Luther Norris, a noted Sherlockian collector in Los Angeles, and flourished for a few years. Enthusiasts now operate a Solar Pons website (*solarpons.com*).

August Derleth (born February 24, 1909; died July 4, 1971) was a prolific writer in many branches of fiction, with a special interest in books that reflected and interpreted rural Wisconsin. For Sherlockians, he continues to be acknowledged as, in Julian Wolff's words, "the greatest serious imitator of the Master." He is also the first writer to create a novel, as opposed to a short story, in the Canonical tradition. Derleth's work is unique in having inspired the publication of pastiches of its own, tales by Basil Copper, beginning with *The Dossier of Solar Pons* (1979).

NICHOLAS MEYER. A new kind of pastiche became instantly popular with the publication of Nicholas Meyer's *The Seven-Per-Cent Solution* in 1974. Although its Foreword speaks of "a surfeit of forgeries" already in existence, there had been nothing like it — a novel-length serious text presented as an authentic Canonical tale, one of Watson's manuscripts newly discovered and committed to print. (A possible exception: *A Study in Terror*, Ellery Queen's 1966 novelization connecting Holmes with the Jack the Ripper murders.) This one was a sensation, achieving success both in hardback and in paperback, and then becoming a well-received film.

The Seven-Per-Cent Solution purports to tell the true story of the events of 1891, the period of Holmes's obsession with Professor Moriarty, which in this interpretation is not his successful investigation and defeat of the master-criminal's gang, but his descent into drug-induced paranoia, Moriarty being an innocent mathematics teacher and Holmes's childhood tutor:

> "Dr. Watson, your friend is persuaded that I am some sort of —"
> he groped for the words — "criminal mastermind. Of the most
> depraved order," he added with a helpless shrug, throwing up
> his hands. "Now I ask you, sir: in all honesty — can you see in
> me the remotest trappings of such an individual?"

Watson takes Holmes under his care and entices him to Vienna, where the young Dr. Sigmund Freud is gaining renown for his cures of cocaine addicts. So much of the story is quite plausible: Freud did himself use cocaine, break the habit, and become interested in the treatment of addiction. Meyer's narrative continues: Holmes, weaned from his drugs, stumbles into a mystery and of course solves it, averting "a European war." Final revelations follow as Freud hypnotizes Holmes to find out about the traumas of his childhood.

Meyer (born 1945) already had one minor movie script to his credit. He told interviewers that he had always enjoyed Sherlock Holmes in a casual way, but became seriously interested while he was working in New York as a film-industry publicist: "There was this little bar I used to go to after work; one evening I saw a young lady there whose acquaintance I sought to make. We got onto the subject of Holmes, and I was astounded by how much this young woman knew about those stories. After that I went back and reread the entire canon." He wrote *The Seven-Per-Cent Solution* when the screen-writers' strike of 1973 deprived him of more immediate work, and it made him an immediate success. After the book, and the film that followed, he became a director as well as a writer, delivering *Time After Time* (1979), a film about H. G. Wells and Jack the Ripper that intrigued many Sherlockians, and *Star Trek II: The Wrath of Khan*, among other successes.

A sequel to Meyer's remarkable work was *The West End Horror* (1976), in which he brings Holmes and Watson into contact with George Bernard Shaw, Bram Stoker, and Gilbert and Sullivan. *The Canary Trainer* (1993) takes Holmes to Paris, where he encounters the Phantom of the Opera.

THE 'BOOM' PERIOD. Many imitators followed, none of them as successful, or as well written, as the original; some were workmanlike, others appallingly bad. Among the scores of titles were *Sherlock Holmes vs. Dracula, or, The Adventure of the Sanguinary Count* (1978) by Loren D. Estleman and *The Demon Device* by Robert Saffron and *The Incredible Umbrella* by Marvin Kaye (both 1979). Such novel-length pastiches, mostly in trade-paperback format, made up a body of material many times longer than the original Canon. In a few cases these books were convincing, well-told mystery stories involving Holmes — an outstanding example being *The Quallsford Inheritance* (1986) by Lloyd Biggle, Jr. Also receiving much acclaim from Sherlockians have been three titles by Canadian author Beth Greenwood: *Sherlock Holmes and the Case of the Raleigh Legacy* (1986), *Sherlock Holmes and the Case of Sabina Hall* (1988), *Sherlock Holmes and the Thistle of Scotland* (1989).

But the 1970s and 1980s brought many other books about which the complaints jostle one another for priority. To begin with, the Watsonian style is not so easy to imitate, especially for American writers who put American slang and idiom into his mouth and make a hopeless muddle of British titles of nobility. Watson's (that is to say, Doyle's) prose is invariably clear; sentences like these, not difficult to find in pastiches, make the sensitive reader wince:

- I was aware of what he spoke.
- "Let me disagree on that point," stated Holmes.
- I can only say, with medical retrospect, that it was like the sensation in the *glans penis* at the moment of *ejaculatio*, only it rapidly spread throughout my entire body in one hot glorious wave of molton pleasure.

The authentic Watson also knows the subtleties of the usage of "shall" and "will," and can spell. He is, as Sherlockians have enjoyed pointing out, unreliable about dates, train times and other such details, but perhaps not so unreliable as authors who have their Victorian characters send telegrams from a railway station, mention "blocks" as a unit of distance, or imagine that Holmes might eat waffles for breakfast. Still more important, Watson's stories have a dignity which the pastiches frequently lack, presenting as they do riots in the streets of Cambridge, explicit sexual encounters of various kinds, and astonishing behaviour on Holmes's part. In one he plays his violin to entertain the patrons of an Italian restaurant; in another he rides a horse. Nicholas Meyer started this trend by compelling the Holmes of *The Seven-Per-Cent Solution* to wield a coal-shovel as he helps propel a rushing railway train. Dramatic physical action is not unknown to the Holmes of the Canon, who wields a screwdriver in "Lady Frances Carfax" and wrestles in the grass in "The Naval Treaty," but for the authors of pastiches it is his daily routine.

They also portray him rubbing shoulders with every possible figure of history or fiction. Among the characters who have been introduced into pastiches of these two decades are Prince Albert of Monaco, Annie Besant, Professor Challenger, Aleister Crowley, Benjamin Disraeli, Alfred Dreyfus, Friedrich Engels, Fu Manchu, William Ewart Gladstone, W.G. Grace, Adolf Hitler, Karl Marx, Hercule Poirot, Ramanujan, Theodore Roosevelt, Rupert of Hentzau, Tarzan, and Virginia Woolf — virtually everyone, historical or fictional, whose lifespan overlapped with Holmes's.

In story after story, as the fame of these characters perhaps suggests, Holmes finds himself required to solve mysteries on which the fate of the civilized world depends. The outcome of World War I turns on his actions, or the black arts of a master-magician will enable him to rule the world, or the huge gold reserves that stabilize international economics may disappear. In *The Earthquake Machine* (1976), by Austin Mitchelson and Nicholas Utechin, Holmes is cabled to come at once: "Your country at stake." In several of the books, as he did in Meyer's *The Seven-Per-Cent Solution*, Holmes averts a war. Such a motif was still being used at the end of the 1980s, in *Sherlock Holmes and the Mark of the Beast* (1989) by Ronald C. Weyman. The extreme is reached in the frankly parodic *The Strange Case of the End of Civilisation as We Know It*, the published script of a British television film starring John Cleese (1977). Even when an author cannot possibly twist his plot to include international spies, assassinations, wars, statesmen, and Armageddon, he may at least have Holmes call the case "the most serious I have yet encountered" or make equally extravagant mutterings.

A disproportionate number of these novel-length pastiches involve Irene Adler or Mycroft Holmes; a disproportionate number follow Nicholas Meyer's lead in reinterpreting the relationship between Holmes and Moriarty, or in shedding new, if somewhat questionable, light on Holmes's character and origins. (Meyer attributed his introduction of adultery and murder into Holmes's childhood memories to the speculations of that solid Sherlockian scholar Trevor S. Hall in *Sherlock Holmes: Ten Literary Studies* [1969].) A book whose title is *Exit Sherlock Holmes* (1977, by Robert Lee Hall) can hardly do otherwise than end with Holmes's departure from the scene, and in a thoroughly unexpected way; *The Last Sherlock Holmes Story* (1978, by Michael Dibdin) makes and keeps a similar promise. *The Adventure of Sherlock Holmes'*

Smarter Brother (1975, by Gilbert Pearlman, based on a Gene Wilder film of the same year) also delivers what its title promises, and reveals Moriarty behind the villainy into the bargain.

A few of these works, including *Smarter Brother*, are intended strictly for laughs, like the Twain and Leacock works of nearly a century earlier. So are the much-acclaimed works of Robert L. Fish, short stories appearing in *Ellery Queen's Mystery Magazine* and collected in *The Incredible Schlock Homes* (1966) and its sequels. In the likes of "The Adventure of the Spectacled Band" and "The Adventure of the Snared Drummer," Schlock Homes of Bagel Street indulges in puns and slapstick:

> "You have arrived at a crucial moment, Watney!" said he, his keen eyes glittering. "If this litmus paper remains blue, then all is well. If it turns red — then I am afraid we shall have to depend upon store-bought whiskey for our afternoon libations!"

But others are attempts at serious fiction using Holmes and Watson. By and large, they lack the complexity and verbal texture of the originals, as well as the modest (but achievable) ambitions in plot and social significance.

By 1980, many Sherlockians had come to dread any work ostensibly about Holmes that included an author's note explaining the origin of the manuscript in a battered tin dispatch-box inherited from a great-uncle or bought by a friend at an estate auction. A Sherlockian "boom" — so called at the time — had begun in the early 1970s thanks to Nicholas Meyer's books and a successful North American tour of the play "Sherlock Holmes" starring John Wood. It continued through the mid-1980s thanks to the television series starring Jeremy Brett as Holmes. But publication tailed off a little when, at the end of the 1980s, Dame Jean Conan Doyle made it known that she wanted the appearance of pastiches to stop. It seemed best, she suggested, that authors should invent their own characters. In the United States, where most such material was published, she still controlled some copyrights on the Canonical stories, and was able to enforce that preference, so that publication of commercial pastiches ceased. Elsewhere, some have continued to appear.

IN RECENT DECADES. Fewer novel-length pastiches have appeared in the past two decades, although there have been a few, including a series of well-written short novels by John Hall: *Sherlock Holmes and the Disgraced Inspector* (2000), *Sherlock Holmes and the Hammerford Will* (2001), and others. More like the fanciful pastiches of a previous decade is *Sherlock Holmes'*

Lost Adventure: The True Story of the Giant Rats of Sumatra (2004) by Lauren Steinhauer; and Stephen Kendrick's *Night Watch* (2001) stands in the same tradition by introducing a very young Father Brown as a foil for Holmes in a mystery with a not very convincing theological flavour. Among the best Sherlockian reading of recent years has been a series of books by Larry Millett: *Sherlock Holmes and the Red Demon* (1996), *Sherlock Holmes and the Ice Palace Murders* (1998), *Sherlock Holmes and the Rune Stone Mystery* (1999), *Sherlock Holmes and the Secret Alliance* (2001), and *The Disappearance of Sherlock Holmes* (2002). Although they are set in Minnesota, improbably far from Holmes's usual haunts, they capture both Watson's authorial tone and Holmes's style and personality. They also introduce and develop a locally based detective, publican Shadwell Rafferty, with whom Holmes has a thoroughly convincing rapport.

Most serious pastiches had been written at novel length until close to the turn of the century, but a number of authors are now writing successful Holmes short stories — the genre in which most of the Canon actually is cast. This format compels the author to keep a plot within reasonable bounds, with Holmes solving a single mystery with a manageable number of clues and suspects, and keeps foreign travels and intergalactic complications to a minimum. In this vein, two anthologies edited by Marvin Kaye — *The Game Is Afoot* (1994) and *The Confidential Casebook of Sherlock Holmes* (1998) — can stand on the shelf beside *Murder in Baker Street* (2001), *Murder, My Dear Watson* (2002), and four other volumes edited by Martin H. Greenberg, Jon Lellenberg, and Daniel Stashower. More good reading for a chilly autumn night appears in the oddly titled *The Mammoth Book of New Sherlock Holmes Adventures* (1997), edited by Mike Ashley. There are also collections of short stories by individual authors, most importantly June Thomson, whose much-admired oeuvre includes *The Secret Journals of Sherlock Holmes* (1993), *The Secret Files* (1993), *The Secret Chronicles* (1994), *The Secret Documents* (1997), and *The Secret Notebooks* (2004).

The range of styles in Sherlockian novels has expanded far beyond pastiches — that is, imitations of the original adventures — to include *The Childhood of Sherlock Holmes* (2000) by Mona Morstein and *The Secret Diary of Dr. Watson* (2001) by Anita Janda. Both books work effectively on the reader's emotions. The same is true of *Eye of the Crow* (2007) by Shane Peacock, first in a series of novels about "The Boy Sherlock Holmes" intended in part for adolescent audiences. Nick Rennison's *Sherlock Holmes: The Unauthorised Biography* (2006) returns to the genre created by William S. Baring-Gould with *Sherlock Holmes of Baker Street* a generation earlier, the full-length and largely convincing narrative of Holmes's life. A single period, the "Great Hiatus" during which Holmes was absent from London and thought dead, is addressed in novels of very different kinds: *Sherlock Holmes, the Missing Years* (1999) by Jamyang Norbu and *The Shadow of Reichenbach Falls* (2008) by John R. King.

In a category of its own, both witty and grotesque, is *A Samba for Sherlock* (1997), a translation of the Portuguese *O Sangô de Baker Street* by Jô Soares. The 2003 best-seller *The Curious Incident of the Dog in the Night-time* by Mark Haddon, a narrative from the point of view of an autistic boy, caught many Sherlockians' attention on the strength of its title, though its plot has little to do with Holmes.

VARIATIONS ON A THEME. Of special interest have been a few novels that look at Holmes and his milieu from a less-familiar viewpoint. The earliest of these were a pair of sensitive and brilliant novels by John Gardner (not the American novelist of the same name, but a British author of detective fiction). They are *The Return of Moriarty* (1974, British edition titled simply *Moriarty*) and *The Revenge of Moriarty* (1975). Their premise is that, like Holmes, Moriarty escaped death at the falls of the Reichenbach. *The Return of Moriarty* thus tells in a new way the events of "The Empty House," in April 1894; its strength is the portrayal, exciting but not melodramatic, of Moriarty's underworld empire, where sophisticated ingenuity is coupled with the rough work of thugs and whores. *The Revenge of Moriarty* is set two years later, as the Napoleon of Crime, having escaped to America when London was made too hot to hold him, returns, and incidentally plans the theft of the Mona Lisa from the Louvre. Holmes figures in both books, though their chief detective is Inspector Angus McCready Crow of Scotland Yard. Even at the end of the second volume, Moriarty escapes his clutches; the scene was thus set in 1975 for a third Gardner epic, which, however, did not appear until the posthumous publication of the starkly titled *Moriarty* in 2008.

Other attempts in that genre included *I, Sherlock Holmes* (1977), ostensibly Holmes's own memoirs, by Michael Harrison, and books focusing on Mycroft Holmes, Mrs. Hudson, and even Dr. Watson's alleged second wife, "Amelia." Undoubtedly the funniest such works were M.J. Trow's *The Supreme Adventure of Inspector Lestrade* (1985) and fifteen other increasingly surrealistic novels about the life and work of Inspector Sholto Lestrade of Scotland Yard, most of which have little to do with Sherlock Holmes. The most successful were eight novels by Carole Nelson Douglas, beginning with *Good Night, Mr.*

Holmes (1990) in which Irene Adler finally receives a convincing and sympathetic treatment. They begin with close fidelity to the events of "A Scandal in Bohemia" but shortly move far away, becoming prolix and sensational as the series goes on.

Beyond all these works are a multitude of exceptions and special treatments, from *Sherlock Holmes, Bridge Detective* (1973, by George Gooden and Frank Thomas) to *Trouble in Bugland* (1983, by William Kotzwinkle), in which Inspector Mantis, an insect in Sherlockian garb, solves mysteries in a world of Victorian insects.

Several prolific authors have been tempted to write novels not about Sherlock Holmes but about his followers. *The Case of the Baker Street Irregulars* (1940) by Anthony Boucher is a *roman à clef* featuring a number of prominent Sherlockians, thinly disguised. Gladys Mitchell's *Watson's Choice* (1955) is about British enthusiasts; Julian Symons's *A Three Pipe Problem* (1975) is about an actor. Jerry N. Williamson's *The Tulpa* (1980) is a horror novel that includes a scene of bloodshed at a Sherlockian society dinner.

BIBLIOGRAPHY. A history of the pastiche genre is found in *The Sincerest Form of Flattery* (1983) by Paul D. Herbert, which includes a long bibliography of work up to that date. More recent is *The Alternative Sherlock Holmes: Pastiches, Parodies and Copies* (2003) by Peter Ridgway Watt and Joseph Green. The most extensive listing and analysis of pastiches, including scripts and related material, is in the form of a database maintained online (*illustriousclients.org/?name=Content&pid=5*) by Philip K. Jones; another site with extensive lists, including an index of historical and fictional characters who appear in pastiches, is maintained by Adrian Nebbett at *www.schoolandholmes.com*.

THEATRE

The stage adaptations of the Canon that can be presumed to be closest to Doyle's ideal are his own plays of *The Speckled Band* (1910) and *The Crown Diamond* (1921). The former, originally titled *The Stonor Case*, was a success in the original production with H.A. Saintsbury as Holmes; Charles Millward took over when the play was brought to New York after almost five months on the London stage, but Saintsbury returned in a 1921 revival. The script was published (by Samuel French) in 1912. As for *The Crown Diamond*, its run was short, its revivals have been few, and the script was not published until 1958. With minor alterations, it became the short story "The Mazarin Stone" just a few months after its first performance, in Bristol, with Dennis Neilson-Terry as Holmes. The scripts of both plays are now available in such volumes as *The Uncollected Sherlock Holmes*, edited by Richard Lancelyn Green, and Leslie S. Klinger's *The Apocrypha of Sherlock Holmes*. Neither work was anywhere near as successful as the much greater play, loosely based on a draft by Doyle, that had established Holmes's image on the stage before the turn of the century.

WILLIAM GILLETTE. For two generations of Americans, the face of Sherlock Holmes was the face of William Gillette, who played Holmes from 1899 through 1932, to unvarying acclaim. His principal vehicle was *Sherlock Holmes*, a play he wrote himself, in circumstances described by P.M. Stone in a special supplement to the *Baker Street Journal* in 1953:

> Some enterprising reporter for a New York newspaper had reported that A. Conan Doyle had stated that, should anyone ever suggest a play based on the Sherlock Holmes stories, his own choice would be William Gillette for the leading role. Doyle had, in fact, said nothing of the kind, and at that time had not even met the actor. Later, however, Charles Frohman, the famous theatrical producer, saw the newspaper paragraph, and, realizing its potential, turned it over to Gillette.... A year or more later, Gillette received a second and more urgent message from Frohman requesting him to prepare at once a stage version of the great detective's career, the producer having meanwhile secured Doyle's permission....
>
> Following an exhaustive study of the renowned detective's achievements, as set forth by the indefatigable Dr. Watson, Gillette wrote to Conan Doyle, inquiring as to how many liberties he could take with his famous literary character. Doyle is reported to have replied that Gillette could "marry the detective — murder him — or do anything he pleased."

Any qualms Doyle may have had about Gillette were apparently stilled when the two men met in May 1899, and the author found the actor "the living image of Sherlock Holmes," as biographer John Dickson Carr puts it.

The resulting play script, though publicly described as being by Doyle and Gillette jointly, was entirely Gillette's work. The play had its premiere October 23, 1899, at the Star Theatre in Buffalo, and then moved to New York for a run of seven months at the Garrick Theatre. From September through April

William Gillette poses in deerstalker and tweed suit, his costume in the title role of "Sherlock Holmes." The picture was a publicity still by New York theatrical photographer Otto Sarony in 1899, when the long-running play had its premiere.

it ran at the Lyceum Theatre in London, where Dr. Watson had met Mary Morstan in *The Sign of the Four* fourteen years previously. Productions were numerous, if not continuous, over the next few years, sometimes in New York and sometimes in other cities across North America. Gillette returned to the role in 1915 and again in 1923, and beginning in the fall of 1929 a "Farewell Tour" took him to dozens of communities. Gillette's last recorded appearance in his great play came March 19, 1932, in Princeton, New Jersey.

The play is melodramatic to a modern audience, its dramatic climax — in which a lighted cigar glows in a darkened dungeon, tricking the villainous Moriarty into believing that Holmes is still in the room — likely to draw snickers. The heroine, Alice Faulkner, gets Holmes at the end. In a plot largely drawn from "A Scandal in Bohemia" and "The Final Problem," though with echoes from several other Canonical tales skillfully woven into the story, the subsidiary villain, James Larrabee, is as thoroughly foiled as Moriarty himself. Gillette did not carry even the principal members of his company with him through his career, so that many Dr. Watsons and many Miss Faulkners were seen; on the farewell tour Wallis Clark and Peg Entwistle played those roles.

The play was revived occasionally after Gillette's death, but returned to general favour in 1974, when the Royal Shakespeare Company mounted a production in England (brought to America 1974–76) starring John Wood. Frank Langella played the title role on stage in 1977 and then in an HBO television production of the play in 1981. The text is available from Samuel French, Inc., the chief publishers of play scripts, who first issued it in 1922, and a text was also published by Doubleday in 1935. The play was a major attraction of the 1994 summer season for the Shaw Festival in Niagara-on-the-Lake, Ontario, with a text "revised by Christopher Newton," and Jim Mezon starring as Holmes. The revised script, with commentary by theatrical and Sherlockian experts, was published in a spiral-bound volume under the title *The Shaw Festival Sherlock Holmes*. Earlier, Gillette had recorded an adaptation of his play for ABC radio in 1935, having done a half-hour version of "The Speckled Band" in 1930, and Carleton Hobbs starred in it on BBC radio in 1953.

A lesser play by Gillette is *The Painful Predicament of Sherlock Holmes*, a brief comedy in which the great detective has no lines whatsoever to speak. He presented it first in 1905, and occasionally thereafter; its chief claim to historical fame is that a very young Charlie Chaplin played Billy, the page, at the London production in October 1905 (then taking the role in the full-length play two weeks later). The text of *The Painful Predicament* was published in 1955.

William Hooker Gillette, the actor who started this branch of the Holmes industry, was born July 24, 1853, in Connecticut, which remained his home until his death. Gillette made his professional debut in 1875, and reached fame in 1896 when he wrote and starred in a play about the American Civil War, *Secret Service*. It was not long after that triumph that he began work on *Sherlock Holmes*, and *Secret Service* remained in his repertoire for the next three decades. He was still playing Holmes as he neared eighty, P. M. Stone recalls:

> On Gillette's first entrance, as he slowly removed his overcoat and seated himself at the foot of the staircase before sending up his card to Miss Faulkner, the entire house stood up, and, after an impressive moment of silence, extended to the distinguished actor a tumultuous greeting in tribute to the genuine affection and admiration in which he was held. No doubt his thoughts drifted back to that auspicious evening of September 13th, in 1875, when he had made his first important theatrical appearance at the old Globe Theatre in Washington Street [in Boston].

If enthusiasts of Holmes admired Gillette, he returned their respect, attending the 1934 dinner of the Baker Street Irregulars and being listed as a BSI member in 1935. The mansion (with a working railroad in its grounds) that he built with his vast earnings from the stage is near Hadlyme, Connecticut, and is now operated as Gillette Castle State Park. He died April 29, 1937. An exhibition in his memory was staged in 1970–71 at the Nook Farm Visitors' Center in Hartford, Connecticut, and the published catalogue includes photographs of him in various plays, as well as fragments of valuable information. Also informative is *Molding the Image*, a brochure produced to accompany a 1983 exhibition of Gillette material at the University of Minnesota. As of 2009, two Sherlockians have let it be known that books about Gillette are actively in preparation.

The best-known image of Gillette is a cartoon by "Spy" (Leslie Ward) that appeared in *Vanity Fair* magazine February 27, 1907. That fully coloured drawing has been reproduced at least twice as a print for modern Sherlockians' walls. Gillette is also acknowledged to have been Frederic Dorr Steele's ideal Holmes, though not directly the model for his illustrations. It is generally thought that the curved pipe now associated with Holmes, but not mentioned in the Canon or seen in early illustrations, was introduced by Gillette, who found that his speeches were more audible over it, and his face more visible, than through a straight pipe.

MODERN PLAYS. The only important Sherlockian play for several decades after William Gillette was *The Return of Sherlock Holmes* by Harold Terry and Arthur Rose, produced in Cardiff and London in 1923–24 (starring Eille Norwood) and revived in 1930 and 1953. It was largely based on "Lady Frances Carfax," "Charles Augustus Milverton," and "The Empty House." A number of minor productions can also be unearthed, including *Sherlock Holmes* by Ouida Rathbone, which had just four performances (one in Boston and three in New York) in 1953.

Also in 1953, Holmes came to the stage of the Sadler's Wells Ballet Theatre, London, in the production *The Great Detective*, choreographed by Margaret Dale and with music by Richard Arnell. Kenneth Macmillan danced both the Great Detective, in deerstalker and inverness, and "The Infamous Professor," i.e. Moriarty; Stanley Holden was "His Friend, the Doctor," i.e. Watson. Such a *jeu d'esprit* was not seen again until the National Tap-Dance Company of Canada staged *The Hound of the Baskervilles* in 1987.

A landmark production was *Baker Street*, a musical which opened on New York's Broadway February 16, 1965, after tryouts in Boston and Toronto. The music and lyrics were by Marian Grudeff and Raymond Jessel; the book, taken chiefly from "A Scandal in Bohemia" and "The Final Problem," was by Jerome Coopersmith. Fritz Weaver appeared as Holmes, Peter Sallis as Watson, Martin Gabel as Moriarty, and Inga Swenson as Irene Adler. *Baker Street* is a beautiful piece of entertainment, if no more plausible than any other work in which a love interest must be balanced with a heart-stopping Sherlockian plot. Not surprisingly, some of the best songs are put in the mouth of Irene Adler — "Letters" and "Finding Words for Spring" — and one can forgive the authors for giving her a duet with Holmes, "What a Night This Is Going to Be." More unexpected, and perhaps the most touching moment of the play, is the song given to Watson, "A Married Man." And Holmes does not lose his dignity when he sings his solo in Act I, scene 7:

> I have waited in vain
> For someone to explain
> What love conceivably can offer
> The cerebral type of man,
> But no one ever has
> And no one ever will
> For no one ever can —
> But, ah!

The cold, clear world of the intellect
Is the world that I revere.
In the pure, dry air of the scientist
I am in my proper sphere....

Baker Street ran on Broadway for 311 performances; there have been a few revivals. The book and lyrics were published in 1966 (*Baker Street: A Musical Adventure of Sherlock Holmes*), and several 33-rpm records were released with some or all of the music, including the original cast album from MGM Records in 1965, now available on CD.

To put Irene Adler on stage and make her sing is an almost irresistible temptation. Alessandro Gebbia notes one achievement that fortunately has never been staged: "Peter H. Wood's *Uno Scandale in Bohemia* (1990) imagines Giacomo Puccini, the famous Italian opera composer, trying to adapt Doyle's 'A Scandal in Bohemia,' translated into Italian in 1895, before moving to Sardou's La Tosca. Wood's work is the hilarious libretto presented to the reader in the double version of English and macaronic Italian." More seriously, a chamber opera version of "A Scandal in Bohemia," by Thomas Whitman and Nathalie Anderson, had its premiere at Swarthmore College in Pennsylvania in 2009.

Since the Sherlock Holmes boom that followed the 1974 revival of Gillette's *Sherlock Holmes*, there have been dozens of minor plays and a few major productions. Among the more significant ones (scripts are available in print in most cases):

- *Sherlock's Last Case*, by Matthew Lang, first produced in London in the summer of 1974, and subsequently staged in several other British cities. It came to Broadway in the summer of 1987 with Frank Langella in the title role.
- *The Incredible Murder of Cardinal Tosca*, by Alden Nowlan and Walter Learning, first produced by Theatre New Brunswick (Fredericton) in January 1978. Later that year it was seen in Toronto and elsewhere in Canada.
- *The Crucifer of Blood*, by Paul Giovanni, first staged on Broadway in 1978–79 with Paxton Whitehead as Holmes and Glenn Close as the heroine, Irene St. Claire. The high point of the production was the spectacular staging of a boat chase down the foggy Thames, based on the scene in *The Sign of the Four*. A television production in 1991

starred Charlton Heston (who had also appeared in *Crucifer* in Los Angeles in 1981, with Jeremy Brett as Watson).

- *The Secret of Sherlock Holmes*, by Jeremy Paul, starring the Holmes and Watson made familiar by Granada Television in the 1980s: Jeremy Brett and Edward Hardwicke. It opened in London September 22, 1988, and played for a long run, but constant rumours of a North American tour were never borne out.

- *Sherlock Holmes, the Musical*, by Leslie Bricusse, opened in Exeter in October 1988 and played in London for about two weeks, with Ron Moody as Holmes. A touring revival in 1993 was not a box office success.

- *Sherlock Holmes — the Last Act!* by David Stuart Davies, a British expert who has also written a number of pastiches. Roger Llewellyn has performed this one-man tour de force, based on the reminiscences of an elderly Holmes, since 1999 in countless cities, many nations and three separate continents.

- *Sherlock Holmes, the Final Adventure* by Steven Dietz "seems to be given a new production in North America every month," Roger Johnson wrote in the *Sherlock Holmes Journal* in 2008. It was first produced at the Actors' Theatre of Louisville, Kentucky, in 2007.

Two books attempt to provide an inventory of Sherlockian plays: *On Stage: Sherlock Holmes: Comedy, Drama and Musicals* (1997) by Charles Hall and Peter Blythe and *Sherlock Holmes on the Stage* (2008) by Amnon Kabatchnik.

RADIO

The old-fashioned medium of radio seems perfectly suited to the stories of Holmes and Watson. Holmes has been heard over the air in North America, as well as in the Scandinavian countries and elsewhere, but above all, Holmes on radio is a British genre, having begun in 1938 with a single half-hour production of "Silver Blaze." Five years later Arthur Wontner, by then well known as a Holmes in film, starred in "The Boscombe Valley Mystery"; his Watson was Carleton Hobbs, later to be the greatest of radio Holmeses himself. Occasional other British productions followed, notably a 1954 series of twelve episodes starring John Gielgud as Holmes and Ralph Richardson as Watson, produced by Harry Alan Towers for the BBC Light Programme.

CARLETON HOBBS. Even before the Light Programme gave Gielgud the chance to play the great detective, its BBC rival, the Home Service, had found the definitive radio Holmes. He was Carleton Hobbs (born June 18, 1898; died August 2, 1978), trained at the Royal Academy of Dramatic Arts, who had had a distinguished career on the stage and in films since 1924, as well as in radio. He was first heard October 15, 1952, in "The Naval Treaty," which was presented as part of "The Children's Hour," like sixteen programs (including six stories each attempted twice) from 1952 through 1957. Hobbs was then transferred to the Light Programme, where he starred in "The Hound of the Baskervilles" in six episodes in 1958, and in fifty-six further programs, his last being appropriately "His Last Bow" in July 1969. Most of the performances lasted thirty minutes, but there were ninety-minute interpretations of "A Study in Scarlet," "The Sign of the Four," "The Valley of Fear," and (with a different supporting cast from that of the 1958 series) "The Hound of the Baskervilles." All the stories were based on the Canon; by the end of his radio career Hobbs had presented all but two of the original tales ("The Creeping Man" and "The Veiled Lodger") at least once, eight twice, and five three times. The majority of the Hobbs broadcasts were based on adaptations by Michael Hardwick, prolific writer and broadcaster and well-known Sherlockian. (Hobbs himself became an honorary member of the Sherlock Holmes Society of London.) Hardwick wrote an appreciation of Hobbs on the latter's death in 1978:

> There was some correspondence in *Radio Times* once about the authentic nature of the voice of Holmes. In "The Stock-broker's Clerk" Watson refers to his "high, somewhat strident tones." Carleton Hobbs's tones were not noticeably high, and certainly not strident. Incisive is perhaps the word; the sharp edge which commands, varied with the warmth which endears. Hobbo was passing through his sixties when he recorded those series, which put him a couple of decades beyond Mr. Holmes's prime; but such is radio's deception with voice age, and such Hobbo's art, that he convinced utterly.

Throughout his radio career, Hobbs was complemented by the voice of Norman Shelley as Watson.

GORDON AND LOVELL, RATHBONE AND BRUCE. Holmes came to American radio in 1930 in the voice of William Gillette himself, who starred in "The Speckled Band" for half an hour on the evening of October 20. A week later a continuing series began, starring Richard Gordon as Holmes and Leigh Lovell as Watson; it stretched to a hundred programs, the last of them being heard in May 1933. That series was carried (as was Gillette's broadcast) on NBC's two networks. It began with Canonical tales and ended with such plausible imitations as "The Case of Vamberry, the Wine Merchant" and "The Singular Affair of the Aluminum Crutch." The scripts were the work of Edith Meiser, a young actress, director, and writer whose work demonstrated her devotion to the Canon. Meiser (born May 9, 1898, died September 26, 1993) was a Vassar graduate whose stage debut in 1921 had been followed by the making of reputations in directing, writing, and (with the firm of McKnight and Jordan) production; she also appeared in several films. Meiser maintained a life-long interest in the Canon, joining the Adventuresses of Sherlock Holmes and becoming, in 1991, one of the first women to be admitted as a Baker Street Irregular. A note by Bill Nadel and Ray Stanich in *Prescott's Press* in 1991 describes

> what would be a truly phenomenal second season of exploits on NBC's two major radio networks (the Red and the Blue) as well as their West Coast pickups.... The Holmes cast of Richard Gordon, Leigh Lovell, Lucille Wall, and even Miss Meiser herself would be performing the mystery scripts three times a week, all under the sponsorship of the G. Washington Coffee Company. An avid enthusiast of the Holmes Canon could pick up all three outings of the show each week, if he or she was fortunate enough to live in the Mid-west. Some would even sit by their radios with the Memorial Edition of the tales, checking on the faithfulness of Miss [Meiser's] adaptation.

As the golden age of North American radio continued, a second important series of Holmes exploits was broadcast from Hollywood. Its principal performers: Basil Rathbone and Nigel Bruce, delivering half-hour episodes as Holmes in the intervals of making their films in the same roles. These performances began with "Silver Blaze" on October 2, 1939; by the time they concluded with "The Singular Affair of the Baconian Cipher," on May 27, 1946, a total of 219 episodes had been broadcast. From 1939 through 1942, the Rathbone-Bruce broadcasts were on the NBC "Red" network, thereafter on the Mutual network. To modern listeners, familiar with at least a few of the episodes through scratchy recordings, the commercial sponsors are better known: the Household Finance Corp., Bromo-Quinine, Petri Wine. Edith Meiser was responsible for the scripts until late 1943; Denis Green, a British radio writer, and "Anthony Boucher" (William Anthony Parker White), by then a recognized Sherlockian, then took over. "Clearly, Green and Boucher were serious about their Sherlockianism," say Robert and William Persing, reviewing the series in the *Baker Street Journal* in 1991. They judge one typical episode "a striking mystery, Canonically inspired, and played intelligently," one strength of the series being the meatier roles given to Watson than Bruce was allowed to play in the Rathbone films of the same era.

> The series as a whole (though not always in its individual parts) posits a middle ground, halfway between the intellectual mysteries of the Watsonian stories and the action-adventure, melodramatic world of the Universal films.... In the plotting, too, the quality varies considerably.... As a radio program, it is sharply acted, well-written, and makes good use of its radio format. (The show's use of sound effects is particularly evocative, and they are used as important clues in more than one adventure.)

Audio recordings of many of these adventures are now on the market for a new generation of listeners and collectors.

When Rathbone abandoned the role of Holmes in 1946, it was briefly played for the ABC network by Tom Conway, with Nigel Bruce returning as Watson. Next to try was John Stanley, in a total of seventy-eight programs for Mutual in 1947–48. Other actors have taken to the air from time to time, less ambitiously.

MERRISON AND WILLIAMS. Sherlock Holmes had returned to BBC radio occasionally since Hobbs and Shelley, and in 1987 when plans were made to do a new version of *The Hound of the Baskervilles*, one question was obvious. "If someone says to you, why are they doing that old workhorse yet again," said producer-director David Johnston, "tell them this: because we're going to do it better than it's ever been done before." He was speaking to the writer of the script, Bert Coules, who tells the story in a little book titled *221BBC* (1998). Their version of *The Hound* was broadcast in two parts, May 27 and June 3, 1988, with Roger Rees as Holmes and Crawford Logan as Watson.

On the strength of that success, the BBC commissioned Coules to write more scripts, but new actors were cast: Clive Merrison (born 1945) as Holmes and Michael Williams (1935–2001) as Watson. They appeared in *A Study in Scarlet* and *The Sign of the Four*, broadcast on BBC Radio Four in 1989, and then embarked on the *Adventures* and *Memoirs* in 1991, with the intent of dramatizing all sixty of the Canonical tales, the first time any radio team had done that. Other writers were involved, but Coules remained throughout, and for most of the project the producer-directors were Enyd Williams and Patrick Rayner. After all the short stories had been presented, Merrison and Williams did *The Valley of Fear*, and finally, on May 26, 1998, their own new version of *The Hound of the Baskervilles* (with a cameo appearance by Judi Dench, Williams's wife, as Mrs. Hudson).

The results were congenial to a Sherlockian ear, as Roger Johnson wrote:

> Both actors have what I should call ageless voices, unlike some of their predecessors. Hobbs and Shelley were permanently middle-aged, even when they were young; David Buck sounded too old to be consorting with Barry Foster's energetic young Holmes. Merrison and Williams sound *right* together. They also share with Hobbs and Shelley the helpful fact that their voices contrast, by which I mean that Merrison sounds like Holmes and not like Watson, while Williams sounds like Watson and not like Holmes. Williams as Watson is clearly a normal, intelligent, educated man — a bit of a romantic, but essentially practical and level-headed. Merrison's Holmes has something of the theatrical manner of Jeremy Brett's interpretation ... the manic-depressive genius that is Sherlock Holmes.

The whole project was so successful that Coules was called on to create additional scripts. Williams had died in 2001, but Merrison returned to the studio accompanied by Andrew Sachs as Watson for "The Further Adventures of Sherlock Holmes" in 2002 and 2004.

FILM

It is plausibly said that Sherlock Holmes has appeared in more films, and been represented by more actors, than any other character. Ronald DeWaal in his *World Bibliography* estimated the number of films as "over 150" as of 1974. They range from early, ephemeral pieces and long-lost comedies to modern feature films, as well as the classic Basil Rathbone movies of the 1940s which for four decades defined the public image of Holmes. Several books have been published on the subject, some of them also addressing television productions:

- *Sherlock Holmes on the Screen* (1977), by Robert W. Pohle Jr. and Douglas C. Hart.
- *The Films of Sherlock Holmes* (1978), by Chris Steinbrunner and Norman Michaels.
- *Sherlock Holmes Screen and Sound Guide* (1994) by Gordon E. Kelley.
- *Sir Arthur Conan Doyle at the Cinema* (1996) by Scott Allen Nollen.
- *Starring Sherlock Holmes* (2001, new edition 2007) by David Stuart Davies.
- *Sherlock Holmes on Screen* (2002) by Alan Barnes.

The earliest in the genre is a mere eighteen feet of sixteen-millimetre film titled *Sherlock Holmes Baffled* — "clearly made for viewing on a mutoscope or peepshow machine," according to Michael Pointer, who discovered it. It was filmed April 26, 1900. The films of the following two decades — several from Denmark, others from Italy and Germany, as well as England and the United States — were mostly short and, as DeWaal puts it, "pseudo-Sherlockian," treating Holmes as a figure of fun. Comic actor Mack Sennett made several Holmes comedies in 1911 and1912, directed by film pioneer D.W. Griffith.

After the 1916 film of William Gillette's play was released, however, other serious films followed, including forty-seven starring Eille Norwood. All but one of his films co-starred Hubert Willis as Watson. They began with a full-length "Hound of the Baskervilles" in 1921 and went on with forty-five two-reelers (length about thirty-five minutes apiece) based on individual cases, chosen in an unusual order. The first series (1921) began with *The Dying Detective* and *The Devil's Foot* before continuing with the inevitable *A Scandal in Bohemia*. *The Final Problem* was held until last of all, concluding the third series of films (1923). Later that year Norwood co-starred with Arthur Cullin as Watson in a full-length *Sign of the Four*. Eille Norwood (real name Anthony Brett; born October 11, 1861; died December 24, 1948) also had a career as a stage actor, and did play Holmes on the stage in 1923 in *The Return of Sherlock Holmes*. Arthur Conan Doyle — who had no opportunity to see most of the great Holmesian actors — thought very highly of Norwood, paying this tribute in *Memories and Adventures*:

> He has that rare quality which can only be described as glamour, which compels you to watch an actor eagerly even when he is doing nothing. He has the brooding eye which excites expectation and he has also a quite unrivalled power of disguise. My

only criticism of the films is that they introduce telephones, motor cars and other luxuries of which the Victorian Holmes never dreamed.

Many succeeding films, of course, would do the same.

Norwood was succeeded on screen by Arthur Wontner, who made *The Sleeping Cardinal* (retitled *Sherlock Holmes' Fatal Hour* for an American audience) in 1930, *The Missing Rembrandts* in 1932, *The Sign of Four* in 1932, *The Triumph of Sherlock Holmes* (*The Valley of Fear*) in 1934, and *The Silver Blaze* (*Murder at the Baskervilles*) in 1936. Wontner (1875–1960) maintained an interest in Holmesian matters, accepting an honorary membership in the Sherlock Holmes Society of London, and was judged by some as the finest portrayer Holmes ever had — "the veritable fathomer of Baker Street in person," said Vincent Starrett.

Among the other portrayers of Holmes in the early film period:

- John Barrymore in *Sherlock Holmes* (retitled *Moriarty* in England), 1922.
- Clive Brook in *The Return of Sherlock Holmes*, 1929, and *Sherlock Holmes*, 1932.
- Raymond Massey in *The Speckled Band*, 1931.

BASIL RATHBONE. Steinbrunner and Michaels in *The Films of Sherlock Holmes* explain how the screen's most influential Holmes came to be:

> In 1939, at a Hollywood cocktail party — so legend has it — Twentieth Century-Fox studio head Darryl Zanuck suddenly turned to a fellow guest, British actor Basil Rathbone, and declared he would make a perfect Sherlock Holmes....
>
> "Hi there, Sherlock, how's Watson?" Variants of the chant were to haunt Rathbone the rest of his career. In his autobiography, *In and Out of Character*, Rathbone laments at "being 'typed,' more completely 'typed' than any other classic actor has ever been or ever will be again...."

The films that star Rathbone as Sherlock Holmes — fourteen of them, made in two brief bursts — were successes when they first appeared and have been perennials ever since. It is difficult to find a week when one of them is not being shown on some television station's late movie, and video rental has given them a whole new audience. A full study of them is *Ready When You Are, Mr. Rathbone* (1992), by Roger Johnson.

Only two of the fourteen films were made by Twentieth Century-Fox, and they are the two generally considered best, and certainly the two most faithful to Holmes's late-Victorian environment. Steinbrunner and Michaels again:

> Here, quite innovatively, Holmes was sent back some fifty years and more to the original time in which the stories were set, accentuating the rich Victorian details separating that more peaceful epoch with a disordered 1939, where war-clouds were already gathering. It has been said that converting *Hound* into a "costume classic" was less a daring than a commercial move, very right for audiences thirsting for escapist entertainment; nonetheless, the idea of a gaslit Holmes was strikingly original, quite set apart from the many modern-dress Sherlocks familiar to thirties moviegoers.

The Hound of the Baskervilles was released in March 1939; it co-starred Richard Greene as Sir Henry Baskerville and Wendy Barrie as Beryl Stapleton. While *The Hound* follows the original story, *The Adventures*, released six months later, is only loosely based on anything Canonical apart from the villainy of Professor Moriarty. The plot has to do with an attempted theft of the Crown Jewels, and ends with a shootout and Moriarty's presumed death at the Tower of London. The heroine, Ann Brandon, was played by Ida Lupino, and a bearded Moriarty by George Zucco.

Two years later, Rathbone began to play Holmes again, grinding out a dozen films for a competing studio, Universal, between the fall of 1942 and the summer of 1946. In these short features (each runs slightly longer than an hour) Holmes was returned to the present day, wearing fedora and trench-coat and jumping onto automobile running-boards. None is based in any significant way on Canonical material; the films frankly attempted to show a Holmes tackling "problems of the present day," which in several cases meant the Nazi evils of World War II. These are the Rathbone films made for Universal Studios:

- *Sherlock Holmes and the Voice of Terror*, 1942, vaguely based on *His Last Bow* but transferred to the World War II era; starring Evelyn Ankers, Reginald Denny, Thomas Gomez.

- *Sherlock Holmes and the Secret Weapon*, 1942, in which Moriarty is hired by the Nazis to steal the new invention; starring Lionel Atwill (as Moriarty), William Post Jr., Kaaren Verne.
- *Sherlock Holmes in Washington*, 1943, about counter-espionage and kidnapping on an American train; starring Marjorie Lord, George Zucco, Henry Daniell.
- *Sherlock Holmes Faces Death*, 1943, vaguely based on "The Musgrave Ritual" but set at an army convalescent home; starring Hillary Brooke, Arthur Margetson, Halliwell Hobbes.
- *The Spider Woman*, 1944, about a series of suicides that turn out to be murders; starring Gale Sondergaard, Vernon Downing, Alec Craig.
- *The Scarlet Claw*, 1944, about a series of killings in a Québec village that are thought to be supernatural but of course prove to be murders; starring Gerald Hamer, Miles Mander, Arthur Hohl. An epilogue to this film, released shortly after the Québec Conference that set the direction for the last year of the war, gives Holmes an opportunity to speak of a golden Anglo-American future.
- *The Pearl of Death*, 1944, more or less based on "The Six Napoleons"; starring Evelyn Ankers, Ian Wolfe, Rondo Hatton.
- *The House of Fear*, 1945, about a group of men living together in a castle who die mysteriously one by one; starring Aubrey Mather, Paul Cavanagh, Holmes Herbert.
- *The Woman in Green*, 1945, about a series of women murdered and mutilated in London; starring Hillary Brooke, Henry Daniell (as Moriarty, who dies again), Paul Cavanagh.
- *Pursuit to Algiers*, 1945, about the attempt to return King Nikolas to Algiers aboard ship; starring Marjorie Riordan, Leslie Vincent, Martin Kosleck.
- *Terror by Night*, 1946, about the transportation of the Star of Rhodesia diamond from London to Edinburgh; starring Alan Mowbray (as Colonel Moran), Renee Godfrey, Mary Forbes.
- *Dressed to Kill*, 1946, in Britain retitled *Sherlock Holmes and the Secret Code*, about the search for stolen engraving plates for Bank of England notes, the clues being concealed in music-boxes; starring Patricia Morrison, Edmond Breon, Frederick Worlock.

Basil Rathbone as a hawk-nosed Holmes and Nigel Bruce as Watson question Hillary Brooke in a scene from "Sherlock Holmes Faces Death," released in 1943. The plot draws in part from "The Musgrave Ritual" — hence the name of Hillary Brooke's character, Sally Musgrave — and has only incidental references to World War II, but the costumes make clear that the events are set in the 1940s.

Besides Rathbone and Bruce as Holmes and Watson, the films include two continuing characters: Dennis Hoey as Lestrade and Mary Gordon as Mrs. Hudson. Several other actors provided what Steinbrunner and Michaels call "a sort of stock company," appearing in various roles, although the two films that require Moriarty present him through different actors.

But the memorable figure is Basil Rathbone (born June 13, 1892; died July 21, 1967). "The physical resemblance of Rathbone to the Sidney Paget illustrations was quite striking," says one critic, while another maintains that he looked like the Holmes drawn by Frederic Dorr Steele. The energy and arrogance Rathbone shows, at least in his finer scenes, are certainly those of

Holmes, although the portrayal cannot be called subtle. Rathbone even snaps, "Elementary, my dear Watson!" now and then, a phrase that never crossed Holmes's lips. He came to the character late in his acting career, having first reached the stage in 1911 and first appeared in film in 1921. In 1930 he played New York detective Philo Vance in *The Bishop Murder Case*. Through the 1930s he was seen in adventure films, and he returned to that genre even after his early appearances as Holmes. In 1940, for example, he made *The Mark of Zorro* (he was the villain, opposite Tyrone Power), and there were other films late in his career, even including *Ghost in the Invisible Bikini*, co-starring Rathbone and Boris Karloff. He also made stage appearances and did much radio work, but never escaped the image of Sherlock Holmes with which he remains associated twenty-five years after his death. He says a few words about Holmes in his autobiography, *In and Out of Character* (1962).

Rathbone's Holmes is complemented in all these films by Nigel Bruce (born February 4, 1895; died October 8, 1953), who plays a decent but dunder-headed Watson. Scene after scene requires Bruce to make a fool of himself with women and children, in awkward physical situations, or simply by lagging hopelessly far behind the insight and energetic action displayed by Holmes. In some of the later films, as Rathbone's enthusiasm was visibly failing, Bruce did get fatter parts to play. "In the climax in at least two of the films," Steinbrunner and Michaels note, "it is he who saves Holmes after the latter has stupidly allowed himself to be trapped by the enemy." But Bruce's Watson is most memorable for the fool he manages to make of himself — quacking like a duck to distract a child in *Dressed to Kill*, for example. Already an experienced actor before he fell in with Rathbone, Bruce is deservedly given much of the credit for the success of their films.

During the years they were making their films together, Rathbone and Bruce also presented Holmes and Watson on radio in more than two hundred half-hour episodes.

THE ERA OF COLOUR. Holmes was brought to the screen in colour for the first time in *The Hound of the Baskervilles*, a 1959 film starring Peter Cushing (1913–94), already a veteran of the horror films for which he would be best remembered. Few Sherlockians are neutral about this *Hound*, made by Hammer Film Productions, a British studio also known for its horror films, and it does emphasize the chilling and grotesque aspects of the story. Some liberties are taken, particularly with the character of Cecile (Beryl) Stapleton as played by Marla Landi, and with other aspects of the plot as well. The film also stars André Morell as Watson and, oddly, Christopher Lee as Sir

Henry Baskerville. Three years later, Lee appeared as Holmes instead, in *Sherlock Holmes und das Halsband des Todes* (1962), released in English in 1964 as *Sherlock Holmes and the Deadly Necklace*. This German production had Thorley Walters as Watson. Its plot is melodramatic, dealing with attempts by Moriarty (Hans Söhnker) to steal an ancient Egyptian necklace. Then in 1966 came *A Study in Terror* (and the subsequent Ellery Queen novelization) pitting Holmes against Jack the Ripper. John Neville played Holmes, and Donald Houston was Watson.

The next important Holmes film was *The Private Life of Sherlock Holmes*, a 1970 comedy created by Billy Wilder. The film emphasizes its exploration of the relationship between Holmes (Robert Stephens) and Watson (Colin Blakely) and throws Holmes into a complex relationship with an attractive woman (played by Genevieve Page). Christopher Lee appears as Mycroft Holmes, and the script gives Holmes an opportunity to meet a grateful Queen Victoria when he has foiled the obligatory enemy scheme. Barbara Roden analysed "The Wilder Side of Sherlock Holmes" in *Canadian Holmes* in 1996, writing that

> This is, after all, the film that contains the notorious scene in which Holmes *seems* (please note the italics) to say that he is gay; and how seriously can one really take a Sherlock Holmes adventure which concerns (among other things) missing midgets, mysterious monks, a Russian ballerina who wants Holmes to father her child, and the Loch Ness monster?

The film was considerably cut before release, with entire subplots being excised, though a laser disc version is now available with parts of the deleted material restored.

They Might Be Giants, released in 1971, is not a Victorian exploit, nor is it conventional in any other way. It stars George C. Scott as a retired judge who becomes convinced that he is Holmes, and Joanne Woodward as his psychiatrist, conveniently named Dr. Watson, who is caught up in increasingly surrealist adventures with him. Steinbrunner and Michaels say this about it:

> In truth, *They Might Be Giants* is every bit as fragile and tender as its cinematic predecessor, and indeed, like *Private Life*, was misunderstood, mutilated, and a box-office failure.... The climax is both ambivalent and poignant. Fleeing the police (sent by his brother), Justin [Holmes] and Mildred make their way to

Central Park. There, in the dusk, they hear he clatter of horses' hoofs. Justin knows it is the forces of evil — Moriarty — and it may mean their deaths. Mildred Watson by this time has "crossed over," and shares in all of Justin's fancies. Together they will resist the unseen foe hurtling towards them, or die — as the screen is wiped into color.

There are few more touching scenes in all of Holmesian cinematography.

In 1975 Gene Wilder starred as Sigi Holmes in *The Adventure of Sherlock Holmes' Smarter Brother*, a lunatic affair also starring Marty Feldman as Orville Sacker of Scotland Yard and the delicious Madeline Kahn as the music-hall singer ("Miss Liar!") whose blackmailing case Sherlock Holmes's brother must handle. There are brief appearances by Douglas Wilmer as Sherlock and Thorley Walters as Watson.

The film based on Nicholas Meyer's novel about Holmes and Freud, *The Seven-Per-Cent Solution*, was a popular as well as a Sherlockian success, and did much to fuel the Sherlockian "boom" that lasted through the late 1970s. Despite its modest budget (reports said it was made in twelve weeks for $4.2 million), it presented a constellation of stars: Nicol Williamson as Holmes, Alan Arkin as Sigmund Freud, Vanessa Redgrave as the chanteuse who must be rescued. The second half of the plot departs considerably from that in Meyer's novel. A review in the *New York Post* was less than complimentary:

> There's only one conceivable suspect in the case, and the story quickly devolves into an extended chase, complete with speeding locomotives and do-or-die sword fights.... The film is also dotted with the recurring, inter-cut image of a young boy ascending a staircase — an image that is apparently supposed to whet our appetite for a big psychological revelation.

Other reviewers enjoyed the film more, particularly praising director Herbert Ross. (The screenplay was the work of Meyer himself.) "The Seven-Per-Cent Solution" also starred Robert Duvall as Watson and Laurence Olivier as Moriarty. It opened October 24, 1976.

The other important and successful Holmes film of the modern era is the greatly admired *Murder by Decree*, released in 1979 and starring Christopher Plummer (born December 13, 1927) as Holmes and James Mason as a deliciously doddering Watson. A scene in which Holmes loses patience with

Watson's finicky attempt to eat green peas is one of the gems of Sherlockian cinema. The film presents Holmes investigating the Jack the Ripper murders. The solution — based on some of the more improbable speculations of recent Ripperologists — involves Masonic rituals and a government cover-up to protect noted politicians and royalty; the long-drawn-out final scene of the film, in which Holmes confronts the prime minister (played by John Gielgud), is not its high point. More affecting is the role of Geneviève Bujold as a young woman hidden away in an asylum because she knows the guilty secret. A novelization of the film, by Robert Weverka, was published in 1979 (and copyright by "Saucy Jack Inc.").

A few other feature films have appeared in recent years:

- In 1978 Peter Cook (as Holmes) and Dudley Moore (as Watson and other characters) appeared, along with a galaxy of British comedy stars, in a parody version of *The Hound of the Baskervilles*.
- Steven Spielberg produced *Young Sherlock Holmes* in 1985, starring Nicholas Rowe as an eighteen-year-old Holmes who solves his first case in the company of schoolmate Watson (Alan Cox). It involves several murders, together with — in one reviewer's contemptuous summary — "an Egyptian cult that pours boiling hot goop over virgins during formal dress ceremonies with a lot of men shaved bald and chanting weird things." The film also uses spectacular special effects, created by Pixar Animation in its earliest days, to represent drug hallucinations. Sophie Ward appears as the winsome Elizabeth.
- *Without a Clue*, released in 1988, was a comedy based on the premise that Watson (Ben Kingsley) was the brains of the partnership, Holmes (Michael Caine) an actor who bumbles through his role, even saying that one victim "was bludgeoned to death with a blunt excrement."

All these films were produced in an era when big-screen theatrical release was the important way of reaching viewers, and distribution through rental or individual purposes was a mere afterthought. They were all, of course, also issued on videotape, and subsequently on DVD for home viewing and Sherlockian collecting. Even as the last few were appearing, however, the media universe was changing, with a number of Sherlockian films being made specifically for television.

In 2009, director Guy Ritchie is at work on a new film, to be titled simply *Sherlock Holmes*, with Robert Downey Jr. in the title role, Jude Law as Watson, and Rachel McAdams as Irene Adler. "I never agreed with the idea of the fairly stuffy Edwardian-type gentleman," co-producer Lionel Wigram told an interviewer, defending the new film's emphasis on physical action. "I've been thinking for the last ten years that there must be a way to reinvent Sherlock Holmes." Many producers have thought so, and as the film was being put together, rumours spread that Holmes and Watson would be presented as homosexual in addition to being, in Wigram's words, "more modern, more bohemian."

TELEVISION

For a contemporary viewer it is hard to see past Jeremy Brett and to remember that before he took to the screen as Holmes in 1984 there had been many other television Holmeses, some of them much admired. A surprisingly detailed history of Holmes in television appears as a long chapter in Peter Haining's *The Television Sherlock Holmes* (1986), which is chiefly about the Brett productions but which puts them properly in context. The first appearance of the great nineteenth-century detective on the great twentieth-century medium of entertainment came November 27, 1937, in a single broadcast from New York's Radio City. Louis Hector played Sherlock Holmes. The script, "The Three Garridebs," was published three years later as part of a textbook on broadcast production.

There have been other single television shows over the years, including a half-hour program starring Basil Rathbone in 1953. Among them:

- A 1972 movie of *The Hound of the Baskervilles* starring Stewart Granger (with Bernard Fox as Watson and William Shatner as Stapleton).
- "Sherlock Holmes in New York," made for NBC television in 1976; it starred Roger Moore as Holmes, Patrick Macnee as Watson, Charlotte Rampling as Irene Adler, and John Huston as Moriarty, in a plot that brings Holmes to New York to solve a bank robbery with implications for international affairs. A novelization by D.R. Bensen was published the same year.
- "The Return of the World's Greatest Detective," a ninety-minute series pilot in 1976 starring Larry Hagman as "Sherman Holmes."
- "Masks of Death," starring Peter Cushing in his last appearance as Holmes, with John Mills as Watson, produced in 1984.
- "The Return of Sherlock Holmes," an improbable confection starring Michael Pennington as a Holmes lately thawed out from cryogenic

preservation of his body. Margaret Colin is a young Jane Watson who joins him for adventures that include a visit to London Bridge in Lake Havasu City, Arizona. There were speculations that the 1987 film was intended as the pilot for a series.

- "Hands of a Murderer," broadcast in 1990, starring Edward Woodward as Holmes and John Hillerman as a goateed Watson; the plot has to do with Moriarty (rescued from the scaffold), Mycroft Holmes (kidnapped), and international espionage (foiled).
- "Sherlock Holmes, The Golden Years: Incident at Victoria Falls," made in 1991, with Christopher Lee as an aged Holmes investigating a South African jewel theft in the company of Theodore Roosevelt and other prominent figures. Patrick Macnee plays Watson, and Jenny Seagrove is Lillie Langtry.
- "Sherlock Holmes and the Leading Lady," also with Christopher Lee and Patrick Macnee (1992). Morgan Fairchild is a harshly American Irene Adler.
- A second film about a Holmes emerging from cryogenic storage: "1994 Baker Street: Sherlock Holmes Returns," with Anthony Higgins as Holmes and Debrah Farentino as Dr. Amy Winslow, which aired in 1993. The plot puts Holmes in San Francisco, tracking down an evil descendant of Professor Moriarty.
- Four films starring Canadian actor Matt Frewer as Holmes and Kenneth Welsh as Watson: "The Hound of the Baskervilles" (2000), "The Sign of Four" (2001), "The Royal Scandal" (2001) and "The Case of the Whitechapel Vampire" (2002).

But the characteristic form in television is the series — a structure essentially based on Arthur Conan Doyle's invention of linked short stories featuring the same central characters — and several series have brought Sherlock Holmes to the small screen. The first was a set of six program in the fall of 1951 on Britain's BBC; they starred Alan Wheatley as Holmes and Raymond Francis as Watson, with Iris Vandeleur as Mrs. Hudson. In the fifth episode, "The Red-Headed League," Sebastian Cabot appeared as Jabez Wilson. A second British series was aired in 1964–65; it consisted of thirteen episodes starring Douglas Wilmer as Holmes and Nigel Stock as Watson. David Burke, later to be a well-known Watson, appeared in one episode, "The Beryl Coronet."

In 1968 came Peter Cushing — nine years after his melodramatic film of *The Hound of the Baskervilles* — with fifteen episodes on the BBC, co-starring

Nigel Stock as Watson. Edward Hardwicke, later to be a great Watson, played a minor role in "The Greek Interpreter." Two of the episodes were adapted for television by Michael and Mollie Hardwick, whose hand was behind so much that was Holmesian in Britain for a generation. One enthusiast, Percy Metcalfe, wrote to the *Sherlock Holmes Journal* to protest:

> The series is infinitely inferior to the last one — Douglas Wilmer, to my mind, gave a far more realistic Sherlockian representation than does Peter Cushing, experienced actor though he undoubtedly is.... Not only have the titles been mixed up, but also the text has been tampered with to an extraordinary degree. Take the Dancing Man, for instance.... Why the prolonged love scenes and all that rubbish about Mrs. Cubitt being pregnant? It held up the action of the story.

It is perhaps just as well that such a critic had not seen the 1954–55 television series that appeared in the United States, starring Ronald Howard as Holmes and Howard Marion Crawford as Watson. That the Canon was "tampered with" in these thirty-nine episodes — a full year's series, as television then counted it — is suggested by a mere list of some episode titles:

- "The Case of the Cunningham Heritage," first of the series, broadcast on NBC October 18, 1954.
- "The Case of the Shoeless Engineer."
- "The Case of the Laughing Mummy."
- "The Case of the Jolly Hangman."
- "The Case of the Baker Street Bachelors."

It is almost a shock to see "The Case of the Red-Headed League" half-way down the list.

But the Ronald Howard shows were much more authentic than their titles suggest. They were the work of Sheldon Reynolds, a young writer-director who was determined to undo what Basil Rathbone had done a decade earlier; he would put Holmes back in Baker Street and back in the 1890s, and present the detective as "not an infallible, eagle-eyed, out-of-the-ordinary personality, but an exceptionally sincere young man trying to get ahead in his profession." Watson, in turn, was no buffoon but, in Crawford's words, "a normal man, solid on his feet, a medical student who gives valuable advice." The shows were filmed at a studio near Paris, with location shots actually in London, and the producers spent much effort to recreate the Baker Street flat and other authentic scenes.

Their work was well received both by critics and by Sherlockians. The effusions of Edgar W. Smith, writing in the *Baker Street Journal*, are remarkable, coming as they do from a scholar with a pure devotion to the written Canon:

> The two films which our Committee on Canonicity reviewed last night are authentic in every detail; they capture the full flavor of the times in which Holmes and Watson lived, and they portray faithfully the characteristics and the mood which are, to us, the essence of these tales.... the conception of the Master, conveyed by Ronald Howard, is the very conception suggested by Sidney Paget in the pages of the old Strand Magazine.

Half a century later, no one would offer equally credible praise for "Sherlock Holmes in the 22nd Century," an animated series aimed at children, produced for Britain's ITV network in 1999 and broadcast in the United States by Fox Kids. There has been, however, a good deal of enthusiasm for a series featuring Vasily Livanov (born 1935) as Holmes and Vitaly Solomin as Watson, filmed and broadcast in the Soviet Union between 1979 and 1986. Little known in English-speaking countries at first, the eleven episodes are now available on DVD with subtitles.

JEREMY BRETT. The image of Basil Rathbone as the definitive Holmes was supplanted in the public mind only when Jeremy Brett came to the screen in 1984, in a series of episodes, most of them an hour long, made for Britain's Granada Television. The quality of the early Granada productions was high, and their appeal was tremendous, to the point that a 1991 retrospective in the *Sherlock Holmes Review* was titled "Lifting the Curse of Basil." Jeremy Brett (original surname Huggins; born November 3, 1935) was quickly transformed from a Shakespearean actor, also known for his work in light comedy, into the best-known Sherlock Holmes of the electronic era by far. Brett stars in three dozen hours of drama made for the small screen by Granada, a production company based in Manchester:

First series (1984)
"A Scandal in Bohemia," with Gayle Hunnicutt as Irene Adler
"The Dancing Men," with Betsy Brantley as Elsie Cubitt

"The Naval Treaty," with David Gwillim as Percy Phelps
"The Solitary Cyclist," with Barbara Wilshere as Violet Smith
"The Crooked Man," with Norman Jones as Henry Wood
"The Speckled Band," with Jeremy Kemp as Grimesby Roylott
"The Blue Carbuncle," with Frank Middlemass as Henry Baker

Second series (1985)
"The Copper Beeches," with Natasha Richardson as Violet Hunter
"The Greek Interpreter," with Charles Gray as Mycroft Holmes
"The Norwood Builder," with Matthew Solon as John Hector
    McFarlane
"The Resident Patient," with Nicholas Clay as Percy Trevelyan
"The Red-Headed League," with Roger Hammond as Jabez
    Wilson
"The Final Problem," with Eric Porter as James Moriarty

Third series (1986)
"The Empty House," with Patrick Allen as Sebastian Moran
"The Abbey Grange," with Anne Louise Lambert as Mary
    Brackenstall
"The Musgrave Ritual," with Michael Culver as Reginald Mus-
    grave
"The Second Stain," with Patricia Hodge as Hilda Trelawney
    Hope
"The Man with the Twisted Lip," with Clive Francis as Neville
    St. Clair
"The Priory School," with Alan Howard as the Duke of Hold-
    ernesse
"The Six Napoleons," with Eric Sykes as Horace Harker

Fourth series (1987)
"The Sign of Four," with Jenny Seagrove as Mary Morstan [two
    hours]
"The Devil's Foot," with Denis Quilley as Leon Sterndale
"Silver Blaze," with Peter Barkworth as Colonel Ross
"The Bruce-Partington Plans," with Jonathan Newth as Valentine
    Walter
"Wisteria Lodge," with Donald Churchill as John Scott Eccles

"The Hound of the Baskervilles," with Kristoffer Tabori as Henry Baskerville [two hours]

Fifth series (1991–93)
"The Illustrious Client," with Anthony Valentine as Baron Gruner
"The Creeping Man," with Charles Kay as Professor Presbury
"Thor Bridge," with Daniel Massey as Neil Gibson
"The Boscombe Valley Mystery," with Peter Vaughan as John Turner
"Lady Frances Carfax," with Cheryl Campbell in the title role
"The Master Blackmailer" ("Charles Augustus Milverton"), with Robert Hardy as Milverton [two hours]
"The Last Vampyre" ("The Sussex Vampire"), with Richard Dempsey as Jacky Ferguson [two hours]
"The Eligible Bachelor" ("The Noble Bachelor"), with Paris Jefferson as Hatty Doran [two hours]

Sixth series (1994)
"The Three Gables," with Claudine Auger as Isadora Klein
"The Dying Detective," with Jonathan Hyde as Culverton Smith
"The Golden Pince-Nez," with Frank Finlay as Professor Coram
"The Red Circle," with John Hallam as Black Gorgiano
"The Mazarin Stone," with Jon Finch as Count Sylvius, and Charles Gray as Mycroft Holmes, taking Brett's place
"The Cardboard Box," with Ciaran Hinds as Jim Browner

The episodes were shown first on British television; they had their first North American airing, generally about a year after the British viewing, on the *Mystery!* series of the PBS network, and have been repeated several times in subsequent years, as well as being distributed in various packages in CD form.

The greatest strength of the Granada series is its detailed re-creation of the Victorian scene. Success in that respect was no accident, as Cox, the producer until late in the series, wrote in a 1991 memoir:

We had a wonderful design team who re-created 221-B Baker Street inside and out with absolute devotion. We produced a 70 page document on 221-B and all that went in it, with over

Jeremy Brett as Holmes and David Burke as Watson in a publicity still from the original series of "The Adventures of Sherlock Holmes," 1984–85. The street scene shows how elaborate (and authentic, compared to previous attempts) were the sets created by Granada Television. Burke was later replaced as Watson by Edward Hardwicke.

a thousand entries. They also made a similar attack on the factual records of the period. If you want to know what offices and restaurants were found in Baker Street in 1890, look at our exterior set.

The "70-page document" was subsequently published by Calabash Press as *The Baker Street File* (1997). Cox went on to talk about the extraordinary fidelity he and his colleagues had maintained to the Canonical text, with long stretches of dialogue lifted directly from Doyle's page. When the Granada scripts depart from the Canon, therefore, it is of special interest. Cox cites an example in connection with "The Norwood Builder":

I think that even Inspector Lestrade, who was certainly ahead of his time in the study of fingerprints, had access to the necessary tests of blood and bones. The bones and the blood have to be human bones and blood. Therefore, "enter the tramp," as Holmes says at one point in the story when theorizing over possible solutions. The tramp in our film becomes Oldacre's victim when he needed a corpse to pass off as his own. Holmes of course was familiar with the language of tramps, as he was with all forms of secret writing, noticed the signs left by the doomed man, and began to establish that the remains in the yard were not those of Jonas Oldacre. Why Watson chose to conceal this aspect of the case I simply do not understand.

The Granada scriptwriters and directors can be seen to have taken the Canon seriously, though not always literally. Watson is consistently presented as unmarried; changes were necessary in "The Sign of the Four" to avoid any implication that he marries Mary Morstan at its conclusion. Another feature of interest in the adaptation for television is that each episode begins, not with a Baker Street scene, but with a glimpse of the crime which Holmes will soon be seen investigating.

The productions are rich with detail that a viewer cannot fully absorb the first time through, with Canonical and period allusions, loving touches to the set design and properties, and even carefully chosen music. In "The Illustrious Client," for example, while Baron Gruner leafs through his "lust diary," the music is the "Catalogue Song" aria from Mozart's *Don Giovanni*, in which that predecessor of the Baron enumerates his own conquests. The music for the series in general is the responsibility of Patrick Gowers; the violin solo, supposedly by Holmes, that is its theme is played by Kathy Gowers, his daughter. The photography is beautiful, even though, as Brett said, "I wished we could do it in black and white" to achieve a stark quality. His frequently abrupt physical movement contributes to such an effect; directors (a number of them as the series has progressed) often posed Brett to duplicate the moments of action captured in Sidney Paget's original drawings.

Brett's Holmes has been complemented by two Watsons. In the first two series, the doctor's part was played by David Burke (born May 25, 1934), who established himself as something better than the stereotypical buffoon. "He is the most ordinary man in the world," Burke told one interviewer. "At the same time he is the best kind of English gentleman." That style of Watson was maintained by Burke's successor, Edward Hardwicke, who first appeared in "The Empty House," looking remarkably like a Burke who had been aged by sorrow and the passage of several years after Holmes's supposed death. In subsequent episodes, and in *The Secret of Sherlock Holmes* on London stages, he has presented a Watson who is sensible, reliable, and moderately intelligent, with experience useful to Holmes from such fields as medicine and military life. Hardwicke (born August 7, 1932, son of the noted actor Sir Cedric Hardwicke) became very close to Brett as the series progressed. In one interview Brett called Hardwicke "the best friend a man's ever had," and in another "England's greatest actor, I believe."

The enthusiasm with which Sherlockians greeted Brett's interpretation of Holmes, and the impetus his work gave to the growth of the Sherlockian cult in the 1980s, can hardly be exaggerated, even though not all viewers were equally enthusiastic about his interpretation of the great detective. Speculation about future productions arose after each new series of episodes: would the entire Canon be filmed? In the end it was not. Devotees agonized with Brett when he suffered a mental collapse in 1987, rejoiced when he returned to work, and looked cautiously at the two-hour productions of 1992 and 1993 as Granada, after the departure of producer Michael Cox, took greater and greater liberties with the authentic Holmes. By 1993 — as was evident even in the finished productions — Brett was seriously ill, suffering from physical ailments as well as his life-long manic depression. In the final episodes of the last Sherlock Holmes series, he barely appeared. Brett died September 12, 1995; some of the memorials that followed were fundraisers for the British charity MDF, The Bipolar Organisation.

Some of Jeremy Paul's scripts for the series appear in booklet form, accompanied from photographs, by Ian Henry Publications Ltd. *A Centenary Celebration of Sherlock Holmes, 1887–1897*, with text by Kenneth Harris and edited by Michael Cox (of Granada) and Andrew Robinson, includes excellent reproductions of scenes from the series. Other printed works of interest are *Jeremy Brett and David Burke: An Adventure in Canonical Fidelity* (1986) by R. Dixon Smith, published by the University of Minnesota Libraries, and *Bending the Willow: Jeremy Brett as Sherlock Holmes* (1996), a biography by David Stuart Davies.

OTHER MEDIA

MUSIC. The tune now most associated with Sherlock Holmes is the theme for the Granada television series starring Jeremy Brett, composed by Patrick

Gowers and performed by Kathy Gowers on solo violin. A recording with other material from the series is widely available on CD. Stage and screen have provided other music as well, including the tunes for the musical *Baker Street* and other stage works, and soundtracks from film and television.

Sherlockians themselves like to sing, mostly in a comic vein, a term that may perhaps include the mock-serious rendition of "God Save the Queen" in honour of Queen Victoria. *Singalong with Sherlock Holmes*, compiled by Jim Ballinger and published by the Metropolitan Toronto Reference Library in 1995, includes some material by Ballinger himself, and rather more material devised by other Sherlockians and set to familiar tunes on the principle of the "filk songs" beloved of science fiction enthusiasts:

> Oh, give me a home where Sherlockians roam
> And Watson is faithful and true,
> Where seldom is heard a non-Canonical word,
> And anything may be a clue.

The Adventuresses of Sherlock Holmes, based in New York, like to sing the "ASHenpoof Song," not to mention the "Reindeer Song." A venerable tradition of the Baker Street Irregulars is "Aunt Clara," a 1940s comic song traced to its source in *We Always Mention Aunt Clara* (1990) by W.T. Rabe. The traditional repertoire also includes several songs written by Harvey Officer and set to familiar tunes that appeared first in his *Baker Street Song Book* (1943), such as this one to the Londonderry Air:

> O Sherlock Holmes, the Baker Street Irregulars
> Are gathered here to honour you today,
> For in their hearts you glitter like a thousand stars,
> And like the stars, you'll never pass away....

The 1943 *Song Book* also includes the score for a piece of serious instrumental music, Officer's "Baker Street Suite" for violin and piano; a recording on 78-rpm records was issued in the same year. Since Harvey Officer, a number of other Sherlockians have been known as musical entertainers, including James Montgomery of Philadelphia (for decades the bard of the Baker Street Irregulars), Ballinger during his years with the Bootmakers of Toronto, and currently Karen Campbell, accompanied by Craig Brtnik, also in Toronto. A little Irregular music can be heard on *Voices from Baker Street*, a collection of early Sherlockian recordings issued as vinyl records in 1961 and 1965, and as a CD in 2009.

Before there was such a thing as a Sherlockian, however, there was a Sherlockian song, appearing in editions of the *Scottish Students' Song Book* as early as 1897, and incidentally anticipating the truth that had not yet been revealed in "The Empty House":

> You say it is a pity that this splendid man should die.
> I think the Swiss tale is a plant, I'll give my reason why.
> There's a lady in the question, so he's gone and done a "guy,"
> But he'll turn up again, will Sherlock Holmes.
> With his lips hard set and a cigarette,
> As his fingers thro' his hair he combs,
> He's never yet been baffled
> And he's sent them to the scaffold
> By the score, has Sherlock Holmes.

POETRY. Vast amounts of mediocre verse are written by Holmes enthusiasts. There have also been some fine poems, most famous of them being the sonnet "221B" by Vincent Starrett, often read in solemn tones at Sherlockian gatherings. Almost its rival in popularity is "A Long Evening with Holmes" by William Schweickert. Earlier, Helene Yuhasova was the author of sensitive poems published as *A Lauriston Garden of Verses* (1946) and in the *Baker Street Journal*, though in a few cases it was not clear whether a particular verse was by her or by Edgar W. Smith. The long-time leader of the Baker Street Irregulars, Smith himself was among versifiers of the Canonical tales, four of his efforts appearing in 1950 as *A Baker Street Quartette*. Charles E. Lauterbach (died 1962) was a sensitive poet of the Sherlockian world; *Baker Street Ballads* (1971) was a collection of his verses.

GAMES. The obvious way to match wits with Sherlock Holmes is through a game. As early as 1904, enthusiasts could do that with a "Sherlock Holmes" card game marketed by Parker Brothers. Writing in the *Baker Street Journal* in 1964, Helen G. Halbach tried to reconstruct it, and reported on the suits in its deck: Robber, Thief, Police, Burglar, Run, Help, Clue, Stop, and Sherlock Holmes. Clue, introduced by Parker Brothers forty years later, was originally dubbed "the great new Sherlock Holmes game," but in fact there is nothing Sherlockian about it. However, several board games from other sources do allow players to follow supposed Holmesian adventures. Among them are 221B Baker

Street, produced by Hansen, 1975; Sherlock Holmes, from Whitman, 1980; and Sherlock Holmes, Consulting Detective, from Ben Sanders Company, 1981.

The competitive enthusiast can also tackle Holmes's cases through game books, in which each page offers clues and invites the amateur sleuth to make decisions. A series of these has been published in paperback by Berkley as Sherlock Holmes Solo Mysteries. *Murder at the Diogenes Club* (1987) is among them. For the less venturesome, there are "murder dossiers" of *A Study in Scarlet* and *The Sign of [the] Four* — portfolios of reproduced telegrams, letters, newspaper clippings, and photographs, even a sample of bloodstained rope and a gold ring, through which the imaginative follower can join Holmes in examining the minutiae of one of his original cases.

In addition, there are computer games. The earliest Sherlockian games for the desktop computer were on the market by the early 1990s; for example, Icom Simulations Inc. advertised *Sherlock Holmes, Consulting Detective*, consisting of three colour video mysteries on a CD-ROM: "Open the private casebook of Holmes to pick the case you intend to solve.... Over 90 minutes of interactive video really puts you into the game.... When you think you've got a case solved, take it to court." In the same category is *PC-Sherlock*, described as "a game of logic and deduction" and now available for download on a "free old software" web site. *The Case of the Serrated Scalpel* (1992) and *The Case of the Rose Tattoo* (1996), both from Electronic Arts, were very popular in their day

As technology advances, games have become more elaborate in plot and more sophisticated in graphics, and are typically available both on CD-ROM and for download. Legacy Interactive, which takes pride in combining "casual gaming" with social networking, offers *The Lost Cases of Sherlock Holmes* (2008). Another company, Frogwares, has now produced four increasingly complex games in its Sherlock Holmes series: *The Mystery of the Mummy* (2002), *The Silver Earring*, *The Awakened*, and *Sherlock Holmes vs. Arsene Lupin*, with two more, *The Persian Carpet* and *Sherlock Holmes vs. Jack the Ripper*, announced. *The Awakened* received an award in 2007 for "best use of a license," referring to the permission that Frogwares needed from the owners of the Sherlock Holmes character. One website that specializes in game reviews wrote that *The Silver Earring* provides "interesting characters, an engaging plot, and beautiful graphics, yet it's an adventure with few puzzles and a mystery where you don't actually solve the mystery." It is not quite clear whether the last point was a criticism or a compliment.

PORNOGRAPHY. Obscenity is in the eye of the beholder, but there have been some clearly pornographic works that use Sherlock Holmes as their central character. He has appeared in the stories offered by sex comics and *Screw* magazine, for example, and there have been a few appearances in pornographic video including *The Case of the Pilfered Panties*. Several stories with sexual themes are accessible on the web. The most important work in this little genre is *The Sexual Adventures of Sherlock Holmes* (1971, republished 1993), a paperback novel that betrays a deep and sensitive knowledge of the Canon, retelling *A Study in Scarlet* and "The Greek Interpreter" with extensive sexual content. Its orientation is homosexual; it assumes a physical relationship between Holmes and Watson (as other, more mainstream commentators have sometimes suspected) but also, for example, describes the perverted sex life of Enoch Drebber.

CHILDREN'S BOOKS. Although the Sherlockian Canon has sometimes been dismissed as "boys' books," it is not really suitable for children; the usual age at which a precocious reader discovers Sherlock Holmes is twelve or thirteen. Even for that age, some passages are strong meat, and there have been some attempts to bowdlerize, for example, *The Sign of the Four* to remove references to cocaine. Such adaptations and retellings are more possible now that copyright in most of the stories has expired in the United States. An enthusiast who really wants to introduce a younger child to the original Holmes can have some success with "The Priory School" or "The Sussex Vampire," two stories that at least have children as characters.

"Just as the figure of Holmes had a great impact on later detective stories," Sally Sugarman wrote in the *Baker Street Journal* in 2008, "so Holmes and the Baker Street Irregulars had an impact on children's literature." She discusses the ability to go everywhere and overhear everything as valuable for such sleuths as Nancy Drew and Enid Blyton's Famous Five, and notes that the Irregulars themselves, or their modern heirs, have been featured in books by several authors aiming at younger readers. Among them: Robert Newman (*The Case of the Baker Street Irregular*, 1978, and sequels); Jake and Luke Thoene (*The Mystery of the Yellow Hands*, 1995, and sequels); Nancy Springer (*The Case of the Missing Marquess*, 2006); Alex Simmons and Bill McCay (*The Raven League: Sherlock Holmes Is Missing*, 2006); Anthony Read (*The Case of the Ranjipur Ruby*, 2006); Tracy Mack and Michael Citrin (*The Fall of the Amazing Zalindas*, 2006). Head and shoulders above all others is the absurd and hilarious juvenile novel *The Snarkout Boys and the Avocado of Death* (1982) by Daniel Pinkwater.

New tales with a Baker Street flavour can also be written at a younger child's reading level and with content entirely suitable, if not always completely authentic. The best-known author to have attempted that task is Eve Titus, who created the mouse detective of 221B in *Basil of Baker Street* (1970) and three sequels. Her characters formed the basis for the Walt Disney film *The Great Mouse Detective* (1986), with Vincent Price as the voice of the villainous Professor Ratigan. It included the first tentative Disney venture into computer animation, and although its success was feeble, it was rereleased in 1982 (as *The Adventures of the Great Mouse Detective*). Marjorie Weinman Sharmat's *Nate the Great* (1972) and half a dozen sequels present a boy detective whose working costume is a deerstalker and trench coat:

> I, Nate the Great,
> am a detective.
> I am not afraid of anything.
> Except for one thing.
> Today I am going
> to a birthday party
> for the one thing
> I am afraid of.
> Annie's dog Fang.

Somewhat similar is Alan Coren's *Arthur and the Great Detective* (1979). There is also a series of easy-reading books featuring "Sherlock Hound," with no relationship to a Japanese anime series by the same title. For even smaller children there are various Sesame Street picture books featuring Sherlock Hemlock, as well as several "Sherlock Chick" beginners' books by Robert Quackenbush. An impressive but not complete list of Sherlockian children's books appears on Adrian Nebbett's web site at *www.schoolandholmes.com/childrens.html*.

COMICS. Sherlock Holmes has appeared in the comics since before the invention of comic books; "Sherlocko the Monk," drawn by Gus Mager, figured on newspaper comic pages from 1910 to 1913. Mager later created "Hawkshaw the Detective," who appeared in newspapers around 1915, and was collected in magazine format in 1917. There were deerstalkered detectives in conventional comic books from early times, appearing with Mickey Mouse as early as 1945, Bugs Bunny in 1948, Captain Marvel in 1950, Superboy in 1959, Chip 'n' Dale also in 1959, Mickey Mouse in 1967, and Little Lulu in 1976. *Mad* magazine published "Shermlock Shomes" in 1953 and "The Hound of the Basketballs" the following year. Both editorial cartoons and comic strips in the daily newspapers are still apt to make Sherlockian allusions at any time, although the most familiar date from decades ago: the many *Peanuts* strips by Charles Schulz that present Snoopy the beagle wearing his deerstalker hat. (He appeared on television in the same guise in *It's a Mystery, Charlie Brown*, 1974.)

Full Sherlockian adventures first saw publication in comic-book form in *Classics Illustrated* in 1944, as part of "Three Famous Mysteries." Four years later the same magazine, now titled *Classic Comics*, presented "The Adventures of Sherlock Holmes" (actually *A Study in Scarlet* and *The Hound of the Baskervilles*). *A Study in Scarlet*, much improved, appeared again in 1953 along with "The Speckled Band." All these were, though abbreviated, plausible adaptations of the original tales. Several other publishers tackled Sherlock Holmes in the next three decades. Finally, *Cases of Sherlock Holmes* was published beginning in 1981 — a series of magazines in which the complete text of the Canonical stories would appear, with exquisite illustrations by Canadian artist Dan Day. Although the series (originally published by Renegade Press in California) staggered and eventually stopped, the dozen volumes that did appear were received with enthusiasm. Day's black-and-white illustrations generally model Holmes and Watson on Basil Rathbone and Nigel Bruce, and convey both Victorian atmosphere and physical energy, even passion, to bring the stories to life. A checklist of such publications is *Sherlock Holmes in the Comic Books* (1985, with updates), privately distributed by Charlotte Erickson of Palo Alto, California. Many classic comics are reproduced in *Sherlock Holmes in America* (1981), by Bill Blackbeard.

With the growing popularity of more sophisticated comics and graphic novels for adults, Holmes has appeared from time to time in formats easily overlooked by traditional collectors and libraries. Among titles that have been noted by Sherlockian completists are *Honour Among Punks: The Complete Baker Street Graphic Novel* (2003, based on material first published in 1990–91) and *Holmes: Haydn's Head* (2005). The feature film scheduled to be released late in 2009, starring Robert Downey Jr., is reported to be "based on an unpublished comic book by Lionel Wigram." The most literary of all these works is probably the two volumes of *The League of Extraordinary Gentlemen* (1999–2003), featuring Professor Moriarty though not Holmes himself. A version of *The Hound of the Baskervilles* described as "faithful to Conan Doyle's vision and free from the deerstalker hat and calabash pipe" was announced for 2009 by a London firm called SelfMadeHero.

VIII

FANS AND FOLLOWERS

PARODIES OF THE HOLMES TALES, appearing in England and America at the turn of the century (Doyle's friend Robert Barr wrote one in 1892), indicate how quickly the stories attracted enthusiasts who recognized their distinctive qualities. The preface to *His Last Bow*, published in 1917, is addressed to "the friends of Mr. Sherlock Holmes." But those friends were not yet organized. The first Sherlock Holmes societies were formed in the 1930s, and their successors exist today in more than a dozen countries — embracing, to be sure, only a small number of those who enjoy the stories. To be a "Sherlockian" (in England, a "Holmesian") is to do more than read Sherlock Holmes with delight; it is to enter a world of trivia questions, films, parodies, interlocking societies, little magazines, T-shirts, nostalgia, and a dedication bordering on mania. Much Sherlockian activity is still conducted face-to-face or through the printed word, but increasingly Sherlockians communicate by email or on web sites such as Facebook, where important communities of friends and fellow-enthusiasts have developed.

THE BAKER STREET IRREGULARS

Probably because the stories themselves were more popular in America than in Britain, it was in the United States that the greatest Sherlockian activity developed. Originally limited to a few keen fellows in the New York literary set, the Sherlockian community grew widely over several decades. No single membership card or initiation rite separates the acknowledged Sherlockian from the private devotee. What distinguishes Sherlockian societies from fan clubs is the frequent presence of genuine literary scholarship, sometimes of the kind favoured by professors of English, sometimes of the humane kind associated with Christopher Morley, founder of the Baker Street Irregulars, and other appreciative readers. He called such companions "kinsprits": kindred spirits.

THE BEGINNINGS. Christopher Morley (born May 5, 1890; died March 28, 1957) was, *circa* 1930, an editor of the *Saturday Review of Literature*, a magazine published in New York, as well as a poet and novelist. *Parnassus on Wheels* (1917) was a bestseller, though his most successful book, *Kitty Foyle* (1939), was still to come. Writes Robert Keith Leavitt:

> In his early forties, he was stout, lustily active, gregarious, busy, prosperous (in spite of the recent collapse of the Hoboken theater venture) and immensely popular. He rarely lunched with fewer than four people, and often as not, with a group of a dozen or more. Among his countless fascinating traits was the habit of forming clubs on the spur of the moment.

Among these clubs were the Grillparzer Sittenpolizei Verein and the self-explanatory Three Hours for Lunch Club, which gathered often at Christ Cella's restaurant (or speakeasy) on East 45 Street. (*Three Hours for Lunch* is the title of a 1976 biography of Morley by Helen McK. Oakley; scholar Steven Rothman is said to be near completing a new, more comprehensive book.) The talk at Morley's lunches and dinners was often of literature and the theatre, and sometimes of Sherlock Holmes. Morley had been commissioned to write a preface for Doubleday's *Complete Sherlock Holmes* in 1930, and actor William Gillette had been making his Farewell Tour in 1929–32; in Britain, three early books of gentle Holmesiana had been published by 1932. The great detective was in the air.

The development of a Sherlockian society from Morley's congenial circle is traced in *Irregular Memories of the 'Thirties* (1990), edited by Jon Lellenberg, who summarizes it thus:

> The GSPV luncheons became more and more Sherlockian — until finally the Baker Street Irregulars spun out of it, centrifugally, and into life on their own, at a cocktail party at the Hotel Duane, on Madison Avenue, on January 6, 1934: called by Christopher Morley (in his column in the *Saturday Review of Literature*) to celebrate Sherlock Holmes's birthday.

Prohibition had ended a month earlier, and Morley was calling for the invention of "a Sherlock Holmes cocktail" at the Duane. Whether or not it was served, the cocktail party did take place, an affair of fifteen or twenty people, according to Leavitt's recollection. They were of both sexes, and he maintains that after drinks and lunch "we played Sardines with the pretty ladies who were our guests," Sardines being a very heterosexual form of hide-and-seek.

Such frivolity was followed by a frivolous constitution for the BSI, published in the *SRL* February 17, 1934:

> ARTICLE I. The name of this society shall be the Baker Street Irregulars.
>
> ARTICLE II. Its purpose shall be the study of the Sacred Writings....
>
> ARTICLE IV. The officers shall be a Gasogene, a Tantalus, and a Commissionaire....
>
> BUY-LAWS... (2) The current round shall be bought by any member who fails to identify, by title of story and context, any quotation from the Sacred Writings submitted by any other member....
>
> (4) All other business shall be left for the monthly meeting.
>
> (5) There shall be no monthly meeting.

Then on May 13 Morley's column in the *SRL* presented a crossword puzzle that had been composed by his brother Frank Morley, offering it as an entrance examination for the BSI. About three dozen perfect and near-perfect solutions arrived. Morley soon called "the first formal meeting of the Baker Street Irregulars," for June 5 at Cella's restaurant. "Dress informally of course," his typewritten invitation read. "This first meeting will be stag." That meant that such successful solvers of the puzzle as Emily S. Coit and Katherine McMahon were excluded. Exactly eight people, all male, did attend: Earle Walbridge, Malcolm Johnson, Allan Price, Harvey Officer, R.K. Leavitt, Frank Henry, William S. Hall, and Morley.

A dinner meeting held December 7, 1934, attracted several others who would become legends in the Sherlockian world, including Basil Davenport, Elmer Davis, Gray C. Briggs, Harold W. Bell, and Vincent Starrett. Actor William Gillette and illustrator Frederic Dorr Steele were also among those present — as was Alexander Woollcott, prominent and self-important figure in the New York literary scene. Disagreement has existed ever since about whether

Woollcott was invited, how he behaved while he was there, and whether or not he stole Bill Hall's home-made deerstalker hat. The BSI met again in January 1936, but after that not until 1940.

It has been suggested that if the BSI had not been organized in New York when it did, Sherlockian activity in America would have been based on a society founded in the Midwest instead, by Vincent Starrett of Chicago (born October 26, 1886; died January 5, 1974). From 1930 to at least 1934, Starrett was in constant, enthusiastic correspondence with Dr. Gray Chandler Briggs (1882–1942), a St. Louis radiologist whose Sherlockian accomplishments included an early identification of the house in Baker Street that might have been 221B. (Their correspondence, edited by Jon Lellenberg, was published in 1989 as *Dear Starrett — Dear Briggs*.) Another important correspondent was Logan Clendening (1884–1945), a Kansas City physician, humourist, and writer on literary topics. It was Clendening who gave Starrett some twenty rarities in 1940, to start his second Sherlockian collection after financial difficulties had forced him to sell his first.

Starrett wrote the first, and still perhaps the greatest, book of American Sherlockiana, *The Private Life of Sherlock Holmes* (1933, new editions 1960 and 2008), in the intervals of his work as a Chicago newspaperman and critic. He was one of the original participants in BSI revels, despite the distance from Chicago to New York, and remained active in Sherlockian affairs. Best known of his many writings is the sonnet "221B," first published in 1942:

> Here dwell together still two men of note
> Who never lived and so can never die:
> How very near they seem, yet how remote
> That age before the world went all awry.
> But still the game's afoot for those with ears
> Attuned to catch the distant view-halloo:
> England is England yet, for all our fears —
> Only those things the heart believes are true.
>
> A yellow fog swirls past the window-pane
> As night descends upon this fabled street:
> A lonely hansom splashes through the rain,
> The ghostly gas lamps fail at twenty feet.
> Here, though the world explode, these two survive,
> And it is always eighteen ninety-five.

Starrett's autobiography is *Born in a Bookshop* (1965). A biography with much attention to Sherlockian matters is *The Last Bookman* (1968) by Peter A. Ruber.

AN ERA OF GROWTH. New societies began to form, starting with The Five Orange Pips of Westchester County, north of New York, which has maintained its traditions of strictly limited (and male-only) membership, eloquent scholarship, and annual black-tie dinners for nearly six decades. Several other societies with similar limitations were formed during the 1940s: the Speckled Band of Boston (founded by James Keddie Sr., 1883–1942), the Hounds of the Baskerville [*sic*] of Chicago (founded by Starrett and a few kindred spirits), the Dancing Men of Providence (founded by Roland Hammond, 1876–1957), the Sons of the Copper Beeches of Philadelphia, the Six Napoleons of Baltimore, and others. The name "scions" was soon adopted for these cadet or branch societies, the BSI being accepted as the parent.

The BSI originally claimed to have a Gasogene as its president, which was Christopher Morley; a Tantalus as its secretary, which was sporadically Bill Hall; and a Commissionaire, "who shall ... conduct all negotiations with waiters." That role was soon taken by Edgar W. Smith (born April 1, 1894; died September 17, 1960). He wrote first to Vincent Starrett, who put him in touch with Morley in 1938. By that time he was completing *Appointment in Baker Street*, a biographical dictionary of figures in the Canon, published that year as the first in a series of Sherlockian reference works Smith would develop. By the time the BSI managed to hold a dinner meeting in January 1940, after a four-year hiatus, Smith was in charge of the arrangements and calling himself "Buttons" in allusion to a Victorian page boy. Soon he was "Buttons-cum-Commissionaire," a title he held to the end of his life as the chief organizer of the Irregulars. Smith, as an executive of General Motors (he loved to call it "the Franco-Midland Hardware Company," and used its secretarial resources freely for Sherlockian purposes), was a modest, efficient organizer. Morley was impressed, though unenthusiastic about the activities he directed:

> Now the scholarly group of Baker Street find themselves swaddled, or saddled, with a publishing business, an annual meeting, and a province of pulp. They have about 30 scionist branches whose letters have to be answered. But not by me.

The "province of pulp" included considerable Sherlockiana from Morley's own pen, articles that have been collected and annotated in *The Standard*

Doyle Company (1990), edited by Steven Rothman. It also included several of Smith's works: *Baker Street and Beyond* (1940), a gazetteer, and *Baker Street Inventory* (1945), a bibliography, are the most important. Smith was also represented — along with Morley, Leavitt, and other familiar names — in a hardbound anthology edited by Starrett and published by Macmillan in 1940 under the title *221B: Studies in Sherlock Holmes*.

Still more striking was *Profile by Gaslight* (1944), which Smith edited. In this anthology appeared some classic essays of Sherlockian scholarship — setting the standard to which later writers would aspire, establishing the habit of "playing the game" with the pretense that Holmes and Watson were historical characters, and providing the received wisdom on many Sherlockian issues. For example, James Keddie, Sr., ("The Mystery of the Second Wound") addressed the apparently reconcilable references to Watson's war injury, which affected him in the shoulder in one story, in the leg in another. Edgar W. Smith ("The Long Road from Maiwand") discussed the time that expired between Watson's injury in Afghanistan and his encounter with Holmes in London, a complex calculation that determines the date of *A Study in Scarlet*. Robert Keith Leavitt ("Annie Oakley in Baker Street") talked about ballistics, Charles S. Goodman ("The Dental Holmes") about that canine tooth that was supposedly knocked out of Holmes's mouth by an amateur boxer, Vincent Starrett ("The Singular Adventures of Martha Hudson") about the long-suffering landlady. The volume also presented Rex Stout's straight-faced tour de force, "Watson Was a Woman." ("That Was No Lady," retorted Dr. Julian Wolff in the next chapter.)

The success of *Profile by Gaslight* made the founding of a Sherlockian magazine inevitable. The first issue of the *Baker Street Journal* appeared in January 1946, with Smith as editor and New York bookseller Ben Abramson as publisher. Leftover essays from the anthology, and similar serious works, shared space with a long pastiche, letters, editorial notes (from Smith, and from Morley as "Clinical Notes by a Resident Patient"), and reports from the scion societies. That remained the pattern of the *BSJ* until Abramson, haemorrhaging money, had to abandon it after the first issue of volume 4 (in 1949). In a much less ambitious format — thinner, and typewritten where the Old Series had been professionally typeset — a New Series of the *BSJ* was begun in January 1951. The magazine continues to appear quarterly nearly sixty years later as the most important journal for the discussion of Sherlock Holmes. The *BSJ* was edited until 1960 by Smith; then until 1977 by Julian Wolff; then briefly by John Linsenmeyer, then Peter Blau, and then (as "Fred Porlock") George Fletcher; 1985 through 1992 by Philip A. Shreffler; 1993–95, by William R.

Cochran; 1996–99, by Donald Pollock; and from 2000, by Steven Rothman of Philadelphia. Information is on a web site: *www.bakerstreetjournal.com*.

Two other prominent Sherlockians of the 1940s were both pseudonymous: Anthony Boucher and Ellery Queen. Boucher, actually William A.P. White (1911–68), came to Sherlockian notice with the novel *The Case of the Baker Street Irregulars* (1940), a mystery novel about a murder solved by BSI members. He became prominent both in Sherlockian circles (as founder of the Scowrers and Mollie Maguires of San Francisco, the first major Sherlockian society to welcome women as well as men) and among mystery enthusiasts in general; Bouchercon, the leading international convention for mystery lovers, is named in his memory. Ellery Queen was a partnership of Frederic Dannay and Manfred E. Lee, who wrote novels about a detective (also named Ellery Queen) and edited *Ellery Queen's Mystery Magazine* (founded 1941 and a frequent vehicle for Sherlockian tales for the past five decades). *The Misadventures of Sherlock Holmes* (1940), edited by Queen, was a collection of parodies and pastiches of the Holmes tales.

THE EARLY MODERN ERA. The BSI was no longer entirely a New York organization, for prominent members included out-of-towners such as James Montgomery (1898–1955) of Philadelphia, James Keddie, Jr. (1907–83) of Boston, James Bliss Austin (1903–88) of Pittsburgh, and Clifton R. Andrew (1892–1963) of Akron. The centre of Sherlockian activity began to shift from New York and the BSI to local societies, established in most larger cities and some smaller ones (New Haven, Austin) where one or two enthusiasts managed to light a fire. In the postwar years it became increasingly common for Sherlockians, travelling for business or pleasure, to meet one another and attend the gatherings of one another's "scions." Newsletters sprang up here and there.

Scholarship was flourishing, not only through the *Baker Street Journal* but in privately published pamphlets — only some of which, now extremely rare, have been republished in recent years. In a class by itself was the work of Jay Finley Christ (1884–1963) of Chicago, which included many newspaper pieces and pamphlets as well as *An Irregular Guide to Sherlock Holmes* (1947), an idiosyncratic index to names and key references in the Canon. Virtually without exception, Sherlockians were treating Holmes and Watson as real people, the Canon as history, and Doyle as "the Literary Agent." For example, essayists in *The Illustrious Client's Case-Book*, published in 1948 by the Sherlockians of Indianapolis, consider such matters as Watson's middle name and Holmes's prowess at boxing. That was still the fashion in 1962, when *Sherlock Holmes of Baker Street*, a straight-faced "biography" of the great man, appeared to great acclaim. It was the work of William S. Baring-Gould (1913–67), an executive of Time Inc. and intensely scholarly Irregular whose *magnum opus* was the posthumously published *Annotated Sherlock Holmes* (1967), with hundreds of notes discussing obscurities in the Canon.

Julian Wolff (born January 11, 1905; died February 12, 1990) succeeded to the title of Commissionaire of the BSI, as well as editor of the *Baker Street Journal*, when Edgar W. Smith died in 1960. Wolff was a physician specializing in industrial medicine (and during World War II an army doctor) and had first come to Sherlockian notice through the maps he had drawn to accompany Smith's *Baker Street and Beyond*. They were later published as *The Sherlockian Atlas* (1952) and have been seen on Christmas cards and in other media over the years. Wolff's later creative works included *A Practical Handbook of Sherlockian Heraldry* (1955) and several brochures.

THE SHERLOCK HOLMES BOOM. One might say that the Sherlockian world became more organized in the Julian Wolff era. It even briefly boasted a *Who's Who and What's What* (1961 and 1962), edited by Bill Rabe (1921–92), then of Detroit. Rabe's Sherlockian organization, the Old Soldiers of Baker Street (Old SOBs), moved with him in and out of the United States Army, to Detroit and later to Sault Ste. Marie, Michigan, tossing off publications, audio recordings, and other treasures along the way.

More lasting reference works became available: *The Annotated Sherlock Holmes*, edited by William S. Baring-Gould, in 1967; *The World Bibliography of Sherlock Holmes and Dr. Watson*, Ronald DeWaal's first massive volume, in 1974; Jack Tracy's *Encyclopaedia Sherlockiana*, in effect an index to the Canon, in 1977. In 1980 came DeWaal's second bibliography, *The International Sherlock Holmes*. Newsletters and journals proliferated, including *Baker Street Miscellanea*, founded in 1975 by Bill Goodrich and John Nieminski of Chicago and Donald Pollock, then of Boston. *BSM* took Doyle more seriously, and imposed more consistent standards of originality and quality, than most other Sherlockian publications. It continued quarterly publication until 1994.

In 1979, Peter Blau of Washington, D.C., introduced a newsletter — originally nameless, now titled *Scuttlebutt from the Spermaceti Press* — offering for cognoscenti a monthly summary of Sherlockian news, announcements, and reports of new books, articles, and memorabilia. Blau was already known as the nerve and communications centre for Sherlockians everywhere, as well as the organizer of one of the more active local societies, the Red Circle of Washington, D.C. A petroleum geologist originally from Massachusetts, Peter Blau (born 1932) joined the Baker Street Irregulars in 1959, carries on an extensive correspondence across America and beyond, and maintains huge computerized files of Sherlockian addresses, bibliographical information, and references. He briefly edited the *Baker Street Journal* (1982–83).

Equally prominent in the Sherlockian world, beginning in the 1960s, was John Bennett Shaw (born October 10, 1913, died October 2, 1994), of Tulsa and later Santa Fe. An oilman, funeral director, and insatiable book collector, Shaw became known as the most fanatical of "completist" collectors, seeking to own every Sherlockian item, every variant, every ephemeral object. His generosity to young enthusiasts, and to scholars in search of obscure material, was recognized in tributes he received in a special issue of the *Baker Street Journal* in 1990. Wrote one friend, Jon Lellenberg:

> He has been behind the founding of more scion societies than anyone else, or anyone likely to come after him. His enthusiasm for the cause is boundless and contagious, and his aphorismic advice, more serious than it seems upon first hearing, is legend today: All it takes to start a BSI scion society is two people and a bottle; in a pinch, you can dispense with one of the people.

Shaw said in a 1991 interview for the *Sherlock Holmes Review* that he had some ten thousand books and pamphlets in his collection: "My particular favorite are four Sherlock Holmes books, printed in Germany and dated 1890 to 1897, which belonged to the Czarina of Russia." In the 1980s Shaw conducted several summer "workshops" at which veteran and neophyte Sherlockians could listen to talks, watch films, attempt to answer Shaw's quizzes (famous for their puns), and talk far into the night. The original workshop of that kind was at Notre Dame University, Shaw's alma mater in Indiana, July 31 through August 4, 1977. The devotees who tried to attend Shaw workshops or similar conventions converged on New York each January for what became known as "the birthday weekend," which expanded far beyond its original fixture, the annual dinner of the Baker Street Irregulars.

Involvement in the Sherlockian movement swelled after two 1974 books from mainstream publishers, and the movie made from one of them, attracted widespread attention. The more successful of the books was *The Seven-Per-Cent Solution* by Nicholas Meyer, a Hollywood screen writer, who daringly juxtaposed Holmes and Sigmund Freud in the first modern "pastiche," or imitation of the Canonical stories. In his novel Holmes consults Freud for help in curing the cocaine addiction that has caused him to imagine, and fear, Professor

Moriarty. It was made into a successful 1976 film, starring Nicol Williamson as Holmes. The other 1974 comet was *Naked Is the Best Disguise* by Samuel Rosenberg, a New York writer who has identified his book as the first to take Doyle seriously in literary terms. He proposed a "Conan Doyle Syndrome," juxtaposing death, darkness, the written word, and cross-dressing or sexual perversity, finding it in story after story in the Canon. Sherlockians were generally outraged, but interested.

A further influence on the public interest in Holmes was a revival of William Gillette's turn-of-the-century play *Sherlock Holmes*, presented by the Royal Shakespeare Company. It played in England in the summer of 1974, and then came to North America for thirty-two performances in Washington and 219 (between November 1974 and January 1976) in New York, followed by a tour touching Toronto, Detroit, Los Angeles, Denver, and Chicago. In 1979 *Baker Street Miscellanea* found it necessary to publish "A Symposium on Collecting Sherlockiana During the Holmes Boom," with comments from several noted figures, including John Bennett Shaw:

> There can be no doubt that there was and still is a Boom, a revival, a resurgence of interest in Sherlock Holmes, a proliferation of books, pamphlets, plays, films, recordings, tapes, articles in periodicals, art and craft objects, and much more. Endlessly! I know this well, probably better than most. I know this as a collector, for I write a dozen or so letters a day to fellow Holmesians, to book-sellers, publishers and so on. I know because I have no space in my library (a room built on to the house in 1970 specifically to house my Holmes collection). I know because I am stretching my avocational budget to the breaking point, buying and housing old and new materials.

The flood of material was acquired not only by the long-time collectors but by a throng of new Sherlockians, for whom new societies were formed, new periodicals optimistically launched.

THE IRREGULARS TODAY. By general consent, the BSI remains the parent society of Sherlockian groups in the United States, although its role is limited to approving new groups' names (to avoid duplication) and trying to keep track of them. The BSI itself meets each January, for an annual dinner on a Friday night, and has sponsored a number of other events, including "Silver Blaze" outings to New York's Belmont racetrack and weekend tours to the "Valley of Fear" in Pennsylvania and "the Country of the Saints" in Utah where much of *A Study in Scarlet* is set.

It also maintains an active publishing program, inspired by the sort of thing done by the Irregulars under Edgar W. Smith's leadership half a century earlier. In addition to the longstanding *Baker Street Journal* (lately augmented with a *Christmas Annual* each winter), there are now several series of books. They include the *Manuscript Series*, presenting facsimiles and other texts with annotations; the *International Series* of anthologies introducing the Sherlockian work of other lands to North American audiences; and the *Baker Street Irregulars History Series*, initially a series of four narratives by Jon Lellenberg culminating with *Irregular Crises of the Late 'Forties*, although books by other hands, taking the story closer to the present, are now in progress. A Baker Street Irregulars Trust (*www.bsitrust.org*) has been established "to assemble, preserve, and make available for study relevant materials" about the history of the BSI, its members, and kindred subjects. The Trust's archives are deposited with the Houghton Library at Harvard University.

The leadership of the BSI passed from Julian Wolff to Thomas L. Stix, Jr., in 1986, and then to Michael Whelan in 1997. Both chose to use the title "Wiggins" in honour of the urchin who leads Holmes's original Baker Street Irregulars, rather than being the "Commissionaire" as Wolff had been. Stix (born July 11, 1923, died September 9, 1998) was a New York stockbroker who became a BSI member in 1961 and followed his father, Tom Stix Sr. (1896–1974) into the Irregulars' inner circle. Whelan (born September 26, 1938) is a retired businessman who received his investiture as a BSI member in 1974. His address for BSI purposes is 7938 Mill Stream Circle, Indianapolis, Indiana 46278.

One cannot apply for BSI membership, which is awarded to Sherlockians who have made a mark in published scholarship or in their local societies. Some prominent Sherlockians from overseas have been similarly "investitured." Such honours are awarded on the sole initiative of the BSI's benevolent dictator (the organization has no formal governing body). Membership has since 1944 involved an investiture, or *nom de plume*, which may be a Canonical story title, character, or other allusion. Nathan L. Bengis (1906–79), a New York teacher and book collector, was "The Lion's Mane"; Richard J. Sveum, a Minneapolis medical researcher, is "Dr. Hill Barton." Since 1949 an investiture has been accompanied by a Victorian shilling, the silver coin with which Holmes paid his original assistants their daily wage. As of spring 2009, 613 people had received BSI investitures over the signature of Morley, Smith, Wolff, Stix, or Whelan, authorizing them to, in the Canonical phrase, "go everywhere, see everything, overhear everyone." There were 311 Irregulars still living.

The single most prominent member of the BSI is surely Peter Blau of Washington, who continues to produce his monthly *Scuttlebutt* newsletter and is the nominal secretary of the organization. A few of its other prominent members are John Bergquist of Minneapolis; Ray Betzner of Thorndale, Pennsylvania; Susan Dahlinger of Highland, New York; Tom Francis of Boston, chair of the BSI Trust; Los Angeles lawyer and editor Leslie S. Klinger; Jon L. Lellenberg of Chicago, who also serves as American representative of the Estate of Dame Jean Conan Doyle; Warren Randall of Long Island, New York; Susan Rice of New York City; Albert M. Rosenblatt of Poughkeepsie, a New York supreme court judge, along with his wife, Julia Carlson Rosenblatt; Steven Rothman of Philadelphia, editor of the *Baker Street Journal*; Bob Thomalen of Eastchester, New York.

Since Christopher Morley's day, the BSI had admitted only two women, both under exceptional circumstances. (Lee Offord in 1958 may have been accidental, her name being androgynous; Lisa McGaw in 1982 was dubbed "Mrs. Hudson" for her service as organizer of the William Gillette Memorial Luncheon.) Wolff had steadfastly ignored pressure to open BSI membership to successful Sherlockian women, but after his death Stix took that step, extending membership in January 1991 to six prominent women, including Sir Arthur's daughter, Dame Jean Conan Doyle; author Edith Meiser; one of the early solvers of the crossword puzzle, Katherine McMahon; Julia Carlson Rosenblatt, co-author of *Dining with Sherlock Holmes* (1976, 1990); and Evelyn Herzog and Susan Rice, leaders of the Adventuresses of Sherlock Holmes. Further investitures to women came in subsequent years.

SHERLOCKIAN LIFE

Franklin D. Roosevelt, president of the United States in the 1940s, was reputed to be a Sherlockian; Isaac Asimov, polymath and science fiction author, was an enthusiastic Baker Street Irregular. Other well-known figures in the field have included Nobel Prize winning physician Philip S. Hench, prominent authors such as Poul Anderson and Howard Haycraft, journalist Elmer Davis, and sportswriter Red Smith. Sherlockians today come from all walks of life and most social classes — although full involvement in travel and collecting does generally require a healthy disposable income. No generalization about the participants in a local Sherlockian society is entirely valid beyond a common interest in Sherlock Holmes, but certain other interests are widely found: detective fiction (of course), Victorian England, science fiction. Many Sherlockians are also members of groups celebrating such Victorian figures as Charles Dickens, William Morris, and Gilbert and Sullivan. And, by and large, they are friends. While the full range of personalities is, of course, represented, the presumption is that Sherlockians will have something in common and enjoy one another's company. Several marriages have grown out of friendships made in Sherlockian organizations; countless other intimate friendships have grown up.

Still, most Sherlockian activity is carried on alone. One reads the Canon (although it is easy to neglect that simple activity in favour of derivative entertainment), keeps up with the scholarship and fantasy being written about it by Sherlockian colleagues, watches video, corresponds avidly by email and sometimes through that quintessential Victorian invention, the letter, writes the occasional article for newsletter publication, and looks forward to the monthly or quarterly meeting of a nearby society, at which the same activities can be enjoyed in the company of a few friends. It may even be true that the most important Sherlockian activity takes place not so much on the printed page, but in the theatre of the mind, where for a Sherlockian there is always an immediate escape to 1895:

> When the world closes in with its worries and cares
> And my problems and headaches are coming in pairs
> I just climb in my mind up those seventeen stairs
> And spend a long evening with Holmes.

So wrote Bill Schweickert in "A Long Evening with Holmes," first published in *Canadian Holmes* in 1984. But there are livelier and more sociable activities as well.

LOCAL SOCIETIES. More than four hundred active Sherlock Holmes societies, the great majority of them in the United States, appear on a list maintained by Peter Blau of Washington (*members.cox.net/sherlock1/Sherlocktron.html*). Such societies are called "scions" in Sherlockian parlance, the word indicating that they are offshoots of a national society (in the United States, the BSI). Most local groups take their name from some Canonical reference, and often elaborate it in the titles of their officers. The secretary of the Great Alkali Plainsmen of Greater Kansas City, for instance, is "Stangerson," after a character in *A Study in Scarlet*, in which the great alkali plain appears. Groups range from the very small to some that draw as many as one hundred people to meetings, and from the new and unstable to some that have been in operation for decades. In a few cases, meetings (typically three to ten times a year) have formal programs of films, lectures, music, and quizzes, but many of the societies devote their meeting time to informal discussion and socializing. Many publish some sort of newsletter. Except for a hidebound few, all welcome women and men on equal terms, and generally there is no admission requirement beyond interest and the payment of modest dues.

The smaller scion societies are often built around the enthusiasm of one individual, and can wither when that person leaves or burns out. Larger ones can go on almost indefinitely, and may be governed by clique, consensus, or, in a few cases, elaborate formal procedures. Among the most venerable societies are the Speckled Band of Boston; the Three Garridebs of Westchester County, New York; the Five Orange Pips, also of Westchester; the Sons of the Copper Beeches of Philadelphia; the Red Circle of Washington; the Six Napoleons of Baltimore; the Illustrious Clients of Indianapolis; Hugo's Companions of Chicago; the Norwegian Explorers of Minneapolis; the Scowrers and Molly Maguires of San Francisco. Local Sherlockian societies have all the strengths and weaknesses of other volunteer and hobby organizations, including enthusiasm and camaraderie on the one hand, a field for petty politics and ego display on the other. Some groups have dissolved amid personal rivalries, while others seem unaffected by dissension.

The quality and enthusiasm of a scion does not always reflect the size of its home city. Perhaps the most-admired and liveliest local Sherlockian society anywhere is the Occupants of the Empty House of Southern Illinois, which meets for dinner monthly in the tiny town of Du Quoin and publishes a small but erudite newsletter, the *Camden House Journal*.

Canada. Sherlockians in Canada have been closely associated with those in the United States for more than forty years. Among the scion societies of the Baker Street Irregulars in the 1940s was The Canadian Baskervilles, headed by Humfrey Michell of Lennoxville, Québec, and Ron Graham of Hamilton, Ontario. At about the same period, the Baker Street Squires briefly flourished in Toronto.

Both organizations were long extinct by 1971, when the Metropolitan Toronto Central Library began to form a Sherlock Holmes and Arthur Conan Doyle collection in its literature department. A few Canadian Sherlockians, most prominent of them being Toronto judge S. Tupper Bigelow (1901–93), maintained their attachment to the BSI and the Sherlockian community in the United States. They, and others, were attracted to a "Weekend with Sherlock" conducted by the library December 4 and 5, 1971. When it was over, diehards agreed that a new Sherlockian society in Toronto should be formed. Inevitably, it took its name from the only Canonical reference to Toronto, as the place where Sir Henry Baskerville acquired his boots, and the first meeting of The Bootmakers of Toronto was held February 4, 1972. The first president — dubbed "Mr. Meyers" — was Derrick Murdoch (born December 7, 1909; died May 21, 1985), a newspaper columnist. His successor was True Davidson, mayor of the Toronto suburb of East York.

The Bootmakers (*www.bootmakers.ca*) grew steadily to reach a high point in the 1990s, when it could claim to be the largest active Sherlockian society in North America, with attendance of eighty to one hundred people at five to seven meetings each year, and membership of more than two hundred. A

A few members of the Bootmakers of Toronto pose in Victorian garb (and one as Holmes himself) at the society's annual dinner in January 2008. Vintage costume is not to everyone's taste, but dressing up can be fun, especially when it involves Duchess of Devonshire hats for the ladies and toppers or bowlers — or deerstalkers — for the gentlemen. Photo by Philip Elliott.

newsletter, *Canadian Holmes*, founded early in the society's history, became a quarterly magazine circulated far beyond the Toronto area. The society has shrunk somewhat in recent years but continues vigorous, with half a dozen meetings a year, mostly at the Toronto Reference Library.

Prominent members of the group since its early days have included Cameron Hollyer (1926–2000), curator of the Arthur Conan Doyle collection at the Toronto Public Library until his 1991 retirement; Bob Coghill, a teacher and librarian; lawyer Clifford S. Goldfarb; retired teacher Doug Wrigglesworth; and Maureen Green (1939–2006) and Edwin Van der Flaes, a Toronto couple who are the best-known Canadian faces in American Sherlockian circles; and myself (born 1949), author of *In Bed with Sherlock Holmes* and other writings. Members who have contributed substantially over the years are honoured with the rank of Master Bootmaker (MBt).

The Bootmakers of Toronto came to think of itself as an independent national group — "the Sherlock Holmes Society of Canada" — rather than a scion of the Baker Street Irregulars, although close contact with American Sherlockians continues. It issues charters to its own scions elsewhere in Canada: Montréal, Halifax, Vancouver, Winnipeg, Saskatoon, Edmonton, Calgary and Ottawa.

THE ADVENTURESSES OF SHERLOCK HOLMES. A group of students at Albertus Magnus College in Connecticut, a small Roman Catholic women's institution, discovered a common interest in Sherlock Holmes in the fall of 1965, and two years later had defined themselves as a Sherlockian society under the name of the Adventuresses of Sherlock Holmes (a title said to be have been coined by Julian Wolff). In 1968 a group of them went to New York to be on the fringes of the BSI celebrations of Sherlock Holmes's birthday, and to meet a few of the prominent Sherlockians with whom they had corresponded. That evening — January 5, 1968 — six of them mounted a brief, cold picket line outside Cavanagh's Restaurant as the Irregulars arrived for a dinner from which, because of their sex, the Adventuresses were barred. John Bennett Shaw and Peter Blau invited them inside for a drink before dinner.

In subsequent years the Adventuresses (*www.ash-nyc.com*) gradually gained legitimacy and reputation. Four of the original members — Evelyn Herzog, Pat Moran, Mary Ellen Couchon, and Linda Patterson (later Ripley) — continued their Sherlockian interests, and were soon joined by Sherlockian women with no Albertus Magnus connection. By the mid-1980s most Sherlockian women held, or aspired to, ASH membership. The centre of activity was New York, where beginning in 1975 the Adventuresses, or ASH, began holding an annual dinner on the same evening as that of the BSI. From 1979 men were also admitted. With the admission of women to the BSI beginning in 1991, the ASH dinner in January disappeared, but the society holds spring and fall dinners as well as other events, and is known for its (generally good-natured) teasing of male Sherlockians about sex discrimination, and for its determination not to let the men outdo the women in hearty social activity.

Investitures in the style of the BSI were adopted by the Adventuresses, and available only to women, with a few exceptions, until 2008. The only visible officer is the Principal Unprincipled Adventuress, who has always been, and remains, Evelyn Herzog. The ASH published a newsletter in 1975 and 1976, transforming it into a magazine, *The Serpentine Muse*, in 1977. It continues to be published quarterly.

JANUARY IN NEW YORK. The chief festival of the Sherlockian world is an annual gathering in New York on the first or second weekend of January to celebrate Sherlock Holmes's birthday. The natal day was established as January 6 by Christopher Morley, the founder of the BSI, who wrote in the *Saturday Review of Literature* in 1933 that Holmes had been born in January, and, he added, "I nominate January 6th," that being the date of the issue in which his column appeared. Later he wrote in the *Baker Street Journal* that January 6, 1854, had been selected as the likely birthday by an unidentified member of the Irregulars, based on "zodiacal and astrological study." Other writers have stitched together more of a rationale for the January 6 date, partly involving Holmes's apparent affection for *Twelfth Night*, which he quotes more often than any other Shakespearean play — which is to say twice, at most. Finally, in 1957, Nathan Bengis clinched it by looking at the early paragraphs of *The Valley of Fear*, which take place on January 7, year not specified. The story begins with Holmes sitting at the table, in a somewhat cranky mood, with his untasted breakfast in front of him. The obvious explanation is a hangover, the result of a little birthday celebration the previous night. Ergo, January 6.

Sherlockians happily accept that date, and the New York venue for the party, despite the inconveniences of travelling to the metropolis in early January. The centre of the activity is the Algonquin Hotel on New York's West 44 Street, famous as the home of literary activity since the "Round Table" made its home there in the 1920s. Some Sherlockians are able to stay at the Algonquin, while others choose less expensive hotels nearby. By some time on the Thursday of the week in question, an acute eye will spot the occasional deerstalker at the Algonquin's lobby bar, and that evening parties of Sherlockians are likely to form up there to head out for supper at someone's favourite restaurant. The formal event for that evening is a Distinguished Lecture sponsored by the Baker Street Irregulars, and it need hardly be added that conversation and refreshment will continue far into the night in various participants' hotel rooms.

Friday begins (officially, for the wise will have breakfasted privately first) with the Martha Hudson Breakfast at the Algonquin. By the time breakfast is over, the early birds are gathering for another meal, the William Gillette Memorial Luncheon at the Old Homestead Restaurant in the Chelsea neighbourhood. Those who were too late in applying for reservations, or who decided against a heavy lunch, will be sightseeing instead, or getting a head start on the afternoon's shopping, which may well include visits to the local mystery bookstores. The Mysterious Bookshop often invites Sherlockian authors to be on hand to sign their books and meet their readers.

On the Friday evening the BSI holds its annual dinner. BSI members and guests put on their finest (black tie is popular, though not compulsory) and gather for drinks and dinner. The meal has had a series of venues over the years, most recently settling at the Union League Club on East 37 Street. With the recent advent of women into the Irregulars' ranks, it is no longer true that the cocktail hour will be graced with the presence of only one woman, to be toasted respectfully as "The Woman" and then sent away in a cab as the men go in to dinner. The tradition of The Woman is still maintained — she is usually the wife or widow of a prominent Irregular, and she goes off to dine with previous years' recipients of the same honour. But now a respectable number of women remain on hand to dine with the men. There is room for about 175 people altogether at the BSI dinner, and invitations are greatly coveted. Invested Irregulars can expect them in the mail from Wiggins, the BSI's leader, and are allowed to suggest the names of eligible non-Irregulars whom Wiggins will consider inviting if there is room. The wise Sherlockian attending the BSI dinner will bring a folding satchel to carry away the souvenirs and novelties distributed by friends and advertisers. He (or now she) can expect an evening of convivial conversation and long-drawn-out programming, including a series of original presentations and a number of BSI traditions. Someone will read the constitution and buy-laws of the society, someone will recite "Sherlock Holmes's Prayer" as composed by Christopher Morley, there will be a recital of the Musgrave Ritual, a scratchy recording will be played of James Montgomery singing "Aunt Clara," and new Investitures will be announced.

Elsewhere in the city, the Gaslight Gala is taking place — the latest version of an alternative dinner aimed at those who were not eligible to attend the BSI event. The Gala has been held lately at the Manhattan Club on West 56 Street, and is acknowledged, by those who have tried both events, to be somewhat livelier than that at the BSI dinner, the entertainment more original, and certainly the crowd rowdier and more high-pitched.

The January weekend in New York continues with private parties, visits to bookstores, outings to the theatre if anything Sherlockian is playing, and hours of conversation with friends new and old. Sherlockian dealers do business at the Algonquin Hotel on the Saturday morning, and the final highlight of the weekend is a Saturday afternoon cocktail party. This gathering began as a private party thrown by Julian Wolff each year for "Irregulars and their ladies." With annually growing crowds, the increasing number of Sherlockians who are not Irregulars attending other parts of the weekend's festivity, and the arrival of women as Irregulars themselves, it long ago became a general-admission event with tickets offered for sale.

Unlike most conventions, the January Sherlockian weekend has no registration desk, no organizing committee, and no published agenda. The date is determined by the leadership of the BSI, events are organized by their volunteer sponsors, and the word goes out along the grapevine and through the newsletters: meet in New York on the stated weekend, order lunch and dinner tickets from these sources, prepare for much to drink and little time to sleep, and enough talk to make even a Sherlockian hoarse.

CONVENTIONS, WORKSHOPS, TOURS. At other times of the year, too, Sherlockians gather. The weekend workshops organized by John Bennett Shaw (first at Notre Dame University in 1977) set the pattern for similar events sponsored by colleges, other institutions, or local Sherlockian societies here and there, and one or two full-fledged events of the kind are typically held each year. A weekend conference is likely to include several formal papers, some films or dramatic presentations, quizzes, music, a banquet allowing the opportunity for participants to show off Victorian costumes if they wish, and many late-night hours of conversation. Events of this sort are usually in the summer, and because of the work involved they generally take place just once, although there are a few repeated events such as an annual May "symposium" in Dayton, Ohio. The longstanding "Autumn in Baker Street" weekend at the Bear Mountain resort north of New York is no longer held, but lives in Sherlockian anecdote. At any such event one can expect to see many Sherlockians from the immediate neighbourhood, particularly members of the sponsoring society if there is one. Out-of-towners will also be there — some who happened to be in the area, others whose passionate enthusiasm for Sherlockian society means that they attend every such event within a thousand-mile radius of home. Finally there will be a few prominent names, mingling with local neophytes who ask them in awed tones about their Irregular friends, their publishing achievements, and their deep knowledge of the Canon.

Other special events are held here and there: theatre parties, picnics, light-hearted sporting competitions. An outing to the race track by a group of Sherlockians becomes a "Silver Blaze" event, in honour of the story by that title, if the track authorities will make one of the day's races a special feature and allow the Sherlockians to give a prize to the owner of the winning horse. A Silver Blaze outing, usually to New York's Belmont track, is an annual festivity for the Baker Street Irregulars; in May of each year, the Red Circle of Washington arranges a Silver Blaze at Pimlico, near Baltimore, and the Bootmakers of Toronto hold one in July at Woodbine.

Occasionally, Sherlockians pack their suitcases (if not Victorian carpet-bags) to travel farther afield. The most ambitious of these trips have been half a dozen excursions to Switzerland's Reichenbach Falls and other points of interest, organized by the Sherlock Holmes Society of London, the most recent being in 2005. The first such "pilgrimage," in 1978, included a banquet in honour of Adrian Conan Doyle, then living in Lausanne, and a carefully staged combat between Holmes (played by Sir Paul, later Lord, Gore-Booth, the society's president) and Moriarty (played by Charles Scholefield, another prominent member) at the brink of the dreadful falls. The London society, unhampered by the expenses of transatlantic travel, has also made journeys in pursuit of Holmes's traces in Oxford, Winchester, Portsmouth and other parts of England. On the western side of the Atlantic, the Baker Street Irregulars have made visits to the Valley of Fear in Pennsylvania and Mormon country in Utah. From New York, there have twice been Sherlockian cruises to Bermuda.

Despite what outsiders often assume, Sherlockians do not necessarily frequent "murder mystery weekends" — events in which a house party in a grand hotel, or a chartered railway coach, is disrupted by a murder in which victim, suspects, and police are played by actors scattered through the crowd. Some Sherlockians enjoy such activities and seek them out (they are often sponsored by specialist travel agencies) while others do not, but they rarely if ever form part of the entertainment on a strictly Sherlockian occasion.

When a Sherlockian travels, the first hope is to find a special event at the end of the journey; failing that, visitors are always welcome at the regular meetings of local societies. Some such gatherings, such as the annual dinner of the Three Garridebs in May, the now-defunct dinner of The Master's Class in Philadelphia on the Sunday of the New York "January weekend," and the Bootmakers of Toronto annual dinner in late January, are particularly well known. But if nothing is scheduled, a travelling Sherlockian will pick up the telephone anyway to see whether any of the locals are free for dinner. Someone is always happy to greet the visitor, talk about matters of common interest, and raise a glass to the honour of Sherlock Holmes. (In imitation of formal Victorian dinners, Sherlockians often drink toasts. Toasts are proposed chiefly to the health and memory of characters in the Canon, or to their author. A toast to "the Queen," meaning Victoria rather than Her present Majesty, is also popular, even in the American republic. This custom may owe something to the one-time vogue for propounding what would now be called trivia questions, with the loser of a challenge buying the next round. Having identified Grimesby Roylott, the company might cheerfully drink to his downfall. Probably from such origins, the traditional toasts of the Baker Street Irregulars are "The Woman"; "Mrs. Hudson"; "Mycroft"; and "Dr. Watson's Second Wife.")

OVERSEAS

Enthusiasm for Sherlock Holmes is of course not limited to North America. It is particularly intense in Britain, where the earliest readers of the Canon lived, and where it is easy to imagine that Holmes walked these very streets, rode these very railway lines. Although British and American activity developed mostly in isolation, there are now close ties between the Sherlockians of Canada and the United States and the "Holmesians" (their preferred term) of Britain.

EARLY HOLMESIANS. Sherlockian interest began in Britain before there was anything of the sort in the United States. The father of it all was Ronald Arbuthnot Knox (1888–1957), Roman Catholic priest (later Monsignor), scholar, and Bible translator, who chose to make a sectarian point in a satirical way in a paper delivered to an Oxford University student society in 1912. His theme was the merits and limitations of textual "higher criticism" for the understanding of the Bible, and he chose to convey his meaning by trying to apply the Biblical techniques to a more popular Canon. The title he chose was "Studies in the Literature of Sherlock Holmes." Among the students who heard the paper was the young Christopher Morley, later to be founder of the Baker Street Irregulars, who described the impact of Knox's work thus:

The device of pretending to analyse matters of amusement with full severity is the best way to reproach those who approach the highest subjects with too literal a mind. This new frolic in criticism was welcome at once; those who were students at Oxford in that ancient day remember how Mr. Knox was invited around from college to college to reread his agreeable lampoon.

"Studies in the Literature of Sherlock Holmes" eventually formed a chapter in Knox's book *Essays in Satire* (1928).

The gage was picked up at England's other ancient university, Cambridge, where Sydney (later Sir Sydney) Roberts (1887–1966), an authority on the works of Samuel Johnson, found time to reply to Knox in *A Note on the Watson Problem*, a pamphlet published (1929) by the Cambridge University Press. Other writings by Roberts followed: *Doctor Watson: Prolegomena to the Study of a Biographical Problem* in 1931 (based on an article published in 1930), *Holmes and Watson: A Miscellany* in 1953. Knox had used Sherlock Holmes as a tool in making a theological argument, but Roberts found in Holmes a life-long interest, and established a learned tradition that many British enthusiasts have followed ever since.

In or about 1934, a Sherlock Holmes Society was founded by the pioneer Sherlockians in Britain, including Roberts and H. W. Bell. Also on hand from the beginning was novelist and theologian Dorothy Sayers, whose creation Lord Peter Wimsey owed much to Sherlock Holmes. It flourished for only a couple of years, running into interpersonal difficulties and finally being dissolved even before World War II put an end to such frivolities. Any hope of its revival was dashed by the 1941 death of Archie MacDonell, the Scots novelist who had been its secretary and principal moving spirit. The story of the early society is told in detail by Richard Lancelyn Green in the *Sherlock Holmes Journal* in 1993.

THE SHERLOCK HOLMES SOCIETY OF LONDON. A revival of the society came in 1951. The train of events began with the Festival of Britain, a period of cultural events organized by the government as a way to celebrate the return to peacetime conditions (despite continuing austerity and food rationing). Among the Festival's events was a Sherlock Holmes exhibition sponsored by the Borough of St. Marylebone, the local government in the area of London that included Baker Street. Collectors who lent memorabilia for the exhibition, and others whose interest was stimulated by the exhibition, agreed to form what they called the Sherlock Holmes Society of London. Sydney Roberts became the founding president; R. Ivar Gunn was chairman (his widow, Margaret Gunn, was for many years a central presence in the councils of the SHS); Colin Prestige, a Kent lawyer and expert on the operettas of Gilbert and Sullivan, was among the founders.

For many years the face of British Sherlockians was the merry and erudite "Don" — Edward A.D. St.G. Hamilton, sixth Marquess of Donegall (1903–75). A former war correspondent, he was associated in his obituaries with "journalism and jazz," and his career had many other features, from his presence at the coronation of George V in 1911 (he was the youngest person in Westminster Abbey for the occasion) to achievements in boating and skiing. As for his Sherlockian merits, James Edward Holroyd said in the *Sherlock Holmes Journal* that

> It would be difficult to imagine anyone, here or overseas, who more wholeheartedly exemplified Holmes's own dictum of "playing the game for the game's own sake" than Lord Donegall. His favourite adventure was "The Empty House," no doubt in part because it originally appeared in the *Strand Magazine* in October, 1903, the month of his birth.... His library, divided between London and Switzerland, was one of the most comprehensive in the field.

Holroyd himself (ca. 1902–85) was probably the most erudite of all British Sherlockians. He it was who first suggested the idea for the 1951 Sherlock Holmes exhibition, and before long he became one of the founders of the SHS. He was author of *Baker Street By-Ways* (1959) and *Seventeen Steps to 221B* (1967), and for many years wrote a column of pithy observations, "The Egg-Spoon," for the society's *Sherlock Holmes Journal*.

Prominent members of the Sherlock Holmes Society of London (*www.sherlock-holmes.org.uk*) have included these:

- Guy Warrack, distinguished orchestral conductor and author of *Sherlock Holmes and Music* (1947).
- Sir Paul (later Lord) Gore-Booth (1909–84), for a long period the society's beloved president, in the intervals of his work in a notable diplomatic career.
- Stanley MacKenzie (died 1995), whose Sherlockian collection, identified in the 1960s as "probably the largest in Europe," was based on

theatrical items he managed to acquire during a long career as a professional stage manager.

- Anthony (Tony) Howlett, a barrister to whom is attributed the unexceptionable answer "Yes" when he was asked, "Is Sherlock Holmes real or fictional?" His widow, Alfreda Howlett, currently serves as President of the society.

Among other names of importance are those of Philip and Patsy Dalton, (Captain) W.R. (Bill) Michell, Philip Porter, Nicholas Utechin, Heather Owen, Pamela Bruxner, David Stuart Davies and Kathryn White, and Roger Johnson. The SHS has a highly formal structure including both a President and a Chairman, as well as two Honorary Secretaries (Catherine Cooke in charge of meetings, and Robert Ellis in charge of memberships; his address is 13 Crofton Avenue, Orpington, Kent BR6 8DU). Most of its meetings are held in London, but the SHS is known for its expeditions both to Switzerland on several occasions and, annually, to one or another British region where the details of one or two Canonical stories can be investigated first-hand.

Publication of *The Sherlock Holmes Journal* began in May 1952, carrying Sherlockian scholarship and news, originally by SHS members and then by Americans and others as well. The *SHJ*, published twice a year, is now one of the world's finest Sherlockian journals. It is currently edited by Roger Johnson and Heather Owen. There is also a monthly newsletter, the *District Messenger*. Among other achievements of the society is its involvement in the making of the forty-three-minute film "Mr. Sherlock Holmes of London," produced in 1971.

Although the Sherlock Holmes Society of London is the national society for British Sherlockians, enthusiasts in other parts of the country have found it worth while to establish local societies. Two of these with a particularly high profile are the Northern Musgraves, based in Yorkshire, and the Franco-Midland Hardware Company, specializing in correspondence activity for those unable to meet in person.

RICHARD LANCELYN GREEN. By the 1990s it was widely recognized that a young businessman with an ancestral house in Cheshire and a flat in London was the owner of the world's outstanding collection of Doyleana and Sherlockiana, and quite possibly the world's outstanding authority on such matters himself. Richard Lancelyn Green came by his bookmanship honestly; born July 10, 1953, he was the son of prolific author Roger Lancelyn Green and had been brought up to both erudition and prosperity. He also worked hard at collecting, learning, and eventually writing.

At the beginning of the 1980s Green collaborated with John Michael Gibson on two volumes that presented newly discovered works by Arthur Conan Doyle. They were quickly followed (1983) by the massive *Bibliography of A. Conan Doyle*, part of a series of scholarly bibliographies issued by the Clarendon Press, Oxford. Several more books followed, some of them again with Gibson. Especially valuable was Green's own *The Uncollected Sherlock Holmes* (1983), with an introduction 137 pages long that could have been published in itself as a biography of Doyle. However, it came to be generally understood that Green cherished the ambition of writing a full-length, definitive biography, when the long-awaited "Doyle papers," particularly family letters, should at long last become available.

Meanwhile, Green took an active part in Sherlockian affairs, travelling, giving talks, and continuing to write, though he could be prickly about perceived slights and shy in public situations. Friends, and he had many of them, who visited his London home reported that it was chock-a-block with books, papers, and artifacts, many of them unique. A good many of the items in the 1983 *Bibliography* could be listed only because Green had somehow unearthed copies of them. He owned a copy of *Beeton's Christmas Annual* for 1887, of course, but also many Doyle manuscripts and letters — and Doyle's waistcoat, and family photographs, and the silver cigarette case that Doyle had presented to Sidney Paget on the occasion of the latter's wedding.

On March 28, 2004, Green was found dead in his bed, in circumstances that left open the possibilities of suicide, murder, or accident. He had been at the centre of a controversy over the imminent sale of Doyle papers and souvenirs from the estate of Dame Jean Conan Doyle, which Green had argued should go to the British Library rather than being dispersed and perhaps eluding scholars like himself. His death drew international media attention, and left his Sherlockian friends mourning — sentiments that were eventually expressed in *To Keep the Memory Green* (2007), a volume of tributes and recollections edited by Steven Rothman and Nicholas Utechin.

Green bequeathed his collection to the city of Portsmouth, which had been Doyle's home for a time, and the Arthur Conan Doyle Collection Lancelyn Green Bequest is now being catalogued by the Portsmouth Central Library and City Museum (*www.conandoylecollection.co.uk*).

HARDWICK AND HARRISON. Two other British Sherlockians, active chiefly outside the circle of the SHS, are deserving of special mention. The younger was Michael Hardwick (1924–91), author of several pastiches — *Prisoner of the Devil* (1979) was particularly admired — and of much other Sherlockian writing as well. He was, for example, responsible for dozens of scripts for the series starring Carleton Hobbs as Holmes on BBC radio. In collaboration with his wife, Mollie, he wrote a minor biography of Arthur Conan Doyle, *The Man Who Was Sherlock Holmes* (1964), and one of the most widely used of Sherlockian reference books, the breezy *Sherlock Holmes Companion* (1962). Alone he produced its successor, *The Complete Guide to Sherlock Holmes* (1986). Michael and Mollie together dramatized several Canonical tales in *Four Sherlock Holmes Plays* (1964), *The Game's Afoot* (1969), and *Four More Sherlock Holmes Plays* (1973). Nor was their work limited to Sherlockian writings; they were associated with *The Duchess of Duke Street* on British television, and with the novelizations of many episodes of "Upstairs, Downstairs."

The other unique figure among British Sherlockians was still more remarkable: Michael Harrison (born April 25, 1907; died September 13, 1991). His work was usefully summarized by Roger Johnson in the *Sherlock Holmes Journal*:

> His first important work in the field of Sherlock Holmes resulted from a seven-book contract, and the subject was suggested to him by the publisher. That book was the classic *In the Footsteps of Sherlock Holmes* [1958]. Others were to come, but this painstaking and engagingly discursive investigation of Holmes's England should be on every Sherlockian's bookshelf. Even here, though, Michael's occasional hastiness could be seen.... The book was deservedly well-received; a revised edition appeared in 1972, and the author produced a second volume in the same vein, *The London of Sherlock Holmes* [1972], equally invaluable to an understanding of the metropolis in which the detective lived.
>
> *The World of Sherlock Holmes* [1973] followed, and another of the author's quirks became apparent: the tendency to suppose — or even to invent — and then to present the supposition as fact....
>
> Michael Harrison's last books in his field were all published in America. This was a loss for the British reader, as two of them, at least, are among the very best. In 1976, he was invited to compile a *Festschrift* in honour of Dr. Julian Wolff's 70th birthday; the result was *Beyond Baker Street*, which contains not a single dud among its 25 essays. And in 1984 appeared the long-awaited

A *Study in Surmise*, in which the author set out what he believed to be the real inspiration for Sherlock Holmes....

Michael Harrison felt that he had been rather snubbed by what he saw as the Sherlockian Establishment in Britain, but he remained on cordial terms with many individuals here.

Particularly striking is *I, Sherlock Holmes*, a purported autobiography of the sleuth, rich like most of Harrison's writing with Victorian detail. His non-Sherlockian books, which were many, ranged from *Fanfare of Strumpets* (1971), about society prostitution, to *Fire from Heaven* (1976), about spontaneous human combustion. There were also a number of novels.

In the United States, he was beloved for his great talent at story telling and knowledge of the Victorian and Edwardian eras. His books sometimes sound rather like transcriptions of the hours he could spend rambling; they are poorly indexed, subjects change on a whim, references are lacking, and details sometimes questionable, but the reader who seeks entertainment and the spirit of the age is well rewarded. In old age Harrison made several visits to North America to find appreciative audiences, not only for his talk but for his courtly Edwardian presence, with a gallantry to women and a striking appetite for liquor.

OTHER LANDS. In the more distant English-speaking lands, and even outside the English-speaking world, there have been clusters of Sherlockian enthusiasts, often led by a single energetic figure. At one time they seemed remote, but modern communication and travel have brought them into closer connection with North American Sherlockian activities, and the Baker Street Irregulars have drawn attention to such worldwide links with the publication of an "International Series" of anthologies that so far includes three volumes:

- *Japan and Sherlock Holmes* (2005), edited by Yuichi Hirayama, Masamichi Hugirashi, and Hirotaka Ueda. It appears that nowhere in the world does the passion for Holmes equal that felt in Japan. Although Sherlockian activity in that country began with the Baritsu Chapter, founded chiefly by Americans during the postwar occupation, the real father of Sherlockian enthusiasm in Japan is Kouki Naganuma, a deputy minister of finance in the postwar period who wrote several books about Holmes. In 1977, a Japan Sherlock Holmes Club was founded by Tsukasa Kobayashi (born 1929) and his wife, Akane Higashiyama. The two, along with photographer Masaharu Uemura, demonstrated their enthusiasm and knowledge in *Shārokku Hāmuzu no Rondon* (1984), translated into English and published as the sumptuous *Sherlock Holmes's London* (1986). The Japan Sherlock Holmes Club (*www.holmesjapan.jp*) may now be the largest such organization in the world, with more than one thousand members, including those in, at last report, eleven branches around the country. The single most active Sherlockian in Japan is Kiyoshi Tanaka (born 1952), an engineer, illustrator, and prolific writer in both Japanese and English. Japanese Sherlockians have been responsible for many books, seminars, and other activities; the world's first statue of Sherlock Holmes was unveiled in 1988 in Karuizawa Town, Nagano. Attempting to explain the wild popularity of Holmes in his country, Tanaka, as well as citing all the reasons that obtain in English-speaking lands, has added this one: "The stories take place in the Victorian age in England, which corresponds to the dawn of civilization during the Meiji era in Japan — when we modelled our society after those of England and other European nations, and introduced things to Japan such as gas lamps and carriages, etc. Thus, the atmosphere of the stories makes readers feel nostalgic for "the good old days'."

- *Scandinavia and Sherlock Holmes* (2006), edited by Bjarne Nielsen, who serves as president of the Sherlock Holmes Klubben i Danmark (*www.sherlockiana.dk/shklub/*). Reviewer Roger Johnson called the book "a fascinating selection of writings, in English, from Danish and Swedish scholars (and one Norwegian, Nils Nordberg). The history of Holmesian scholarship in Scandinavia, recounted in the twin introductions by Mr Nielsen and Mattias Boström, includes such familiar names as Storm-P [Henry Storm-Peterson], A. D. Henriksen, Tage La Cour, Henry Lauritzen, and Åke Runnquist from the past, and, among today's luminaries, Mia Stampe Lagergaard, Jens Byskov Jensen, Ted Berman, and Hans-Uno Bengtsson." The Swedish enthusiasts are online at *www.sherlockholmes.se*.

- *Australia and Sherlock Holmes* (2009), edited by Bill Barnes and Doug Elliott. Much of the material in the volume is reprinted from *News from the Diggings* and *The Passengers' Log*, publications respectively of the Sherlock Holmes Society of Australia and the Sydney Passengers, now merged into a single society under the latter name (*www.sherlock.on.net*).

Among other leading groups now active are the Societé Sherlock Holmes de France (*www.sshf.com*) and 221B — Deutscher Sherlock Holmes Klub (*www.221b-dshc.de*) in Germany. Less is heard in recent years of the once prominent Crew of the S.S. *Friesland* of Holland, led by Cornelis Helling.

THE PRINTED WORD

Although there are Sherlockians whose chief interest is television or film, most are strongly oriented to the printed word. Many of the pioneers in the field were journalists or novelists — Christopher Morley, founder of the Baker Street Irregulars, was both — and writing about Sherlock Holmes came naturally. "Never has so much been written by so many for so few," said Morley about the *Baker Street Journal* in its second year, 1947. In the early years, and even more during the "boom" of the 1970s and 1980s, there were quarterlies and newsletters, monographs and pamphlets. The volume of printed matter has abated a little in the past two decades, but still more is written on Sherlockian themes than almost anyone can find time to read.

DEFINITE ARTICLES. The traditional genre is the literary article, the written equivalent of the orally delivered "paper." The early volumes of the *Baker Street Journal* include many such articles, some with titles or epigraphs in Latin (dedicated readers could swallow such phrases in those days, or at least knew where to look them up) and most with wit as well as learning. As generation succeeded generation, there was perhaps less erudition in the average piece of Sherlockian writing, but articles, considered "scholarly" if they had footnotes, continued to be the staple of the *BSJ* and the growing number of other Sherlockian magazines. In general they were the work of men and women who loved books, but rarely were they written in the style of English professors. Edgar W. Smith, the most eloquent Sherlockian of them all, was an executive in the automobile industry. Edward F. Clark Jr., whose "Study of an Untold Tale" in the *BSJ* in 1963 was arguably the acme of Sherlockian essays — clear, clever, knowledgeable, solid, informative, and interesting — was a Wall Street lawyer. Before 1970 there were certainly Sherlockian books, but those of any size were chiefly anthologies, rather like the journals but fatter. Vincent Starrett's *The Private Life of Sherlock Holmes* was admired not only because it was so good but because it was so unusual.

Sherlockian writing followed something of a trajectory over the years that followed. Morley and his contemporaries knew, and mostly acknowledged, that they were writing in tribute to the creations of Arthur Conan Doyle; sometimes they even nodded to Doyle's other works as they commented lovingly about

Sherlock Holmes. Later, through the 1950s and 1960s, the Sherlockian "game" made it a faux pas to acknowledge Doyle as anything more than "the Literary Agent." A narrow circle of enthusiasts wrote with passion on questions about which only a Sherlockian could be truly passionate, and maintained the pretense that Holmes and Watson and their associates were historical characters about whom facts can be unearthed and theories proposed.

A striking example was the practice of Sherlockian "chronology," the attempt to assign dates, as exact as possible, to each of Holmes's published (and even unpublished) cases. Although many of the stories do mention dates ("The Reigate Squires" takes place "in the spring of '87," for example), they can be frustratingly vague, and they can certainly be inconsistent. There has never been consensus, among those who care deeply about such matters, on whether *A Study in Scarlet* takes place in 1881 or 1882, or *The Sign of the Four* (leading to Watson's marriage, a pivotal event in the biography of the Baker Street partners) in 1887 or 1888. The work of chronology has slowed down, but not stopped altogether in recent decades, as earlier writers have come to most of the possible conclusions in their conflicting but enthusiastic researches. The major works of Sherlockian chronology are these:

- William S. Baring-Gould, *The Chronological Holmes* (1955).
- Harold Wilmerding Bell, *Sherlock Holmes and Dr. Watson: The Chronology of Their Adventures* (1932).
- T.S. Blakeney, *Sherlock Holmes: Fact or Fiction?* (1932).
- Gavin Brend, *My Dear Holmes* (1951).
- Jay Finley Christ, *An Irregular Chronology* (1947).
- Vincent Delay, *Holmes and Watson: A New Chronology of Their Adventures* (2008, translated from the French).
- Henry T. Folsom, *Through the Years at Baker Street* (1963, 1964, 1990).
- John Hall, *I Remember the Date Very Well* (1993).
- Ernest B. Zeisler, *Baker Street Chronology* (1953).

The findings of these and other chronologists were conflated in *The Date Being?*, a 1970 brochure by Andrew Jay Peck with a revised and expanded edition (1996) edited by Peck and Leslie S. Klinger.

In addition to scholarship of this kind, Sherlockian journals have always published much other material. There have always been quizzes, sometimes ingenious and sometimes descending to the level of trivia questions. There have always been pastiches and parodies, of varying qualities. And there has always been poetry, although contemporary Sherlockian verse does not ascend to the art practised in the 1950s by Charles E. Lauterbach; nor does the genre of "tale-in-verse" seem still to exist. With the development of offset printing in the 1960s, the range of possibilities grew wider, and Sherlockians could be offered photographs and drawings, reproductions of news clippings, manuscript facsimiles, and much more. At various times, the journals have also found room for dramatizations, prayers, personal reminiscences, television reviews, jokes, and even recipes. Sherlockians came to write more openly about sex than they used to, and more in simple explanation of the customs and circumstances of the Victorian era, providing information which many readers of the 1940s might have been able to remember for themselves. By 1990, a growing amount of Sherlockian history was also seeing print, as well as straightforward news about the expanding world of Sherlockian societies and activities — and, always, a number of articles in the traditional sense.

THE BOOM AND WHAT FOLLOWED. During the "boom" in the last quarter of the twentieth century, the number of Sherlockian magazines and newsletters burgeoned. The majority of the important ones have now ceased publication, and others have shrunk, victims of waning interest and the inevitable shift of energies onto the Internet. The *Baker Street Journal* (*www.bakerstreetjournal. com*) now has a circulation of between 800 and 1,000 copies four times a year, half what it was two decades ago, but remains the largest Sherlockian magazine. (Its business address: PO Box 465, Hanover, Pennsylvania 17331.) Comparable in stature is the British *Sherlock Holmes Journal* (*www.sherlock-holmes.org.uk/ journal.php*), published twice a year. Smaller magazines include *The Serpentine Muse*, published by the Adventuresses of Sherlock Holmes (*www.ash-nyc.com*); *Prescott's Press*, published by the Three Garridebs of Westchester County (*3garridebs.homestead.com*); and *Canadian Holmes*, published by the Bootmakers of Toronto (*www.bootmakers.ca*). But there are also a multitude of other publications; the *BSJ* publishes an annual list of "Sherlockian Periodicals Received," which for 2007 included forty titles. Among the newsletters that are of interest to an audience beyond the membership of a local club are these monthlies:

- *Scuttlebutt from the Spermaceti Press* (*members.cox.net/sherlock1/ scuttle.htm*), written and published by Peter Blau of Washington with a more or less exhaustive summary of Sherlockian news and publications.
- *The District Messenger* (*www.sherlock-holmes.org.uk/district.php*), a British equivalent to Blau's newsletter, edited by Roger Johnson for the Sherlock Holmes Society of London.

- *The Camden House Journal* (Box 21, Zeigler, Illinois 62999), with meeting reports and announcements of the Occupants of the Empty House, a society in the southern Illinois region, as well as the continuing series of papers presented to the Occupants, nearly all of them original and thought-provoking.

The list of important Sherlockian serials that have ceased publication is a sad one:

- *Baker Street Miscellanea*, privately published from 1975 to 1994 under the editorship, at various times and in various combinations, of Donald Pollock, Jon Lellenberg, Ann Byerly, and William Goodrich. It consistently presented ground-breaking material and took a special interest in Doylean studies at a time that other Sherlockian media mostly ignored the author.
- *The Sherlock Holmes Review*, published 1986–96 at Zionsville, Indiana, under the editorship of Steven Doyle.
- *Wheelwrightings* (1978–92) and *Plugs and Dottles* (monthly, 1980–98), both chiefly edited by Robert C. Burr of Peoria, Illinois, on behalf of a local society, the Hansoms of John Clayton. The latter, in particular, exemplified what was lively and good-humoured in the Sherlockian world.
- *The Holmes and Watson Report*, published six times a year from 1997 to 2004 by Brad Keefauver of Peoria and demonstrating a zest, not to say madness, remarkable even by the usual standards of Sherlockians.
- *Sherlock Magazine*, which was *The Sherlock Holmes Gazette* at its founding in 1991, then *Sherlock Holmes the Detective Magazine*, and then simply *Sherlock* before adopting its final title. Published by a succession of companies and edited by a number of individuals with, apparently, varying visions, it was for most of its life the glossiest and most commercial of Sherlockian publications, and incorporated a good deal of material about mystery writing in general. It ceased publication about the end of 2006, following Issue 68, leaving behind generic content on its web site (*www.sherlockholmes.com*) but no indication that there had once been a magazine.

The years following the so-called "boom" were a productive period for Sherlockian books as well as for journals. Among the many other items that would appear on a bibliography for this period are such volumes as these:

Monographs — *A Study in Surmise: The Making of Sherlock Holmes* (1984) by Michael Harrison; *The Elementary Methods of Sherlock Holmes* (1987) and *Sherlock and The Ladies* (1988) by Brad Keefauver; *God and Sherlock Holmes* (1984) by Wayne Wall; *In Bed with Sherlock Holmes* (1985) by Christopher Redmond; *On the Scent with Sherlock Holmes* (1978) by Walter Shepherd; *The Making of Sherlock Holmes* (1984) and *The Sherlock Holmes Murder File* (1985) by Kelvin I. Jones.

Anthologies — *A Touch of the Class* (1981), representing work by members of The Master's Class of Philadelphia; *Studies in Scarlet* (1989), edited by David Hammer; *A Singular Set of People* (1990), edited by Marlene Aig and David Galerstein. *Sherlock Holmes by Gas-Lamp* (1989), edited by Philip A. Shreffler, consists of highlights from the first forty years of the *Baker Street Journal*.

Scrapbooks and coffee-table books — *The Sherlock Holmes Scrapbook* (1974) by Peter Haining; *Sherlock Holmes: The Man and His World* (1979) by H.R.F. Keating; *Sherlock Holmes in America* (1981) by Bill Blackbeard; *Sherlock Holmes: A Centenary Celebration* (1986) by Allen Eyles; *Elementary, My Dear Watson* (1986) by Graham Nown; *The Pictorial History of Sherlock Holmes* (1991) by Michael Pointer; *The Life and Times of Sherlock Holmes* (1992) by Philip Weller with Christopher Roden.

Cookbooks — *Sherlock Holmes Cookbook* (1976) by Sean Wright and John Farrell; *Dining with Sherlock Holmes* (1976, 1990) by Julia Carlson Rosenblatt and Frederic H. Sonnenschmidt; *Sherlock Holmes Cookbook* (1989) by Charles A. Mills. In addition there have been books on such specific topics as film and television, travel (and Victorian London), and Sherlockian history.

As with magazines, Sherlockians seem to be writing less in book form since the dawn of the Internet era. From the early 1990s to the present, pastiches continue to appear, and there has if anything been a growing volume of Doyleana, but a bibliography of more traditional Sherlockian material would be meagre, indeed. It is perhaps symbolic that in 1996 Calabash Press embarked on a series of *The Case Files of Sherlock Holmes*, intending a volume of essays on each of the sixty stories; only four have appeared: "The Musgrave Ritual," "The Speckled Band," "The Dying Detective," and "The Blue Carbuncle." In addition there are these few volumes:

> **Monographs** — *The Baker Street Briefs* (1994), collected writings by S. Tupper Bigelow; *Sidelights on Holmes* (1998) by John Hall; *The Science of Sherlock Holmes* (2006) by E.J. Wagner; *Sherlock Holmes and a Question of Science* (2006) by Christopher Lindsey.
>
> **Anthologies** — *Violets & Vitriol* (2004), edited by S.E. Dahlinger; *Ladies, Ladies* (2007), edited by Patricia Guy and Katherine Karlson.
>
> **Scrapbooks** — *The Mysterious World of Sherlock Holmes* (2008) by Bruce Wexler. There are also a few reference books. *Encyclopedia Sherlockiana* (1994) by Matthew E. Bunson is not on any account to be confused with the better-known volume by Jack Tracy under almost the same title, which is more comprehensive and reliable on persons and places mentioned in the Canon, although Bunson does also cover films and some other odd matters. *The Bedside, Bathtub & Armchair Companion to Sherlock Holmes* (1999) by Dick Riley and Pam McAllister is uneven and frequently derivative. *The Canonical Compendium* (1999) by Stephen Clarkson is a massive, complicated index to names and topics in the Canon, with page references to five frequently used editions.

BIBLIOGRAPHY. Sherlockian writings up to 1980 (including editions of the Canon, scholarship both serious and tongue-in-cheek, pastiches and many other genres) are fully listed in three bibliographies compiled by Ronald B. DeWaal. His first book, and winner of a major award for bibliographic achievements, was *The World Bibliography of Sherlock Holmes and Dr. Watson* (1974), with a total of 6,221 entries. It was followed in 1980 by *The International Sherlock Holmes* (1980). Neither volume has a subject index, though entries are arranged in broad categories. It was a long wait before the 1994 publication of *The Universal Sherlock Holmes*, again by DeWaal but with extensive editorial involvement by the publisher, George Vanderburgh of The Battered Silicon Dispatch-Box. This edition was sold as unbound sheets and amounted to four volumes of entries — a total of 24,703 items, including all that had appeared in the two earlier volumes as well as thousands of new ones. A fifth volume provides assorted indexes, but again there is no detailed subject access. The *USH* is additionally awkward because within any section, individual items from the first volume and then the second volume precede the new ones, rather than being merged in a single alphabetical sequence. Nevertheless, this large and irregular work contains a treasure of information on what has been written and done about Sherlock Holmes over the years. It has been converted to web access by the University of Minnesota Libraries (*special. lib.umn.edu/rare/holmes.phtml*) and additional entries are added to the web site from time to time by librarian Timothy J. Johnson.

The only real subject index to Sherlockian scholarship is *Bigelow on Holmes* (1974), edited by Donald Redmond from a card-index originally prepared by S. Tupper Bigelow for his private use. The card index itself is now held in Toronto Reference Library, and was kept up to date by Redmond until entries closed in 1999.

PUBLISHERS. Since *Profile by Gaslight* in 1944, from Simon & Schuster, a few important Sherlockian books have been issued by mainstream publishers. Doubleday ventured to publish Jack Tracy's *Encyclopaedia Sherlockiana* in 1977, for example, no doubt feeling some affection for the subject because of its still definitive *Complete Sherlock Holmes*. Many pastiches, which can be expected to have a general readership, have come from general publishers (Scribners, McGraw-Hill, Dutton, Putnam, St. Martin's Griffin, Carroll & Graf, Doubleday again), and even more have appeared in trade paperback editions, likely to be found on drugstore racks, from Pinnacle, Signet, Warner, Ace, Ballantine, and the like.

But a good deal of Sherlockian literature has always been privately published and distributed by the author through specialized channels. Such materials can be frustrating for the would-be collector, to say nothing of the bibliographer. Half a century ago private publication typically involved negotiations with a local printing company; nowadays computerized word processing and typesetting are the first steps in a sequence that can end with production by a "books on demand" firm a continent away. Any Sherlockian society and, indeed, any individual can produce books of a sophisticated appearance, and can negotiate to offer them for sale on Amazon.

Somewhere in the middle come the products of small presses, themselves little more than hobby activities, specializing in Sherlockian material. Several have come and gone over the years, including Edgar W. Smith's The Pamphlet

House and, more recently, Jack Tracy's Gaslight Publications and Samuel Gringras's Magico Magazine. At present three such small presses are in business:

- Gasogene Books, a part of Wessex Press (*www.wessexpress.com*) in Indianapolis, Indiana. Proprietor: Steven Doyle.
- Calabash Press, a part of Ash-Tree Press (*www.ash-tree.bc.ca/calabash.html*) in Ashcroft, British Columbia. Proprietors: Christopher and Barbara Roden.
- The Battered Silicon Dispatch-Box (*www.batteredbox.com*) in Flesherton, Ontario, and Sauk City, Wisconsin. Proprietor: George Vanderburgh.

BOOK DEALERS. Sherlockian books, except the few issued by trade publishers, cannot reliably be found in general bookstores. Current titles are bought, if not from the authors or publishers, then online, or from specialist dealers such as the mystery bookstores that exist in most major cities. Typically such dealers also carry used and rare books, and are as comfortable dealing by mail as selling to their walk-in clientele. Among the best-known such stores are these:

- The Mysterious Bookshop, 58 Warren Street, New York, New York 10007 (*www.mysteriousbookshop.com*).
- Sleuth of Baker Street, 1600 Bayview Avenue, Toronto, Ontario M4G 3B7 (*www.sleuthofbakerstreet.com*).
- Murder One, 2–4 Hoxton Square London N1 6US, England (*www.murderone.co.uk*).
  There is an Independent Mystery Booksellers Association with a list of its members online at *www.mysterybooksellers.com*.

More advanced Sherlockian collectors will also have a use for dealers who work only by mail, specializing in used and rare material. Many general rare book dealers handle Sherlockiana from time to time; one or two who formerly specialized in such material, such as Gravesend Books of Pocono Pines, Pennsylvania, and Sherlock in L.A. of Oceanside, California, are no longer in business. Two higher-end firms that may be of interest are James Pepper Rare Books of Santa Barbara, California (*www.jamespepperbooks.com*), and Peter L. Stern & Company, Inc., of Boston (*www.sternrarebooks.com*).

PRIVATE COLLECTIONS. Some Sherlockians maintain a short shelf of well-loved volumes. Others are casual collectors of books and other material about Sherlock Holmes. A few are enthusiasts, and a very few are "completists," keen to acquire a copy of everything, however banal or rare, that touches on Holmes. Even in an era when fewer people seem to use and covet books, a collection can become valuable in monetary terms (and a good collection is inevitably expensive to acquire), and is certainly valuable as a resource for a Sherlockian who seeks, as many do, to write about Holmes for publication or to impress fellow members of a society.

Some Sherlockian collectors are chiefly interested in editions of the Canon. First editions can be expensive, but need not be — a copy of the first American edition of *The Hound of the Baskervilles*, in "good" condition, was listed for $184 from a Connecticut dealer on the used-book web site Alibris.com in May 2009. Later, often obscure and fugitive, editions are also of interest to some collectors, as they were to Nathan L. Bengis of New York, whose unprecedented library of editions of *The Sign of the Four*, collected in the 1950s, is now at the Toronto Public Library. A striking collection could be formed of paperback editions alone, including some from the middle decades of the twentieth century with lurid cover illustrations by the masters of pulp publishing. Other collectors specialize in the non-Sherlockian works of Arthur Conan Doyle; or pastiches and other derivative works; or classic pamphlets and books of Sherlockian scholarship. Some of the latter now fetch breathtaking prices, although the intelligent collector will make careful comparisons between dealers before reaching for the credit card.

One of the greatest Sherlockian collections was that of James Bliss Austin of Pittsburgh (whose achievement in that field was paralleled by his collecting and scholarship in Japanese art). After his death his Sherlockiana was offered for sale by the beneficiaries of his will, the generality of the collection fetching $151,000 from Pepper & Stern, then in business together, who offered most of the material for resale through their catalogues at eye-popping prices. Austin's two greatest treasures were auctioned separately later: the manuscript of *The Valley of Fear* (it sold for $260,000) and a copy of *Beeton's Christmas Annual* containing the first publication of *A Study in Scarlet* ($52,000). John Bennett Shaw of Santa Fe was known as a voracious completist; shortly before his death in 1994, his collection was acquired by the University of Minnesota. Peter Blau of Washington is a prominent collector as well as authority on Sherlockian matters. Much specialized information aimed at Sherlockian collectors is maintained on a web site (*www.bestofsherlock.com*) by a young California scholar, Randall Stock.

LIBRARY COLLECTIONS. Four public institutions — one in Canada, one in the United States, and two in England — have sizeable collections of Sherlockian material, and treasures can be found at a number of other locations.

What claims to be "the world's largest gathering of material related to Sherlock Holmes and his creator Sir Arthur Conan Doyle" is at the Elmer L. Andersen Library of the University of Minnesota (222 21st Avenue South, Minneapolis, Minnesota 55455). The Sherlock Holmes Collections (special. lib.umn.edu/rare/holmes.phtml) — the plural is important — began with the holdings of a New York Sherlockian, James C. Iraldi, who sold his collection to the university in 1974. They grew tremendously with the acquisition of the treasures, including first and other early editions of the Canon, assembled by Philip S. Hench, a physician at Minnesota's Mayo Clinic and member of the Sherlockian society in the Minneapolis area, the Norwegian Explorers. That collection was donated to the university by his widow in 1979. The Minnesota holdings grew enormously with the addition of the John Bennett Shaw collection, delivered to Minneapolis in 1993, and the collection of Allen Mackler, received by bequest in 2006 (and including Mackler's impressive full-size restoration of the 221B sitting room). The collections are now managed by curator Timothy J. Johnson, with their growth and use supported by a group of Friends of the Sherlock Holmes Collections.

The Canadian repository is the Toronto Reference Library (789 Yonge Street, Toronto, Ontario M4W 2G8), part of the Toronto Public Library (*www. torontopubliclibrary.ca*). Its Arthur Conan Doyle Collection was formed in 1971 with the purchase of materials that had belonged to a British mystery enthusiast, Arthur Baillie. The library soon also acquired the collection of S. Tupper Bigelow, a long-time Sherlockian who was a retired Toronto judge, the many variant editions of *The Sign of the Four* that had been part of the collection of Nathan L. Bengis of New York, and a collection assembled by British bookseller Harold Mortlake. Founders of the collection included Cameron Hollyer and Mary McMahon of the library's Literature Department; in an advisory role were the library's director, John Parkhill, and an external friend, Donald A. Redmond of Queen's University. The collection includes the works of Arthur Conan Doyle and associated material (including some Doyle manuscripts) as well as Sherlockiana in general. The whole collection is housed in a comfortable room with Victorian furniture, still called Room 221B although it is on the fifth floor of the library's modern building. Since the 1991 retirement of Cameron Hollyer, the collection has been under the curatorship of Victoria Gill and more recently Peggy Perdue. *A Checklist of the Arthur Conan Doyle Collection*, compiled by Donald A. Redmond, was issued in 1973 (second edition 1977).

A major Holmes collection can be found at what would have been Holmes's neighbourhood library: the Marylebone Library (109–117 Marylebone Road,

London NW1 5PS, England). That library was a service of the old Borough of St. Marylebone at the time its collection was formed from books and other materials donated for the Sherlock Holmes exhibition that was the Borough's contribution to the Festival of Britain in 1951. With changes in local government, the library is now operated by the City of Westminster. The collection is under the curatorship of Catherine Cooke, who edited an inventory, *The Contents of a Lumber-Room*, published by the library in 1986.

The newest major Sherlock Holmes collection is in the British city of Portsmouth, at the Central Library (Guildhall Square, Portsmouth PO1 2DX, England) and City Museum. The Arthur Conan Doyle Collection Lancelyn Green Bequest (*www.conandoylecollection.co.uk*) was, as the title indicates, given to Portsmouth by the will of collector Richard Lancelyn Green, who died in 2004. The library's web site notes that there are "five prioritised areas of the collection — the Doyle family photographs and papers, spiritualist photographs and papers, dramatisations, Victorian and Edwardian World and Sherlock Holmes Phenomena." Much of the material has not yet been catalogued and made available for use, but Portsmouth has mounted two major public exhibitions. At present, the web site explains, "The exhibition's displays explore the life of Arthur Conan Doyle and the creation of Sherlock Holmes. It features a range of interactive displays, a 'new' Sherlock Holmes mystery, and narration by Stephen Fry, the Patron of the collection."

A number of other libraries have good collections of Sherlockiana and Doyle material, ranging from the Library of Congress in Washington to the Humanities Research Center of the University of Texas at Austin and the Lilly Library of Indiana University at Bloomington. A recent development is the Baker Street Irregulars Trust archive at Houghton Library, Harvard University.

THE INTERNET

Probably the majority of Sherlockian activity now takes place through the medium of the Internet. Fifteen years ago there was no such thing as a Sherlockian web site; now there are dozens, including one (*members.cox.net/sherlock1/Sherlocktron.html*) that is the direct descendant of the first known electronic Sherlockian presence, Sherlocktron. In the early 1990s it was a dial-up bulletin board operated by Willis G. Frick of San Clemente, California. Today it is "an Internet information center" with listings of societies, publications, "purveyors" (of merchandise from tea to chessboards) and web links.

Web sites come and go unpredictably, but as of early 2009, these are some of the major and apparently stable Sherlockian sites online:

- Sherlockian.Net (*www.sherlockian.net*), operated by myself, with several hundred web pages consisting primarily of links to Sherlockian and collateral material, as well as some essays and other specific material, and a page discussing "how to write a term paper" about Holmes or Doyle.
- 221B Baker Street (*221bakerstreet.org*), operated by Michael Sherman, with texts of most of the Canonical stories as well as Sidney Paget illustrations and other material.
- The Best of Sherlock Holmes (*www.bestofsherlock.com*), operated by Randall Stock, with lists and links emphasizing manuscripts, rare books, and electronic products such as e-texts and computer games.
- The Diogenes Club (*www.diogenes-club.com*), operated by David Coulter, with texts (the Canon and a number of collateral works), a set of summaries of the stories, and much other material.
- Le Musée de l'Holmes (*www.sherlock-holmes.org*), a sizeable site in French operated by Sébastien Canevet, with subsidiary sites in six other languages under the rubric of "Sherlock Holmes International."
- Camden House (*www.ignisart.com/camdenhouse*), operated by David Soucek and others, with texts of the stories, a large collection of illustrations ("Pinacotheca Holmesiana"), and other material.
- Sherlock Peoria (*www.sherlockpeoria.net*), operated by Brad Keefauver, including Keefauver's lively blog and much other entertaining material.

John Bergquist of Minneapolis maintains an authoritative survey of Sherlockian Resources on the Internet at *www.tc.umn.edu/~bergq003/holmes*.

Several online discussion groups and online societies for Sherlockians are in operation using various technologies. "The longest established online group for the discussion of Sherlock Holmes and kindred topics" is the Hounds of the Internet (*www.sherlockian.net/hounds*), which operates through a listserv, distributing messages from any member to all the others by email. Founded in 1992 by Alan Block, it has been operated since 1995 through a server at Kent State University. There have been three listowners in succession to Block: Les Moskowitz, Steve Clarkson, and since 2004 Alex Braun. One story is offered for discussion each week, although the Hounds can touch on any Sherlockian subjects that may come to mind.

In the late 1990s the Hounds had almost a monopoly on electronic Sherlockian discussion; the group was large and active, and carried many contributions to scholarship as well as news, gossip, and wit. In recent years it has dwindled considerably, because of the development of other groups and newer technologies for conversation, and also because the Hounds have not been immune from the kind of interpersonal conflict that plagues any voluntary association. A linkage called WelcomeHolmes, founded by Jim Hawkins in 1999 and operating on the Yahoo Groups service, now claims to be "the web's largest Holmes discussion group." It operates a spinoff web site at *www.welcomeholmes.com*.

Other places for Sherlockian talk, each with a different way of contributing to the Web 2.0 world, include The Sherlock Holmes Social Network, a social site (*sherlockholmes.ning.com*); Holmesian.net, an online forum (*www.holmesian.net/forums*); and a Sherlockian community on LiveJournal (*community.livejournal.com/221b_bakerst*). Facebook has, at last count, six "Sherlock Holmes" groups, each with more than one hundred members, as well as a number of smaller ones, and a large group called "Sherlock Holmes Club and Purveyors of Sherlockiana." At the other extreme of electronic sophistication, there is a longstanding Sherlockian newsgroup, alt.fan.holmes, where discussion has become as desultory as on most otherparts of Usenet.

IX

A LASTING INFLUENCE

EVERYONE KNOWS WHO SHERLOCK HOLMES IS. *Holmes* is so universally recognized as the name of a detective that in 1986, when British police created a powerful computer system for cross-referencing the reports and clues associated with complicated cases, they dubbed it HOLMES, for Home Office Large Major Enquiry System. The name is even in the definitive *Oxford English Dictionary*:

> **Sherlock Holmes** *v. trans.*, to make deductions about, to assess, to deduce....

The dictionary also provides evidence for the existence of "sherlocked," "Sherlock-holmesing," and other variations.

To be sure, most of the great unobservant public, who could hardly tell a weaver by his tooth or a compositor by his left thumb, are inclined to identify Sherlock Holmes by his clothes and tools, rather than by his essential traits of principle and brain. The deerstalker hat, the Inverness cape, the magnifying glass, the curved pipe, perhaps the violin: these, in the general estimation, make a detective. But the deerstalker is the invention of illustrator Sidney Paget, the cape its inauthentic if plausible companion; actor William Gillette added the curved pipe, which was enthusiastically adopted by Frederic Dorr Steele for his illustrations. (The "calabash" pipe with its flaring bowl is a still more recent misconception — Robert S. Ennis, writing in the *Baker Street Journal* in 1997, traced it to vaudeville comedian Robert Woolsey in a 1936 film.) Only the magnifying glass, as a tool for observation, and the violin, as a tool for ratiocination, are wholly authentic, although it must be admitted that, in an age before tobacco was understood to be literally poisonous, Sherlock Holmes did smoke. His blue-wreathed image has come down now through a hundred years, and however debased and simplified from the realities of the Canon, it has become a part of England's culture — and of the world's.

One indication of widespread acceptance is that Holmes and his creator have figured on postage stamps issued by Nicaragua (1972), Switzerland (2007), and half a dozen smaller countries (*www.trussel.com/detfic/sholmes. htm*). The United Kingdom itself issued a set of five stamps picturing selected Canonical cases in 1993. In addition, Sherlockian connections to "local post" issues and other forms of stamps and coins are summarized in at least three pamphlets by enthusiasts, including Benton Wood's *The Philatelic & Numismatic Holmes*, 1990 and 1995.

MEMORIALS

Apart from Anne Shirley, whose home "Green Gables" is the chief tourist attraction of Prince Edward Island, there can be few fictional characters whose home is eagerly sought by tourists. But seekers do look for 221B Baker Street, and find no such house. The number 221 is part of an office block long occupied by the Abbey National Building Society, a savings and loan institution, and lately redeveloped for residential use. Just up the way is the "Sherlock Holmes Museum" at 239 Baker Street, whose proprietor, John Aidiniantz, succeeded after long effort in persuading the Royal Mail that mail addressed to 221B should be delivered to him (it was formerly taken to the public relations department of Abbey National). The museum, which charges a hefty admission fee, is decorated and furnished in Victorian style and includes a reconstruction of the 221B sitting room as well as some Holmesian artifacts and souvenirs. There is little else to see in Baker Street itself, apart from artwork in the Underground station and souvenirs at the Park Plaza Sherlock Holmes Hotel (*www.parkplazasherlockholmes.com*).

But there are many other places to which Sherlockians can, and do, make pilgrimages.

MUSEUMS AND SITES. The most extensive and reputable of museums devoted to Sherlock Holmes is at Meiringen, Switzerland; it is housed in what was formerly the English church at that village near the Reichenbach Falls. The Sherlock Holmes Museum, on Conan Doyle Place, was opened May 5, 1991, by Dame Jean Conan Doyle, in a ceremony attended by some hundred members of the Sherlock Holmes Society of London during one of that society's pilgrimages to Switzerland. The centrepiece of the museum is a reconstruction of the 221B sitting room, done by Tony Howlett, a prominent member of the SHS and mastermind of the museum, and architects John and Sylvia Reid. The museum is associated with a nearby and longstanding hotel which honours Holmes's memory: Park-Hotel Sauvage "Englischer Hof," 3860 Meiringen, Bernese Oberland, Switzerland (*www.sauvage.ch*).

A second Sherlock Holmes Museum in Switzerland is found in the "Maison Rouge" at Lucens, a short distance from the Château de Lucens. Adrian Conan Doyle, who lived for a time in the Château, established the museum in 1965, and it has been reopened in a nearby landmark house, rue des Greniers 7, 1522 Lucens (*www.lucens.ch/TOUR/Sherlock.html*). Here, too, exhibits include a reconstruction of the 221B sitting-room.

At Crowborough, East Sussex, where Doyle lived in his last years, there was for about a decade a museum and archive operated by the "Conan Doyle (Crowborough) Establishment" (*www.the-conan-doyle-crowborough-establishment.com*), headed by Brian W. Pugh. Under the management of its founder, local historian Malcolm Payne, the museum was part of the "Crowborough Cross" hotel from 1989 to 1995 before being moved to the nearby grand house called Groombridge Place and subsequently to a local school, but its treasures are currently in storage. The Establishment provides research material about Doyle on request, for a fee, and took pride in organizing support for a statue of Doyle that was erected in Crowborough in 2001. Doyle's house is now a retirement home, Windlesham Manor.

Other former Doyle residences are also possible places of pilgrimage; there has beenintermittent interest in finding some way to preserve his house "Undershaw" at Hindhead, Surrey, which has fallen on hard times and is threatened by highway construction. An hour's drive from Hindhead, or two hours from Crowborough, is Minstead, near the Doyles' summer cottage, where Sir Arthur and Lady Doyle lie buried in the churchyard; the markers that stood over their former graves, in the grounds at Windlesham, are now in the Minstead church belfry.

Restorations of the 221B sitting room can be seen in more places than Meiringen alone. Devotees and casual tourists both visit the "Sherlock Holmes" pub (*www.sherlockholmespub.com*) in London's Northumberland Street, and for many a Sherlockian it is the first and most important stop on a tour of the city. The cozy replica there, in an upstairs room separated from viewers by a railing and window, includes much of the memorabilia originally assembled for the Festival of Britain exhibition in 1951. At least one privately created 221B replica welcomes serious visitors; it is in the home of Dennis Dobry near Reading, Pennsylvania. Another sitting room was formerly on view in the "S. Holmes, Esq." pub of the Holiday Inn Union Square, San Francisco, but it has been closed, and word in the Sherlockian world is that the owners would welcome an offer.

Also now closed is the exhibition in Holmes's honour that formerly attracted tourists to the Granada Television studios near Manchester. It included portions of the sets on which the Jeremy Brett television productions were done. Kathryn White and David Stuart Davies, two prominent British Sherlockians, helped to plan the exhibit, in which one could see not only the sitting room of 221B Baker Street but part of the "Bar of Gold" opium den, as well as the façade of Bradley's tobacco shop. Since the closing in 1999, Granada has converted the Baker Street locale to part of the set for its soap opera "Coronation Street."

The libraries that collect Sherlockian and Doylean material are natural places of pilgrimage, if not strictly museums. The University of Minnesota now has the 221B replica created by the late Allen Mackler, and the Toronto Reference Library does house its collection in a "Room 221B" with some Victorian ambiance. Gillette Castle in Hadlyme, Connecticut, is a state park and museum celebrating the work of William Gillette, which consisted largely of impersonating Holmes; it is supported by a Friends organization (*www.friendsofgillettecastle.org*). The visitor to Universal Studios in Hollywood will see a little of Basil Rathbone.

STATUES AND PLAQUES. The world's first statue of Sherlock Holmes stands, or rather sits, in the village square in Meiringen, Switzerland. The work of British sculptor John Doubleday, it was unveiled during a visit by touring members of the Sherlock Holmes Society of London on September 10, 1988. Less than a month later, a second statue, this one by Japanese sculptor Yoshinori Satoh, was unveiled in Karuizawa Town, Nagano, Japan, erected by Japanese Sherlockians to mark the place where the Canon was first translated into Japanese. The world's third such statue, by Gerald Ogilvie Laing, was installed in Edinburgh in 1989 by the Federation of Master Builders, close to Arthur Conan Doyle's birthplace in Picardy Place. Admirers of Doyle were regretful that it was Holmes, rather than his creator, who was represented, and horrified that Doyle's birthdate was misstated in the inscription on the base. A fourth statue, again by John Doubleday, stands outside Baker Street station in London; it was unveiled as the highlight of a 1999 festival organized by the Sherlock Holmes Society of London.

Plaques associated with Holmes can be seen on two houses where Doyle lived: the little house in Bush Villas, Elm Grove, Southsea, and his house in Tennison Road, South Norwood, London. The home of Holmes himself is not so commemorated, presumably because of the difficulty of finding 221B Baker Street, but in the Baker Street station of the Underground there are tiles and other artworks symbolic of Holmes.

Two other sites in London have Sherlockian plaques. One is the Criterion Bar — the building in Piccadilly Circus (no longer a bar) where Watson met his friend Stamford in the incident that led to his acquaintance with Holmes. That plaque was erected by enthusiastic Sherlockians in 1953. The following year, other enthusiasts managed to put a plaque in the room where, according to *A Study in Scarlet*, Holmes and Watson actually set eyes on one another: the old pathology laboratory (now a curator's office) at St. Bartholomew's Hospital. Visiting Sherlockians wanting a look at that plaque generally come away with tales to tell about the difficulty of finding it, as Bart's is far from making it a public attraction — but it does exist and can be seen.

There are several plaques in the area of Switzerland's Reichenbach Falls, where Holmes met Professor Moriarty in mortal combat. The first was erected in 1952 at the supposed Englischer Hof, now known as the Park-Hotel Sauvage. A pair of plaques was erected in 1957 near the Falls, and yet another in 1992 at the precise spot where Holmes and Moriarty presumably met.

RESTAURANTS AND BUSINESSES. Holmes's own favourite restaurant appears to have been Simpson's in the Strand, London, but few of the many hostelries named in his honour are at the same gastronomic level as that distinguished establishment. The one known exception was Sherlock's on Sheppard, in Toronto, which — like Simpson's — specialized in roast beef, but which is long out of business. A number of bars and restaurants with long reputations, including Sherlock's Home in Minneapolis, Holmes and Watson Ltd. in Troy, New York, the Sherlock Holmes in Edmonton, and Professor Moriarty's in Saratoga Springs, are gone as well.

Surviving Sherlockian restaurants, most with highly collectible menus and beer coasters, include Sherlock's Pub and several related establishments in locations in Texas and neighbouring states (*www.sherlockspubco.com*); Baker Street, "one of the finest bars New York City has to offer" (*www.bakerstreetny. com*); the Sherlock Holmes pub in Bahrain (*www.gulfhotelbahrain.com*); and the Sherlock Holmes in Aarhus, Denmark (*www.sherlock-holmes.dk*). Most North American establishments that try to make a Sherlockian connection are pubs with a synthetic British atmosphere, with deerstalkers and similar symbols decorating the menus and perhaps the walls. In England itself, the Sherlock Holmes pub in London's Northumberland Street is by no means the same place as the Park Plaza Sherlock Holmes Hotel, in Baker Street itself; the latter has its own eating places including Sherlock's Bar & Grill, although the coyly named Ristorante Moriarti is now defunct. In York Place, Edinburgh, is the Sir Arthur Conan Doyle pub, near the author's birthplace.

Businesses in many cities have borrowed the Holmes name with, perhaps, even less justification — although one can defend Sherlock Security Systems in Brooklyn, and certainly Sherlock Bones (*www.sherlockbones.com*) of Oakland, a detective agency billing itself as "tracer of missing pets." Also reported are several tobacconists, including Sherlock Pipes & Tobaccos of Colorado Springs, and various firms called Sherlock Homes, doing business in such lines as real estate on Long Island (*www.gosherlockhomes.com*), neighbourhood development in Alberta (*www.sherlockhomes.ca*), housebuilding in Nashville (*www.sherlockbuilders.com*), and home inspection in Oklahoma. The connection with Baker Street is not entirely clear, but painters are very familiar with Sherlock Extension Poles and similar tools made by the Wooster Brush Company of Ohio.

SOUVENIRS. The Sherlockian restaurants and bars are lavish sources of coasters, matchbooks, menus, and similar trophies for collectors. Promotional items from businesses with Sherlockian names are also in abundance (at least one collection boasts a rubber jar-opener bearing the advertisement of Sherlock Homes Real Estate of Wescosville, Pennsylvania). From 1992 to 2006, London's Baker Street boasted the Sherlock Holmes Memorabilia Company, selling souvenirs, but it has fallen victim to financial difficulties. Collectibles include many classes of material:

- Stuffed toys, intended more or less for children; any number of deer-stalkered dogs, in particular, have appeared on the market.
- Plastic and cloth figures of Snoopy, the dog from the *Peanuts* comic strip, in the Holmes gear he sometimes also affects in print.
- Pipes, whether intended for actual smoking or only as novelties (a calabash filled with after-shave lotion was available from Avon, the door-to-door sales firm, in the 1970s).
- Clothing, ranging from neckwear (the Baker Street Irregulars has produced several versions of its own tie; the Sherlock Holmes Society of London has both a tie and a ladies' scarf) to jockey shorts with vaguely Holmesian motifs. There are also many T-shirts and sweatshirts, especially those produced by Sherlockian societies for their members and friends.

- Magnifying glasses, including a "Sherlock Hose" model produced in the 1960s by B.F. Goodrich of Canada.
- Busts of Holmes, produced for connoisseurs, including Royal Doulton "toby jugs" in two sizes.

Small entrepreneurs produce keychains, mugs, letter-openers and other artifacts — not all of the finest quality — for the Sherlockian market. An important source of the more desirable items is Classic Specialties of Cincinnati, Ohio (*www.sherlock-holmes.com*). Few collectibles of this kind have serious artistic value, although a bust of Holmes produced by Edgar P. Smith in the 1960s, as by "Oscar Meunier," is widely admired. For completist collectors the tchotchkes are of course essential, but otherwise their value is in demonstrating how extensively the culture of the English-speaking world has been penetrated by the image, however distorted, of a detective with a magnifying glass and a fore-and-aft cap. Many collectibles of an earlier era are pictured in *The Sherlock Holmes Collection* (1987) by Charles Hall, a Sherlockian in Scotland; the book also reproduces film stills, cartoons and illustrations.

THE COMMON IMAGE

Clearly the customers of businesses that use the name of Sherlock Holmes are not all Sherlockians. The proprietors recognize the appeal of the great detective to every part of the public, and a level of name recognition that few other figures can claim. "Sherlock" stands with Elvis, Marilyn, Romeo, and Madonna as a given name that has become familiar to all. Even toddlers know it, at least in the form of "Sherlock Hemlock," a deerstalkered character on the children's television program *Sesame Street* and in its spinoff toys, games and, books, including *Sherlock Hemlock and the Great Twiddlebug Mystery* (1972). (For a new generation, Holmes and Watson are a cucumber and a tomato, respectively, in the "Veggie Tales" video *Sheerluck Holmes and the Hounds of Baker Street*.) The excitement surrounding the projected release of a 2009 feature film with a new image for Holmes, portrayed by Robert Downey Jr., is an indication that viewers continue to find his figure fascinating even if they are fuzzy about the details.

ALLUSIONS. "I hear of Sherlock everywhere," Mycroft Holmes tells Watson in "The Greek Interpreter." The alert reader still hears of Sherlock everywhere a hundred years later, encountering jokes about "amazing deductions" at income tax season and references to unusually perceptive politicians as "the Sherlock Holmes" of the public service. Cartoons, the expression of the contemporary culture in printed form, are full of such references:

- "Garfield," June 2, 1992: "Somebody ate the piece of cake I was saving.... Any suspects, Sherlock?"
- "Pardon My Planet," June 20, 2008: "So what are we planting now? . . . Why, the same as always — a lemon tree, my dear Watson."

The "lemon tree" joke, like many popular references, is based on one of two phrases that have become associated with Holmes even though they appear nowhere in the Canon:

- "Elementary, my dear Watson." Holmes often addresses his companion as "my dear Watson," and several times uses the word "elementary," most strikingly in "The Crooked Man":

"Excellent!" I cried.
"Elementary," said he.

But the two are never juxtaposed, although Basil Rathbone and a thousand subsequent actors have done their best. The first use of "Elementary, my dear Watson," is attributed to comic writer P.G. Wodehouse in *Psmith, Journalist* (1915). The apocryphal nature of the phrase does not keep it from being endlessly used and reused:

> "Elementary, my dear Watson," said the famous British detective Sherlock Holmes — a phrase that could also be used to describe the procedure involved in applying for an award at the [University of Calgary] student awards and financial aid office.

It was even listed, as Doyle's own words, in the 1937 edition of *Bartlett's Familiar Quotations*, but has been expunged in subsequent editions. The saving grace is the flexibility in jokes and puns: What school did Sherlock Holmes attend? (Elementary.) John Bennett Shaw, inveterate punster, wrote about the detective's eating and drinking habits in the *Baker Street Journal* in 1967 and titled his article "Alimentary, My Dear Watson."

- "Quick, Watson, the needle!" This phrase is perhaps even more objectionable than the other, suggesting as it does a desperation in Holmes's use of drugs by injection. The half-informed public is fascinated by the detective's drug habit, in the era of "Just say no," and when a Sherlockian gives a talk at a public library, the first or second question from the audience is bound to be about cocaine. Whatever Holmes's unhealthy habits, there is no evidence that he relied on Watson to reach the apparatus for him; indeed, Watson is frequently seen reproaching his friend for his use of drugs. But as a fragment of folk knowledge the phrase has caught on since; apparently Gretchen Finletter coined it in 1946.

The best-known case of Sherlock Holmes is certainly *The Hound of the Baskervilles*, which is also the most often mentioned by non-Sherlockian authors. Cartoonists have had endless fun with it, from Gary Larson's "Parakeet of the Baskervilles" in *The Far Side* to a Gahan Wilson classic in *Playboy* (1959): "It strikes me you've made a great deal of bother over very little, Baskerville." (That was the first cartoon in four pages of drawings by the master of twisted humour; the last of them is captioned, "Extraordinary thing, Watson — the clues indicate the killer to have been a man of your exact build and appearance!")

In more literate circles, the Sherlockian words most often alluded to are from "Silver Blaze":

> "Is there any point to which you would wish to draw my atten-
>   tion?"
> "To the curious incident of the dog in the night-time."
> "The dog did nothing in the night-time."
> "That was the curious incident," remarked Sherlock Holmes.

Now this passage has the merit of exactly capturing Holmes's methods and indeed personality — the almost Zen quality of recognizing that nothing is something. And it has application far beyond the behaviour of animals around a horse-barn. Politicians act in some of the same way, newspaper allusions suggest:

> The dog-that-did-not-bark aphorism applies almost too closely
> for comfort to the universities' reaction to the Government's
> plan to abolish the long-standing University Grants Committee.
> (*Times Higher Education Supplement.*)

The report of Mr. Justice William Parker's inquiry effectively ends Mr. Stevens's political career, but it does not answer a central question about Mr. Mulroney's initial handling of the Stevens affair and several similar problems. That question, as Sherlock Holmes put it in Silver Blaze, is: why didn't the dog bark? Or at least bark sooner? (*Globe and Mail*, Toronto.)

"Sometimes, as mystery fans know," Jim Coyle of the *Toronto Star* wrote in March 2009, "dogs not barking is a clue." The allusion is apparently so well understood that the *Washington Post* was able to use the headline "The War That Didn't Bark" (November 4, 2008) without feeling the need to explain it.

In the 1970s a new phrase became popularly associated with Sherlock Holmes: "seven-per-cent solution." It had been in the Canon all along, in *The Sign of the Four*, but it was brought to prominence by Nicholas Meyer's novel *The Seven-Per-Cent Solution* (1974) and the successful movie made from it. Suddenly the phrase was everywhere that a percent sign might be:

- Andres wanted a wine with a lower alcohol content (seven per cent was the solution). — *Saturday Night*.
- A 5% Solution? — *Time* discusses a scaled reduction of weapons under the Strategic Arms Limitation Treaty.

There was a new burst of such constructions in Canada in 1991, when a new national "Goods and Services Tax," with a 7 percent rate, was introduced; half the editorials about the tax, and advertisements for stores that were offering temporary tax savings, spoke of "the 7-per-cent solution." The percent solution has entered the language to the point that many of its users probably no longer think of the Sherlock Holmes connection.

Apple Corporation, makers of Macintosh computers and the software that runs them, took advantage of the very name of "Sherlock" by giving that label to the search facility that was part of Mac Operating System versions 8 and 9 and the early releases of Mac OS X, between 1998 and 2007. It was represented by a deerstalker-and-magnifying-glass icon. A quite different Sherlock is " a shared infrastructure for the management and distribution of survey data in Quebec university libraries. . . . Sherlock, like its famous namesake, provides a magnifying glass for the detailed examination of survey data and meta-data files in both English and French."

LITERATURE. References to Holmes are not limited to the newspapers, but can be found in every sort of writing. His name may be dropped, or there will be some mention of the Baskerville hound or the Speckled Band, without warning in any novel or memoir. (Not every such reference, however, betrays first-hand acquaintance with the Canon: one sees, for example, the suggestion that looking for a hidden object in plain view is one of Holmes's insights, whereas in fact it was the accomplishment of the Chevalier Dupin in Edgar Allan Poe's "The Purloined Letter.")

Vladimir Nabokov alludes to Holmes here and there in *Pale Fire* (1962), a verse-and-annotations experimental novel that stretches out tentacles into most of western culture. Even more impressive is the Holmesian influence on T.S. Eliot (1888–1965), a poet whose creative roots are in the Edwardian period and who repeatedly writes of London fog and an era that is past. Eliot's best-known allusion to Holmes is in "Macavity," one of the comic poems that make up *Old Possum's Book of Practical Cats* (1939) and were eventually converted into the musical drama *Cats*. Macavity is "the mystery cat... the Napoleon of Crime," with obvious similarities to Professor Moriarty. More important are references here and there in Eliot's more serious verse, including an extract from "The Musgrave Ritual" that is dropped without warning into a tense scene in *Murder in the Cathedral* (1935). Eliot had some scholarly interest in Holmes, corresponding occasionally with American Sherlockians, and did acknowledge the influence of the Canon on his work.

More recently, serious literature has drawn on the Sherlock Holmes tradition in the form of Umberto Eco's *The Name of the Rose* (Italian 1980, English translation 1983). This large and dense novel — on which was based a successful 1986 film starring Sean Connery — is about a mediaeval monk, one William of Baskerville, who turns detective. Eco is himself a scholar and theoretician interested in semiotics, the science of "meaning," and co-editor of *The Sign of Three* (1983), which deals with logic, symbolism, and other matters, in a dense and difficult way, including much discussion of Holmes. Naturally, then, similar deep things are readily found in *The Name of the Rose*.

The writers most strongly influenced by Holmes, of course, have been the creators of subsequent detective stories, whose very genre was largely formed by the precedents Doyle set. It can be said that most detective fiction is either a following of Doyle or a rebellion against him, but there are works that explicitly draw on Sherlockian motifs, such as some of the books of Julian Symons (born 1912), a British master of traditional detection. His *A Three Pipe Problem*

(1975) is about a young actor whose reputation rests on his role as Sherlock Holmes. *Watson's Choice* (1955) by Gladys Mitchell is in the same category. Most of Ellery Queen can be seen as a tribute to Holmes. And some pastiches — stories explicitly about Holmes, though not by the original author — attract and retain reader interest on their own merits. Walter R. Brooks's Freddy the Pig, one of the great characters of children's literature, would hardly have achieved that eminence without his decision in *Freddy the Detective* (1932) to emulate his idol, Sherlock Holmes.

The great detective has even edged his way into science fiction, both overtly (*The Science-Fictional Sherlock Holmes*, a volume of short stories edited by Robert C. Peterson, appeared in 1960) and more subtly. The master of the genre, Robert A. Heinlein, produced *The Moon Is a Harsh Mistress* in 1966; its central figure is a masterful computer called Mycroft. *Earthman's Burden* (1957), by Poul Anderson (himself a Sherlockian) and Gordon R. Dickson, is a delightful collection of episodes about extraterrestrials who adopt one Earthly literary culture after another, including, for a period, that of foggy Baker Street. By a less prominent author, but ingenious and of interest, is *Their Majesties' Bucketeers* (1981) by L. Neil Smith. Away from the printed page, Sherlock Holmes is a recurring background figure in the television and movie series "Star Trek": it is a popular Sherlockian belief that Mr. Spock, played by Leonard Nimoy, is somehow related to Holmes. In a classic episode of *Star Trek: The Next Generation*, Commander Data recreates the Baker Street interior as a holographic environment in which he assumes the role of Holmes ("Elementary, Dear Data," 1988).

ADVERTISING. Who has not seen a caricature of a hawk-nosed face, surmounted by a deerstalker hat, in some newspaper or Yellow Pages advertisement? Sherlock Holmes is a commonplace whenever the headline suggests searching, or investigating, or hunting down some product or service or benefit: "Give us a clue! If you're listed incorrectly in your phone book, please tell us now," "You don't have to be a great detective to tell which is the better copy.," "Looking for the best kitchen value?," "Why people drive themselves to the airport is a mystery to me." Many such ads are simplistic, with unimaginative drawings of Holmes or, at best, familiar portraits of Basil Rathbone (not, presumably for copyright reasons, Jeremy Brett). But a few advertisers, over the years, have done better, creating sympathetic and humorous text as well as elaborately posed photographs. An example of such sophistication is "The case of the disappearing files," a double-page magazine advertisement from Xerox of Canada:

"My dear fellow, haven't you found that file on 'The Case of the One Armed Man' yet?"

"I know it's here somewhere. What we need is more filing space to organize all our paperwork."

"But, how did you know this new Xerox 4000 Copier could solve all our filing problems?"

"Elementary, my dear fellow. I spoke to the people at Xerox yesterday."

Then there are the advertisers who have used Holmes as the principal character in a booklet or brochure — such as Boeing Computer Services (*The Great Training Mystery*), State Farm Fire and Casualty Co. (*Surelocked Homes*), and the Ontario Chiropractic Association (*The Discoveries of Inspector Spine*). More substantial and noncommercial, but similar in using Holmes to deliver a message, is *The Life Insurance Conspiracy* (1976) by Peter Spielmann and Aaron Zelman; astonishingly, Holmes has also been used several times as the central character in textbooks of computer programming. A 1989 campaign from the Canada Post Corporation, "Following Your Mail Closely," involved brochures explaining registered mail and other special services, which were distributed across Canada in counter displays consisting of striking foot-wide cardboard silhouettes of Holmes.

Television commercials starring Holmes were ephemeral in a period before the widespread use of video recorders; they have ranged from the seemingly authentic to the absurd. At the latter extreme is a 1992 commercial presenting one baby dressed as Holmes (that is, in a deerstalker) and another as Watson (in a bowler hat) discussing the relative merits of different brands of diaper. The message, as in decades of print ads, is simple: Sherlock Holmes sees the details that others miss, unravels the mysterious, and understands the truth when others, including the viewer and the perennially befuddled Watson, can see nothing.

ACADEMIC SCHOLARSHIP

What Sherlockians do is one thing, and what English professors do is generally another. When Fordham University Press was persuaded, in 1975, to take over publication of the *Baker Street Journal* — an arrangement that lasted for some seventeen years — it was with no pretense that the *BSJ* would be publishing academic literary scholarship. Despite the trappings of footnotes and formal style, and an erudition that might startle many professors, Sherlockian writers typically have been playing an elaborate game, making tongue-in-cheek assumptions about the historic existence of Holmes, Watson, and their associates, pretending to analyze history rather than literature, attributing inconsistencies in the tales to Watson's medical handwriting rather than to Doyle's indifference. The traditional article of this kind still has a place in Sherlockian publications, although its style is less predictable than it was in the 1940s.

However, the time did come when a growing number of English professors, passing as Sherlockians, found themselves unable to throw off their professional inclinations completely. The *Baker Street Journal* in the 1980s published articles about "The Semiotic Watson," "Mythological Archetypes in the Sherlockian Canon," and "The Two-Author Theory of 'The Blanched Soldier'," as well as more traditional studies of "Automobiles in 'His Last Bow'" and whether Holmes might have been left-handed. The *BSJ* even began mentioning the name of Doyle from time to time, in sober studies about the Canon's sources and comparisons of the Canonical tales with other Victorian writings. And a journal that sometimes aspired to serious scholarship flourished during the same era: *Baker Street Miscellanea*, which quickly acknowledged support from Northeastern Illinois University — not from a department of English, to be sure, but from "the Advisory Committee on Popular Culture." That term provides the slightly derisory title under which professors of English classify detective stories, science fiction, romances, and other books that large numbers of people actually and happily read. (Publishers have a slightly less condescending term for them: "genre fiction.") Scholars, those who notice Arthur Conan Doyle and Sherlock Holmes at all, frequently include the Canon and its study under this rubric, and one Sherlockian book (*Dr. Joe Bell*, by Ely Liebow) was actually published in 1982 by the "Popular Press" of Bowling Green University in Ohio, known as a centre for such study.

In recent years, things have gone much further, as serious literary presses have begun to publish works about Sherlock Holmes, and serious literary journals have begun to make room for articles about him. Such things were rare before the 1980s, and there was a tradition of scholarly disdain for Holmes and Doyle, on the part of academics who were not by inclination Sherlockians. The standard explanation is snobbery: that academics shy away from discussing literature that ordinary people read and like, in favour of the elite and obscure, which may seem to need more explicating. "Entrance into those rarefied reading lists quite often demands that the writer be either 'dull' or 'difficult' in order to satisfy the critic's sense of hierarchy," Kathryn White suggested in *ACD: the Journal of the Arthur Conan Doyle Society*. The neglect of Doyle in the late twentieth century was fully consistent with the attitude in university English departments, as recently as fifty years ago, that nineteenth- and twentieth-century writings were not quite deserving of scholarly attention; at the turn of the twentieth century, Oxford barely tolerated the study of English literature from any period. Beyond that conservatism, however, there may have been a sense that little in Doyle was important or enduring. It is quite true that most of his books now languish unread, and even Sherlock Holmes is better known as a simplified cliché than from the pages of the works in which he first appeared. White again: "We may, perhaps, agree that Conan Doyle did not write great literature, but his work should not be dismissed without fair trial."

From time to time, non-Sherlockian academics would speak or write about Doyle with an air of astonished discovery. One example was a 1971 paper by Jay Macpherson, of the University of Toronto's Victoria College, on "Sherlock Holmes as a Figure of Romance." Another was a 1990 paper by McGill University's Paul Piehler, which included a devastating examination of why so rich a mine as the Canon has been largely ignored by his colleagues in English departments. Papers like these, sounding like announcements that a new continent has just been discovered, could sound patronizing or defensive or merely naïve, and were bound to hit many high points very briefly. They could, of course, report their authors' awareness that the detective story, with its "puritan" virtues and predictability, owes most of its hereditary traits to the genes of Sherlock Holmes. Beyond that, they could reveal that Holmes is a romantic hero or a "mythic" figure; they could tell their readers that Doyle was a genius at recording the details of Victorian society; they could note with astonishment that the Canon, like Doyle's other work, draws on the dark side of the psyche, with sexual ambivalences and fears of death. These generalizations are the essential underpinnings of scholarship, but the Canon's readers knew them all along.

A few scholars did dare to do genuinely useful things, both in Sherlockian journals and elsewhere. Absolutely conventional in its method, for example, and instructive in its results, was a 1972 article in the *Baker Street Journal* by Donald J. Watt: "The Literary Craft of *The Hound of the Baskervilles*." Most important was a large amount of research about Doyle's life, his methods, and the influences on him, published in such early books as Donald Redmond's *Sherlock Holmes Among the Pirates*, Owen Dudley Edwards's *The Quest for Sherlock Holmes*, and Kelvin Jones's *Conan Doyle and the Spirits*, as well as in various journals. A typical step forward would involve proof that Doyle saw, knew, or read something, coupled with speculation that some element of his work is the result of that encounter or knowledge. Southern Illinois University

Press followed with *The Quest for Sir Arthur Conan Doyle*, edited by Jon L. Lellenberg, in 1987, which consolidated the state of biographical research as of that time. Bibliographical scholarship had also become established; the *World Bibliography of Sherlock Holmes and Dr. Watson* (1974), compiled by Ronald B. DeWaal, then humanities librarian at Colorado State University, received an award as the best work of bibliography published in the United States that year. McGill-Queen's University Press published Donald Redmond's *Sherlock Holmes: A Study in Sources* in 1982, and a further milestone was the 1983 appearance from Oxford's Clarendon Press of *A Bibliography of A. Conan Doyle*, by Richard Lancelyn Green and John Michael Gibson.

One of the first genuinely academic papers about Doyle's work was a long piece by Audrey Jaffe in a 1990 issue of the Berkeley-based little journal *Representations*, titled "Detecting the Beggar: Arthur Conan Doyle, Henry Mayhew, and 'The Man with the Twisted Lip'." In it, she examines "The Man with the Twisted Lip" using the modern critical technique of "deconstruction," which examines not the author's intent or the reader's subjective reaction, but the actual words of a text, which may be subversive of both. This tale, Jaffe reports, "both constructs and disables detective fiction's fantasy of social control"; she continues to examine the story in terms of "exchange ... transformation ... exposure." Two decades later, one of the most recent academic papers is "The Hound of the Baskervilles: Modern Belgian Masters, Paralyzing Spectacles, and the Art of Detection" in the journal *English Literature in Transition* in 2009. In that piece, Nils Clausson of the University of Regina argues that *The Hound* "is constructed around an opposition between science and art, and it is as an artist rather than as a scientist that Holmes conducts his investigation of the death of Sir Charles and the plot to murder Sir Robert [*sic*]. In contrast to the amateur scientists in the novel, Holmes is repeatedly associated with art, specifically with sculpture, drama, and painting and painters." Assertions of this kind, which can lead to interesting insights and arguments, are the business of literary scholars, and have less appeal to traditional Sherlockians who simply seek to enjoy Sherlock Holmes. But the latter still dominate: the Modern Languages Association's *International Bibliography* lists only a few articles each year about Doyle and Sherlock Holmes from the hundreds of scholarly journals it indexes (apart from numerous articles from the *Baker Street Journal* which it also deems worthy of listing).

A striking way to see the contrast is to compare two volumes in which selected Sherlock Holmes stories are accompanied by essays about them. The first to appear was *The Baker Street Dozen* (1987), edited by Pj Doyle and

E.W. McDiarmid, both mainstream Sherlockians. The brief essays it contains include an appreciation of "The Red-Headed League" by a well-known red-headed Sherlockian, Ann Byerly; ruminations on "The Five Orange Pips" by Isaac Asimov, who justifiably calls Doyle "a most careless plotter" in view of the many holes in the fabric of this tale; and Richard Lancelyn Green on "The Reigate Squires," commenting mostly on handwriting. Seven years later, in 1994, came *Sherlock Holmes: The Major Stories with Contemporary Critical Essays*, edited by John A. Hodgson. Titles here include "Sherlock Holmes: Ethics, Logic, and the Mask" and "'The Speckled Band': The Construction of Woman in a Popular Text of Empire," as well as a reprinting of Jaffe's 1990 article from *Representations*, which the editor identifies as an example of "new historicist criticism."

Ordinary readers do not find today's literary analysis entirely congenial or even, always, comprehensible. Semiotics and deconstructionism may be passing out of fashion, but their replacements are likely to be no more easily grasped; even educated non-academic readers are still struggling with the Marxist, Freudian, and feminist approaches that were new in earlier decades. Samuel Rosenberg's *Naked Is the Best Disguise*, published in 1974, outraged many Sherlockians precisely because of its reliance on a Freudian view of the world. But it seems certain that every approach can find something of interest in the Canon, drawing the reader's attention to such matters as Holmes's elitist disdain for physical labour (a significant point for Marxists), the infantile breast fixation of Watson (Freudians), and the constrained role of damsel-in-distress allocated to most of Doyle's heroines (feminists).

It will come as no surprise to Sherlockians, or ordinary readers of the Canon, that there is something manly about Sherlock Holmes and the life's work created for him by Doyle. It is no surprise, either, that a detective, whose job is to chase down criminals, can be seen as an advocate of the existing social structure, which in the London of 1895 included the Queen and Empire. Academic scholars have examined and documented these generalizations, and put them into context, in books such as these:

- Rosemary Jann, *The Adventures of Sherlock Holmes: Detecting Social Order* (1995).
- Charles R. Putney, Joseph A. Cutshall King, and Sally Sugarman, editors, *Sherlock Holmes: Victorian Sleuth to Modern Hero* (1996).
- Michael Atkinson, *The Secret Marriage of Sherlock Holmes and Other Eccentric Readings* (1996).

- Joseph A. Kestner, *Sherlock's Men: Masculinity, Conan Doyle, and Cultural History* (1997).
- Diana Barsham, *Arthur Conan Doyle and the Meaning of Masculinity* (2000).
- Catherine Wynne, *The Colonial Conan Doyle: British Imperialism, Irish Nationalism, and the Gothic* (2002).

Let is be said that there is no real "secret marriage," only the struggle that Holmes experiences with his feelings about Irene Adler; that, according to Kestner, *The Hound of the Baskervilles* "presents two forms of atavistic masculinity," Stapleton and Selden; and that *The Valley of Fear* provides, according to Wynne, an examination of "a criminal Irishness." The untrained reader may be inclined to dismiss these statements as self-evident, rather like Rosenberg's discovery that in many Sherlock Holmes stories, bloodshed is associated with some form of writing, or the assertion by some other scholar that windows are of great significance in the Holmes tales, as someone is constantly entering, leaving, or looking through them. The achievement of these academic scholars is much like Holmes's own achievement, in identifying which of many perfectly obvious facts to choose as the focus of attention, and then suggesting how to interpret it.

It does no harm to such scholarship, of course, that so much in the writings about Sherlock Holmes can be used so easily to illuminate subjects that were already of interest in the last years of the twentieth century, such as the roles of the sexes and the stability of capitalist institutions. As new concerns arise, it would be no surprise to see an interpretation of Sherlock Holmes that positioned him as a symbolic figure in the tension between civilization and terrorism. (Doyle's non-Sherlockian novel *The Tragedy of the Korosko*, about Islamic terrorism in Egypt, has lately been hailed as prescient.) Serious attention to the four novels and fifty-six short stories about Sherlock Holmes has barely begun.

THE APPEAL OF SHERLOCK HOLMES

The constitution of the Baker Street Irregulars defines its purpose as "the study of the Sacred Writings," that is, the Sherlock Holmes tales. Such "study," and publication of elegantly written mock scholarship with the full apparatus of footnotes, is an honoured activity in the Sherlockian world. But it lost some of its novelty as English professors began to trespass on the territory, taking the texts seriously and seeking not so much to entertain as to bolster their authors' scholarly reputations. The original purpose of Sherlockian activity, after all, was enjoyment — an exaggeration, not an abandonment, of the childish excitement with which the original readers, and succeeding generations, read the Sherlock Holmes tales. There is something compelling about Holmes, something about this figure, or at least about the stories that tell of his adventures, so that they have been continuously in print since their first publication, have been translated into dozens of languages, have made their way onto the screen and into the awareness of billions of people. (Not only people: a precocious pig also caught the Baker Street bug, according to the 1932 children's classic *Freddy the Detective* by Walter R. Brooks.) The enthusiasm and apprehension that greeted news of a new film in 2009, with Holmes portrayed by a star who looks very little like Basil Rathbone, is sufficient evidence that Holmes is not yet a spent force.

Fred Strebeigh addressed the central issue in a 1987 article in *Smithsonian* magazine, describing the phenomenon of Sherlockian enthusiasm, which he did not hesitate to call a "cult."

> What pulls Americans so strongly, 100 years after his literary birth, toward Sherlock Holmes? Isaac Asimov, the well-known science-fiction writer (invested by the Irregulars as "The Remarkable Worm Unknown to Science"), suggests that Holmes may be "the most successful fictional character of all time" because he represents the triumph of the "gifted amateur who could see clearly through a fog." Dr. David Musto ("Dr. Anstruther"), of the Yale Medical School and the Yale Sherlock Holmes Society, says that Holmes appeals to modern readers because he represents a life unencumbered by the petty details of human existence. When you read a Holmes story, says Musto, "you encounter a world in which people have breakfast but never use the toilet." Holmes' world is an "exciting place, but it's also peaceful — a world of modified danger."
>
> Other Sherlockians give different answers. At a meeting of an inner circle of the Irregulars ... I heard a range of explanations of Holmes' appeal: the human scale of nineteenth-century London,... the influence of the age of radio that began in the 1930s,... the mythic vitality of the characters.

More from Asimov, writing in *Newsday* in 1984:

Sherlock Holmes is the epitome of intelligence and he is always on the side of good. He defeats the villains by his superior brains, but he avoids becoming a villain in his turn by not using shrewdness and trickery. He *is* shrewd and he is not above using trickery, as in donning a clever disguise. That, however, is not his chief weapon. His chief weapon is a combination of acute observation and keen, logical deduction.... Before the end of a story, he is sure to reveal his line of reasoning and all seems plain and clear.... The audience, meeting such a rare character, cannot help but be delighted. How wonderful to have intelligence made so plain and straightforward that any reader can feel he might be that intelligent, too, with a bit of luck. (This is especially so when Watson is presented as brave and loyal, but as so dense and misunderstanding that almost any reader feels smart by comparison.)

Thirdly, Karl E. Meyer in in 1986:

Why Holmes?

A good tuppence answer is that Doyle knew what he was doing, that Victorian London taken in the right dose is pure tonic and that Holmes as freelance knight errant appeals to American impatience with lumbering institutions.... What is distinctive about Holmes is his immutability — the scenes change, but never his personality. He is the first in a line of always-the-same characters reaching one extreme in Superman and Sam Spade, another in the Lone Ranger and John Wayne, and a third (just to be argumentative) in Ronald Reagan.

And finally, Paul M. Chapman writing in, ironically, the last issue of *Sherlock Magazine* before it ceased publication (2006):

Part of Holmes' lasting hold on the popular psyche is the appeal of nostalgia, of the cherished image of a better, more certain time. The Victorian period was an age of hero-worship, a currency which has become debased and devalued in our more iconoclastic milieu. If Holmes is to be valued still it should not be for his obvious weaknesses and failings — which fatuous commentators would highlight as providing evidence of his modernity — but for his strength, certainty, and pragmatic morality, timeless values which should ensure that he will continue to inform our culture in both obvious and subtle ways for some time to come.

Some replies emphasize the person of Sherlock Holmes, others the gaslit era in which he moves; there may even be a few that acknowledge the storytelling skill of Arthur Conan Doyle.

No one could contemplate meeting Sherlock Holmes in the flesh and making friends with him; brusque and insulting rejection would be all too likely. So mercurial and egotistical a figure might be a stimulating acquaintance, but no more. Unless, to be sure, one imagined him as a lover, for it is said that women like dangerous and unpredictable men, and there is not much doubt that some women readers (and women viewers of Jeremy Brett as Holmes, most of all) are half in love with Sherlock Holmes. But a thrilling lover may make a bad husband. Holmes is indeed a heroic figure of the kind Meyer suggests, but in the nature of things heroic figures walk alone. Lois Lane never quite makes contact with Superman, the Lone Ranger is forbidden the community of his former brethren in the Texas Rangers, and even King Arthur is betrayed by the one friend he thought he had. As perceptive writers have been saying for decades, the man to choose for a friend would be Watson rather than Holmes — not so much because of his supposed stupidity (he is not, in the Canon, unusually stupid) but because of his ordinary decency, the comfort with which he moves in normal society. Watson is the man who marries, repeatedly, and Watson stands flat-footed on the ground while Holmes moves eerily through London, in the city but not of it. His hobbies, talents, and vices are affectations, his friendships nonexistent, his only relative as improbable a man as he is himself.

It is impossible to imagine Holmes in any activity but detection, the business of establishing justice when the ordinary mechanisms of society fail. Frequently acting around or above or against the law, he is guided by his own principles, and seems as arbitrary as God in his dealings with ordinary mortals. Here, much more than in his personality, lies his appeal to the modern reader, indeed much of the appeal of all detective stories. One can be scared half to death by the Baskerville hound, but it is a healthy kind of fear, with the necessary catharsis coming predictably in Chapter XIV. This experience is in fact a comfort to readers who have to double-lock their doors for fear of real-life burglars, and whose purses can be snatched at any moment on the filthy city street. Vengeance is mine, says Sherlock Holmes within the safe confines of the page. Shortly before what he expects will be his death, in "The Final Problem," he tells Watson that "The air of London is the sweeter for my presence." The police whose deficiencies he supplies are not actually corrupt, as the reader sometimes suspects modern police of being, but they are certainly bumblers, and the reader rejoices at the idea of a powerful, incorruptible, almost superhuman figure bringing murderers to justice and, when necessary, humbling kings.

Superheroes exist in modern literature and film too, of course, including the ones Meyer mentions, but the appeal of Holmes is greatly increased by his Victorian context. Victorian London is not being met as a new world, like Middle Earth or even the England of Shakespeare. It was the home of our great-grandparents and the immediate source of our own civilization. Most of the streets Watson mentions in his narratives can still be walked by the Sherlockian pilgrim. The people he describes speak intelligible English, bet on horse races, eat toast and take their fiancées to the theatre — why, once or twice Sherlock Holmes even uses the telephone. But just as London seems familiar, there comes reference to paregoric, a J pen or a governess, and the reader is reminded of a century-wide gulf. Perhaps most important in making Holmes's world different from our own is the absence of the internal combustion engine, with all its implications for urban sounds and smells, rapid movement across the city, and social instability. Hansom cabs — the horse-drawn predecessors of taxis — catch the imagination of modern readers precisely because they emphasize the limited mobility (and, one may imagine, the calm) of a society without cars.

The age of Holmes (say 1880 to 1905) is far enough in the past that today's readers do not know it first hand, as Christopher Morley and the other early Sherlockians did, but its details are not entirely obscured either. The mind's-eye picture of London, *circa* 1895, and the scene presented in most movies about the period, is delightfully cozy: swirling fog outside the sitting-room window, trapezoidal gas-lamps casting a yellow glow on the cobblestones while a hansom rattles past. For a middle-class Briton, it must seem, everything was secure, from domestic comfort to economic prospects, masculinity, and the glory of Empire. A little attention to social history makes clear how unrealistic is this picture, summed up by Vincent Starrett as "that age before the world went all awry." The world has always been awry, and so were the 1890s, with as many difficulties of social change, unemployment, starvation, alcoholism, and rumoured war as any other decade, including the present one. The careful reader of the Canon, indeed, will notice evidences of these problems, for Doyle knew his era well and got the details mostly right. But the average reader of detective fiction hardly wants realism. It is better to imagine one's hero striding

319

through a world in which there were no systematic wrongs, so that the righting of individual wrongs (Grimesby Roylott bitten by his own poisonous serpent, James Windibank horsewhipped) completes the work of justice.

Farewell and hail. Arthur Conan Doyle wrote in the 1927 Preface to *The Case-Book of Sherlock Holmes* that his detective

> must go the way of all flesh, material or imaginary. One likes to think that there is some fantastic limbo for the children of imagination, some strange, impossible place where the beaux of Fielding may still make love to the belles of Richardson, where Scott's heroes still may strut, Dickens's delightful Cockneys still raise a laugh, and Thackeray's worldlings continue to carry on their reprehensible careers. Perhaps in some humble corner of such a Valhalla, Sherlock and his Watson may for a time find a place, while some more astute sleuth with some even less astute comrade may fill the stage which they have vacated.

Doyle was utterly wrong. Famous even by 1927, Sherlock Holmes and his Watson are world-famous now, and if they live in "some fantastic limbo" they live also on the television screen, the advertising billboard, and always the printed page, to say nothing of the never-vacated stage of the active imagination. "So they still live," Vincent Starrett wrote in *The Private Life of Sherlock Holmes*, "for those that love them well." But they live also for those who do not particularly love them but merely know that they existed — that they still exist, like Robin Hood or Cinderella. Meanwhile, who now reads Richardson or Fielding or Thackeray, or even Charles Dickens?

There is no need to imagine a more astute sleuth, for any shortcomings of the original Holmes have long since been supplied by the fancy of generations of readers. Duller and duller Watsons, meanwhile, have been provided to the point of satiation by screen writers, an injustice that rankles with readers who understand the fine qualities that made the original Watson a worthy companion for Holmes. As for the beaux and belles, the Cockneys and (especially) the reprehensible worldlings, it is easiest to imagine them as clients and witnesses and villains as Holmes continues his brilliant work of detection, ranging across that "fantastic limbo" to right the wrongs and shine light on whatever may be in darkness.

Sherlock Holmes, who was conceived on a page of Arthur Conan Doyle's notebook and brought to birth in a shilling paperback, has escaped his creator's control. Surviving embarrassing distortions by advertisers and film directors, surviving parodies and caricatures, the decay of time and the damage of dog-eared pages, he has earned eternal life. Readers who can never get enough of his dancing grey eyes, his sardonic remarks, his courage, and his energy have poured out a hundred and twenty years of affection on the stories of Sherlock Holmes, and on the character himself. In response to that passion, he has become for them — for us — a person, a companion, a friend. The Sherlock Holmes whom Arthur Conan Doyle wrote has become the Sherlock Holmes we love.

APPENDIX

THE SIXTY TALES

EACH STORY TITLE IS LISTED (with its conventional **ABBR**eviation, devised by early Sherlockian scholar Jay Finley Christ, in capitals) along with its date of first publication.

A **STUD**y in Scarlet[1]	[December] 1887
The **SIGN** of the Four[1][2]	February 1890

THE ADVENTURES OF SHERLOCK HOLMES

A **SCAN**dal in Bohemia	July 1891
The **RED**-Headed League	August 1891
A Case of **IDEN**tity	September 1891
The **BOSC**ombe Valley Mystery	October 1891
The **FIVE** Orange Pips	November 1891
The Man with the **TWIS**ted Lip	December 1891
[3]The **BLUE** Carbuncle	January 1892
[3]The **SPEC**kled Band	February 1892
[3]The **ENG**inee**R**'s Thumb	March 1892
[3]The **NOBL**e Bachelor	April 1892
[3]The **BERY**l Coronet	May 1892
[3]The **COPP**er Beeches	June 1892

THE MEMOIRS OF SHERLOCK HOLMES

[3]**SILV**er Blaze	December 1892
[3]The **YELL**ow Face	February 1893
[3]The **STOC**k-broker's Clerk	March 1893
[3]The "**GLOR**ia Scott"	April 1893
[3]The **MUSG**rave Ritual	May 1893
[3]The **REIG**ate Squires[4]	June 1893
[3]The **CROO**ked Man	July 1893
[3]The **RESI**dent Patient	August 1893
[3]The **GREE**k Interpreter	September 1893
[3]The **NAVA**l Treaty	October–November 1893
[3]The **FINA**l Problem	December 1893
The **HOUN**d of the Baskervilles[1]	August–April 1901–02

APPENDIX: THE SIXTY TALES

THE RETURN OF SHERLOCK HOLMES

[3]The **EMPT**y House   September 1903
[3]The **NORW**ood Builder   October 1903
[3]The **DANC**ing Men   December 1903
[3]The **SOLI**tary Cyclist   December 1903
[3]The **PRIO**ry School   January 1904
[3]**BLAC**k Peter   February 1904
[3]**CHA**rle**S** Augustus Milverton   March 1904
[3]The **SIX N**apoleons   April 1904
[3]The Three [3] **STU**dents   June 1904
[3]The **GOLD**en Pince-Nez   July 1904
[3]The **MISS**ing Three-Quarter   August 1904
[3]The **ABBE**y Grange   September 1904
[3]The **SECO**nd Stain   December 1904

The **VALL**ey of Fear[1]   September–May 1914–15

HIS LAST BOW

WISTeria Lodge[5]   August 1908
[3]The **CARD**board Box[6]   January 1893
[3]The **RED** Circle[7]   March–April 1911
[3]The **BRUC**e-Partington Plans   December 1908
[3]The **DYIN**g DetectiveNovember 1913
The Disappearance of **LADY** Frances Carfax   December 1911
[3]The **DEVI**l's Foot   December 1910
His **LAST** Bow[8]   September 1917

THE CASE-BOOK OF SHERLOCK HOLMES

[3]The **ILLU**strious Client   November 1924
[3]The **BLAN**ched Soldier   October 1926
[3]The **MAZA**rin Stone   October 1921
[3]The Three [3] **GAB**les   September 1926
[3]The **SUSS**ex Vampire   January 1924
[3]The Three [3] **GAR**ridebs   October 1924
The Problem of **THOR** Bridge   February 1922
[3]The **CREE**ping Man   March 1923
[3]The **LION**'s Mane   November 1926
[3]The **VEIL**ed Lodger   January 1927
[3]**SHOS**combe Old Place   March 1927
[3]The **RETI**red Colourman   December 1926

---

1   Novel length; others are short stories.
2   In many editions, just *The Sign of Four*.
3   In the original publication, "The Adventure of" preceded this title.
4   In its earliest publication, "The Reigate Squire"; in most American editions, "The Reigate Puzzle."
5   Formally, "The Adventure of Wisteria Lodge." First published as "The Singular Experience of Mr. John Scott Eccles: A Reminiscence of Mr. Sherlock Holmes."
6   Appeared in the earliest book edition of *The Memoirs*, in its appropriate chronological place, but suppressed thereafter, and introduced into *His Last Bow* twenty years later.
7   Originally subtitled "A Reminiscence of Sherlock Holmes."
8   Subtitled "The War Service of Sherlock Holmes" or "An Epilogue of Sherlock Holmes."

INDEX

"SH" always means "Sherlock Holmes." A page number in **bold** type indicates the page where a term or topic is principally discussed. Routine mentions of Holmes, Watson, Doyle, and London are not indexed, and the *Baker Street Journal* is not indexed when it is mentioned in the text only as the place where something was published. Mentions of places are indexed as specifically as possible (city in preference to state, for example). Definite articles are omitted at the beginning of titles.

A to Z Atlas, 142
Aarhus, Denmark, 302
"Abbas Ruby," 213
"Abbey Grange," 29, 47, 60, 64, 98, 124, 156, 158, 161, 188, 207, 246
Abbey National, 46, 147, 299
Abbreviations, 12
ABC radio, 224, 231
Abduction, 61
Abdul Hamid II, 177
Abramson, Ben, 262
Academic scholarship, 310ff
ACD: the Journal, 311
Ace, 291
Achilles tendon, 48
"Actor's Duel," 102
Actors' Theatre, 228
Adams, 53
Addleton tragedy, 56
Adelphi Theatre, 114
Adler, Irene, 17, 43, 45, 51, 63, 160, 161, 203, 217, 226, 227, 242, 243, 245, 315
"Adventure in Canonical Fidelity," 250
Adventure of SH' Smarter Brother, 217, 240
"Adventure of the Two Collaborators," 211
"Adventure of the Unique *Hamlet*," 212
Adventure of (formulaic title), 16
Adventures of Arthur Conan Doyle, 137
Adventures of Conan Doyle, 135
Adventures of Gerard, 103, 106
Adventures of SH, 16ff, 211
Adventures of Solar Pons, 214
Adventures of the Great Mouse Detective, 255
Adventuress, 51
Adventuress, 52
Adventuresses of SH, 16, 52, 230, 251, 272–73, 287
Adventuring in England, 141
Advertising, 309–10
Affaire Lerouge, 199
Afghan Wars (*see also* Maiwand), 48, 175

Afghanistan, 48, 262
Africa, 125, 167, 172, 177, 179
Agatha, 161
Agony column, 165
Aidiniantz, John, 299
Aig, Marlene, 289
Aikin, Bruce, 160
Air Force, 132
Aircraft, 109
Akron, 263
Alberstat, Mark, 118
Albert of Monaco, Prince, 217
Albert Victor, Prince, 195
Albert, Prince Consort, 186, 187
Alberta, 303
Albertus Magnus College, 272
Alcoholism, 98, 134, 171
Aldgate station, 149
Alexander II, 177
Alexander III, 177
Alexander, Arthur M., 142
Alfred the Great, 150
Algonquin Hotel, 273, 274, 275
Alibris, 293
Alice's Adventures in Wonderland, 181
Alimentary, 305
Allahakbarries, 117
Allen, Grant, 74, 167, 180, 201
Allen, Patrick, 246
Alleyn, Roderick, 202
Allingham, Margery, 203
Allusions, 304–05
Alsace, 176
Alt.fan.holmes, 297
Altamont, 33, 174
Alternative SH, 222
"Aluminum Crutch," 230
Always 1895, 269
Amateur Boxing Association, 118
Amateur Cracksman, 97, 184
Amateur sport, 117
Amateurism, 210
Amazon, 291
America (*see* United States)
American Magazine, 75, 88
Amputation, 104, 172
Anaesthetics, 69, 171
Ancient Order of

Hibernians, 30
And on the Eighth Day, 202
Andersen, Elmer L., 294
Anderson, Nathalie, 227
Anderson, Poul, 268, 309
Andrew, Clifton R., 263
Andromeda Strain, 111
Angel, 17
Angels of Darkness, 114
Anglican (*see* Church of England)
Anglo-American Union, 126, 174, 236
Animation, 255
Anime, 255
Ankers, Evelyn, 235, 236
Annandale (surgeon), 69
"Annie Oakley in Baker Street," 262
Annotated editions, 10, 81
Annotated Lost World, 110
Annotated SH, 81, 83, 91, 264
Another Scandal in Bohemia, 52
Anstruther, Dr., 48, 316
Anthropology, 170
Antibiotics, 171
Anti-Semitism, 160
Apocrypha, 83, 113
Apocrypha of SH, 113, 222
Appeal (criminal), 190
Apple Corporation, 307
Appleby, John, and *Appleby's End*, 202
Appledore Towers, 160
Appointment in Baker Street, 261
Arabia, 177
Archbishops, 168
Arctic, 100, 105, 118
Aristocracy, 157
Arizona, 243
Arkin, Alan, 240
Armageddon, 217
Armenia, 177
Army, 97, 122, 152, 184, 264
Arnell, Richard, 226

Arsène Lupin Contre Herlock Sholmès, 201
Arthur & George, 121, 138
Arthur and the Great Detective, 255
Arthur Conan Doyle, 136
Arthur Conan Doyle and the Meaning of Masculinity, 314
Arthur Conan Doyle Collection Lancelyn Green Bequest, 281, 295
Arthur Conan Doyle Museum, 131
Arthur Conan Doyle Society, 95, 311
Arthur Conan Doyle: A Life in Letters, 98, 137
Arthur Conan Doyle: A Memoir, 135
Arthur Conan Doyle: Beyond Baker Street, 136
Arthur Conan Doyle: Beyond SH, 136
Arthur, King, 62, 186, 318
Artillery, 122
Arts and Crafts Movement, 185
"As They Would Have Told It," 211
ASH, 272
Ashcroft, British Columbia, 292
"ASHenpoof Song," 251
Ashley, Mike, 219
Ash-Tree Press, 292
Asimov, Isaac, 268, 313, 316
Assassin, 56
Assizes, 190
Associated Sunday Magazines, 31
Association football, 117
Assyria, 109
Asteroid, 50
Astrology, 273
Astronomer, 50
Atavism, 170, 315
Atkinson, Michael, 314
Atlantic City, 130
Atlantic Ocean, 61
Atlantis, 111
Atwill, Lionel, 236
Audible, 93
Audio (*see* Recording)

Auger, Claudine, 247
Aunt Clara, 52, 251, 274
Austen, Jane, 165
Austin, James Bliss, 30, 263, 293
Austin, Texas, 263, 295
Australia, 21, 29, 125, 129, 172, 173, 200
Australia and SH, 284
Austria, 99, 194
Austria-Hungary, 175, 177, 178
Author's Edition, 78
Autism, 220
Autocrat of the Breakfast-Table, 184
Automobile racing, 116
"Automobiles in His Last Bow," 311
Autumn in Baker Street, 275
Avon, 303
Avventure di SH, 92
Awakened, 253
Axelrad, Arthur M., 148

B.F. Goodrich, 304
Bachelor of Medicine, 100
Baconian Cipher, 230
Bacteria, 171
Bagel Street, 218
Bahrain, 302
Baillie, Arthur, 294
Baker Street, 145ff, 163, 278, 303; illustration, 143
— 221B, 26, 40, 46, 48, 54, **58**, 86, 143, 147–48, 247, 260, 299, 302
— 221B, reconstructions, 58, 294, 299, 300, 301
— & Waterloo Railway, 147
— (musical), 44
— (play), 226–27, 251
— *and Beyond*, 262, 264
— and Pimlico bus, 149
— Bachelors (story), 244
— *Ballads*, 252
— bar, 302
— *Bazaar*, 147
— *Briefs*, 290
— *By-Ways*, 279

— *Chronology*, 286
— *Dozen*, 313
— *File*, 248
— *Inventory*, 262
— Irregulars, 13, 30, 56, 79, 80, 90, 115, 131, 222, 225, 230, 251, 252, 254, **257ff**, 259, 270, 272, 273–75, 276, 277, 283, 285, 303, 315
— Irregulars (original), 55, 155
— Irregulars History Series, 267
— Irregulars Trust, 267, 295
— *Journal*, 10, 39, 196, 252, **262**, 263, 265, 267, 268, 285, 287, 289, 310, 311, 313
— *Miscellanea*, 63, 74, 87, 90, 208, 211, **264**, 266, 288, 311
— *Quartette*, 252
— *Song Book*, 251
— Squires, 270
— station, 143, 146, 148, 149, 299, 301, 302
— *Suite*, 251
Baker, disappears, 67
Baker, C. Douglas, 196
Baker, Edward, 145
Baker, Henry, 18, 155, 156, 159, 246
Baker, Michael, 98
Bakerloo Line, 147
Balfour, Arthur, 152, 181
Balkans, 175, 176, 177
Ball, Alec, 90
"Ballad of Reading Gaol," 190
"Ballad of the Ranks," 112
Ballantine, 291
Ballet, 226
Ballinger, Jim, 251
Ballistics, 196, 262
Ballooning, 109
Baltimore, 261, 270, 276
Bangladesh, 179
Bangs, John Kendrick, 211
Bank of England, 144, 236
Bantam Classics, 79
Baptists, 168, 186
Bar of Gold, 301
Barclay, Nancy, 162

Baring-Gould, Sabine, 180
Baring-Gould, William S., 10, 44, 81, 83, 180, 203, 219, 264, 286
Baritsu Chapter, 283
Barkworth, Peter, 246
Barnes & Noble, 79
Barnes, Alan, 233
Barnes, Bill, 284
Barnes, Julian, 121, 138
Barr, Robert, 101, 167, **180**, 201, 211, 212, 257
Barrie, James, 101, 112, 117, **181**, 211
Barrie, Wendy, 235
Barrister, 189, 195
Barrymore, John, 234
Barsham, Diana, 314
Bart's (*see* St. Bartholomew's)
Bartlett's Familiar Quotations, 305
Barton, Dr. Hill, 267
Basil of Baker Street, 255
Baskerville family, 24, 157
Baskerville, Sir Charles, 170
Baskerville, Sir Henry, 64, 173, 235, 239, 247, 271
Baskerville, Sir Robert, 313
Baskerville, William of, 308
Baskervilles Investments Ltd., 132
Bathroom, 58
Battered Silicon Dispatch-Box, 94, 290, 292
Bavaria, 52
Bayswater, 145
Bayswater Road, 145
BBC Home Service, 229
BBC Light Programme, 228, 229
BBC radio, 224, 231, 282; Radio Four, 231
BBC television, 138, 243, 244
Beaconsfield, Lord (*see* Disraeli)
Beagle voyage, 182
Bear Mountain, 275
Bear, Greg, 111
Beare, Geraldine, 74

Beaulieu, 107
Beck, Adolf, 194
Bedside, Bathtub & Armchair Companion, 290
Beecher, Henry Ward, 181
Beekeeper's Apprentice, 44
Beery, Wallace, 110
Beeswing, 60
"Beetle-Hunter," 109
Beeton's Christmas Annual, 12, 70, 85, 281, 293
"Before My Bookcase," 116
Begg, Paul, 196
Belfast, 166
Belgium, 123, 125, 178, 179
Bell, Alexander Graham, 169
Bell, Harold W., 259, 278, 286
Bell, Joseph, 49, 59, 68, 99, 138, 200
Bell, Laura, 51
Bellamy, Maud, 37
Bellinger, Lord, 186
Bells, 184
Belmont racetrack, 266, 276
Ben Sanders Company, 253
Benda, W.T., 90
Bending the Willow, 250
Bengal, 179, 197
Bengis, Nathan L., 138, 267, 273, 293, 294
Bengtsson, Hans-Uno, 284
Bensen, D.R., 242
Benson, Arthur, 140
Bentley, Edmund Clerihew, 202
Berg Collection, 72
Bergem, Phillip G., 98
Bergin, Patrick, 111
Bergquist, John, 268, 296
Berkeley, 53, 313
Berkey, Jim, 43
Berkley, 253
Berkshire, 140, 190, 193
Berlin, 171
Berman, 284
Berman, Ruth, 210
Bermuda, 276
Berner Street, 195
Bernhardt, Sarah, 51, 63, 183
Bertillon, Alphonse, and Bertillonage, 197
"Beryl Coronet," 19, 62, 161, 243
Besant, Annie, 217
Best Detective Stories, 204
Best of Sherlock, 13, 70, 293, 296
Best of SH, 296
Best Science Fiction

of Arthur Conan Doyle, 109
Betzner, Ray, 268
Beyond Baker Street, 282
Beyond the City, 102, 104
Bhurtee, 22
Bible, 67, 91, 168, 198, 277; scholars, 12
Bibliography, 66, 72, 78, 92, 93, 137–38, 198, 281, 290–91, 312
Bibliography of A. Conan Doyle, 10, 15, 31, 32, 34, 66, 72, 85, 102, 103, 105, 112, 137–38, 281, 313
Bicycle, 196
Big Sleep, 203
Bigelow on Holmes, 291
Bigelow, S. Tupper, 10, 270, 290, 294
Biggle, Lloyd, 216
Bignell Wood, 101
Bill of rights, 151
Billy, 54, 55, 101, 224
Bimetallic question, 53
Binomial theorem, 50
Biographies, 133ff
Bipolar Organisation, 250
Birlstone, 30, 95, 160
Birmingham, 21, 100, 140, 141, 181
Birthday weekend, 265, 272, 273–75, 277
Bishop Murder Case, 238
Bishops, 150, 168
Bismarck, Otto von, 175, 176
"Black Baronet," 213
Black dog, 67
Black Gorgiano, 247
Black Mask, 97
"Black Narcissus," 214
"Black Peter," 28, 144
"Black Spaniel," 37
Black tie, 261, 274
Blackbeard, Bill, 256, 289
Blackmail, 28
Blacks, 160
Blackwall Tunnel, 144
Blakeley, Colin, 239
Blakeney, T.S., 286
"Blanched Soldier," 35, 48, 171, 177, 311
Blau, Peter, 262, 264, 268, 269, 272, 287, 293
Blitz, 142
Block, Alan, 296
Bloemfontein, 122
Bloodstains, 196
Bloody Business, 193
Bloody Murder, 198, 200, 208
Bloody Sunday, 193
Bloomington, 295
Bloomsbury, 145

"Blue Carbuncle," 16, 18, 79, 155, 156, 165, 188, 207, 246, 290
Blythe, Peter, 228
Blyton, Enid, 254
Board of Agriculture, 158
Board schools, 152
Boarding-house, 161
Bobbies, 191
Bodymaster, 30
Boeing Computer Services, 310
Boer War, 35, 122
Bohemia (and King), 17, 42, 51, 177, 194, 208
Bohemian, 242
Bombay, 180
Bonaparte (*see* Napoléon)
Boobus Britannicus (*see also* Watson), 47
Book of Common Prayer, 168
Book of the Queen's Dolls' House, 114
Booker Prize, 121
Bookman, 47, 116
Book-of-the-Month Club, 79
Booksellers, 292
Boom, 81, 216, 218, 240, 264ff, 285, 287, 288
Booth, Charles, 159
Booth, Martin, 136
Bootlace, 59
Bootmakers of Toronto, 251, 271–72, 276, 277, 287
Borden, Lizzie, 44, 194
Born in a Bookshop, 261
Boroughs, 150; "the Borough," 144
Boruvka, Lieutenant, 206
"Boscombe Valley Mystery," 17, 60, 87, 157, 166, 207, 228, 247
Bosnia, 175
Boston, 184, 225, 226, 261, 263, 264, 268, 270, 292; *Sunday Post*, 78
Boswell, James, 47
Botany, 170
Bottle, for Sherlockians, 265
Boucher, Anthony, 222, 231, 263
Bouchercon, 263
Boulevard assassin, 56
Bow Street, 190; Runners, 191
Bow windows, 148
Bowling Green University, 311
Boxing, 118ff, 263
Boy SH, 219
Boyce, D.G., 153
Brackenstall, Mary,

158, 161, 246
Bradford, Edward, 193
Bradley, Alan, 42
Bradley's tobacco shop, 301
Braille, 93
Brain fever, 171
Brandon, Ann, 235
Brandy, 172
Branger, Tobias, 119
Brantley, Betsy, 245
Brattleboro, Vermont, 119
Braun, Alex, 296
Breasts, 314
Brend, Gavin, 148, 286
Breon, Edmond, 236
Brett, Anthony, 233
Brett, Jeremy, 42, 49, 51, 194, 218, 228, 242, 245ff, 301, 309, 318; illustration, 248
Brewster, John, 93
Bricusse, Leslie, 228
Bridges, 144, 169
Brigadier Gerard (play) (*see also* Gerard), 112
Briggs, Gray Chandler, 90, 147, 259, 260
Bristol, 222; *Observer*, 87
Britannia, 175
British Association, 27
British barrow, 56
British Campaign in France and Flanders, 124
British government, 53
British Journal of Photography, 130
British Library, 97, 133, 281
British National Association of Spiritualists, 127
British Pharmacopoeia, 43
British Rail, 149
British South Africa Company, 173
British superiority, 140
Brixton bus, 169
Broad arrow, 190
Broadmoor, 190
Broadway, 226–27
Brock, H.M., 90
Brodribb, John Henry, 184
Brodie, Geoffrey, 132
Bromet, Geoffrey, 132
Bromo-Quinine, 230
Brook, Clive, 234
Brooke, Hillary, 236, 237
Brooklyn, 181, 303; bridge, 169
Brooks, Walter R., 308, 316
Brown, Father, 202, 219
Brown, Ivor, 135
Browner, Jim, 247
Brtnik, Craig, 251
Bruce, Nigel, 47,

230, 238, 256; illustration, 237
"Bruce-Partington Plans," 32, 53, 64, 75, 109, 149, 154, 156, 157, 178, 187, 246
Brunel, Isambard Kingdom, 181
Brunton, 21
Bruxner, Pamela, 280
BSI (*see* Baker Street Irregulars)
Buck, David, 232
Buckfastleigh, 25
Buckingham Palace, 144
Buckingham Palace Mansions, 101
Buckinghamshire, 140
Bucks Row, 195
Budd, George Turnavine, 100
Buddhism, 67
Buffalo, 174, 222
Bugs Bunny, 255
Building society, 147
Bujold, Geneviève, 241
Bulgaria, 177
Bunson, Matthew E., 290
Burke, David, 243, 249, 250; illustration, 248
Burke's Peerage, 158
Burma, 179
Burr, Robert C., 288
Bush Villas, 100, 302
Bushman, 170
Busts, 54, 304
Buttons, 261
Buy-Laws, 259, 274
Byerly, Ann, 87, 88, 288, 313

Cabell family, 25
Cabinet, 151
Cabot, Sebastian, 243
Cabs, 149
Caine, Hall, 75
Caine, Michael, 241
Calabash Press, 248, 289, 292, 298
Calcutta, 179, 180
Caleb Williams, 1988
Calgary, 272
California, 256, 293
Cambell, Cheryl, 247
Camberwell, 144
Cambridge, 156, 216; University 117, 278
Cambridgeshire, 140
Camden House, 148, 296
Camden House Journal, 169, 270, 288
Campbell, Karen, 251
Campbell, Maurice, 25
Campbell-Bannerman, Henry, 154
Campion, Albert, 203
Canada, 53, 70, 76, 95, 124, 125, 166, 172, 173, 180, 189, 216, 243, 256, 270, 294, 304

Canada Post, 310
Canadian Baskervilles, 270
Canadian Holmes, 24, 160, 196, 239, 269, 272, 287
Canals, 141, 144
Canary Murder Case, 202
Canary Trainer, 215
Canevet, Sébastien, 296
Cannon Street station, 141, 149
Canon, 12, 38, 113
— abbreviations, 12
— annotated editions, 10
— conventions, 16
— cross-references, 16
— errors, 46
— time lapses, 15
— word count, 12
Canonical Compendium, 38, 290
Canonical Index, 10
Canonicity, 245
Canterbury, 168
Cape Colony, 122, 172
Cape (*see also* Inverness), 84
Capital punishment, 188, 190
Capitalist institutions, 315
Capitalization, 70, 72
"Captain Jones of the 'Rose'," 74
Captain Marvel, 255
Captain of the Polestar, 102, 105
"Cardboard Box," 20, 22, 31, 64, 82, 166, 181, 197, 247
Cardiff, 226
Carey, Peter, 28
Carfax, Lady Frances (*see* Lady)
Caribbean, 172
Carlyle, Thomas, 116
Carnegie, Andrew, 174
Carr, John Dickson, 57, 75, 98, 107, 122, 131, 134, 213, 222
Carrados, Max, 201
Carrington, Hereward, 130
Carroll & Graf, 291
Carroll, Lewis, 138, 181
Cartoons, 84, 91, 305, 305
Cartwright, 56
Case Files of SH, 290
Case for Spirit Photography, 129
"Case of Identity," 17, 59, 64, 86, 155, 162
Case of Oscar Slater, 121
"Case of the Baker Street Bachelors," 244
Case of the Baker

Street Irregular, 254
Case of the Baker Street Irregulars, 222, 263
Case of the Cottingley Fairies, 130
"Case of the Cunningham Heritage," 244
"Case of the Jolly Hangman," 244
"Case of the Laughing Mummy," 244
"Case of the Missing Marquess," 254
"Case of the One Armed Man," 309
"Case of the Pilfered Panties," 254
"Case of the Ranjipur Ruby," 254
Case of the Rose Tattoo, 253
Case of the Serrated Scalpel, 253
"Case of the Shoeless Engineer," 244
"Case of the Velvet Claws," 202
"Case of the Whitechapel Vampire," 243
"Case of Vamberry," 230
Case-Book of SH, 34ff, 75, 77, 90, 94, 319
Casebook of Solar Pons, 214
Casement, Roger, 125
Cases of SH, 256
Castle Rouge, 52, 196
Catalogue Song, 249
Catharsis, 318
Catholicism, 22, 67, 97, 99, 105, 126, 153, 154, 160, 168, 178, 180, 272, 277
Cats, 38
Cavalry, 122
Cavanagh, Paul, 236
Cavanagh's Restaurant, 272
Cawnpore, 179
Cecil, Robert (*see* Salisbury)
Cella, Christ, 258, 259
Centenary Bibliography of German, 91
Centenary Celebration of SH, 250
Central Criminal Court, 144, 190
Central Park, 240
Cerebral type of man, 226
Certain Gracious Lady, 187
Ceylon, 172, 179
Chairs, 58
Challenger, HMS, 109
Challenger, Professor, 99, 109, 217
Chamberlain, Joseph, 181
Chamberlain, Neville, 181

Chancellor of the Exchequer, 151
Chandler, Raymond, 203
Channel tunnel, 123
Chapel Noir, 52, 196
Chaplin, Charlie, 224
Chapman, Eliza Ann, 195
Chapman, Paul M., 317
Chapside, 145
Character names, 68; copyright, 77
Charing Cross station, 141, 149
"Charles Augustus Milverton," 28, 156, 160, 161, 164, 206, 226, 247
Charlington, 27
Charteris, Francis, 121
Chase scene, 15
Château de Lucens, 131, 300
Checklist of the Arthur Conan Doyle Collection, 138, 294
Chelsea, 144, 274
Chemistry, 169
Chenai, 180
Cheshire, 141, 280
Chess, 37
Chesterton, G.K., 62, 202
Chicago, 77, 260, 261, 263, 266, 268, 270; *Tribune*, 76
Chief Constable, 192
Childhood of SH, 219
Children's books, 254–55, 308
Children's Hour, 229
China, 140; 184; Chinaman, 204
Chip 'n' Dale, 255
Chiropractic, 310
Chivalry, 134
Christ Cella's, 258, 259
Christ, Jay Finley, 12, 38, 138, 263, 286
Christian IX, 157, 178
Christiania, 92
Christianity, 63, 67, 128, 175, 182
Christie, Agatha, 201, 202, 205
Christie's, 133
Christmas Annual (see also *Beeton's*), 267
Christmas cards, 264
Christmas Carol, 182
Christmas story, 18
Chronicles of Addington Peace, 25
Chronicles of Sir Arthur Conan Doyle, 95
Chronicles of Solar Pons, 214
Chronological Holmes, 286
Chronology, 83, 286
Chronology of the Life of Sir Arthur Conan Doyle, 137

Chujoy, Anatole, 92
Church of England, 108, 151–53, **168–69**; churchgoing, 22
Churchill, Donald, 246
Churchill, Lord Randolph, 181
Churchill, Winston, 182
Cincinnati, 304
Cinderella, 320
Ciphers, 21, 27, 79, 199
Circle Line, 149
Circular Staircase, 202
Circus, 139
Citizenship, 140
Citrin, Michael, 254
City and South London Electric Railway, 149
City of London, 144, 151, 166, 192
Civic affairs, 181
Civil law, 190
Civil rights, 151
Civil War, English, 108
Civil War, U.S., 174, 181, 225
Clara, Aunt, 52, 251
Clarence, Duke of, 195
Clarendon Press, 281, 313
Clark, Edward F., Jr., 57, 285
Clark, John D., 203
Clark, Wallis, 224
Clarkson, Stephen, 38, 290, 296
Class, 155ff, 208
Classic Comics, 256
Classic Specialties, 304
Classics Illustrated, 256
Clausen, Christopher, 208
Clausson, Nils, 313
Clay, Nicholas, 246
Cleek, Hamilton, 201
Cleese, John, 217
Clendening, Logan, 260
Cleveland, 193
Cleveland Street, 194
Cleveland, Grover, 174
"Clinical Notes by a Resident Patient," 262
Cloister and the Hearth, 106
Close to Holmes, 142
Close, Glenn, 227
Clothing, 163
Clubs, 258
Clue, 252
Coal and Iron Police, 190
Coal-tar, 169
Cocaine, 42, 183, 211, 215, 254, 265
Cochran, William R., 262
Cockneys, 56, 320
Cocktail, 259
Cocktail party, 275

Code (*see* Ciphers)
Coffee, 89
Coffin, 33
Coghill, Bob, 272
Coins, 193
Colin, Margaret, 243
Collectors, 93, 265, 266, 279, 280, 292–93
Collier, P.F., publisher, 14, 15, 78
Collier, Peter Fenelon, 75
Collier, Robert J., 75
Collier's, 26ff, 74, 88, 213; illustration, 89
Collins, Wilkie, 199
Colonial Conan Doyle, 315
Colonial Office, 172; Secretary, 151
Colonies, 172–73
Colorado Springs, 303
Colorado State University, 313
Colours, 24
Colt, Emily S., 259
Combs, Oilock, 211
Comics, 91, 254–56
Coming of the Fairies, 130
Commissionaire, 259, 261, 264, 267
Commissioner, 193
Common law, 77, 189
Commons, House of, 150, 151, 181, 186
Communism, 177, 206
Complete Guide to SH, 282
Complete SH, 9, 22, 38, 77, 78, **79**, 90, 258, 291
Completist collector, 265, 292
Computers, 53, 73, 307, 309; games, 201; programming, 310
Conan, 97
Conan Doyle (book), 112, 135, 136
Conan Doyle (Crowborough) Establishment 95, 137, 300
Conan Doyle and the Latter-Day Saints, 13
Conan Doyle and the Parson's Son, 121
Conan Doyle and the Spirits, 126, 312
Conan Doyle Bibliography, 138
Conan Doyle Estate Ltd., 77, 133
Conan Doyle Place, 299
Conan Doyle Syndrome, 266
Conan Doyle, (Dame) Jean, 77, 101, 104, 131, 132, 137 157, 218, 268, 281, 300; estate, 268

Conan Doyle, Adrian, 57, 75, 80, 101, 104, 131, 134, 135, 212, 213, 276, 300; wife, Anna, 132
Conan Doyle, Arthur (*see* Doyle)
Conan Doyle, Denis, 101, 104, 131, 212
Conan Doyle, Detective, 119
Conan Doyle, His Life and Art, 131
Conan Doyle, Jean (Lady) (Leckie), 64, 101, 123, 124, 130, 133, 157
Conan Doyle, Kingsley, 100, 123, 131, 133
Conan Doyle, Malcolm (*see* Conan Doyle, Adrian)
Conan Doyle, Mary (daughter), 100, 124, 131, 133
Conan Doyle, Nina, 132
Conan Doyle: A Biographical Solution, 135
Conan Doyle: Portrait of an Artist, 136
Conan Doyle: The Man Who Created SH, 137
Conan Doyle's Stories for Boys, 78
Conan Doyle's Tales of Medical Humanism, 104
Concordance, 93
Condensed Novels, 211
Conferences, 275
Confidential Casebook of SH, 219
Congo, 125, 179
Congregationalism, 181
Congress of Protestant Foreign Missions, 67
Connecticut, 225, 272, 293
Connery, Sean, 30, 308
Conservative Party, 152, 153, 154, 181, 182
Constables, 193
"Construction of Woman," 314
Consulting detective, 40
Contents of a Lumber-Room, 295
Continental Op, 203
Contracts, 189
Conventions, 275
Convict, 190
Conway, Tom, 231
Cook, Peter, 241
Cooke, Catherine, 280, 295
Cooper, James Fenimore, 167

Cooper, Joe, 130
Coopersmith, Jerome, 44, 226
"Copper Beeches," 19, 27, 43, 63, 79, 162, 173, 246
Copper, Basil, 214
Copyright, 14, 76ff, 92, 94, 132, 189, 218, 309; Term Extension Act, 76
Coram, Professor, 158, 247
Coren, Alan, 255
Coren, Michael, 136
Cornhill, 145
Cornhill Magazine, 186
Cornish horror, 33
Cornwall, 33, 140
Cornwell, Patricia, 196, 206
Coronation Street, 301
Cosmopolitan, 76, 212
Costello, Peter, 49, 119
Costume, 271, 275
Cottingley fairies, 130, 138
Couchon, Mary Ellen, 272
Coules, Bert, 231
Coulter, David, 296
"Country of the Saints," 13, 267
County Cup, 118
Court Circular, 165
Courts, 190
Covell, Walter, 93
Coward, Noel, 101
Cox, Alan, 241
Cox, Don Richard, 136
Cox, Michael, 247, 250
Coyle, Jim, 307
Craig, Alec, 236
Crawford, Howard Marion, 244
Crawford, Virginia, 182
Cream, Neill, 194
Created and creator, 115
Creative Multimedia, 94
Credit, 156
"Creeping Man," 36, 109, 158, 171, 229, 247
Crelling, Jack, 169
Cremorne Gardens, 163
Crew of the SS *Friesland*, 285
Crichton, Michael, 111
Cricket, 116ff, 184
Crime, 188ff, 192ff
Crime d'Orcival, 199
Crime of the Congo, 125
Crime, Detective, Espionage, 198
Crimean War, 175
Crimes Club, 120
Criminal Investigation

Cooper, Joe, 130
Department, 192, 193
Criminal Law Amendment Act, 187
Crinoline, 163
Criterion Bar, 92, 302
Crockford's Clerical Directory, 169
Crooked Man," 15, 22, 56, 64, 162, 179, 180, 246, 305
Crosby, the banker, 56
Crossword, 259
Crow, Angus McCready, 220
Crowborough, 95, 101, 122, 300
Crowborough Edition, 78
Crowley, Aleister, 217
Crown Diamond, 34, 35, 114, 221
Crown Jewels, 235; Irish, 194
Crows, 14
Croxley Master, 103, 105, 119
Croydon, 144, 166
Crucifer of Blood, 227–28
Crusoe, Robinson, 63
CRW Publishing, 80
Cryogenics, 242–43
Crystal Palace, 187
Cubitt, Hilton and Elsie, 27, 58, 161, 245
Cuff, Sergeant, 199
Cullin, Arthur, 233
Cult, 316
Culver, Michael, 246
Cumberland, 141
"Cunningham Heritage," 244
Curious Incident of the Dog, 220
Curious Incident of the Hound, 25, 67
Curious Incident of the Missing Link, 110
Current Encyclopedia, 75
Cushing, Peter, 238, 242, 243–44
Czar, 177, 208; Czarina, 265

Dahlinger, Susan, 268, 290
Daily Chronicle, 116, 124
Daily Life in Victorian England, 165
Daily Mail, 116
Daily Mirror, 165
Daily Telegraph, 120, 165, 171
Dale, Margaret, 226
Dalgliesh, Adam, 203
Dalton, Philip and Patsy, 280
Dame, 157
Dame Blonde, 201
Damsel in distress, 19, 314

"Dancing Men," 27, 60, 79, 155, 158, 199, 244, 245
Dancing Men of Providence, 261
Danger!, 103, 123
Dangerous Game, 141
Daniell, Henry, 236
Dannay, Frederic, 202, 263
"Dark Angels," 213
Dark Water, 138
Dartmoor, 24, 25, 56, 67, 138, 140; Prison, 190
Darwin, Charles, 170, 182
Data, Commander, 309
Date Being?, 286
Dating of cases, 286
Daughter of Time, 203
Davenport, Basil, 259
David Copperfield, 182
Davidson, True, 271
Davies, Bernard, 141
Davies, David Ian, 93
Davies, David Stuart, 10, 228, 233, 250, 280, 301
Davis, Elmer, 259, 268
Davis, Richard Harding, 90
Davos, 100, 119
Day, Dan, 91, 256
Dayton, 275
De Luxe Edition, 79
Dear Starrett — Dear Briggs, 260
Death, 164; death penalty, 188
Death at Dartmoor, 25
Debrett's Peerage, 158
Débuts de SH, 91
Deconstructionism, 313, 314
Deduction, 60
Deductions, 304
Deerstalker hat, 84, 85, 164, 223, 255, 260, 271, 298, 309; on dogs, 303
Delay, Vincent, 286
"Demon Angels," 213
Demon Device, 216
Dempsey, Richard, 247
Dench, Judi, 232
Denmark, 157, 178, 233, 284
Denny, Reginald, 235
"Dental Holmes," 262
Denver, 94, 266
Depression, 250
Depressions, 153
"Deptford Horror," 213
Deputy-Lieutenant, 151
Derbyshire, 141
Derivative, 210
Derleth, August, 213–14
Des Greniers, rue, 300
Descent of Man, 182

Desert Drama (see *Tragedy of the Korosko*)

Detecting Social Order, 314

"Detecting the Beggar," 313

Detective Branch, 192

Detective fiction, 198ff, 269, 308–09; conventions, 13, 204

"Detective Stories Gone Wrong," 211

Detectives, 192; textbook for, 91

Detroit, 264, 266

Deutscher SH Klub, 284

"Devil's Foot," 33, 64, 75, 109, 156, 233, 246

Devon, 24, 25, 140, 180

Devonshire Place, 100

Devonshire, Duchess of, 50, 194, 271

Devoy, Nancy, 22

DeWaal, Ronald B., 10, 66, 138, 232, 233, 264, 290, 313

Dexter, Colin, 205

Diamond Jubilee, 185, 187

Diapers, 310

Dibdin, Michael, 217

Dickens, Charles, 165, 167, 182, 189, 199, 269, 320

Dickson, Gordon R., 309

Dictator, 32

Dictionary of National Biography, 186

Dietz, Steven, 228

Dilke, Charles, 182

Dining with SH, 268, 269

Dinosaur Summer, 111

Dinosaurs, 109, 111

Diogenes Club, 23, 53, 296

Diplomacy, 178

"Disappearance of Lady Frances Carfax" (see Lady)

Disappearance of SH, 219

Discoveries of Inspector Spine, 310

Disintegration Machine, 110

Diskettes, 94

Disney, Walt, 255

Disraeli, Benjamin, 152, 182, 217

Distinguished Lecture, 274

District Line, 149

District Messenger, 280, 287

District Railway, 149

Divorce, 64, 124–25, 181, 182, 185

Divorce Law Reform Union, 29, 124

Dixie, Steve, 160

Dobry, Dennis, 301

Dockers' strike, 153

Docklands, 142

Doctor of Medicine, 100, 172

Doctor Watson: Prolegomena, 278

Doctor, the Detective and Arthur Conan Doyle, 136

Doctor (see Dr.)

"Doctors of Hoyland," 104

Doctors' Stories, 60

Dodgson, Charles Lutwidge, 181

Dog in the night-time, 20, 306

Dog, black, 25, 67

Doings of Raffles Haw, 102, 111

Don Giovanni, 249

Don Murillo, 32

Donegall, Marquess of, 279

Doorbell Rang, 203

Doran, George H., Co., 31, 34

Doran, Hatty, 174, 247

Dorn, William S., 142

Dorset, 140

Dorset Street, 195

Dossier, 253

Dossier no. 113, 199

Dossier of Solar Pons, 214

Dostoevsky, Fyodor, 183

Double entendre, 63

"Double-Barrelled Detective Story," 211

Doubleday, 22, 26, 38, 77–79, 90, 224, 291

Doubleday, John, 301

Douglas, Carole Nelson, 52, 196, 220–21

Douglas, John and Ivy, 30, 64, 207

Douglas, Lord Alfred, 187

Douty, Robert Watson, 30

Dover, 176

Downey, Robert, Jr., 241, 256, 304, 316

Downing Street, 144

Downing, Vernon, 236

Download audio, 93

Doyle Diary, 98

Doyle, Annette, 97

Doyle, Arthur Conan, 95ff and passim
— accused of murder, 25
— American tours, 54, 101, 129, 137, 174
— and Spiritualism, 126ff
— appearance, 96
— autobiography 31, 116, 134
— biography, 133ff, 312

Doyle, Bryan Mary, 98

Doyle, Caroline, 97

Doyle, Catherine, 97

Doyle, Charles, 85, 97, 98, 136

Doyle, Constance, 97, 101, 185

Doyle, Dodo (see Doyle, Bryan Mary)

Doyle, Georgina, 98, 133

Doyle, Ida, 98, 133

Doyle, Innes Hay, 97, 123, 133

Doyle, Jane Adelaide (see Doyle, Ida)

Doyle, John, 97, 133

Doyle, Lottie, 97
— birth, 97, 301
— candidate, 154
— character in fiction, 138
— chivalry, 134
— costumed, 110
— death and burial, 101, 300
— early writings, 19
— estate, 77, 92, 131–33, 212
— fiction, 104ff
— finances, 74
— handwriting, 22, 70, 82, 313
— importance, 311–12
— innovations as author, 198, 200
— interest in crime, 119ff
— killing Holmes, 23
— letters, 98, 137
— life reflected in writing, 49, 82
— litigation, 77
— marriages, 100–01, 104
— medical work, 22, 32, 35, 59, 99–100, 104, 108, 171
— military interests, 123–24
— name, 97
— nationality, 140
— notes, 45
— poetry, 112
— portrait, 87, 96
— prominence, 9, 101
— prose style, 102
— reading, 67, 68
— recognized (see also Literary agent), 46, 285
— sexual and emotional, 26, 29, 105, 134, 135
— Spiritualist efforts, 129
— sportsman, 116–19
— strengths, 312, 317
— style, 216
— voice, 96
— writings about SH, 83

Doyle, Bryan Mary, 98

Doyle, Caroline, 97

Doyle, Louise (Lady) (Hawkins), 64, 100–01, 124, 133

Doyle, Mary (Foley), 97, 98, 99, 107, 136

Doyle, Mary (sister), 97

Doyle, Pj, 313

Doyle, Steven, 288

Dr. Joe Bell: Model for SH, 69, 99, 311

Dracula, 101, 185

Dragnet, 214

Drains, 152

Drayson, Alfred W., 127

Drebber, Enoch, 161, 254

Dressed to Kill, 236, 238

Drew, Nancy, 254

Dreyfus, Alfred, 217

Drood, Edwin, 182

Drugs, 42

Druitt, Montague John, 195

Du Maurier, George, 42, 168

Du Quoin, Illinois, 270

Dual Alliance, 175

Duane, Hotel, 258, 259

Dublin Castle, 194

Duchess of Duke Street, 282

Duet (play), 103, 112

Duet with an Occasional Chorus, 100, 103, 104

Duke Street, 282

Dumb-bell, 30

Duncan, Alistair, 142

Dungeons and Dragons, 57

Dupin, C. Auguste, 61, 198, 199, 308

Durham, 141

Dutton, 291

Duvall, Robert, 240

"Dying Detective," 32, 42, 54, 58, 70, 75, 88, 171, 172, 233, 247, 290

Dynamics of an Asteroid, 50

Dynamite, 109

Ears, 20

Earthman's Burden, 309

Earthquake Machine, 217

East End, 145, 195

East Indies, 178

East York, Ontario, 271

Eastchester, New York, 268

Easter, 62

Easter Rising, 154

Easton Press, 80

Eccles, John Scott, 31, 246

Echo, 165

Eco, Umberto, 61, 308

Ectoplasm, 128, 129

Edalji, George, 119ff, 134, 190

Eddowes, Catharine, 195

Edge of the Unknown, 129, 130

Edgware Road, 145

Edinburgh (see also University), 69, 97, 104, 136, 154, 166, 236, 303

Edinburgh Medical Journal, 69

Editions, 66ff, 78ff, 91ff

Editorial cartoons, 255

Edmonton, 92, 272, 302

Edricson, Alleyne, 107

Education Act, 73, 152

Edward, Prince of Wales (Edward VII), 52, 57, 101, 123, 157, 182, 205

Edwardian Life and Leisure, 165

Edwardian period, 139, 283

Edwardians: The Remaking of British Society, 165

Edwards, Birdy, 30

Edwards, Owen Dudley, 70, 82, 104, 136, 312

"Egg-Spoon," 279

Egypt, 91, 100, 105, 176, 184, 239, 241, 315

Eighty-seventh Precinct, 206

Eire, 154

El Dieff, House of, 131

Elba, 105

Elcock, Howard, 90

Electricity, 108

Electronic Arts, 253

Electronic Holmes Companion, 94

Electronic text, 73, 93

Elementary, 238, 305, 310

Elementary Methods of SH, 59, 289

"Elementary, Dear Data," 309

Elementary, My Dear Watson, 289

"Eligible Bachelor," 247

Eliot, T.S., 308

Elizabeth, 241

Ellery Queen's Mystery Magazine, 202, 218, 263

Elliott, Douglas, 110, 284

Elliott, Philip, 271

Ellis, Robert, 280

Elm Grove, 100, 302

Elmer L. Andersen Library, 294

Elvis, 304

Email, 296

Empire, 139, 172ff, 185, 314, 319

Empress of India, 179

"Empty House," 26, 41, 44, 48, 49, 54, 74, 88, 114, 148, 169, 170, 220, 226, 246, 250, 252, 279

Encyclopaedia, 155

Encyclopaedia Britannica, 83

Encyclopaedia Sherlockiana, 10, 38, 44, 139, 157, 161, 192, 264, 290, 291

Encyclopedia of Mystery and Detection, 209

Encyclopedia Sherlockiana, 290

Endeavour, 60

Ender, Christoph, 94

Engels, Friedrich, 217

"Engineer's Thumb," 18, 169, 172

Engineering, 18, 139, 158, 169, 181

England, 107, 140

"England is England yet," 260

Englischer Hof, 300, 302

English Channel, 123, 176

English Literature in Transition, 313

English professors, 310ff, 315

Ennis, Robert S., 298

Entwistle, Peg, 224

Epilepsy, 98

"Epilogue of SH," 33

Erickson, Charlotte, 256

Ermyntrude, Dame, 107

Ernst, Bernard, 130

Esclaves de Paris, 199

Escott, 161

Espionage, 243

Essays in Satire, 278

Essays on Photography, 130

Essex, 140

Estate, 131–33

Estate (see Conan Doyle, Dame Jean; Doyle, Arthur Conan)

Estleman, Loren D., 216

Estuary, 142

"Ethics of Criticism," 116

Étude en Rouge, 91

European affairs, 174ff

Euston Road, 145

Euston station, 141, 149

Evan, R.J., 152

Evanovich, Janet, 206

Evans, Stewart P., 196

Evening News, 165

Evolution, 170, 182

Exchange rates, 155

"Exciting Christmas Eve," 109

Exeter, 228

Exhibition (1951), 278, 279, 295, 301

Exhibition of 1851, 187

Exit SH, 217

Exploits of Brigadier Gerard, 103, 106

Exploits of SH, 57, 75, 131, 134, 213

Explorers, 109

Exports, 140

Eye of the Crow, 219

Eyles, Allen, 289

Facebook, 257, 297

Facsimile texts, 80, 87

Fainting, 163

Fair use, fair dealing, 76

Fairchild, Morgan, 243

Fairies 138; photographs, 74, 130

Fairy Tale: A True Story, 130

Fall of the Amazing Zalindas, 254

Fall River, Massachusetts, 44, 194

Families, 162

Family and Residences of Arthur Conan Doyle, 98

Famous Five, 254

Famous Stories of Code and Cipher, 79

Famous Tales of SH, 78

Fanfare of Strumpets, 51, 163, 283

Far Side, 306

Farentino, Debrah, 243

Farewell tour, 258

Farmer, Philip José, 63

Farrell, John, 289

Faulkner, Alice, 224

Fear, 318

Federation of Master Builders, 301

Feldkirch, 99

Feldman, Lew David, 131

Feldman, Marty, 240

Felony, 188, 189

Feminism, 104; feminist criticism, 314

Femme Fatale, 52

Fer-de-Lance, 54, 203

Ferguson, Jacky, 247

Festival of Britain, 278, 295, 301

Festschrift, 282

Fiction of Sir Arthur Conan Doyle, 138

"Field Bazaar," 113, 211

Field hospital, 122

Fielding, Henry, 50, 198, 320

Figure, 162

Film, 232ff

Films of SH, 10, 233, 234
Final Adventures of SH, 80, 113
"Final Problem," 20, 23, 44, 45, 49, 224, 226, 233, 246, 319
Final Séance, 130
Finch, Jon, 247
Finding Sherlock's London, 142
"Finding Words for Spring," 226
Fingerprints, 27, 88, 196–97, 249
Finlay, Frank, 247
Finletter, Gretchen, 306
Fire from Heaven, 283
Firearms, 192
Fires Tegn, 92
Firm of Girdlestone, 102, 104
First editions, 293
First floor, 147
First National, 110
First War of Independence, 179
Fish, Robert L., 218
Fishing, 118
"Five Orange Pips," 17, 21, 27, 74, 79, 313
Five Orange Pips of Westchester, 261, 270
Five Sherlockian Walks, 142
Flag, 19
Flanagan, John Richard, 90
Flaubert, Gustave, 41
Fleet Street, 17
Flesherton, Ontario, 292
Fletcher, George, 262
Flying Squad, 192
Fog, 319
Foley, Charles, 98, 133, 137
Foley, Mary (*see* Doyle)
Foley, Nelson, 98
Following Your Mail Closely, 310
Folsom, Henry T., 286
Football, 116
Footnotes, 310
Footprints, 60, 196, 199
For the Sake of the Game, 141
Forbes, Mary, 236
Fordham University Press, 310
Foreign Secretary, 151, 186
Forensic science, 60, 172, 196–97
Forgiveness, 207
Forth Bridge, 169
Foster, Barry, 232
"Foulkes Rath," 213
Four SH Plays, 282; *Four More*, 282
Fox Kids, 245
Fox, Bernard, 242
Fox, Kate and

Margaret, 127
France and French, 28, 39, 44, 57, 91, 105, 106, 108, 123, 162, 166, 175, 176, 179, 182, 190, 197, 200, 205, 284
Franchise Affair, 203
Francis, Clive, 246
Francis, Dick, 206
Francis, Raymond, 243
Francis, Tom, 268
Franco-British Exhibition, 144
Franco-Midland Hardware Company, 261, 280
Franconia, Virginia, 94
Franco-Prussian War, 176
Frank Joseph, Emperor, 177
Frank Leslie's, 75
Frankland, old, 189
Freddy the Detective, 309, 316
Frederick of Prussia, 176
Fredericton, 227
Freedom, 151
Freeman, R. Austin, 60, 201
French, Samuel, 221, 224
Freud, Sigmund, 183, 215, 240, 265; Freudian analysis, 18, 314
Frewer, Matt, 243
Frick, Willis G., 295
Friedman, Kinky, 206
Friends of Gillette Castle, 301
Friends of the SH Collections, 294
Friendship (*see* Watson)
Friston, D.H., 85
Frohman, Charles, 222
Frost, Mark, 138
Fry, Herbert, 143
Fry, Stephen, 295
Fu Manchu, 51, 75, 217
Furies, 33
Further Adventures of SH, 232
Futrelle, Jacques, 201

G. Washington Coffee, 230
Gabel, Martin, 226
Gaboriau, Emile, 199, 200
Gainsborough, Thomas, 50
Galactic SH, 93
Galapagos Islands, 182
Galerstein, David, 289
Game Is Afoot, 141, 219
Game, Sherlockian (*see also* Holmes,

reality), 262, 286, 310
Game's Afoot, 282
Games, 252–53; computer, 201, 253
Garden City Publishing, 77
Gardner, Erle Stanley, 202
Gardner, John, 51, 194, 220
Garfield, 305
Garrick Theatre, 222
Garrick-Steele, Rodger, 25
Garrideb, Nathan, 36, 158, 170
Gaslight Gala, 274–75
Gaslight Publications, 292
Gasogene, 259, 261
Gasogene Books, 82, 292
Gaudy Night, 202
Gazette (Wolfe Pack), 203
Gebbia, Alessandro, 227
General Instruction for the Police, 192
General Motors, 261
Genetics, 170
Genre fiction, 311
Gentlemen, 156
Geology, 170
George V, 279
George Yard Buildings, 195
Georgia, 132; *Georgia Review*, 208
Georgian houses, 145
Gerard, Brigadier, 102, 106
Germany and German, 31, 33, 91, 92, 116, 121, 123, 125, 154, 162, 169, 171, 175, 176, 178, 179, 233, 238, 265, 284
Getsuyo-shobo, 92
Ghana, 172
Ghost in the Invisible Bikini, 238
Ghosts, 35, 127
Giant rat, 57, 178, 219
Gibson, Charles Dana, 75
Gibson, John Michael, 10, 13, 15, 31, 32, 34, 66, 72, 85, 102, 103, 105, 112, 115, 137, 281, 313
Gibson, Maria, 36
Gibson, Neil, 64, 158, 174, 247
Gielgud, John, 228, 229, 241
Gilbert, A., 90
Gilbert, William Schwenck, 158, 183, 215, 269, 279
Gilchrist, 117
Gilchrist, Marion, 121
Gill, Victoria, 11, 294
Gillette Castle, 225, 301

Gillette, William, 43, 90, 222ff, 229, 233, 258, 259, 266, 298, 301; memorial luncheon, 268, 274
Giovanni, Paul, 227
Gladstone, William Ewart, 152, 153, 175, 181, 183, 185, 217
Glamour, 233
Glands, 171
Glasgow, 121, 140, 194
Glass Village, 202
Globe, 165
Globe and Mail, 307
Globe Theatre, 225
"Gloria Scott," 21, 39, 81, 157, 190
Gloucestershire, 141
God, 23, 62, 129, 207, 318
God and SH, 186, 289
God Save the Queen, 251
Godfrey, Renee, 236
Godwin, William, 198
Goethe, 41
"Gold Bug," 199
Gold Coast, 172
"Gold Hunter," 213
Golden Jubilee, 187
"Golden Pince-Nez," 28, 57, 83, 89, 156, 158, 177, 191, 208, 247
Goldfarb, Clifford S., 106, 272
Goldscheider, Gaby, 138
Golf, 101, 119
Golmes, 92
Gomez, Thomas, 235
Good Morning, Irene, 52
Good Night, Mr. Holmes, 52, 220
Good Old Index, 10, 38
Gooden, George, 222
Goodman, Charles S., 262
Goodrich, William, 10, 38, 264, 288
Goodwin, Archie, 203
Gordon, Charles George, 58, 183
Gordon, Mary, 237
Gordon, Richard, 230
Gore-Booth, Paul, 276, 279
Gothic, 19, 27, 32
Governesses, 158, 161–62, 319
Government, 53, 150
Government of Ireland Act, 154
Governor-General, 179
Gowers, Kathy, 249, 251
Gowers, Patrick, 249, 250
Grace, William Gilbert, 117, 184, 217

Grafton, Sue, 206
Graham, Ron, 270
Gramophone, 108
Granada Television, 228, 245ff, 248, 249; studios, 301
Grand Duke, 183
Grand Old Man, 152, 183
Grand Union Canal, 144
Grandes horizontales, 51, 64, 163, 283
Granger, Stewart, 242
Grant, Alan, 203
Graphic novels, 256
Gravesend Books, 292
Gray, Charles, 246, 247
Gray, Dorian, 187
Great Alkali Plainsmen, 269
Great Boer War, 122
Great Britain, 181
Great Detective, 211, 226
Great Eastern, 181
Great Game, 175
Great Hiatus, 44, 81, 169, 220
"Great Keinplatz Experiment," 109
Great Mouse Detective, 255
Great Shadow (Doyle), 102, 106
Great Shadow (Goldfarb), 106
Great Training Mystery, 310
Great Western Railway, 181
Great Wyrley, 120
"Greek Interpreter," 23, 32, 53, 244, 246, 254, 304
Green Flag, 103, 105
Green Gables, 299
Green peas, 241
Green, Anna Katherine, 200
Green, Denis, 231
Green, Joseph, 222
Green, Maureen, 272
Green, Richard Lancelyn, 10, 15, 31, 32, 34, 66, 69, 72, 82, 85, 102, 103, 105, 112, 113, 115, 133, 137, 222, 278, 280–81, 295, 313
Green, Roger Lancelyn, 280
Greenberg, Martin H., 109, 219
Greene, Hugh, 200
Greene, Richard, 235
Greenland, 119
Greenwood, Beth, 216
Gregg shorthand, 93
Gregory, Inspector, 193
Gregson, Tobias, 193
Griffith, D.W., 233

Griffiths, Frances, 130
Grillparzer Sittenpolizei Verein, 258
Gringras, Samuel, 292
Grissons, 119
Grand Duke, 183
Grand Old Man, 152, 183
Grudeff, Marian, 226
Gruner, Baron, 34, 247, 249
"Guards Came Through," 103
Guinea, 155
"Gully of Bluemansdyke," 102
Gunn, Margaret and R. Ivar, 279
Gutenberg, 94
Guy, Patricia, 290
Gwillim, David, 246

Haakon VII, 178
Habitual criminal, 192
Haddon, Mark, 220
Hadlyme, Connecticut, 225, 301
Hafiz, 41
Haggard, H. Rider, 101, 167
Hagman, Larry, 242
Haining, Peter, 113, 242, 289
Halbach, Helen G., 252
Half a man, half a boy, 110
Half-crown, 155
Halifax, 173, 272
Hall, Charles, 228, 304
Hall, John, 218, 286, 290
Hall, Robert Lee, 217
Hall, Trevor S., 217
Hall, William S., 259, 260, 261
Hallam, John, 247
Hallamshire, 141, 193
Hamer, Gerald, 236
Hamilton, Ontario, 270
Hammer Film Productions, 238
Hammer, David, 63, 141, 289, 292
Hammett, Dashiell, 201, 203
Hammond, Roger, 246
Hammond, Roland, 261
Hampshire, 82, 101, 140
Hampstead, 144
Hanbury Street, 195
Handwriting (*see also* Doyle, Watson), 22
Hanging, 188, 190
Hangover, 45
Hansen, 253
Hanshew, Thomas W., 201
Hansom cabs, 149,

260, 319
Hansom, Joseph Aloysius, 149
Hansoms of John Clayton, 288
Hapgood, Norman, 75
Hard-boiled, 203
Harden, John Vincent, 57
Hardin, John Wesley, 57
Hardwick, Michael, 135, 160, 229, 244, 281–82
Hardwick, Mollie, 135, 160, 244, 282
Hardwicke, Cedric, 250
Hardwicke, Edward, 93, 130, 228, 244, 248, 250
Hardy, Robert, 93, 247
Hardy, Thomas, 165, 167
Harker, Horace, 246
Harper & Brothers, 16, 20, 96
Harper's Weekly, 20
Harrington, Hugh, 10
Harris, Kenneth, 250
Harrison, Benjamin, 174
Harrison, Michael, 45, 51, 67, 146, 163, 220, 282–83, 289
Harrow, 144
Hart, Douglas C., 233
Harte, Bret, 211
Hartford, Connecticut, 225
Harvard College and University, 70, 75, 184, 267, 295
Harwood, Nina, 132
Haslemere Estates, 148
Hastings, Captain, 204
Hatherley, Victor, 18, 169
Hats (*see also* Deerstalker), 163
Hatton, Rondo, 236
Hawkins, Jim, 297
Hawkins, Louise (*see* Doyle)
Hawkshaw the Detective, 255
Haycraft, Howard, 208, 268
Hayden, Mrs., 127
Haydn's Head, 256
HBO, 224
Headline Review, 80
Heard, H.F., 212
Hearst, William Randolph, 75
Hearst's, 35, 36, 75, 88
Heart failure, 171
Hebrew, 92
Hebrews (*see also* Jews), 188
Hector, Louis, 242
Heinlein, Robert A., 53, 309

Helling, Cornelis, 285

Hench, Philip S., 268, 294

Henderson, Edmund, 193

Hendon, 109

Henriksen, A.D., 284

Henry VIII, 49, 168

Henry, Frank, 259

Henry, Ian, 250

Henry, O., 90, 212

Henry, Sir Edward, 197

Heraldry, 264

Herbert, Holmes, 236

Herbert, Paul D., 222

Heredity, 100, 169

Herefordshire, 25, 141

Heritage Club, 80

Hero, 62, 317

"Hero as Woman," 104

Hero, 62

Herschel, William, 197

Herzegovina, 175

Herzog, Evelyn, 268, 272, 273

Heston, Charlton, 228

Hewitt, Martin, 201

Hibernians, Ancient Order, 30

Higashiyama, Akane, 283

Higgins, Anthony, 243

High Holborn, 145

Higham, Charles, 105, 109, 135

Higher criticism, 277

Highgate Miracle, 213

Highland, New York, 268

Highlands, 69

Hilda Wade, 180

Hillerman, John, 243

Hillerman, Tony, 206

Hindhead, Surrey, 100, 300

Hinds, Ciaran, 247

Hines, Stephen, 121

Hirayama, Yuichi, 283

His Last Bow, 31, 75, 82, 90

"His Last Bow," 33, 39, 55, 75, 81, 88, 154, 156, 174, 229, 235, 257, 311

Historical novels, 106ff

Historicist criticism, 314

History of Spiritualism, 129

History Series, 267

History, Sherlockian, 287

Hitler, Adolf, 63, 217

HMS Pinafore, 158, 183

Hobbes, Halliwell, 236

Hobbs, Carleton, 224, 228, 229, 232, 282

Hobbs, Don, 93

Hoboken, 258

Hodder School, 99

Hodge, Patricia, 246

Hodgson, John A., 314

Hoehling, Mary, 135

Hoey, Dennis, 237

Hohl, Arthur, 236

Holborn Viaduct, 145

Holden, Stanley, 226

Holder, Alexander, 160

Holdernesse, Duke of, 27, 156, 157, 246

Holdhurst, Lord, 23, 151

Holiday Inn, 301

Holiday, Gilbert, 90

Holland Park Avenue, 145

Holland (see Netherlands)

Holloway, 190

Hollyer, Cameron, 11, 74, 272, 294

Hollywood, 230, 234, 265, 301

Holmes & Watson Country, 141

Holmes and Watson, 45

Holmes and Watson Ltd., 302

Holmes and Watson Report, 288

Holmes and Watson: A Miscellany, 278

Holmes and Watson: A New Chronology, 286

Holmes, Justin, 239–40

Holmes, Mycroft, 23, 32, 39, 53, 217, 220, 239, 243, 246, 247, 277, 304, 318

Holmes, Oliver Wendell, Jr., 184

Holmes, Oliver Wendell, Sr., 68, 184

Holmes, Sherlock, passim

— ancestors, 39

— and women, 28, 37, 43, 63, 239, 315, 318

— artist, 313

— as symbol, 39

— attitude to police, 188, 193, 204–05

— biography, 38, 44, 81, 82, 219, 263, 286

— birth and birthday, 45, 258, 273

— boxer, 119

— chemical work, 41, 44, 58, 86, 89, 169, 196

— children, 203

— death, 44, 45, 62, 217

— drugs, 51, 215, 305–06

— eating and drinking, 305

— friendship, (see under Watson)

— gender, 42

— image, 304ff

— in America, 45

— invention, 200

— knowledge, 40; of law, 189

— left-handed, 311

— letters to, 46

— limits, 14, 40

— meets Watson, 39

— methods, 59, 69

— music, 40

— name, 184, 211, 303

— physical, 217

— profession, 154

— reality, 40, 45, 102, 262, 263, 280, 286, 310

— retirement, 33, 36, 39, 45

— smoking, 58

— social attitudes, 65, 208

— teeth, 262

— traits, 42

— university, 21, 39

— voice, 229

Holmes, Sherman, 242

Holmes, Sherrinford, 45, 68, 71

Holmes, Sigi, 240

Holmes: Haydn's Head, 256

Holmesian.net, 297

Holmesians, 257, 277

Hologram, 309

Holroyd, James Edward, 279

Home counties, 140

Home Office, 121, 197; Home Secretary, 151, 191; HOLMES, 298

Home Rule, 124, 125, 153–54, 183, 185

Homes, Schlock, 218

Homosexuality, 17, 41, 125, 187, 194, 205, 239, 242, 254

Honorary Secretaries, 280

Honour Among Punks, 256

Hoover, J. Edgar, 203

Hope, Lady Hilda Trelawney, 29, 246

Horace, 41

Horgan, Patrick, 93

Hornung, Ernest W., 74, 97, 184, 201

Horror, 198, 238

"Horror of the Heights," 109

Horse-racing, 118, 266, 276

Hoskins, Bob, 111

Hotel Duane, 258, 259

Hottentot, 170

Houdini and Conan Doyle, 130

Houdini, Harry, 129–30, 184

Houghton Library, 267, 295

Hound of the Baskervilles, 24ff,

37, 56, 64, 65, 67, 70, 123, 127, 138, 151, 156, 165, 170, 189, 198, 293, 306, 307, 312, 313, 315

— stage and screen, 226, 229, 231, 232, 233, 235, 238, 241, 242, 243, 247, 256

"Hound of the Basketballs," 255

Hounds of the Baskerville [sic], 261

Hounds of the Internet, 296

Hounsfield, Edith, 88

House of Commons, 150, 151, 181, 186

House of Fear, 236

House of Lords, 150, 157, 181, 186

House of Temperley, 119

House of the Baskervilles, 25

Household Finance, 230

Housekeeper, 54

Housemaid, 161

Houses, 145

Houston, Donald, 239

Hove, Sussex, 133

"How Watson Learned the Trick," 114, 211

Howard, Alan, 246

Howard, Ronald, 131, 132, 244–45

Howlett, Alfreda and Anthony, 280, 300

Hudson, Mrs., 54, 63, 160, 220, 237, 243, 262, 268

Huggins, Jeremy, 245

Hugirashi, Masamichi, 283

Hugo, Victor, 199

Hugo's Companions, 270

Huguenots, 108

Human Personality and Its Survival, 127

Humanities Research Center, 295

Hume, Fergus, 200

Hund von Baskerville, 92

Hungary, 177

Hunnicutt, Gayle, 245

Hunter, Evan, 206

Hunter, Kathryn Montgomery, 60

Hunter, Violet, 19, 27, 43, 63, 160, 246

Hunting the Dartmoor Legend, 24

Huret, Boulevard assassin, 56

Hurlstone Manor, 21, 160

Huston, John, 242

Hutchinson, George, 85

Hyde Park, 145

Hyde, Jonathan, 247

Hydesville, New York, 127

Hydrocarbon, 41

Hypnotism, 105, 109, 215

Hysteria, 183

I Remember the Date Very Well, 286

I, SH, 45, 220, 283

Ian Henry Publications, 250

Ichthyosis, 171

Icom Simulations, 253

Idler, 101, 180, 185

Idylls of the King, 186

Illinois, 270, 288

Illustrated London News, 166

Illustrations, 26, 73, 84ff

"Illustrious Client," 34, 75, 82, 156, 157, 172, 183, 208, 247, 249

Illustrious Client's Case-Book, 263

Illustrious Clients of Indianapolis, 270

Imperial British East Africa Company, 172

Imperialism, 125, 314

Importance of Being Earnest, 187

Impossible, eliminating, 62

In and Out of Character, 234, 238

In Bed with SH, 44, 52, 65, 272, 289

"In Memoriam," 186

"In Memoriam SH," 79

In re: SH, 214

In the Footsteps of Birdy Edwards, 30

In the Footsteps of SH, 146, 282

Incident at Victoria Falls, 243

Income tax, 115, 150, 304

Incredible Murder of Cardinal Tosca, 227

Incredible Schlock Homes, 218

Incredible Umbrella, 216

Independent Mystery Booksellers Association, 292

Index to the Strand Magazine, 74

India, 18, 27, 48, 53, 54, 104, 140, 160, 175, 178, 179–80, 197

— Army, 179

— Mutiny, 15, 22, 179

— India Office, 172, 179

Indiana, 265; University, 70, 295

Indianapolis, 80, 263, 267, 270, 292

Induction, 61

Infamous Professor, 226

Infantry, 123

Inference, 60

Inflation, 155

Influenza, 131

Inner Circle, 149

"Inner Room," 112

Innes, Michael, 201, 202

Innocence of Father Brown, 202

Insight Engineering, 94

Insurance money, 68

Intellectual property (see also Copyright), 77

Intelligence, 317

Interest, 155

International Bibliography, 313

International Series, 267, 283

International SH, 66, 138, 264, 290

International Spiritualist Congress, 129

Internet, 11, 93, 94, 289, 295–97

Interviews and Recollections, 137

Introduction to Bibliography, 72

Inverness cape, 84, 298

Investiture, 267, 273, 274, 316

iPod, 93

Iraldi, James C., 294

Ireland and Irish, 30, 33, 97, 124, 125, 140, 153, 160, 168, 183, 187, 315

— Irish-American, 174

— Church Act, 153

— Crown Jewels, 194

— Free State, 154

— Question, 153–54

Irene at Large, 52

Irene's Last Waltz, 52

Iroquois, 108

Irregular Chronology, 286

Irregular Crises of the Late 'Forties, 80, 267

Irregular Guide, 12, 38, 263

Irregular Memories of the 'Thirties, 258

Irregulars (see also Baker Street Irregulars), 56

Irving, Henry, 101, 106, 184

"Is Disease a Reversion?," 170

Islam, 44, 175, 177, 184, 315

Isle of Wight, 140

Isonomy, 79

It's a Mystery, Charlie Brown, 256

Italy and Italians, 32,

92, 160, 175, 176, 227, 233; restaurant, 216

ITV network, 245

"J. Habakuk Jephson's Statement," 105

Jack the Ripper, 45, 120, 159, 163, 194–96, 214, 215, 239, 241

Jack the Ripper, the Definitive History, 196

Jack the Ripper: A Bibliography, 196

Jack the Ripper: Scotland Yard Investigates, 196

Jackson, 48

Jackson, Steven, 197

Jaffe, Audrey, 313

Jaffe, Jacqueline A., 136

James II, 108

James Pepper Rare Books, 292

James, Henry, 75

James, P.D., 198, 201, 203

Janda, Anita, 219

Jane Annie, 112, 181

Jann, Rosemary, 314

Japan, Japanese, 92, 178, 255, 283–84, 301; art, 293

Japan and SH, 283

Japan SH Club, 283, 284

"Japanned Box," 108

Jeffers, H. Paul, 193

Jefferson, Paris, 247

Jeffries, James J., 119

Jensen, Jens Byskov, 284

Jeremy Brett and David Burke, 250

Jerome, Jerome K., 101, 167, 180, 185

Jersey Lily, 52, 183

Jervis, Christopher, 204

Jessel, Raymond, 226

Jesuits, 99, 126

Jesus of Nazareth, 62, 128, 188

Jewell, Donald G., 118

Jews (see also Hebrew, Hebrews), 121, 160, 168, 195

Jezail bullet, 48

Jim Thorpe, Pennsylvania, 30

John, King, 150

Johns Hopkins University, 119

Johnson, Jack, 119

Johnson, Malcolm, 259

Johnson, Roger, 10, 228, 232, 235, 280, 282, 284, 287

Johnson, Samuel, 47, 142, 278

Johnson, Timothy J., 291, 294

Johnston, David, 231

"Jolly Hangman," 244
Jolnes, Shamrock, 211
Jones, Athelney, 193
Jones, Elwyn, 196
Jones, Kelvin I., 126, 289, 312
Jones, Norman, 246
Jones, Philip K., 222
Journal of Popular Culture, 203
Journal of the Arthur Conan Doyle Society, 95
Jubilee, 185, 187
Jude the Obscure, 167
Judges' Rules, 41, 191
Judiciary, 191
Juliet, 63
Jungle Book, 185
Jupiter, 53
Jurassic Park, 111
Jury, 47, 188
Justice, 188, 206, 319
Justice of the Peace, 190
Juwes, 195

Kabatchnik, Amnon, 228
Kahn, Madeline, 240
Kandahar, 48
Kansas City, 260, 269
Karloff, Boris, 238
Karlson, Katherine, 11, 290
Karuizawa Town, 284, 301
Kay, Charles, 247
Kaye, Marvin, 216, 219
Keating, H.R.F., 289
Keaton, Buster, 210
Keddie, James, Jr., 263
Keddie, James, Sr., 261, 262
Keefauver, Brad, 59, 62, 288, 289, 296
Kehoe, Jack, 30
Keller, Arthur, 47, 90
Kelley, Gordon E., 233
Kelly, Alexander, 196
Kelly, Mary Jeannette, 195
Kelmscott Press, 185
Kemp, Jeremy, 246
Kendrick, Stephen, 219
Kennedy, Bruce, 30
Kensington, 144, 145; Gardens, High Street, 145
Kent, 140, 193
Kent State University, 296
Kenya, 172
Kestner, Joseph A., 314, 315
Key, Jack D., 104, 111, 141, 171
Keys, 139
Khalifa, 184
Khartoum, 44, 184
King (*see also* Edward VII), 62, 150
King James Bible, 168
King Kong, 111
King, John B., 220

King, Joseph A. Cutshall, 314
King, Laurie R., 44, 180, 205, 206
King's Cross station, 141, 149
Kingsley, Ben, 241
Kinsprits, 258
Kipling, Rudyard, 74, 75, 90, 101, 119, 137, 140, 167, 175, 185
Kitchener, Horatio Lord, 122
Kitty Foyle, 258
Klein, Isadora, 161, 247
Klinefelter, Walter, 84, 85, 88, 90
Klinger, Leslie S., 82, 113, 222, 268, 286
Knees, 59
Knight errant, 317
Knighthood, 101, 123, 157
Knox, Ronald Arbuthnot, 204, 277–78
Kobayashi, Tsukasa, 142, 283
Koch, Robert, 171
Koktzwinkle, William, 222
Kolkata, 180
Kombs, Sherlaw, 211
Kosleck, Martin, 236
Kosminski, 195
Krejci-Graf, Karl, 156
Kroll, Baron Ennesfred, 214
Ku Klux Klan, 17

La Cour, Tage, 284
Labour Party, 152
Lachtman, Howard, 137
Ladies, Ladies, 290
Lady, Ladies, 101, 156; Gracious Lady, 187
"Lady Carfax," 33
"Lady Frances Carfax," 32, 56, 75, 161, 217, 226, 247
Lady X, 28
Ladysmith, 122
Laffont, Robert, 91
Lagergaard, Mia Stampe, 284
Laing, Gerald Ogilvie, 301
Laing, Robin, 138
Lake Havasu City, 243
Lamarckian transmission, 100
Lambert, Anne Louise, 246
Lambeth, 144
Lament for a Murder, 202
Lamond, John, 135
Lancashire, 99, 141
Lancelyn Green (*see* Green)
Lancet, 159
Land Act, 153

Land of Mist, 103, 110
Landi, Marla, 238
Landlady, 54, 158
Lane, Lois, 318
Lang, Matthew, 227
Langella, Frank, 224, 227
Langtry, Lillie, 52, 183, 243
Larrabee, James, 224
Larson, Gary, 306
Last Bookman, 261
Last Galley, 103, 105, 106
Last SH Story, 217
"Last Vampyre," 247
Later Adventures, 80
Latin, 285
Latin America, 32
Latter-Day Saints, 13
"Laughing Mummy," 244
Lauriston Garden of Verses, 252
Lauritzen, Henry, 284
Lauterbach, Charles E., 12, 252, 287
Law, British, 41, 189ff
Law, Jude, 241
Leacock, Stephen, 211, 212, 218
Leadenhall Street, 145
League of Extraordinary Gentlemen, 256
Learning, Walter, 227
Leavenworth Case, 200
Leavitt, Robert Keith, 258, 259, 262
Leblanc, Maurice, 201, 211, 212
Leckie, Jean (*see* Conan Doyle)
Leckie, Malcolm, 123
Lecoq, Monsieur 199
Lee, Christopher, 93, 238, 239, 243
Lee, Manfred B., 202, 263
Leech, red, 56, 84
Leeds Mercury, 165
Legacy Interactive, 253
Legion of Honour, 57
Leicestershire, 141
Lellenberg, Jon L., 77, 80, 98, 133, 134, 136, 137, 211, 212, 219, 258, 260, 265, 267, 268, 288, 313
Lemon tree, 305
Lennoxville, Québec, 270
Leo XIII, Pope, 57, 177
Leopold II, 125, 178
Leprosy, 171
Lesbian (*see* Homosexuality)
Leslie, Frank, 75
Lestrade, Inspector G., 14, 17, 193, 196, 220, 237, 249
Lestrade, Sholto, 220
"Letters," 226

Letters to SH, 46, 63
Letters to the Press, 115
Lewtrenchard, 180
Liberal Party, 124, 152, 153, 154, 181, 182, 183
Liberal Unionism, 124, 154
Liberty, 35, 37, 75, 76, 88
Libraries, 270, 272, 293–95, 301
Library of Congress, 97, 295
LibriVox, 93
Licensing hours, 152
Liddell, Alice, 181
Liebow, Ely M., 69, 99, 311
Life and Death of Jonathan Wild, 50
Life and Times of SH, 289
Life Insurance Conspiracy, 310
Life of Sir Arthur Conan Doyle, 98, 122, 134
"Lifting the Curse of Basil," 245
Light, 128
Light, speed, 169
Lilly Library, 295
Limbo, 320
Limited Editions Club, 79, 80, 90
Lincolnshire, 141
Lindsey, Christopher, 172, 290
Linsenmeyer, John, 262
"Lion's Mane," 36, 40, 43, 70, 109, 170, 267
Lippincott, J.B., Co., 13, 14, 72
Lippincott's Magazine, 14, 15
Liquor, 152
List of Seven, 138
Lister, Lord, 69
Listserv, 296
Literary agent, 46, 72, 95, 116, 263, 289
"Literary Craft of the Hound," 312
Literary Estate, 78
Literary Guild, 78, 79
Literary scholarship, 258, 285, 310ff
Literature, 74, 307–09; Victorian, 167–68, 311
"Lost Special," 114
Little Library, 92
Little Lulu, 255
Little Purlington, 141, 169
Little, Brown, 212
Livanov, Vasily, 245
LiveJournal, 297
Liverpool, 140, 141
Liverpool Street station, 141, 149
Llewellyn, Roger, 228
Lloyd George, David, 154

Lloyd, John, 196
Local government, 151
Locations of cases, 141
Loch Ness monster, 239
Locked-room mystery, 23, 198
Locksley Hall, 186
Lodge, Oliver, 101, 129
Logan, Crawford, 231
Logic, 60, 308
London, 142ff, 172 and passim
— Bridge, 144, 243; station, 141
— City of (*see* City)
— County Council, 151
— County cricket, 117
— Lord Mayor, 151
— lost civilization, 139
— School of Economics, 180
— Scottish Border Counties Association, 116
— Underground Limited, 149
— *see also* SH Society
London of SH, 282
London: Illustrated, 143
"Londonderry Air," 251
Lone Ranger, 317, 318
"Long Evening with Holmes," 252, 269
Long Island, 174, 268, 303; cave mystery, 82
"Long Road from Maiwand," 262
Long Stories, 80, 90
Looking Over Sir Arthur's Shoulder, 102
Lord, 157
Lord Mayor, 151
Lord, Marjorie, 236
Lord's, 117
Lord-Lieutenant, 151
Lords, House of, 150, 157, 181, 186
Loring, Sir Nigel, 107, 134
Lorraine, 176
Los Angeles, 82, 214, 266, 268
Lost Cases of SH, 253
Lost Diaries, 211
"Lost Special," 114
Lost World (Crichton), 111
Lost World (Doyle), 103, **109–11**
Lost Worlds in Time, Space and Medicine, 111
"Lot No. 249," 126
Louis of Bavaria, 52
Louis XIV, 108
Louisville, 228
Louvre, 194, 220
Lovell, Leigh, 230

Lovesey, Peter, 205
Lucens, 131
Lucerne, 300
Lucknow, 179
Luke, Charles, 203
Lupin, Arsène, 201, 211, 253
Lupino, Ida, 235
Lutz, Robert, 92
Lycett, Andrew, 137
Lyceum Theatre, 15, 184, 224
Lyons, Laura, 64

Ma'am, the, 98, 134
Macaulay, Lord, 116
Macauley, Charles Raymond, 26, 90
"Macavity," 308
MacDonald, Inspector Alec, 50
MacDonald, Ramsay, 101
MacDonell, Archie, 278
Machen, Wendy, 24
Macintosh computer, 307
Macintyre, Ben, 50
Mack, Tracy, 254
MacKenzie, Stanley, 279
Mackler, Allen, 58, 294, 301
MacLachlan, Don, 58
Macmillan, 262
Macmillan, Kenneth, 226
Macnee, Patrick, 242, 243
Macpherson, Jay, 312
Macy, George, 80
Mad, 255
Madame Tussaud's, 146, 147
"Maddened by Mystery," 211
Madison Avenue, 258
Madonna, 304
Madras, 180
Mafeking, 122
Mafia, 32
Magazines, 72
Mager, Gus, 255
Magico Magazine, 13, 292
Magnifying lens, 59, 84, 298, 304
Mahanoy City, Pennsylvania, 30
Mahdi, 184
Maida Vale, 145
"Maiden Tribute of Modern Babylon," 186
Maigret, Inspector, 205
Maison Rouge, 300
Maiwand, Battle of, 48, 262
Making of SH, 289
Mallard Press, 80
Malone, Edward, 109
Maltese Falcon, 203
Mammoth Book of New SH Adventures, 219

Man Booker Prize, 121
"Man from Archangel," 105
Man in the street, 135
Man Who Hated SH, 135
Man Who Was SH, 135, 282
"Man Who Was Wanted," 212–13
"Man with the Twisted Lip," 18, 92, 139, 144, 156, 162, 246, 313
"Man with the Watches," 114
Manchester, 73, 140, 141, 245, 301
Mander, Miles, 236
Manhattan Club, 275
Manic depression, 250
Manning, Henry Edward, Cardinal, 180
Mantis, Inspector, 222
Manual of the Operations of Surgery, 69
Manuscript Series, 267
Manuscripts, 25, 30, 70ff, 281, 293
Maps, 142, 264
Maracot Deep, 103, 111
Marathon, 116
Marble Arch, 146, 190
Marbot, Jean Baptiste de, 106
Marconi, Guglielmo, 63
Marcus, Stephen, 64
Marfan's syndrome, 171
Margetson, Arthur, 236
Marilyn, 304
Mark of the Beast, 217
Mark of Zorro, 238
Marlborough, Duke of, 182
Marlowe, Philip, 203
Marple, Jane, 202
Marque des Quatre, 91
Marriage (*see also* Divorce), 189
"Marriage of the Brigadier," 106
"Married Man," 226
Marry or murder him, 222
Marsh, Ngaio, 202
Martha, 55
Martha Hudson Breakfast, 274
Martinelli, Kate, 205
Marx, Harpo, 210
Marx, Karl, 217; Marxist criticism, 314
Mary Jane, 161
Mary, Queen, 154
Marylebone, 145, 146, 278, 294–95; Cricket Club, 68; Library, 294–95

INDEX

Marylebone Road, 143, 147, 148, 294
Masculinity, 65, 105, 314, 315
Masks of Death, 242
Mason, Gary, 193
Mason, James, 240
Mason, Perry, 202
Masongill, Yorkshire, 99
Masons, 195, 241
"Masque of the Red Death," 110
Massachusetts, 264
Massey, Daniel, 247
Massey, Raymond, 234
"Master Blackmailer," 247
Master Bootmaker, 272
Master's Class of Philadelphia, 276, 289
Masterpieces of Mystery and Detection, 79
Masterpieces of SH, 78
Matchbooks, 303
Mathematics, 20, 50, 60, 181
Mather, Aubrey, 236
Mauch Chunk, Pennsylvania, 30
Maugham, W. Somerset, 74, 167
Mauser rifles, 122
Mauve, 169
Mayfair, 145
Mayfair, 85
Mayhew, Henry, 313
Mayo Clinic, 294
"Mazarin Stone," 35, 55, 58, 109, 114, 151, 221, 247
McAdams, Rachel, 242
McAllister, Pam, 290
McBain, Ed, 205, 206
McCauley, Peter, 111
McCay, Bill, 254
McCearney, James, 136
McClure, Phillips & Co., 25, 26
McClure's, 20
McCord, James, 68
McCormick, Robert, 76
McDiarmid, E.W., 313
McFarlane, John Hector, 246
McGaw, Lisa, 268
McGill University, 312
McGill-Queen's University Press, 313
McGraw-Hill, 291
McKerrow, Ronald B., 72
McKinley, William, 174
McKnight and Jordan, 230
McMahon, Katherine, 259, 268
McMahon, Mary, 294

McNabb, Janice, 25, 67
McParlan, James, 30
McPherson, Fitzroy, 36
Mdivani, Nina, 132
Mecca, 44, 177, 194
Medical Casebook of Doctor Arthur Conan Doyle, 104, 171
Medicine (*see also* Doyle, medical work), 171–72
Mediums, 127, 184
Meiji era, 284
Meiringen, Switzerland, 299–300, 301
Meiser, Edith, 57, 230, 268
Melas, 53
Melbourne, 200
Melodrama, 224
Memoirs of SH, 19ff, 31, 82
Memoirs of Solar Pons, 214
Memorial Edition, 79, 230
Memories and Adventures, 31, 69, 116, 118, 134, 233
Mendel's Law, 169
Menes, Bonnie, 207
Meredith, George, 101, 167
Merivale, Inspector, 193
Merriman, Charles O., 142
Merrison, Clive, 231–32
Metcalfe, Percy, 244
Methodism, 168
Metropolitan Line, 146
Metropolitan Police, 191–92, 196; Act 192; District 142
Metropolitan Railway, 143, 149
Metropolitan Tabernacle, 186
Metropolitan Toronto Reference Library (*see* Toronto)
Meunier, Oscar, 304
Meyer, Karl E., 317, 318
Meyer, Nicholas, 51, 183, 214–15, 216, 217, 218, 240, 265, 307
Meyers, Mr., 271
Mezon, Jim, 224
MGM Records, 227
Micah Clarke, 102, 107
Michaels, Norman, 10, 233, 234, 235, 238, 239
Michell, Humfrey, 270
Michell, W.R., 280
Mickey Mouse, 255
Microscope, 196
Middle Circle, 149

Middle class, 158
Middle Earth, 319
Middlemass, Frank, 246
Middlesex, 140, 151
Midlands, 141, 181
Mikado, 183
Milan, 92
Miller, Russell, 137
Millett, Larry, 219
Millhone, Kinsey, 206
Mills, Charles A., 289
Mills, John, 242
Millward, Charles, 221
Milos, Andre, 132
Milverton (*see* Charles Augustus)
Milwaukee, 91
Minneapolis, 58, 267, 268, 270, 294, 296, 302
Minnesota, 98, 219
Minstead, 101, 131, 300
Miracle Plays, 67
Mirror of the Century, 73
Misadventures of SH, 16, 212, 263
Misdemeanour, 189
Miserables, 199
"Missing Rembrandts," 234
'Missing Three-Quarter," 29, 84, 117
Missions, 67
Mister (*see* Mr.)
Mitchell, Gladys, 222, 308
Mitchell, Sally, 165
Mitchelson, Austin, 217
Mitre Square, 195
Miurrai, 92
"Modern Belgian Masters," 313
Modern Languages Association, 313
Molding the Image, 225
Mollie Maguires, 30, 67, 207
Molly Maguires, 30
Mona Lisa, 194, 220
Monaco, 217
Monarchy, 150, 186
Money, 154ff, 193
— value of, 16, 56, 70, 145, 150, 155–56, 160
Mongoose, 22
Monier-Williams, Monier, 67
Monkey extract, 36
Monmouth's Rebellion, 108
Monro, James, 193
Monroe Doctrine, 174
Monroe, Marilyn, 304
Mons, 123
Monsieur Lecoq, 199
Montague Place, 100
Montenegro, 45, 175, 203
Montez, Lola, 52

Montgomery, James, 251, 263, 274
Montpellier, 33, 41, 44, 169
Montréal, 272
Moody, Ron, 228
Moon Is a Harsh Mistress, 53, 309
Moonstone, 199
Moor, 180
Moore, Dudley, 241
Moore, Roger, 242
Morality, 206
Moran, Colonel Sebastian, 26, 114, 236, 246
Moran, Pat, 272
Morang, George N. & Co., 72
Morcar, Countess of, 165
Morell, André, 238
Moriarty, 51, 220, 234
Moriarty, Professor James, 23, 26, 30, 39, 44, 45, 49, 62, 68, 170, 207, 215, 276, 302, 308
— fiction, stage and screen, 51, 194, 215, 217, 218, 220, 224, 226, 234, 235, 236, 237, 239, 240, 242, 243, 246, 256, 266
Morley, Christopher, 18, 41, 45, 79, 258ff, 261, 262, 268, 273, 274, 277, 285, 319
Morley, Frank, 45, 259
Mormons, 13, 127, 267, 276
Morning Post, 165
Morris chair, 185
Morris, Jane, 185
Morris, William, 11, 185, 269
Morrison, Arthur, 201
Morrison, Patricia, 236
Morse, Inspector, 205
Morstan, Mary, 15, 43, 48, 64, 68, 224, 246, 249
Morstein, Mona, 219
Mortal Consequences, 209
Mortimer, Dr., 170–71, 198
Mortlake, Harold, 294
Moskowitz, Les, 12, 296
Moström, Matthias, 284
Mother of the free, 140
Motorways, 145
Mount-James, Lord, 29
Mourning, 23, 164
Mouse Detective, 255
Mowbray, Alan, 236
Mozart, Wolfgang, 249
Mr. Fairlie's Final Journey, 214

Mr. Justice Raffles, 97
"Mr. SH of London," 280
Mrs. Hudson, 277
Ms. Holmes of Baker Street, 42
Mulroney, Brian, 306
Mumbai, 180
Mummies, 112
Munro, Grant and Effie, 145, 156, 161
Murder at the Baskervilles, 234
Murder at the Diogenes Club, 253
Murder by Decree, 195, 240
Murder for Pleasure, 208
Murder in Baker Street, 219
Murder in the Calais Coach, 202
Murder in the Cathedral, 308
Murder Ink, 209
Murder Must Advertise, 202
Murder of Roger Ackroyd, 202
Murder One, 292
Murder Rooms, 138
Murder, My Dear Watson, 219
Murderland, 30
"Murders in the rue Morgue," 198
Murdoch, Derrick, 271
Murillo, Ex-president, 57
Murray, John, 31, 34, 80, 81, 90
Musée de l'Holmes, 296
Museums, 299ff
"Musgrave Ritual," 21, 39, 236, 246, 274, 290, 308
Musgrave, Reginald, 154, 158, 160, 246
Musgrave, Sally, 237
Music, 250–52, 279
Musto, David, 316
Mutilation, 20, 104, 108, 121
Mutual network, 230, 231
My Dear Holmes, 148, 286
My Father's Friend, Mr. SH," 131
"My Friend the Murderer," 102
Mycroft, computer, 309
Mycroft, Mr., 212
Myers, Frederick, 127
Mysteries and Adventures, 102
Mysterious Affair at Styles, 202
Mysterious Bookshop, 205, 274, 292
Mysterious World of SH, 290
Mystery booksellers, 292

Mystery fiction, 198ff
Mystery of a Hansom Cab, 200
Mystery of Cloomber, 102, 104
Mystery of Edwin Drood, 182
"Mystery of Marie Roget," 199
Mystery of the Mummy, 253
"Mystery of the Second Wound," 262
Mystery of the Yellow Hands, 254
Mystery Reader, 209
Mystery weekends, 276
Mystery!, 247
MysteryNet, 209
Myth, 62
Myth and Modern Man, 208
"Mythological Archetypes," 311

Nabokov, Vladimir, 308
Nadel, Bill, 230
Nagano, Japan, 284, 301
Naganuma, Kouki, 283
Naked Is the Best Disguise, 17, 266, 314
Name of the Rose, 308
Names (*see also* Holmes, Watson), 68
Nansen, Fridtjof, 119
Napoléon, 28, 105–06, 177; wars, 155, 176, 186
Napoleon of Crime, 50, 194, 220, 308
Narrator, 33–35, 46, 203, 204
Nashville, 303
Natal, 122, 172
Nate the Great, 11, 255
National Tap-Dance Company, 226
"Naval Treaty," 23, 31, 54, 56, 85, 151, 152, 176, 178, 197, 217, 229, 246
Navy (*see* Royal Navy)
Naxos AudioBooks, 93
Nazis, 235, 236
NBC radio, 230; television, 42
Nebbett, Adrian, 196, 222, 255
Neckwear, 303
Neilson-Terry, Dennis, 222
Nelson, G. Patrick, 90
Nero Wolfe of West Thirty-Fifth, 203
Nerve centre, 264
Nesbit, E., 74
Netherlands, 157, 178, 285

Neutrality, British, 175
Never lived, 260
Neville, John, 239
New Annotated SH, 83
New Forest, 101, 107, 133
New Haven, 263
New Jersey, 51
New Oxford Street, 145
New Revelation, 128
New Scotland Yard, 191
New Series, 262
New York, 121, 174, 193, 199, 202, 203, 205, 206, 215, 221, 224, 226, 240, 242, 257, 260, 263, 265, 266, 267, 268, 273, 302
— *Daily News*, 76
— *Post*, 240
— *Public Library*, 70, 72
— state, 108
— *Times*, 90, 120
— *World*, 78
New Zealand, 172
Newcastle, 112
Newcomb, Simon, 50
Newgate, 190;
Newgate Calendar, 198
Newgate Street, 145
Newman, John Henry, 101, 168
Newman, Robert, 254
Newnes, George, 16, 20, 25, 26, 72, 73, 85
News from the Diggings, 284
Newsday, 316
Newsgroup, 297
Newsletters, 263, 264, 269, 270, 273, 285, 287
Newspapers, 78, 124, 165–66; illustration, 88
Newth, Jonathan, 246
Newton, Christopher, 224
Next Generation, 309
Niagara Falls, 61
Niagara-on-the-Lake, 224
Nicaragua, 299
Nicholas II, 177
Nichols, Mary Ann (Polly), 195
Nielsen, Bjarne, 284
Nieminski, John, 264
Night Calls, 138
Night Watch, 219
Nihilists, 28, 177
Nikolas, King, 236
Nimoy, Leonard, 309
1994 Baker Street, 243
Nobel Prize, 268
Nobility, 157
"Noble Bachelor," 19, 64, 126, 155, 156, 157, 158, 174, 247
Nonsense Novels, 211

Nook Farm, 225
Norberton, Sir Robert, 37
Norbu, Jamyang, 220
Norbury, 145
Nordon, Pierre, 112, 135
Norfolk, 27, 140
Norman Shaw Building, 191
Norman, Andrew, 136
Norms, 207
Norris, Luther, 214
North Sea, 144
Northamptonshire, 141
Northeastern Illinois University, 311
Northern Line, 149
Northern Musgraves, 280
Northumberland Fusiliers, 179
Northumberland Street, 58, 300, 303
Northumbria, 141
Norway, 92, 100, 119, 178, 284
Norwegian Explorers of Minneapolis, 270, 294
Norwood, 144
"Norwood Builder," 27, 57, 64, 88, 196, 246, 248
Norwood, Eille, 34, 226, 233
Nostalgia, 284
Notched Hairpin, 212
"Note on the Watson Problem," 278
Notre Dame University, 265, 275
Notting Hill Gate, 145
Nottinghamshire, 141
Nova 57 Minor, 212
Novels, 167
Nowlan, Alden, 227
Nown, Graham, 289

O'Brien, Willis, 111
O'Dell, Jennifer, 111
O'Shea, Kitty, 185
O'Toole, Peter, 130
Oakland, 303
Oakley, Annie, 262
Oakley, Helen McK., 258
Obscenity, 253
Occupants of the Empty House, 270, 288
Oceanside, California, 292
Odessa, 177
Oedipus, 62, 183
Oeuvres Complètes, 91
Officer, Harvey, 251, 259
Official History of the Metropolitan Police, 193
Offord, Lee, 268
Ogonyok Library, 92
Oklahoma, 303
Old Bailey, 144, 190

Old Homestead Restaurant, 274
Old Man in the Corner, 201
Old Possum's Book of Practical Cats, 308
Old Series, 262
Old Soldiers of Baker Street, 264
Oldacre, Jonas, 249
Oliver Twist, 182
Olivier, Laurence, 240
Olympic Games, 115, 116
Omnibus, 149
On Stage: SH, 228
On the Scent, 142, 148, 289
On the Trail of Arthur Conan Doyle, 280
One Voice Recordings, 93
Ontario Chiropractic Association, 310
Opera, 227
Ophthalmology, 100
Opium, 18
Orange Free State, 122
Orchard Street, 146
Orczy, Baroness, 201
Order and disorder, 198, 208, 313, 314
Ordnance Survey, 142
Orel, Harold, 137
Origin of Species, 170, 182
Original Illustrated Strand SH, 80
Orpington, Kent, 280
Orton, Arthur, 194
Oscar II, 178
Oscar Wilde's London, 164
Oslo, 92
Otero, Caroline, 51
Other Victorians, 64
Ottawa, 173, 272
Ottoman Empire, 177
Our African Winter, 116, 129
Our American Adventure, 116, 126, 129
Our Second American Adventure, 116, 129
Out of Doors, 170
Out of the Shadows, 133
Outer Circle, 149
Outline of History, 187
Owen, Heather, 280
Oxford, 13, 156, 181, 205, 276, 281
— Companion to English Literature, 199
— English Dictionary, 298
— Movement, 168
— SH, 69, 81
— Street, 143, 145, 146
— University, 277, 278, 311, 313
— University Press, 81

Oxfordshire, 140

Pacific, 178, 179
Paddington, 144, 145
Paddington station, 141, 149, 181
Page, Genevieve, 239
Pageboy, 54, 55
Paget, Sidney, 20, 26, 80, 84, 85, 88, 91, 190, 200, 237, 245, 249, 281, 298; illustration, 86
Paget, Walter, 85, 90
Paget, Winifred, 88
Paige, Robin, 25
Painful Predicament of SH, 224
Pakistan, 179
Palace of Westminster, 144
Pale Fire, 308
Pall Mall, 53
Pall Mall (newspaper), 165
Pall Mall Gazette, 186
Palmer, William, 194
Palo Alto, 256
Pamphlet House, 291
Pamphlets, 293
Papal States, 176
Paperbacks, 79ff, 293
"Parakeet of the Baskervilles," 306
Parasite, 102, 105, 111
Pardon My Planet, 305
Paregoric, 319
Paretsky, Sara, 206
Paris, 176, 198, 199, 215, 245
Parish, 169
Parish Magazine, 95
Park Lane, 145
Park Plaza SH Hotel, 299, 303
Park Road, 146
Park, William, 121
Parker Brothers, 252
Parker, Justice William, 306
Parker, Lyndon, 214
Parker, Robert B., 206
Parkhill, John, 294
Park-Hotel Sauvage, 300, 302
Parkman, Francis, 108, 116
Parliament, 124, 144, 150, 153, 154, 158, 160, 181, 183, 185, 189
Parnassus on Wheels, 258
Parnell, Charles Stewart, 153, 185
Parody, 210ff, 263
Parsee, 120
Pascal, Janet B., 136
Passengers' Log, 284
Pasteurization, 169
Pastiches, 57, 200, 210ff, 263, 265
Pathology, 169; laboratory, 302
Patient's Eyes, 138

Patterson, Joseph, 76
Patterson, Linda, 272
Paul, Jeremy, 228, 250
Payne, David S., 208
Payne, Malcom, 95, 300
PBS network, 247
PC-Sherlock, 253
Peace, Addington, 25
Peace, Charlie, 194
Peacock, Shane, 219
Peanuts, 256, 303
Pearl of Death, 236
Pearl, Cora, 51
Pearlman, Gilbert, 218
Pearsall, Ronald, 64, 135, 165
Pearson, Edmund, 47
Pearson, Hesketh, 131, 135
Peck, Andrew Jay, 286
Peel, Robert, 153, 191
Peelers, 191
Peerage, 150
Peirce, Charles Sanders, 50, 61
Pencil Productions, 94
Penguin, 79, 80
Pennington, Michael, 242
Pennsylvania, 30, 67, 207, 267, 276
Penny, 155, 165, 166
Pentonville, 190
Penzler, Otto, 205, 209
Peoria, 288
Pepper & Stern, 293
Pepper, James, 292
Per cent, 307
Perdue, Peggy, 11, 294
Perfume, 43
Periodic table, 169
Perry, Anne, 205
Persano, Isadora, 57
Persing, Robert and William, 231
Personalia, 31
Peter L. Stern & Co., 292
Peter Pan, 181
Peterson, Robert C., 309
Petrarch, 41
Petri Wine, 230
Phallic symbolism, 183
Phantom of the Opera, 215
Pharmacopoeia, 43
Phelps, Percy, 246
Pheneas Speaks, 129
Philadelphia, 14, 72, 251, 261, 263, 268, 270
Philatelic & Numismatic Holmes, 299
Phonograph, 169
Photocopying, 76
Photographing Fairies, 130
Photography, 74, 115, 129, 130, 164, 181
Picard, Liza, 165
Picardy Place, 301
Piccadilly Circus, 144, 302

Pictorial History of SH, 289
Picture of Dorian Gray, 14, 187
Piehler, Paul, 312
Pietri, Dorando, 116
Pig, 309, 316
Pike, Langdale, 165
Pilgrimage, 276
Pilot, Roy, 110
Piltdown Man, 110, 138
Pimlico, 149, 276
"Pinacotheca Holmesiana," 296
Pink 'Un, 166
Pinkerton, Allan, and the Pinkertons, 30
Pinkwater, Daniel, 254
Pinnacle, 291
Pipes, 303; curved, 225, 298
Piracy (literary), 14, 15, 73, 78
Pirates of Penzance, 183
Pirie, David, 138
Pitman shorthand, 93
Pittsburgh, 30, 92, 263, 293
Pixar Animation, 241
Planetarium, 146
Plaques, 302
Plaster of Paris, 199
Plato, 39
Playboy, 79, 306
Players Club, 90
Plays, 221ff
Plugs and Dottles, 288
Plum, Stephanie, 206
Plummer, Christopher, 240
Plunket, Andrea, 78
Plymouth, 100
Pocono Pines, 292
Poe, Edgar Allan, 17, 110, 116, 198, 308
Poems of Arthur Conan Doyle, 103
Poet Laureate, 186
Poetry, 252, 287
Pohle, Robert W., Jr., 233
Pointer, Michael, 233, 289
Poirot, Hercule, 202, 204, 217
Poison, 41, 68
Poison Belt, 103, 110, 111
Police 151, 188, 190ff, 204–05, 318
— Act, 191
— and Criminal Evidence Act, 191
— court, 190
— Holmes's attitude to, 16
— state, 191
Polidoro, Massimo, 130
Polish, 195
Politics, 124, 152–54
Pollock, Donald, 263, 264, 288
Pondicherry Lodge, 15, 145

Pons, Solar, 214
Pool, Daniel, 165
Pope, 57, 168, 176
Popular culture, 203, 311
Popular Press, 311
Population, 140
Porlock, Fred, 262
Pornography, 41, 64, 163, 253–54
Porter, Eric, 246
Porter, Philip, 280
Portland, 94, 190
Portman, 146
Portman Rooms, 147, 163
Portman Square, 146
Portrait of a Killer, 196
Portsmouth, 68, 118, 190, 276, 281
Portsmouth Central Library, 281, 295
Portsmouth Literary and Scientific Society, 67, 127
Post office, 139, 147, 164, 166, 299
Post, William, Jr., 236
Potato famine, 153
Potter, Clarkson N., 81
Pottsville, Pennsylvania, 30
Poughkeepsie, 268
Poultry, 145
Pound sterling, 155
Pound, Reginald, 73
Poverty, 159
Power, Tyrone, 238
Practical Handbook of Sherlockian Heraldry, 264
Praed Street 214; Dossier, Irregulars, Papers, 214
Prague, 206
Preface to His Last Bow, 257
Preface to the Case-Book, 319
Prendergast, Jack, 190
Pre-Raphaelites, 185
Presbury, Professor, 158, 247
Presbyterianism, 97, 108, 168
Prescott's Press, 230, 287
President of France, 57; of the United States, 268
Presley, Elvis, 304
Press, Charles, 102
Prestige, Colin, 279
Price, Allan, 259
Price, Vincent, 255
Prime Minister, 152
Prime minister, 23, 151, 181, 182, 186, 191, 241
Prince Edward Island, 299
Prince Henry International Road Competition, 116
Prince of Wales (see Edward)

Princeton, New Jersey, 224
Princetown, 24, 190
Principal Unprincipled Adventuress, 273
Principles of Psychology, 170
Printing (see also Typesetting), 72, 287
"Priory School," 11, 27, 70, 90, 141, 156, 157, 246, 254
Prisoner of the Devil, 281
Prisons, 190, 197
Pritchard, Edward William, 194
Private Life of SH (book), 71, 147, 260, 285, 320
Private Life of SH (film), 239
Privately published, 291
Problem of the Spiteful Spiritualist, 181
"Problem of Thor Bridge" (see Thor)
Procedurals, 205
Professor Moriarty's, 302
Professors (see also Moriarty), 158
Profile by Gaslight, 49, 54, 262, 291
Programming, 310
Prohibition, 259
Project Gutenberg, 94
Prolegomena, 278
Prostitution, 64, 123, 159, 163, 183, 186, 195, 283
Protestantism, 153, 168, 178, 181
Providence, goodness, 23
Providence, Rhode Island, 261
Prudery, 162
Prussia, 176
Psmith, Journalist, 305
Psychic Bookshop, 129
Psychic Press, 121
Psychoanalysis, 183
PsyLogic Systems, 93
Public domain (see also Copyright), 76
Public Health Act, 152
Publishing, publishers, 70, 291–92
Pubs, 302–03
Puccini, Giacomo, 227
Pudd'nhead Wilson, 197
Pugh, Brian W., 24, 95, 137, 300
Punch, 166
Punctuation, 70, 72
Puns, 265
Puritan Pleasures of the Detective Story, 205, 208
Puritanism, 108, 208, 312

"Purloined Letter," 17, 23, 199, 308
Pursuit of the House-Boat, 211
Pursuit to Algiers, 236
Putnam, 291
Putney, Charles R., 314
Puzzle, 206
Pycroft, Hall, 21

Quack, 238
Quackenbush, Robert, 255
Quallsford Inheritance, 216
Quarter sessions, 190
Québec, 108, 173, 307; Conference, 236
Queen, Ellery, 195, 202, 212, 214, 239, 263, 308
Queen (*see* Victoria)
Queen's University, 294
Queensberry, Marquess of, and Rules, 118, 119, 187
Quest for SH, 104, 136, 312
Quest for Sir Arthur Conan Doyle, 134–35, 312
Quick, Watson, 305
Quilley, Denis, 246
Quizzes, 265, 270, 286

Rabbis, Hebrew, 188
Rabe, William T., 10, 52, 251, 264
Racial issues, 160
Racism, 42
Radicals, 181
Radio, 57, 93, 228ff
Radio City, 242
Radio Times, 229
Radix pedis diaboli, 33
Rafferty, Shadwell, 219
Raffles Haw, 102, 111
Raffles, A.J., 97, 184, 201
Raglan, Lord, 62
Railways, 141
Rains, Claude, 111
Raleigh Legacy, 216
Ramanujan, 217
Rampling, Charlotte, 242
Rance, John, 14, 193
Randall, Warren, 268
Random House, 77
Ranston, 146
Rape, 33
Rasputin, 210
Rat of Sumatra, 57
Rathbone, Basil, 9, 42, 91, 93, 131, 230, 231, 232, 234ff, 244, 245, 256, 301, 305, 309, 316; illustration, 237
Rathbone, Ouida, 226

Ratigan, Professor, 255
Rauber, D.F., 203
Raven League, 254
Rawalpindi, 179
Rayner, Patrick, 232
Read, Anthony, 254
Reade, Charles, 106
Reading, 269
Reading Gaol, 190
Reading, Pennsylvania, 301
Ready When You Are, Mr. Rathbone, 235
Reagan, Ronald, 317
Real estate, 303
Real SH, 135
Real World of SH, 49, 119
Realism, 319
Reason, 65
"Recessional," 185
Recordings, audio, 93, 109, 231, 252
Red Army, 92
"Red Circle," 32, 70, 75, 82, 149, 247
Red Circle of Washington, 264, 270, 276
Red Harvest, 203
Red House, 185
Red leech, 56, 84
"Red Widow," 213
Redgrave, Vanessa, 240
"Red-Headed League," 16, 17, 21, 36, 49, 185, 194, 243, 244, 246, 313
Redmond, Christopher, 9, 44, 52, 57, 65, 137, 272, 289, 296
Redmond, Donald A., 11, 14, 67, 68, 73, 78, 138, 169, 291, 294, 312, 313
Redmond, John, 154
Reed, Lawrence L., 138
Rees, Roger, 231
Reform Bill, 152
Reform, political, 150, 152
Refugees, 96, 102, 108
Regent Street, 139, 145
Regent's Park, 143, 145, 146
Reichenbach Falls, 23, 24, 39, 44, 45, 62, 87, 88, 220, 276, 299, 302
Reid, John and Sylvia, 300
"Reigate Squires," 21, 80, 156, 286, 313
Reindeer Song, 251
Religion, 168
Remarkable Worm, 316
"Reminiscence of SH," 31
Reminiscences of John H. Watson, 46
Reminiscences of Solar Pons, 214

Rendell, Ruth, 206
Renegade Press, 256
Rennison, Nick, 45, 219
Reply Paid, 212
Representations, 313, 314
Republic, French, 57
"Resident Patient," 22, 104, 171, 246
Restaurants, 302–03
Resurrection, 62
"Retired Colurman," 37, 63, 141, 169
Return of Arthur Conan Doyle, 131
Return of Moriarty, 51, 220
Return of SH (book), 26ff, 88, 90
Return of SH (film), 234, 242
Return of SH (play), 226, 233
Return of Solar Pons, 214
Return of the World's Greatest Detective, 242
Revenge, 188, 318
Revenge of Moriarty, 51, 194, 220
Reversion, 170
Revolution, 177, 182, 208
Reynolds, Sheldon, 78, 132, 244
Rhodes, Cecil, 172
Rhodesia, 236
Rhys-Davies, John, 111
Rice, Susan, 268
Richardson, Ian, 138
Richardson, Natasha, 246
Richardson, Ralph, 228
Richardson, Samuel, 320
Right of way, 189
Riley, Dick, 290
Riley, James Whitcomb, 101
Rinehart, Mary Roberts, 202
Riordan, Marjorie, 236
Ripley, Linda, 272
Ripper File, 196
Ripper (*see* Jack the Ripper)
Ristorante Moriarti, 303
Ritchie, Guy, 241
Rivals of SH, 200
RMS *Titanic*, 186
Roberts, Sydney, 278
Robin Hood, 31, 62, 320
Robinson Crusoe, 63
Robinson, Andrew, 250
Robinson, Bertram Fletcher, 24, 67
Robinson, Peter, 205
Robson, W.W., 82
Rochester, 127

Rockefeller, John D., 174
Roden, Barbara, 239, 292
Roden, Christopher, 82, 95, 289, 292
Rodin, Alvin E., 104, 110, 111, 141, 171
Rodney Stone, 103, 105, 119
Rogers, Mary, 199
Rogow, Roberta, 181
Rohmer, Sax, 51, 75
Roman Catholic (*see* Catholic)
Roman Hat Mystery, 202
Romance, romanticism, 46, 64, 312
Romeo, 63, 304
Ronald McDonald, 63
Ronder, Eugenia, 37
Roosevelt, Franklin D., 268
Roosevelt, Theodore, 101, 174, 178, 217, 243
Rose, 23
Rose Tattoo, 253
Rose, Arthur, 226
Rosebery, Lord, 152
Rosenberg, Samuel, 17, 266, 314, 315
Rosenblatt, Albert M., 268
Rosenblatt, Julia Carlson, 268, 269
Ross, Colonel, 246
Ross, Duncan, 185
Ross, Herbert, 240
Rossetti, Dante Gabriel, 185
Rothman, Steven, 258, 262, 263, 268, 281
Roughead, William, 121
Round Table, 273
Round the Fire Stories, 103, 114
Round the Red Lamp, 102, 104
Routley, Erik, 205, 206, 208
Rowe, Nicholas, 241
Roxton, Lord John, 109
Royal Academy of Dramatic Arts, 229
Royal Army Medical Corps, 123
Royal Bank of Scotland, 132
Royal Doulton, 304
Royal Infirmary, 69
Royal Mail (*see also* Post office), 299
Royal National Institute for the Blind, 132
Royal Navy, 53, 140, 175
Royal Scandal, 243
Royal Shakespeare Company, 224, 266
Royal Sussex Regiment, 122

Royalties, 70, 72
Roylott, Grimesby, 65, 114, 158, 246, 277, 319
Rubber, 179
Ruber, Peter A., 261
Rudolf, Crown Prince, 194
Rugby, 84, 116ff
Rugeley, 194
Rumbelow, Donald, 159, 196
Runnquist, Ake, 284
Rupee, 180
Rupert of Hentzau, 217
Russell, Clark, 74, 167
Russell, Mary, 44, 180
Russia, 28, 48, 91, 92, 175, 177, 179, 239, 245, 265
Russo-Japanese War, 178
Rutherford, William, 99, 109
Rutland, 141
Ryding, Richard, 48
Rylott, Dr., 114

S. Holmes, Esq. pub, 301
Sabina Hall, 216
Sachs, Andrew, 232
Sacker, Ormond, 45, 71, 240
Sacred Writings, 259, 315
Sadler's Wells, 226
Sadomasochism, 64
Saffron, Robert, 216
Saint (*see* St.)
Saintsbury, H.A., 221
Salaries, 158
Salisbury, Lord, 152, 153, 154, 181, 186
Sallis, Peter, 226
Salt Lake City, 13
Salvarsan, 171
Samba for Sherlock, 220
Sämtliche Romane and Stories, 92
San Clemente, 295
San Francisco, 205, 243, 263, 270, 301
San Pedro, 31
Sand, George, 41
Sangô de Baker Street, 220
Sanguinary Count, 216
Santa Barbara, 292
Santa Claus, 63
Santa Fe, 265
Saratoga Springs, 302
Sardines, 259
Sardou, 227
Sarjeant, William, 42
Sarony, Otto, 223
Saskatoon, 272
Saturday Evening Post, 75, 76
Saturday Night, 307
Saturday Review of Literature, 49, 258, 259, 273

Sauk City, Wisconsin, 292
Sault Ste. Marie, 264
Savage, Victor, 32
Sayers, Dorothy, 199, 202, 278
Scandal, 164, 182
"Scandal in Bohemia," 17, 27, 35, 43, 51, 55, 79, 87, 156, 161, 169, 177, 183, 221, 224, 226, 233, 245
"Scandale in Bohemia," 227
Scandinavia, 157, 178, 228
Scandinavia and SH, 284
Scanning, 94
Scarlet Claw, 236
Scarlet Pimpernel, 201
Scarpetta, Kay, 206
Scheideman, Warren, 87
Scholarly writing, 285
Scholefield, Charles, 276
School and Holmes, 222, 255
Schools, 152
Schreiner, Olive, 167
Schulz, Charles, 256
Schweickert, William, 252, 269
Schwensen, Clara, 97
Science, 169–71
— and art, 313
— and superstition, 24
— fiction, 36, 108, 269, 309
— of SH, 172, 290
— scientific detection, 60
Science-Fictional SH, 309
Scion societies, 261, 263, 265, 269ff, 272
Scotchwoman, 55
Scotland and Scots, 125, 140, 154, 160, 181, 216, 304; border, 116; Office of Works, 97
Scotland Yard, 14, 27, 50, 191–92, 197, 240
Scott, George C., 239
Scott, Walter, 116, 167
Scottish Students' Song Book, 252
Scowrers, 68, 207, 208
"Scowrers," 29
Scowrers and Mollie Maguires, San Francisco, 263, 270
Screw, 254
Scribd, 94
Scribners, 291
Sculpture (*see also* Statues), 304, 313
Scuttlebutt from the Spermaceti Press, 264, 268, 287

Sea stories, 74
Seagrove, Jenny, 243, 246
"Sealed Room," 213
Searching, 93
Sebeok, Thomas A., 61
Second Afghan War, 48
Second Empire, 176
"Second Stain," 29, 46, 61, 150, 151, 156, 174, 186, 246
Second wife (*see also* Watson), 49, 277
Secret Diary of Dr. Watson, 219
Secret Journals, Files, Chronicles, Documents, Notebooks of SH, 219
Secret Marriage of SH, 314
Secret of SH, 51, 228, 250
Secret Service, 225
Secretary of State, 151
Selden, 24
SelfMadeHero, 256
"Semiotic Watson," 311
Semiotics, 308, 311, 314
Sennett, Mack, 233
Serbia, 175
Series, 243
Serpentine Muse, 273, 287
Serrated Scalpel, 253
Servants, 160ff
Sesame Street, 255, 304
"Seven Clocks," 213
Seven-per-cent solution, 307
Seven-Per-Cent Solution, 51, 183, 214–15, 216, 217, 240, 265–66, 307
Seventeen Steps to, 221B, 279
Sex, 20, 34, 35, 63, 105, 163, 167, 203, 210, 216, 266, 287, 312
Sexual Adventures of SH, 16, 254
Shadow of Reichenbach Falls, 220
Shakespeare, William, 45, 63, 72, 184, 245, 273, 319
Shall and will, 216
Sharmat, Marjorie Weinman, 255
Shārokku Hāmuzu, 283
Shatner, William, 242
Shaw Festival, 224
Shaw, George Bernard, 101, 215
Shaw, John Bennett, 63, 265, 266, 272, 275, 293, 294, 305
Sheerluck Holmes and the Hounds, 304

Shelburne, Ontario, 94
Shelley, Norman, 229, 232
Shenandoah Valley, 30
Shepherd, Walter, 289
Sherlock, 288
Sherlock and the Ladies, 289
Sherlock Bones, 303
Sherlock Chick, 255
Sherlock Extension Poles, 303
Sherlock Hemlock, 9, 255, 304
SH — the Last Act, 228
SH (film), 234, 241
SH (game), 252, 253
SH (play, Gillette), 43, 218, 222, 223, 227, 266
SH (play, Rathbone), 226
SH Among the Pirates, 14, 73, 78, 138, 312
SH and a Question of Science, 172, 290
SH and Dr. Watson, 41, 79, 286
SH and Music, 279
SH and the Case of Sabina Hall, 216
SH and the Case of the Raleigh Legacy, 216
SH and the Deadly Necklace, 238
SH and the Disgraced Inspector, 218
SH and the Hammerford Will, 218
SH and the Ice Palace Murders, 219
SH and the Leading Lady, 243
SH and the Mark of the Beast, 217
SH and the Red Demon, 219
SH and the Rune Stone Mystery, 219
SH and the Secret Alliance, 219
SH and the Secret Code, 236
SH and the Secret Weapon, 236
SH and the Thistle of Scotland, 216
SH and the Voice of Terror, 235
SH Arrive Trop Tard, 201, 211
"*SH as a Figure of Romance*," 312
SH Baffled, 233
SH by Gas-Lamp, 289
SH Club and Purveyors, 297
SH Collection, 304
SH Companion, 282
SH Cookbook, 289
SH Faces Death, 236, 237
SH Gazette, 288
SH in America, 256, 289

SH in London, 142
SH in New York, 242
SH in Portrait and Profile, 84, 88
SH in the 22nd Century, 245
SH in the Comic Books, 256
SH in Washington, 236
SH Is Missing, 254
SH Journal, 142, 156, 197, 228, 244, 278, 279, 280, 282, 287
SH Klubben i Danmark, 284
SH Memorabilia Company, 303
SH Murder File, 289
SH Museum, 46, 299
SH of Baker Street, 44, 81, 180, 220, 263
SH on Screen, 233
SH on the Screen, 233
SH on the Stage, 228
SH public house, 58, 300, 302, 303
SH Reference Library, 82
SH restaurant, 302
SH Returns, 243
SH Review, 245, 265, 288
SH Scrapbook, 289
SH Screen and Sound Guide, 233
SH Social Network, 297
SH Society, 278
SH Society of Australia, 284
SH Society of Canada, 272
SH Society of London, 13, 88, 141, 229, 234, 276, 278ff, 287, 300, 301, 303
SH Solo Mysteries, 253
SH the Detective Magazine, 288
"SH the God," 62
SH und das Halsband, 238
SH Versus Jack the Ripper, 195
SH vs. Arsene Lupin, 253
SH vs. Dracula, 216
SH vs. Jack the Ripper, 196
SH Zenshu, 92
SH, Bridge Detective, 222
SH, Consulting Detective, 253
SH, Order and the Late Victorian Mind, 208
SH, the Canon and Sports, 118
SH, the Final Adventure, 228
SH, the Golden Years, 243
SH, the Missing Years, 220
SH, the Musical, 228

SH: A Centenary Celebration, 289
SH: A Study in Sources, 68, 313
"SH: Ethics, Logic, and the Mask," 314
SH: Fact or Fiction?, 286
SH: Nemesis, 201
SH: Ten Literary Studies, 217
SH: The Major Stories, 313–14
SH: The Man and His World, 289
SH: The Published Apocrypha, 113
SH: The Unauthorized Biography, 45, 219
SH: Victorian Sleuth to Modern Hero, 314
SH' Fatal Hour, 234
SH's Greatest Cases, 79
SH's London, 142, 284
SH's Lost Adventure, 219
SH's Prayer, 274
Sherlock Homes, 303
Sherlock Hose, 304
Sherlock Hound, 255
Sherlock in LA, 292
Sherlock Magazine, 288, 317
Sherlock Mews, 146
Sherlock Peoria, 296
Sherlock Pipes & Tobaccos, 303
Sherlock Security Systems, 303
Sherlock Slept Here, 137
Sherlock, cricketer, 68
Sherlock, Jane, 68
Sherlock, search facility, 307
Sherlock, Thomas, 68
Sherlock's Bar & Grill, 303
Sherlock's Home, 302
Sherlock's Last Case, 227
Sherlock's London Today, 142
Sherlock's Men, 314
Sherlock's on Sheppard, 302
Sherlock's Pub, 302
Sherlocked, 298
Sherlockian Atlas, 264
"Sherlockian Periodicals Received," 287
Sherlockian Resources on the Internet, 296
Sherlockian Who's Who, 10, 264
Sherlockian.Net, 94, 296
Sherlockians, 257ff; background, 186
Sherlocko the Monk, 255
Sherlocktron, 11, 269, 295

Sherman Antitrust Act, 174
Sherman, Michael, 296
"Shermlock Shomes," 255
Sherrinford, 45, 68, 71
Shilling, 56, 149, 155, 267
Shinku No Isshi, 92
Shirley, Anne, 299
"Shoeless Engineer," 244
Sholto, Bartholomew, 15
Shomes, Kerlock, 211
Short stories, 38, 199, 202, 219, 243
Short Stories, 80, 90
Shorthand, 93
"Shoscombe Abbey," 70
"Shoscombe Old Place," 37, 70, 74
Shreffler, Philip A., 262, 289
Shropshire, 141
Shroud for a Nightingale, 203
Sidelights on Holmes, 290
Sidney Street siege, 192
Siegfried, 62
Sigerson, 44
Sign of the Four, **14ff**, 42, 46, 48, 56, 64, 65, 67, 70, 78ff, 87, 91, 93, 142, 179, 187, 224, 254, 286, 293, 294, 307
— bibliography, 138
— dossier, 253
— stage and screen, 227, 229, 231, 233, 249
— titled *Sign of Four*, 15, 102, 234, 243, 246
Sign of Three, 61, 308
Signet, 291
Signs of our Times, 138
Silhouette, 147, 310
"Silver Blaze," 20, 37, 79, 85, 118, 155, 228, 230, 234, 246, 306
Silver Blaze races, 266, 276
Silver Earring, 253
Simenon, George, 205
Simmons, Alex, 254
Simon & Schuster, 291
Simpson, 56
Simpson, Joseph, 90
Simpson's in the Strand, 302
Sin, 206
Sincerest Form of Flattery, 222
Singalong with SH, 251
Singing Bone, 201
Singular Adventures of Martha Hudson, 262

"Singular Affair of the Aluminum Crutch," 230
"Singular Affair of the Baconian Cipher," 230
"Singular Experience of Mr. John Scott Eccles," 31
Singular Set of People, 289
Sinhalese, 91
Sir Arthur Conan Doyle Centenary, 131
Sir Arthur Conan Doyle in America, 138
Sir Arthur Conan Doyle Literary Estate, 78
Sir Arthur Conan Doyle, l'homme, 135
Sir Arthur Conan Doyle: Interviews and Recollections, 137
Sir Arthur Conan Doyle's The Lost World, 111
Sir Nigel, 103, 107
6 Messiahs, 138
"Six Napoleons," 28, 70, 160, 236, 246
Six Napoleons of Baltimore, 261, 270
Skene Melvin, David and Ann, 198
Skiing, 100, 119
Skinner, Keith, 196
Skvorecky, Joseph, 206
Slang, 216
Slater, Oscar, 119ff, 134
Sleeping Cardinal, 234
Sleuth of Baker Street, 205, 292
Small presses, 291–92
Smethurst case, 60
Smith, alias, 118
Smith, Culverton, 247
Smith, Denis Nayland, 51
Smith, Edgar P., 304
Smith, Edgar W., 39, 44, 47, 79, 131, 245, 252, **261**, 262, 264, 267, 285, 291
Smith, Elder & Co., 26, 31
Smith, Ernest Bramah, 201
Smith, H. Greenhough, 72, 73
Smith, L. Neil, 309
Smith, R. Dixon, 250
Smith, Red, 268
Smith, Violet, 27, 64, 169, 246
Smith-Mortimer succession case, 56
Smithsonian, 316
Smoking, 299
Snake, 18

"Snared Drummer," 218
Snarkout Boys and the Avocado of Death, 254
Snobbery, 311
Snoopy, 256, 303
Snyder, Laura, 60
Soares, Jô, 220
Soccer, 116ff
Social order, 65
Socialism, 180, 193
Societé SH de France, 284
Societies, Sherlockian, 269ff
Society for Psychical Research, 126, 129
Society of Authors, 115
Sociology, 207
Socrates, 39
Söhnker, Hans, 239
Soho, 145
Solicitor, 189
"Solitary Cyclist," 27, 64, 169, 246
Solly, H. Shaen, 67
Solomin, Vitally, 245
Solomon, 79
"Some Freaks of Atavism," 171
"Some Personalia about Mr. SH," 31, 115
"Some Recollections of Sport," 116
Some Reminiscences of SH, 31
Somerset, 140
Somme, Battle of, 124
Somomy, 79
Sondergaard, Gale, 236
"Song of the Bow," 112
"Song of the Road," 103
Songs of Action, 103, 112
Sonnenschmidt, Frederic H., 289
Sons of the Copper Beeches, 261, 270
Sorbonne, 135
Soucek, David, 296
Soul of Steel, 52
Sound (*see Recording*)
Sources, 67, 283
South Africa (*see also* Boer War), 125, 129, 172, 243
South America, 57, 109
South Norwood, 100, 302
South, American, 21
Southampton, 67
Southend, 144
Southern Illinois University Press, 312
Southsea, 68, 97, 100, 127, 137, 302
Southwark, 144, 145, 186
Souvenirs, 303
Sovereign, 155
Soviet Union (*see also* Russia), 92, 245

Spade, Sam, 317
Spain, 107, 174, 178
Späte Rache, 91
Speakeasy, 258
Special Branch, 192
"Speckled Band," 16, **18**, 63, 65, 81, 158, 194, 224, 229, 246, 256, 290, 307, 314
Speckled Band (film), 234
Speckled Band (play), 103, 112, 114, 221
Speckled Band of Boston, 261, 270
"Spectacled Band," 218
Spencer Blackett, 14, 15
Spencer, Herbert, 170
Spider, 50
Spider Dance, 52
Spider Woman, 236
Spielberg, Steven, 111, 241
Spielmann, Peter, 310
Spillane, Mickey, 201
Spilsbury, Bernard, 60, 193
Spine, Inspector, 310
Spiring, Paul R., 24
Spirit-lamp, 84, 89
Spiritualism, 101, 110, 111, **126ff**, 184
Spock, Mr., 63, 309
Sporting Times, 166
Sports, 29, 116ff
Springer, Nancy, 254
Springfield, Massachusetts, 209
Spurgeon, Charles, 186
Spy, 225
Squire, 22, 158
Sri Lanka, 172, 179
St. Bartholomew's Hospital, 13, 40, 169, 196, 302
St. Clair, Neville and Mrs., 18, 156, 162, 246
St. Claire, Irene, 227
St. James' Gazette, 165
St. John's Wood, 51
St. Louis, 147, 260; Exposition, 90
St. Luke's, London, 67
St. Margaret's Church, 101
St. Martin's Griffin, 291
St. Marylebone (*see* Marylebone)
St. Monica's, 169
St. Pancras station, 141
St. Paul's Cathedral, 144
St. Petersburg, 177
St. Simon, Lord Robert, 157
Staffordshire, 120, 141
Stamford, 302
Stampe, Mia, 284
Stamps, 299
Standard, 165
Standard Doyle Company, 261

Standard Oil, 174
Stanger, Urban Napoleon, 67
Stangerson, 269
Stanich, Ray, 230
Stanley, John, 231
Stapleton, Beryl, 64, 235
Stapleton, Cecile, 238
Stapleton, Jack, 170–71, 242
Star, 165
Star of Rhodesia, 236
Star Theatre, 222
Star Trek, 63, 215, 309
Stark Munro Letters, 100, 103, 104
Starrett, Vincent, 54, 55, 71, 90, 147, 212, 234, 252, 259, 260–61, 262, 285, 319, 320
Starring SH, 10, 233
Stars and Stripes, 19
Stashower, Daniel, 98, 133, 136, 137, 219
State Farm, 310
Statues, 284, 301–02
Statute of Westminster, 173
Stavert, Geoffrey S., 67, 137
Stead, William T., 186
Steamships, 181
Steel true, 131
Steele, Frederic Dorr, 26, 80, 84, 88, 225, 237, 259, 298
Steinbrunner, Chris, 10, 209, 233, 234, 235, 238, 239
Steinhauer, Lauren, 219
Stephen, Harriet, 186
Stephen, Leslie, 186
Stephens, Robert, 239
Stern, Peter, 292
Sterndale, Leon, 246
Stevens, Sinclair, 307
Stevenson, Robert Louis, 167
Stilts, 115
Stix, Thomas L., Jr., 267, 268
Stix, Tom, Sr., 267
Stock, Nigel, 243, 244
Stock, Randall, 11, 13, 70, 293, 296
"Stock-broker's Clerk," 21, 16, 192, 229
Stoddart, J.B., 14, 187
Stoker, Bram, 101, 184, 215
"Stolen Cigar Case," 211
Stone, P.M., 222, 225
Stoner, Helen, 114
Stonor Case, 114, 221
Stonor, Enid, 114
Stonyhurst College, 68, 99
Stop, You're Killing Me, 209
"Storming Party," 112
Storm-Peterson, Henry, 284

Story of an African Farm, 167
Story of Mr. George Edalji, 120
Stout, Rex, 49, 54, 203, 262
Stowe, Harriet Beecher, 181
"Straggler of '15," 105, 106, 112
Strait of Dover, 176
Straker, John, 155
Strand Magazine, 16ff, 72, 73ff, 80, 83, 85, 110, 114, 115, 124, 130, 200, 208, 245, 279, 302
Strange Case of the End of Civilisation, 217
Strangers' Room, 53
Strategic Arms Limitation Treaty, 307
Stratton brothers, 197
Strebeigh, Fred, 316
Street arabs, 56
Stride, Elizabeth, 195
Strumpets, 51
Strychnine, 194
Student, 113
Studies in Hysteria, 183
Studies in Scarlet, 289
"Studies in the Literature of SH," 277–78
Study in Scarlet, 12ff, 38, 40, 45, 46, 48, 56, 59, 61, 63, 67, 72, 78, 80, 85, 91, 92, 114, 189, 193, 199, 200, 229, 231, 254, 256, 262, 267, 269, 286, 293, 302; dossier, 253; illustration, 71
Study in Southsea, 67, 137
Study in Surmise, 67, 283, 289
Study in Terror, 195, 214, 239
"Study of an Untold Tale," 285
Stuttgart, 92
Subcutaneously, My Dear Watson, 43
Submarine, 32
Subway (see Underground)
Sudan, 44, 184
Suffolk, 84, 140
Suffragettes, 33, 104
Sugarman, Sally, 254, 314
Sullivan, Sir Arthur, 158, 183, 215, 269, 279
Sultan, 177
Sumatra, 178; giant rat, 57, 178, 219
Summerlee, Professor, 109
Sunday Dispatch, 212
Sundin, Gunnar, 142
Superboy, 255

Superman, 317, 318
Superstition, 24, 65
Supreme Adventure of Inspector Lestrade, 220
Supreme Court, 184
Surelocked Homes, 310
Sureté, 199, 200
Surfeit of Lampreys, 202
Surrey, 100, 140, 151; shore, 144
Survey data, 307
Susan, 161
Susanna and the Elders, 198
Sussex, 33, 36, 39, 101, 110, 140
"Sussex Vampire," 35, 127, 156, 247, 254
Sutherland, Mary, 17, 155, 160, 162
Sveum, Richard J., 267
Swarthmore College, 227
Sweden, 91, 178, 284
Sweeney, 192
Swenson, Inga, 226
Switzerland, 23, 100, 119, 131, 279, 280, 299
Sydney Passengers, 284
Sykes, Eric, 246
Syllogism, 61
Sylvius, Count Negretto, 114, 247
Syme, surgeon, 69
Symons, Julian, 136, 198, 200, 209, 222, 308
Symposium, 275
"Symposium on Collecting," 266
Syndrome, 266
Syphilis, 100, 171
Szilyagi, Steve, 130

Tabes dorsalis, 100
Tabori, Kristoffer, 247
Tabram, Martha, 195
Tale of Two Cities, 182
Tales of Adventure and Medical Life, 105
Tales of Long Ago, 105
Tales of Love and Hate, 131
Tales of Pirates and Blue Water, 105
Tales of Terror and Mystery, 105
Tales of Twilight and the Unseen, 105
Tallis, Frank, 183
Tamaqua, Pennsylvania, 30
Tanaka, Kiyoshi, 284
Tankerville Club, 164
Tantalus, 259, 261
Tanzania, 172
Tariffs, 174
Tarzan, 63, 217
Taste for Honey, 212
Tea, 180

Technology, 169
Teddy, 22
Tel Aviv, 92
Telegraph, 166, 216
Telephone, 166, 169, 234, 319
Television, 232, 242ff; commercials, 310
Television SH, 242
Teller of Tales, 136
Tennison Road, 100, 302
Tennyson, Alfred Lord, 167, 186
Term paper, how to write, 296
Terror by Night, 236
Terrorism, 315
Terry, Ellen, 184
Terry, Harold, 226
Tess of the D'Urbervilles, 167
Texas, 57, 174, 302; Rangers, 318
Text, electronic, 73, 93, 296
Text, readings, 83
Textbook for detectives, 91
Textbook of Friendship, 41
Textile industry, 181
Textual transmission, 70
Tey, Josephine, 203
Thackeray, William Makepeace, 186, 320
Thames River, 15, 142, 144, 227
"That Was No Lady," 262
Theatre, 221ff
Theatre New Brunswick, 227
Their Majesties' Bucketeers, 309
Thermodynamics, 169
They Might Be Giants, 239–40
Thief in the Night, 97
Thinking Machine, 201
Thistle of Scotland, 216
Thoene, Jake and Luke, 254
Thomalen, Bob, 268
Thomson, Basil, 197
Thomas, Dylan, 137
Thomas, Frank, 222
Thompson, Paul, 165
Thomson, June, 45, 219
"Thor Bridge," 36, 54, 55, 60, 64, 156, 158, 174, 247
Thorndale, Pennsylvania, 268
Thorndyke, Dr., 60, 201, 204
Tonga, 65
Top Nation, 139
"Thou Art the Man," 199
Thought-reading episode, 22
Three Famous Mysteries, 256

"Three Gables," 35, 42, 155, 160, 161, 165, 247
"Three Garridebs," 36, 41, 75, 170, 174, 193, 242
Three Garridebs of Westchester County, 270, 276, 287
Three Hours for Lunch Club, 258
Three Men in a Boat, 101, 185
Three of Them, 103, 104
Three Pipe Problem, 221, 308
"Three Students," 28, 70, 72, 117
Three-body problem, 50
Through the Looking-Glass, 181
Through the Magic Door, 116
Through the Years at Baker Street, 286
Throwback, 170
Thumb, 18; prints (see Fingerprints)
Thy Kingdom Come, 131
Tibet, 44, 194
Tichborne claimant, 194
Tiger in the Smoke, 203
"Tiger of San Pedro," 31
Tilbury, 144
Tiles, 302
Time, 307; Time Inc., 264
Time After Time, 215
Times, 46, 120, 165, 173, 185
Times Higher Education Supplement, 306
Timson, David, 93
Tin dispatch-box, 218
Tin Dispatch-Box, 57
"Tired Captain," 29
Titanic, 186
Titles of nobility, 216
Titus, Eve, 255
"To an Undiscerning Critic," 115
To Keep the Memory Green, 281
To Play the Game, 141
"To Shelve or to Censor," 63
Toasts, 277
Tobacco, 299; ash, 60
Toby, dog, 15
Toilet, 316
Tokyo, 92
Top Nation, 139
Tories, 152
Toronto, 72, 120, 205, 226, 227, 266, 270–71, 292, 302
Toronto Public (Reference) Library,

11, 74, 138, 251, 270, 272, 291, 293, 294, 301
Toronto Star, 307
Torture, 108, 190, 191
Tosca, Cardinal, 227
Tosca, 227
Totem and Taboo, 183
Tottenham Court Road, 159
Touch of the Class, 289
Tourist Guide to the London of SH, 142
Tours, 276
Tower Bridge, 144
Tower of London, 144, 235
Tower, Harry Alan, 228
Toys, 303
Tracy, Jack, 10, 13, 38, 43, 44, 113, 114, 139, 157, 161, 192, 264, 290, 291, 292
Trade Unions Act, 152
Trademarks, 77
Trafalgar Square, 144; riots, 153, 159, 193
"Tragedy of Birlstone," 30
Tragedy of the Korosko, 103, 105, 315
Trains, 141
Tramp, 249
Tranby Croft, 182
Transcriptions, 91
Translations, 91, 315
Transvaal, 122
Transylvania, 185
Trauma, 171
Travel books, 141
Treadmill, 190
Treason, 125
Trelawney Hope, Lady Hilda, 29, 246
Trent's Last Case, 202
Trenton, New Jersey, 206
Trepoff murder, 177, 208
Trepov, Theodore, 177
Trevelyan, Percy, 22, 246
Trevor, "Old," 21
Trial by Jury, 183
Trial of Oscar Slater, 121
Trifles, 59
Trilby, 42, 168
Triple Alliance, Trit, 94
Triumph of SH, 234
Trivia, 277, 286
Trollope, Anthony, 152, 165
Trouble in Bugland, 222
Trouser-knees, 17
Trout in the Milk, 118
Troy, New York, 302
True Conan Doyle, 131, 135
True Crime Files of Sir Arthur Conan Doyle, 121

True Story of SH, 200
True Story of the Giant Rats, 219
Truth about Oscar Slater, 121
T-shirts, 303
Tuberculosis, 100, 171
Tudor times, 160
Tulpa, 222
Tulsa, 265
Turkey, 123, 175, 177, 178
Turner, John, 247
Turner, Martha, 195
Turner, Mrs., 55
Tussaud's, 146, 147
Twain, Mark, 90, 197, 211, 212, 218
Twelfth Night, 45, 273
Twentieth Century-Fox, 234, 235
Twenty Thousand Leagues, 109
Twiddlebug Mystery, 304
Twidle, Arthur, 90
Twisted Lip (see "Man with the Twisted Lip")
"Two Collaborators," 211
221B (anthology), 262
"221B" (poem), 252, 260
"221B Baker Street" (website), 296
"221B Baker Street" (game), 252
221BBC, 231
"Two-Author Theory," 311
Tyburn Tree, 190
Typesetting, 72, 93
Typewriting, 70, 162, 196
Typographical errors, 14, 72, 73, 80, 82

Ueda, Hirotaka, 283
Uemura, Masaharu, 283
Uffa, 57
Ukrainian, 92
Ulster, 125, 153, 154
Ultimate Jack the Ripper Companion, 196
Umberto I, 176
Uncle Bernac, 103, 106
Uncle Tom's Cabin, 181
Uncollected SH, 113, 137, 222, 281
Uncollected Stories, 105
Underground, 32, 147, 149, 299, 302
Undershaw, 100, 300
Union Jack, 19, 173
Union League Club, 274
Unionists, 153
Unions, 152
"Unique Hamlet," 212
United Agents, 77
United Kingdom, 140

United States, 27, 123, 126, 158, **173–74**, 179, 189, 197, 218
United States Steel, 30, 174
Universal SH, 66, 290
Universal Studios, 235, 301
Universities, 28, 50
University of Calgary, 305
University of California at Berkeley, 53
University of Edinburgh, 69, 82, 99–100, 109, 113, 136, 171, 200
University of London, 48
University of Minnesota, 58, 138, 225, 250, 291, 293, **294**, 301
University of Regina, 313
University of Texas, 132, 295
University of Toronto, 312
University of Virginia, 94
University of Wisconsin, 213
Unpublished cases, 17, 56, 285, 286
Upper Baker Street, 146
Upstairs, Downstairs, 160
Urdu, 91
Usenet, 297
USH, 291
Utah, 13, 267, 276
Utechin, Nicholas, 217, 280, 281

V.R. (Victoria Regina), 54
Valentine, Anthony, 247
Valhalla, 320
Valley of Fear, 14, **29ff**, 45, 47, 49, 50, 55, 64, 67, 68, 70, 90, 95, 156, 160, 191, 207, 267, 273, 276, 293, 315
— stage and screen, 229, 232, 234
"Vamberry, the Wine Merchant," 230
Vampires, 35, 185, 243
Van der Flaes, Edwin, 272
Van Dine, S.S., 202, 204
Van Dusen, Augustus S.F.X., 201
Vance, Philo, 202, 204, 238
Vancouver, 272
Vandeleur, Iris, 243
Vanderbilt, 57
Vanderburgh, George, 290, 292

Vanity Fair, 225
Vassar College, 230
Vatican, 176
Vaughan family, 25
Vaughan, Peter, 247
Vauxhall Bridge, 144
Veggie Tales, 304
"Veiled Lodger," 37, 47, 229
Venezuela, 173
Vermissa Valley, 30
Vermont, 185
Verne, Jules, 109, 110, 111
Verne, Kaaren, 236
Vernet, Émile Jean Horace, 39
Veronica, 111
Vestry council, 151
Vetsera, Mary, 194
Vicar, 168, 169
Viceroy, 179
Victoria College, 312
Victoria Falls, 243
Victoria Regina, 54, 74, 140, 150, 154, 156, 168, 179, 182, 185, **186**, 208, 239, 251, 277
Victoria station, 141, 149
Victor*ia* Street, 101, 129
Victor*ia*n age, 152, 186, 287
*Victori*an *London, the Tale*, 165
Vidocq, Fran*ç*ois, 199
Vienna, 100, 18*3*, 215
Vimy Ridge, Battle of, 173
Vincent, Leslie, 236
Violets, 19, 27, 32, 114, 169
Violets & Vitriol, 290
Violin, 41, 249, 298
Visit to Three Fronts, 124
Vital Message, 128
"Voice of Science," 74, 108
Voices from Baker Street, 251
Volunteer Battalion, 122
Von Bork, 154
Von Eckardt, Wolf, 164
Vox populi, 207

Wagner, E.J., 172, 290
Waistcoat, 281
Walbridge, Earle, 259
Wales, 140, 160;
Prince of (*see* Edward)
Walking, 149
Wall Street, 285
Wall, Lucille, 230
Wall, Wayne, 289
Waller, Bryan Charles, 98–99, 136
Walter, Valentine, 246
Walters, Catherine, 51
Walters, Minette, 201
Walters, Thorley, 238, 240

Wanderings of a Spiritualist, 129
Wandsworth, 190
War in South Africa, 123
War of 1812, 173
War of the Worlds, 187
"War Service of SH," 33
Ward Lock and Co., 12
Ward, Leslie, 225
Ward, Sophie, 241
Warner, 291
Warrack, Guy, 279
Warren, Mrs., 160
Warren, Sir Charles, 193, 195
Warshawski, V.I., 206
Warwickshire, 141
Washington, D.C., 264, 266, 268, 269, 270, 276, 287, 295
Washington Post, 307
Washington, George, 56
Waterloo, 103, 106, 184
Waterloo Bridge, 144
Waterloo station, 141
Waterloo, Battle of, 105, 106
Watney, 218
"Watson Was a Woman," 49, 262
Watson, Amelia, 220
Watson, James, 68
Watson, Jane, 243
Watson, John H., 46
— as author, 46
— as gentleman, 249
— as jury, 47, 207
— as killer, 306
— biographer, 47
— brother, 48
— friendship, 41, 48, 239, 318
— gender, 49, 262
— handwriting, 46, 311
— housemaid, 161
— intelligence, 47, 204, 238, 240, 241, 244, 249, 317, 318, 320
— love and marriage, 15, 48, 64, 81, 114–15, 220, 226, 249, 277, 286, 318
— medical career, 48, 82, 172
— name, 18, 263
— prose style, 216
— *Reminiscences*, 13
— wound, 36, 41, 48, 81, 156, 262
Watson, Mildred, 239–40
Watson, Patrick Heron, 69, 99
Watson's Choice, 221, 309
Watt, A.P., 72

Watt, Donald J., 312
Watt, Peter Ridgway, 222
Waugh, Charles G., 109
Wax bust, 54, 114
"Wax Gamblers," 213
Wayne, John, 317
Wayne, Wall, 186
We Always Mention Aunt Clara, 52, 251
Weaver, Fritz, 226
Weaver, Gordon, 121
Weaver's tooth, 59, 139, 298
Web (*see* Internet)
Webb, Beatrice, 180
Webb, Sidney, 180
"Weekend with Sherlock," 270
Weiss, Erich, 129, 184
Welcome to America, Mr. SH, 137
Welcome Holmes, 297
Weller, Philip, 24, 289
Wells Cathedral, 108
Wells, Herbert George, 74, 167, 187, 215
Welsh, Kenneth, 243
Wescosville, Pennsylvania, 303
Wesley, John, 168
Wessex Press, 292
West Africa, 100
West End, 73, 145
West End Horror, 215
West, Arthur Cadogan, 64, 149
Westchester County, 261, 270
Western fiction, 13, 19
Western Morning News, 165
Westminster, 101, 144
— Abbey, 144, 279
— Bridge, 144
— City, 295
Westmorland, 141
Westwood, Frank, 120
Weverka, Robert, 241
Wexler, Bruce, 290
Weyman, Ronald C., 217
Whaling, 28, 100, 118
"What a Night This Is Going to Be," 226
What Jane Austen Ate, 165
Wheatley, Alan, 243
Wheeler, Thomas B., 142
Wheelwrightings, 288
Whelan, Michael, 267
"When the World Screamed," 110
Whigs, 152
Whistle, 192
Whitaker, Arthur, 212
Whitaker's Almanack, 158, 166
White Company, 102, 106–07, 112
White man's burden, 140
White slavery, 64
White, Kathryn, 280, 301, 311, 312

White, William Anthony Parker (*see* Boucher)
Whitechapel, 145
Whitechapel Horrors, 195
"Whitechapel Vampire," 243
Whitehall, 53, 144, 191
Whitehead, Paxton, 227
Whitman, 253
Whitman, Thomas, 227
Whole Art of Detection, 40, 62
Widow of Windsor, 187
Wiggins, 56, 267, 274
Wigglesworth, Belden, 52
Wight, Isle of, 140
Wigmore Street, 146, 147
Wigram, Lionel, 242, 256
Wikipedia, 11, 170
Wild, Jonathan, 50, 198
Wilde, Oscar, 14, 15,138, 164, 168, **187**, 190
"Wilder Side of SH," 239
Wilder, Billy, 239
Wilder, Gene, 218, 240
Wiles, Frank, 90
Wilhelm I, 176
Wilhelm II, 176, 179
Wilhelm, King of Bohemia (*see* Bohemia)
Wilhelmina, Queen, 178
William Gillette Memorial Luncheon, 268, 274
William III, 178
William IV, 186
Williams, Enyd, 232
Williams, Michael, 231–32
Williams, Newton, 15
Williams, Ted, 117
Williamson, Jerry N., 222
Williamson, Nicol, 240, 266
Willis, Hubert, 233
Wilmer, Douglas, 93, 240, 243, 244
Wilshere, Barbara, 246
Wilson Library, Minnesota, 58
Wilson, Gahan, 306
Wilson, Jabez, 155, 161, 243, 246
Wiltshire, 140
Wimsey, Lord Peter, 202, 278
Winchester, 164, 276
Windibank, James, 320
Windlesham, 101, 131, 300

Windows, 315
Windsor, 187
Winning Shot, 102
Winnipeg, 272
Winslow, Amy, 243
Winter, Kitty, 35
Wisconsin, 214
"Wisteria Lodge," 31, 44, 75, 170, 246
With All My Love: An Anthology, 79
Without a Clue, 241
Wodehouse, P.G., 305
"Wold Newton Universe," 63
Wolf Man, 183
Wolfe Pack, 203
Wolfe, Ian, 236
Wolfe, Nero, 54, 63, 203
Wolff, Julian, 58, 214, 262, **264**, 267, 268, 272, 275, 282
Woman in Green, 236
Woman in White, 199
Woman Who Did, 180
Woman, The, 17, 43, 51, 274, 277
Wombwell, George, 139
Women in society, 315
— class, 160, 162, 180
— Doyle's view, 104
— Sherlockian world, 259, 261, 263, 268, 270, 273
Women's Royal Air Force, 132
Wontner, Arthur, 228, 234
Wood, Alfred (Major), 49, 101
Wood, Benton, 299
Wood, Henry, 246
Wood, J.G., 170
Wood, James Playsted, 135
Wood, John, 218, 224
Wood, Peter H., 227
Woodbine racetrack, 276
Woodward, Edward, 243
Woodward, Joanne, 239
Woolf, Virginia, 186, 217
Woollcott, Alexander, 259–60
Woolsey, Robert, 298
Woolwick, 144
Wooster Brush Company, 303
Worcestershire, 141
Wordsworth, 80
Workman, 208
Works of Sir Arthur Conan Doyle, 94
Workshops for Sherlockians, 265
World Bibliography, 10, 66, 138, 232, 264, 290, 312
World of SH, 282
World War I, 31, 33, 97, 112, 122–26,

128, 146, 154, 155, 173, 175, 186, 217
World War II, 92, 182, 235, 236, 237, 264, 278
World Wide Web (*see* Internet)
World's Classics, 82
Worldtainment, 93
Worlock, Frederick, 236
Worm in the Bud, 64
Wormwood Scrubs, 190
Worth, Adam, 50, 194
Wrath of Khan, 215
"Wreck on Loch McGarry," 112
Wrigglesworth, Doug, 272
Wright, Elsie, 130
Wright, Sean, 289
Wright, Theresa, 161
Wright, Willard Huntington, 202
Wynn, Dilys, 209
Wynne, Catherine, 315

Xerox of Canada, 309–10

Yahoo Groups, 297
Yale SH Society, 316
Yale University, 316
"Yellow Face," 20, 145, 156, 160
Yellow Pages, 309
Yeomen of the Guard, 183
Young SH, 241
Yoxley Old Place, 84
Yuhasova, Helene, 252

Zambia, 172
Zanuck, Darryl, 234
Zeichen der Vier, 91
Zeigler, Illinois, 288
Zeisler, Ernest B., 294
Zelman, Aaron, 310
Zen, 306
Zimbabwe, 172
Zionsville, Indiana, 288
Zoology, 170
Zorro, 238
Zucco, George, 235, 236